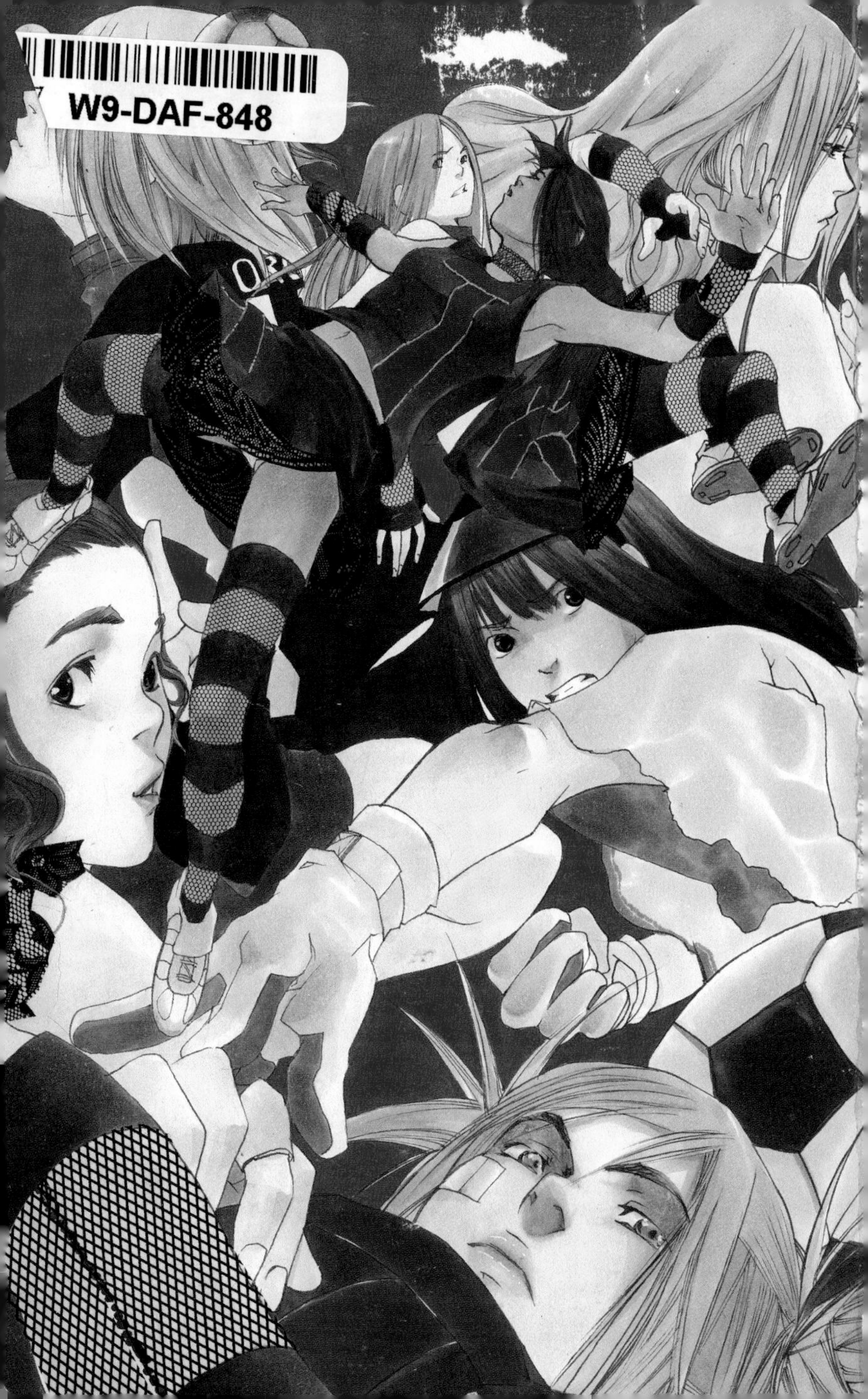

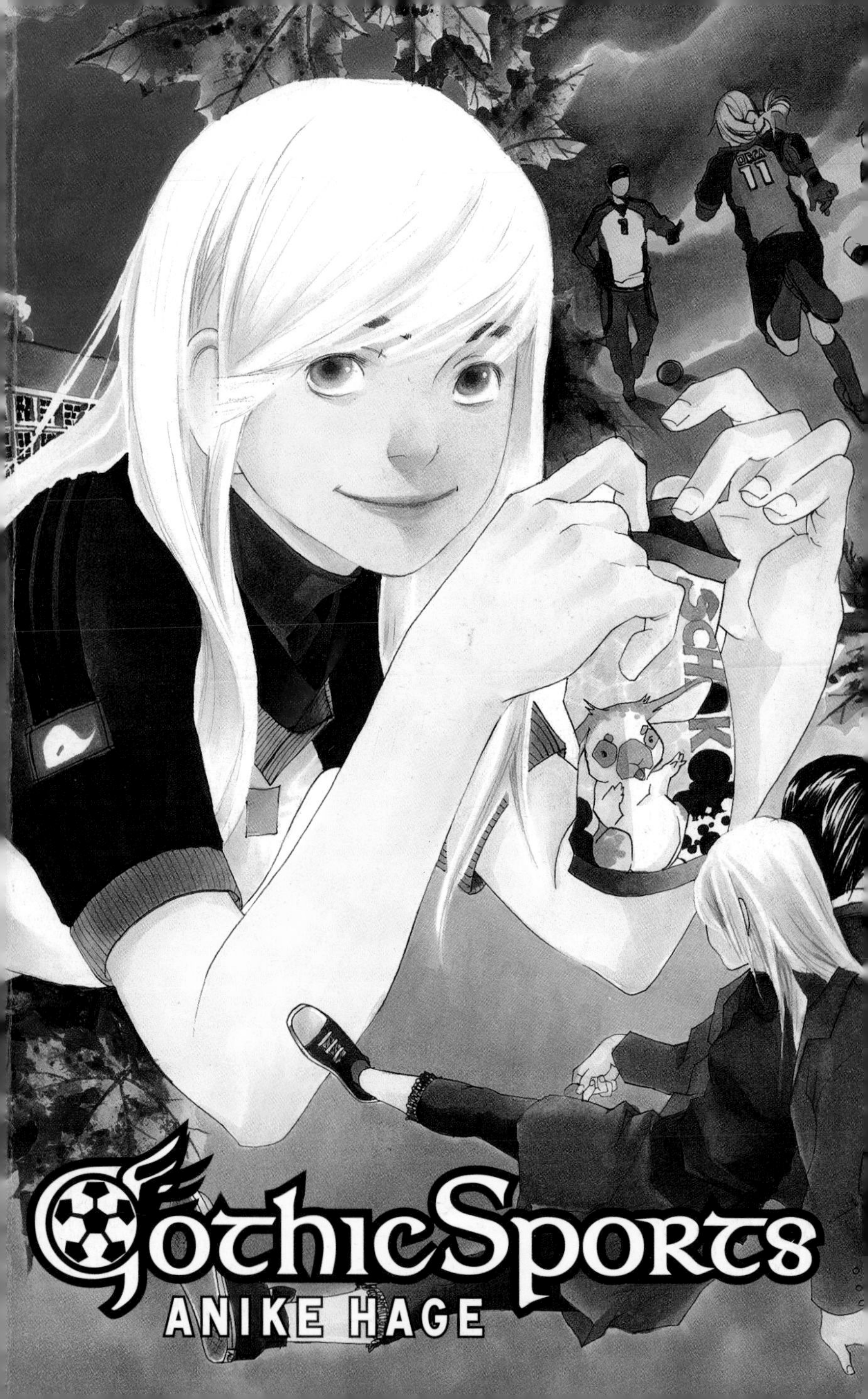
GothicSports
ANIKE HAGE

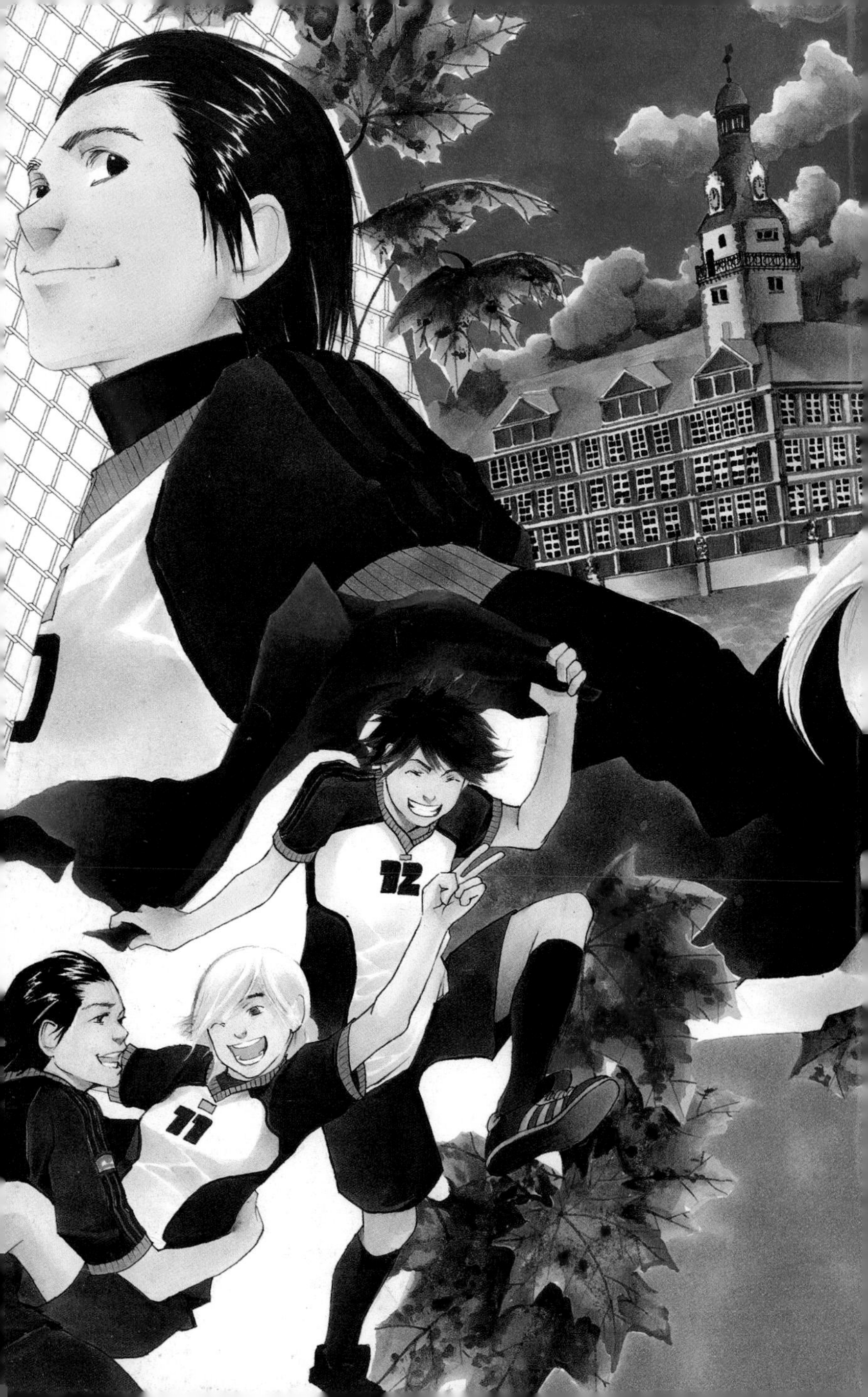

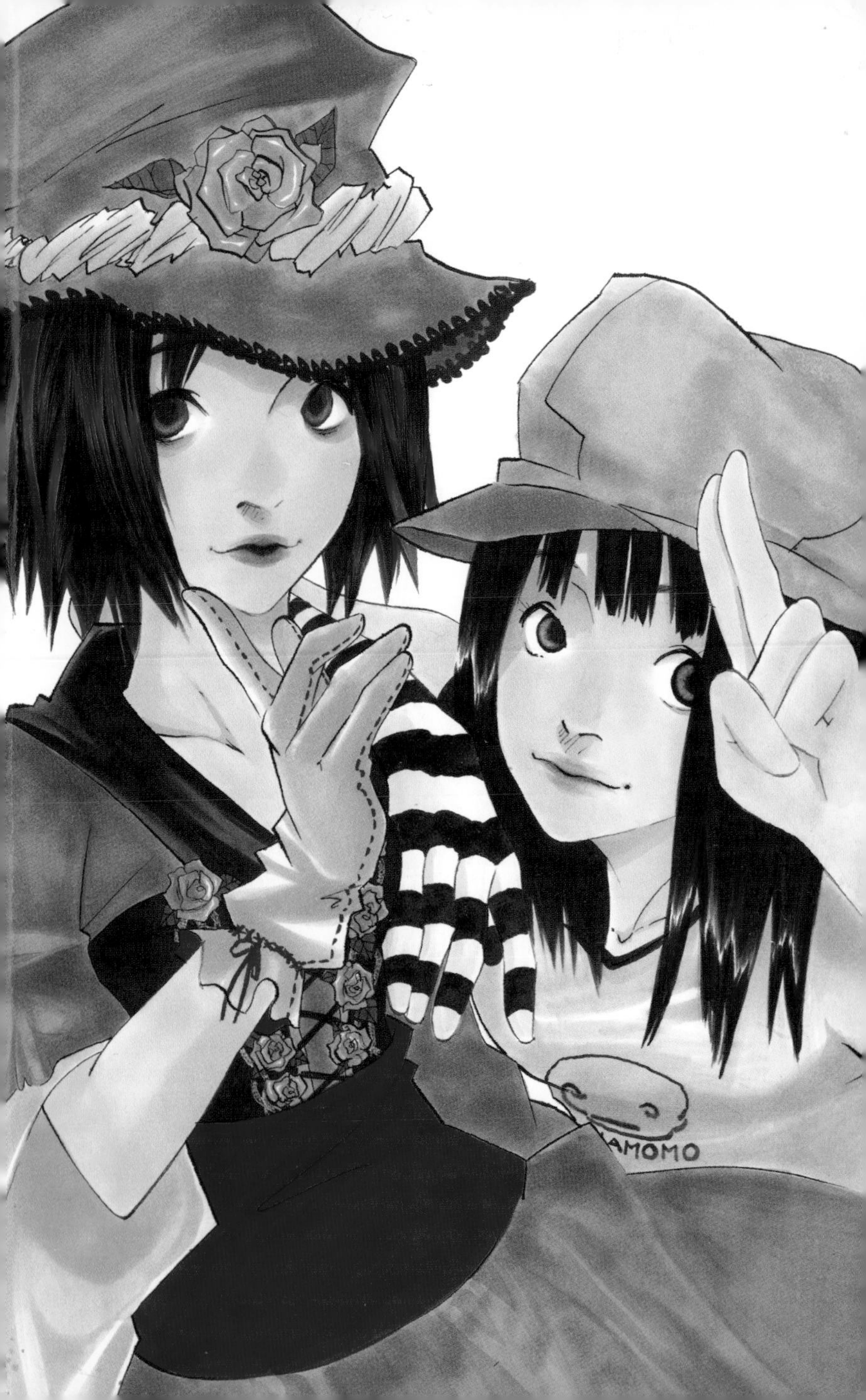
AMOMO

GothicSports

ANIKE HAGE

3

HAMBURG // LONDON // LOS ANGELES // TOKYO

Gothic Sports Volume 3
Created by Anike Hage

Translation - Erin M. Blakemore
English Adaptation - Erin M. Blakemore
Retouch and Lettering - Gavin Highnight
Production Artist - Courtney Geter
Graphic Designer - Jose Macasocol, Jr.

Editor - Peter Ahlstrom
Digital Imaging Manager - Chris Buford
Pre-Production Supervisor - Erika Terriquez
Production Manager - Elisabeth Brizzi
Managing Editor - Vy Nguyen
Creative Director - Anne Marie Horne
Editor-in-Chief - Rob Tokar
Publisher - Mike Kiley
President and C.O.O. - John Parker
C.E.O. and Chief Creative Officer - Stuart Levy

A  Manga

TOKYOPOP and ⊙ are trademarks or registered trademarks of TOKYOPOP Inc.

TOKYOPOP Inc.
5900 Wilshire Blvd. Suite 2000
Los Angeles, CA 90036

E-mail: info@TOKYOPOP.com
Come visit us online at www.TOKYOPOP.com

ISBN: 978-1-59816-994-2

First TOKYOPOP printing: January 2008
10 9 8 7 6 5 4 3 2 1
Printed in the USA

CONTENTS

CHAPTER 13: IMPEDIMENTS   11
CHAPTER 14: VACATION BEGINS   39
CHAPTER 15: CLIMBING   67
CHAPTER 16: SECRETS   95
CHAPTER 17: TRAINING CAMP   123
CHAPTER 18: VACATION ENDS   151

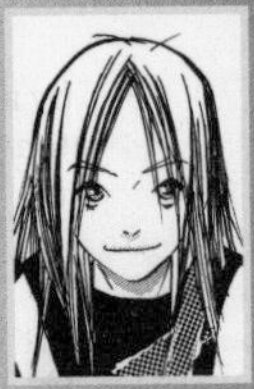

ANYA is fulfilling her dream to start her own soccer team at her high school—and she's stubborn enough to resort to unconventional means if that's what it takes. Her strong dislike of Leon stems partly from his involvement in her hamster's death when they were in elementary school.

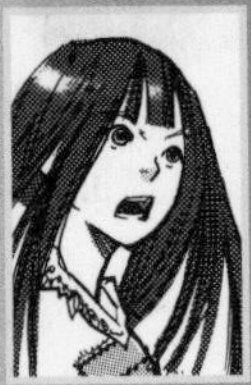

LUISE (LOO) has known Anya since elementary school. They rekindled their friendship when they reunited at Lucrece High. Loo is a real ray of light in Anya's dreary school days.

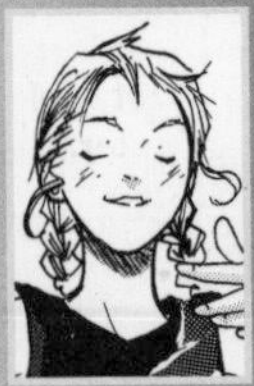

JULIA was a member of the school's soccer team for years, but she never got to play because the coach doesn't believe girls make good soccer players. Instead, she sat on the bench—even during practice! When Anya established her own team, Julia was on board immediately and has become one of the team's most enthusiastic players.

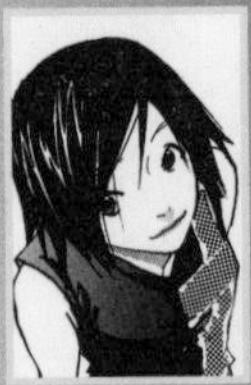

FELICITAS (FILIZ) is (in)famous for her unusual fashion sense, and is also a bit of an outsider in Anya's new class. But when it became clear that there wouldn't be enough people for the new team, she came up with a brilliant way to attract plenty of attention.

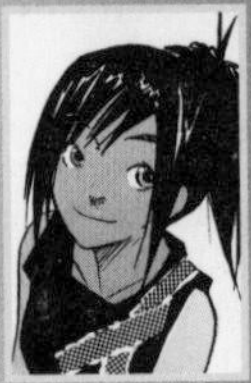

DELIA used to play for the school's basketball team, but decided to help coach the new soccer team for its big game against the official school team. The ambition of the new team has impressed her so much that she's decided to continue training them.

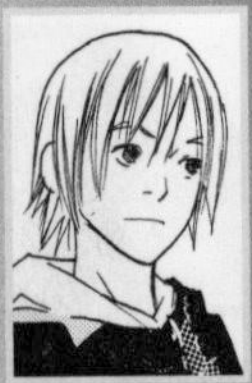

LEON has known Anya since elementary school, but Anya clearly doesn't have any good memories of him, and she has been against Leon's participation on her team from the beginning. The team desperately needs strong players, though, so she's forced to override her distaste for him and let him play—for now.

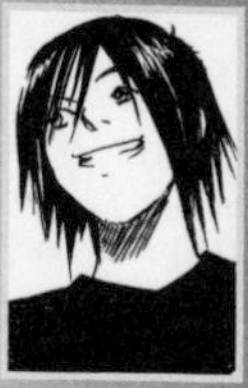

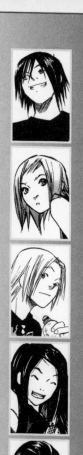

KEVIN has a bit of a temper, which he demonstrated by almost breaking an opponent's arm during the challenge match—after Julia got fouled. He's another of the misfits in Anya's class, and he mostly hangs out with Olga.

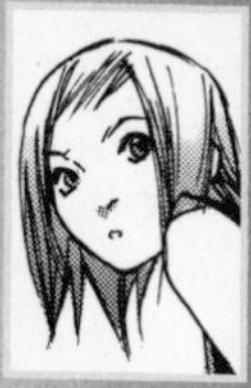

ALEXIA respects the way Anya stood up to the basketball team captain. When she found out from Delia that Anya was forming her own sports team, she was immediately on board.

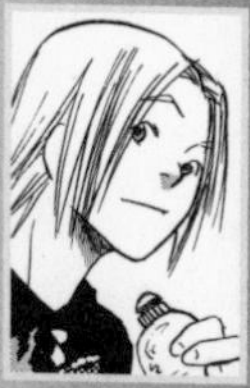

HANNES is Alexia's twin brother, but they don't look alike. Delia talked him into joining the team with his sister.

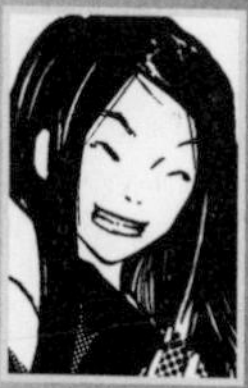

ELLIS would fit better in a ballet class than on a soccer team, as far as Anya's concerned. But this team needs all the players it can get! She has a thing for soccer guys.

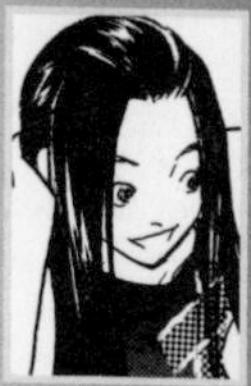

OLGA is another of Anya's classmates that Filiz talked into joining the team, even though her own fashion tastes are more in the Renaissance Fair line. She hangs out with Kevin.

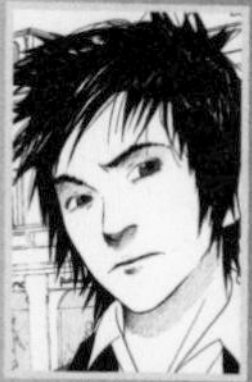

COACH His name hasn't been revealed, but he's the student coach of Lucrece High's official school soccer team. Because he wants nothing to stand in the way of victory, he hasn't allowed the girls on his team any playing time. He's got a low opinion of Anya's upstarts, but Delia has some power over him.

THE STORY SO FAR:

Anya transfers to Lucrece High, dreaming of sharing in the athletic glory of one of its championship sports teams. But joining one of the teams turns out to be harder than she ever expected. The basketball team's queen bee, Marie, thinks Anya is too short and inexperienced, and the soccer coach thinks girls aren't worth giving any playing time. But Anya won't be deterred. Together with some of her new friends, she starts her own soccer team—with a twist; they decide to forego traditional soccer jerseys for Gothic Lolita-style uniforms designed and sewn by the enthusiastic Filiz.

In order to be recognized as an official team by the school, the team needs permission from the principal. Anya manages to convince him to take part in an unusual bet: If the new team plays a match against the well-established school team, he'll entertain the thought of official status for the Gothic Sports team.

In a dramatic and almost hopeless match, Anya's team steps up against the school's most experienced kickers—and loses! But the effort they show is enough to prove to the principal that they're serious, so he approves them anyway. Now the team and their extraordinary new look are the talk of the school—and they've drawn the attention of teams from other schools as well...

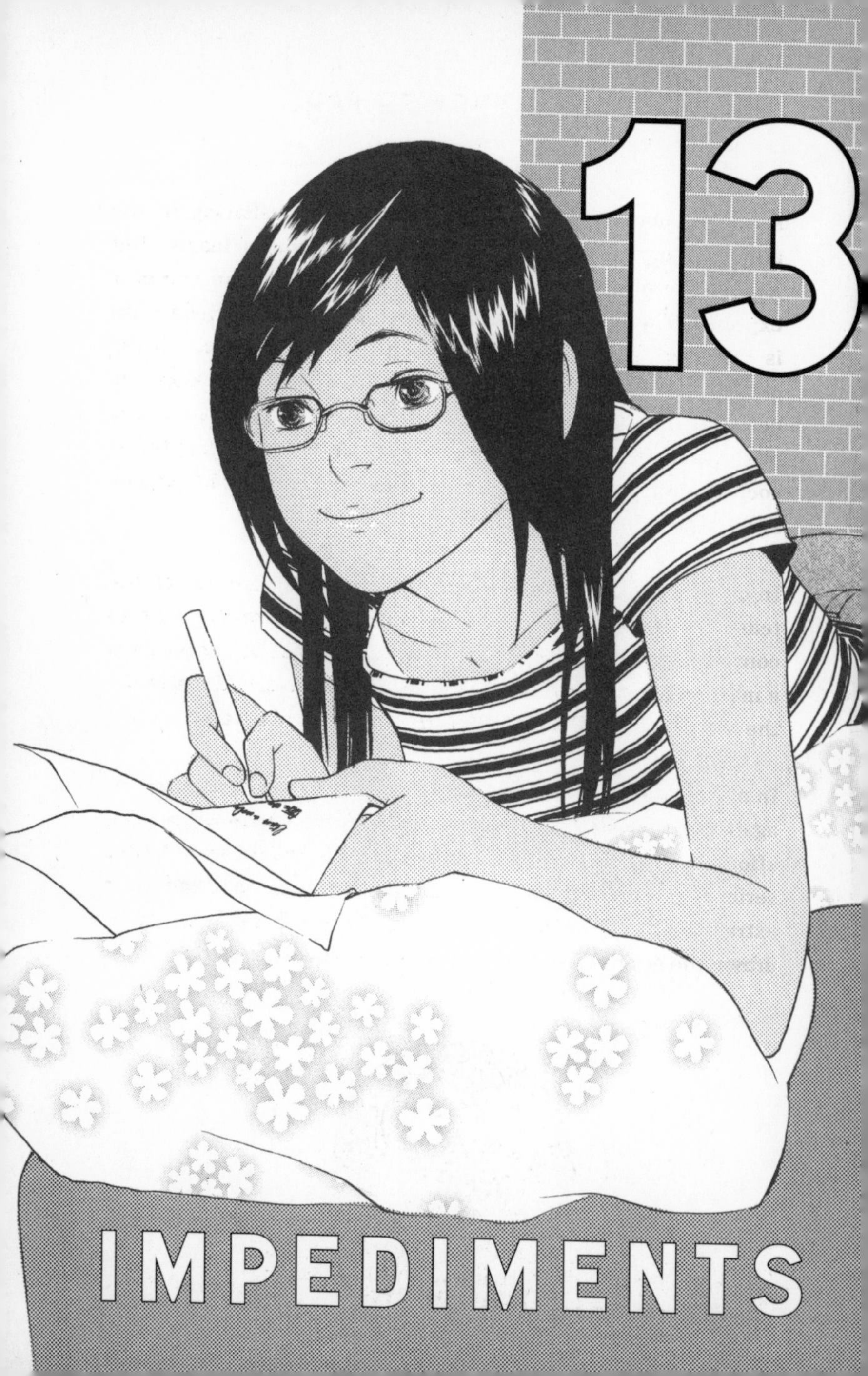
13
IMPEDIMENTS

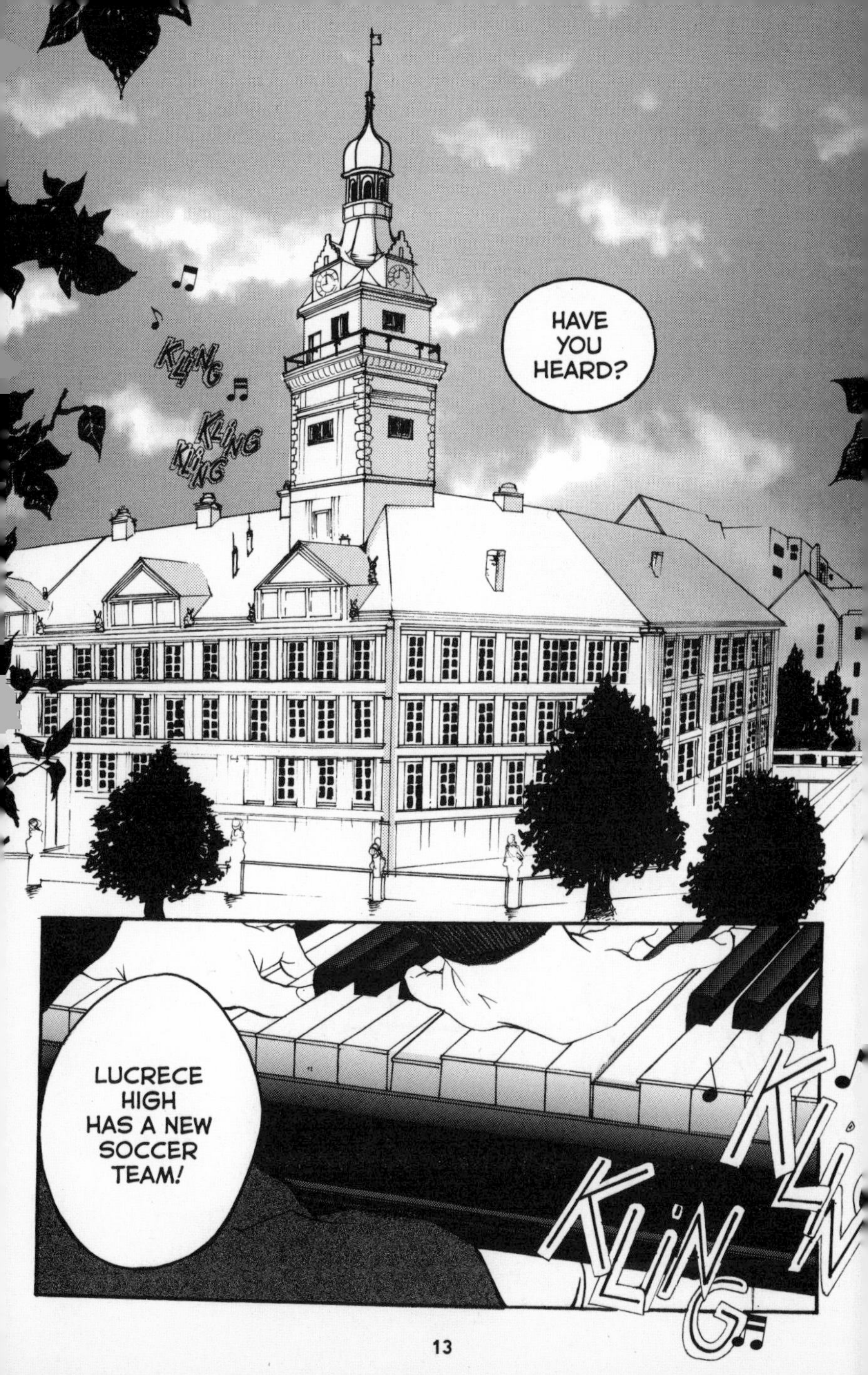
HAVE YOU HEARD?
KLING
KLING
KLING
KLING
LUCRECE HIGH HAS A NEW SOCCER TEAM!

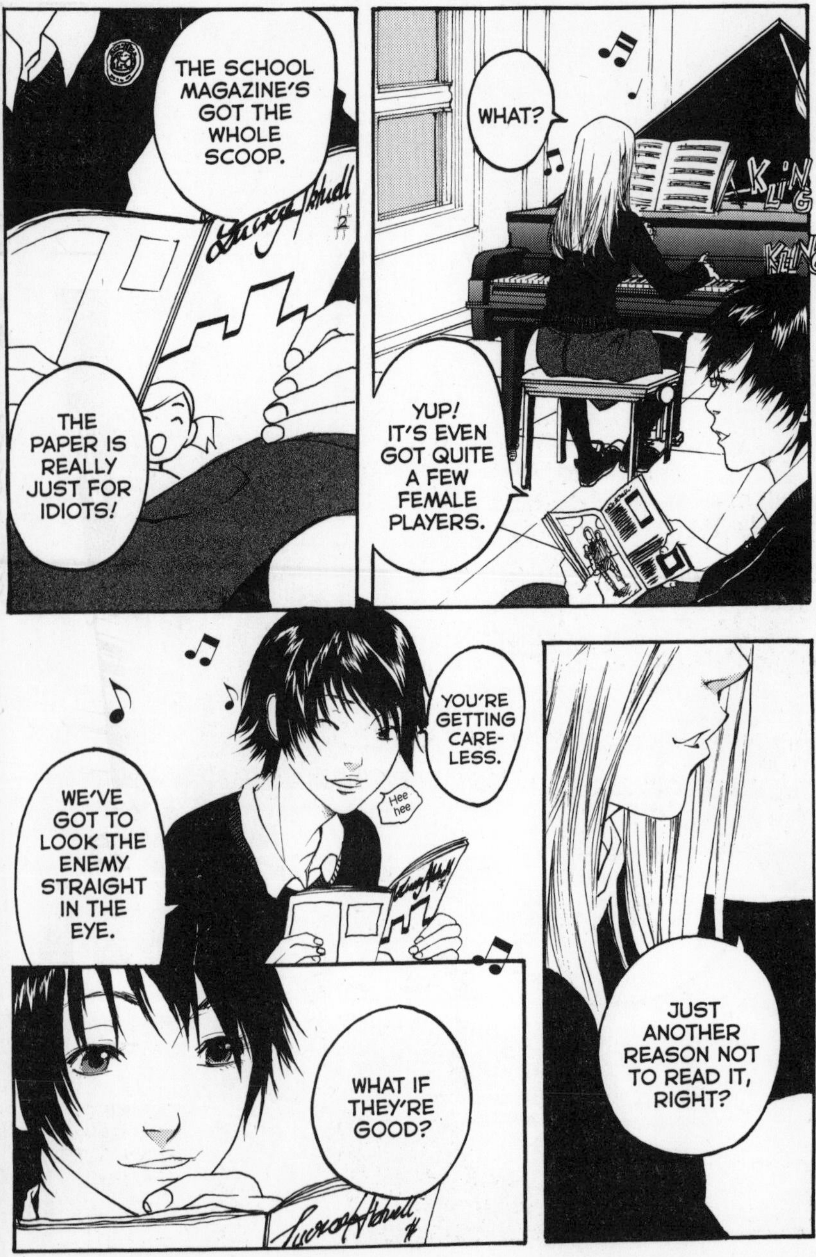
WHAT?
KLING
KLING
YUP! IT'S EVEN GOT QUITE A FEW FEMALE PLAYERS.
THE SCHOOL MAGAZINE'S GOT THE WHOLE SCOOP.
THE PAPER IS REALLY JUST FOR IDIOTS!
JUST ANOTHER REASON NOT TO READ IT, RIGHT?
YOU'RE GETTING CARE-LESS.
Hee hee
WE'VE GOT TO LOOK THE ENEMY STRAIGHT IN THE EYE.
WHAT IF THEY'RE GOOD?

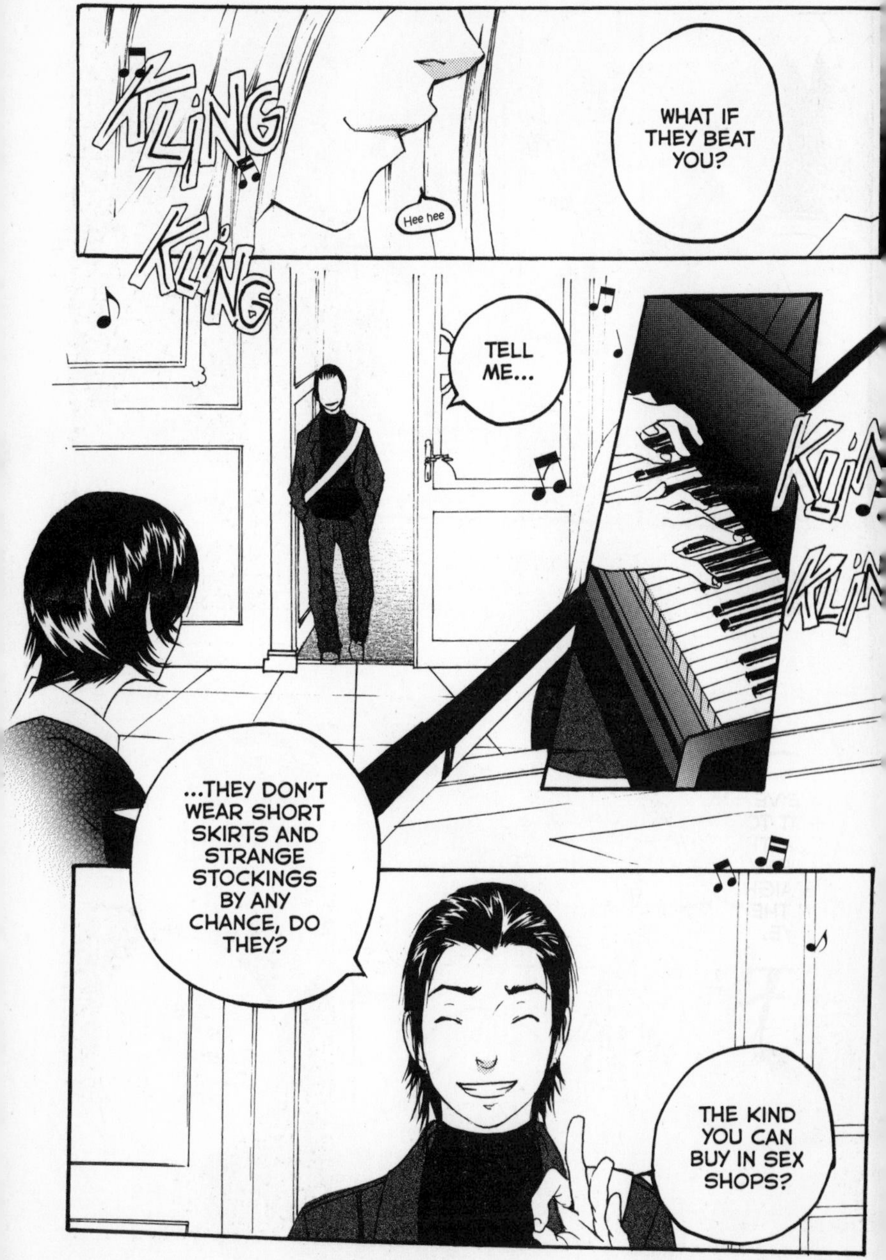

WHAT IF THEY BEAT YOU?
Hee hee
KLING
KLING
TELL ME...
...THEY DON'T WEAR SHORT SKIRTS AND STRANGE STOCKINGS BY ANY CHANCE, DO THEY?
THE KIND YOU CAN BUY IN SEX SHOPS?

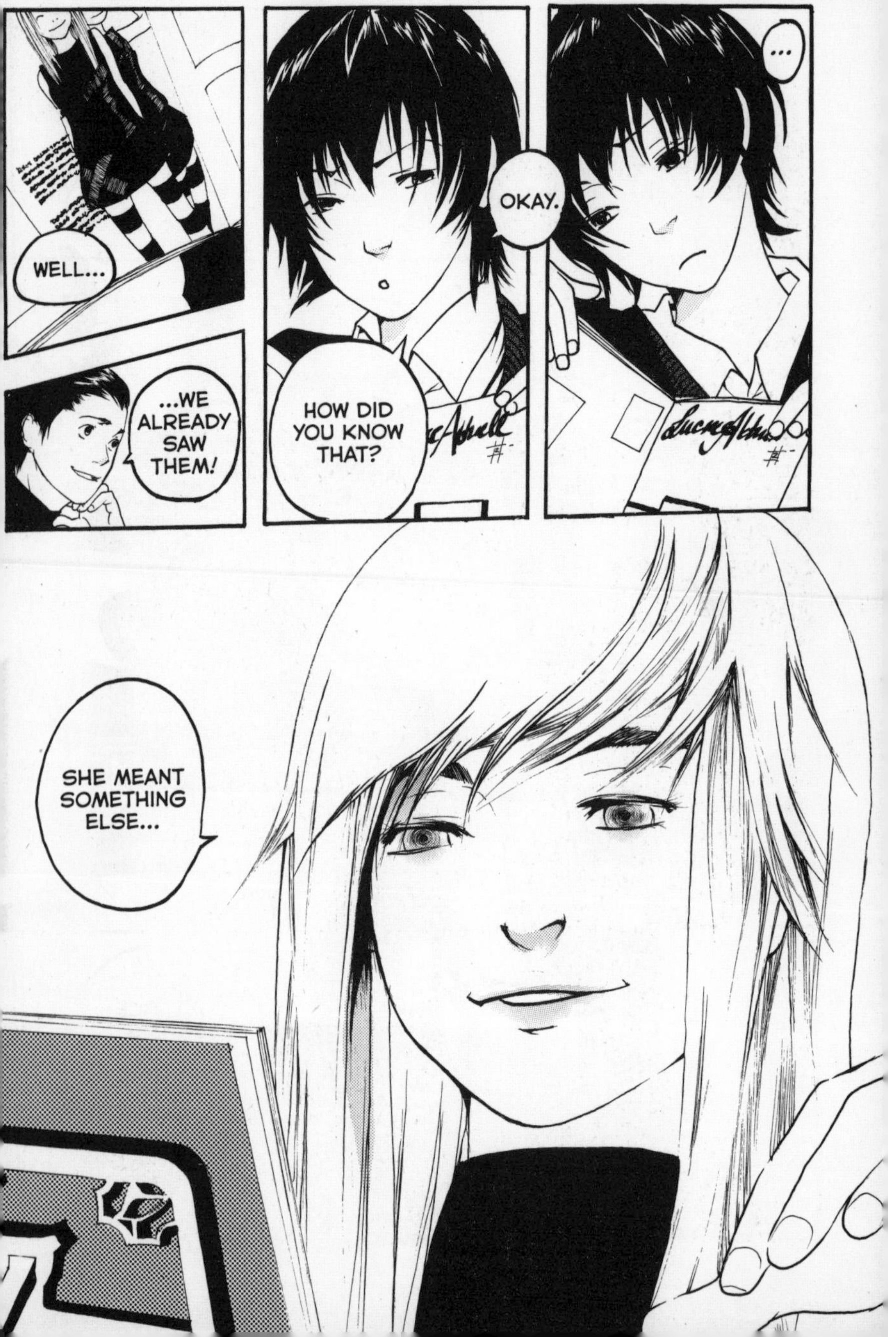
...
OKAY.
HOW DID YOU KNOW THAT?
WELL...
...WE ALREADY SAW THEM!
SHE MEANT SOMETHING ELSE...

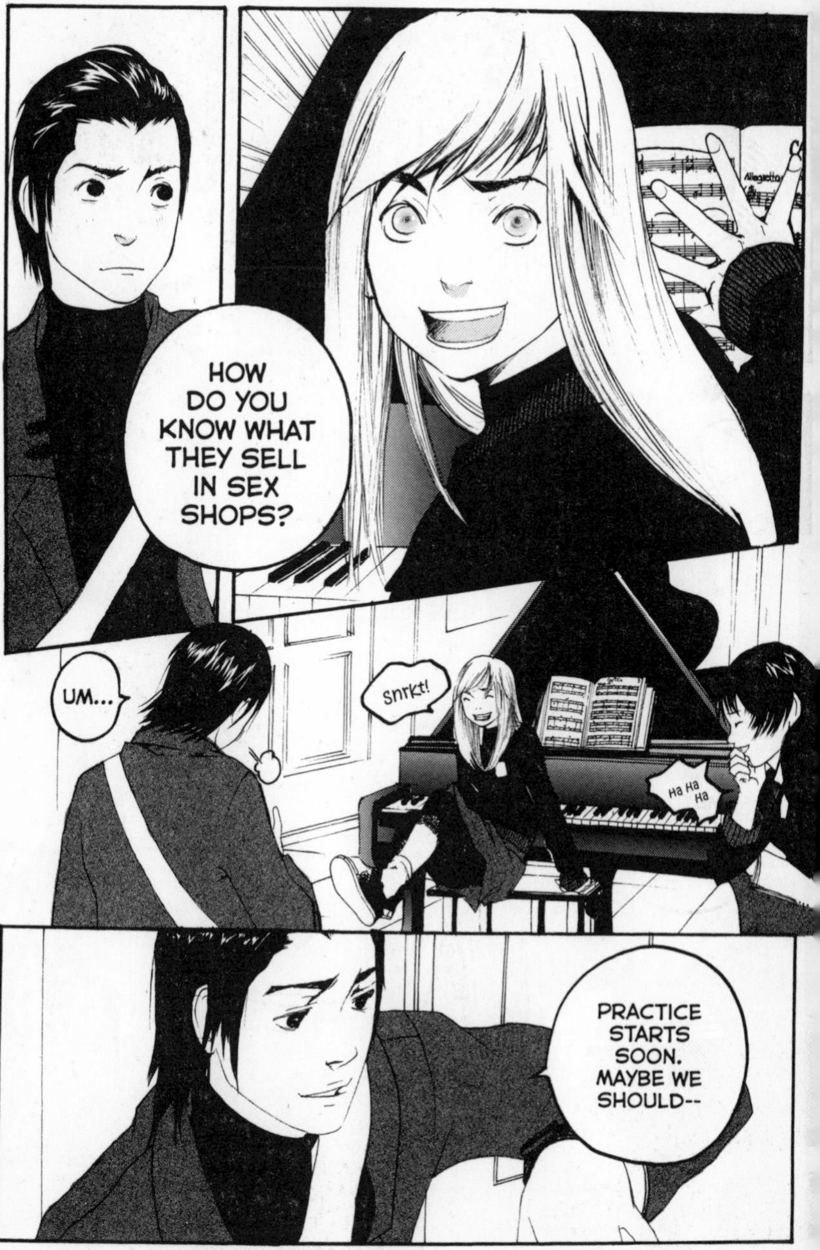
Allegretto
HOW DO YOU KNOW WHAT THEY SELL IN SEX SHOPS?
Ha Ha Ha
Snrkt!
UM...
PRACTICE STARTS SOON. MAYBE WE SHOULD--

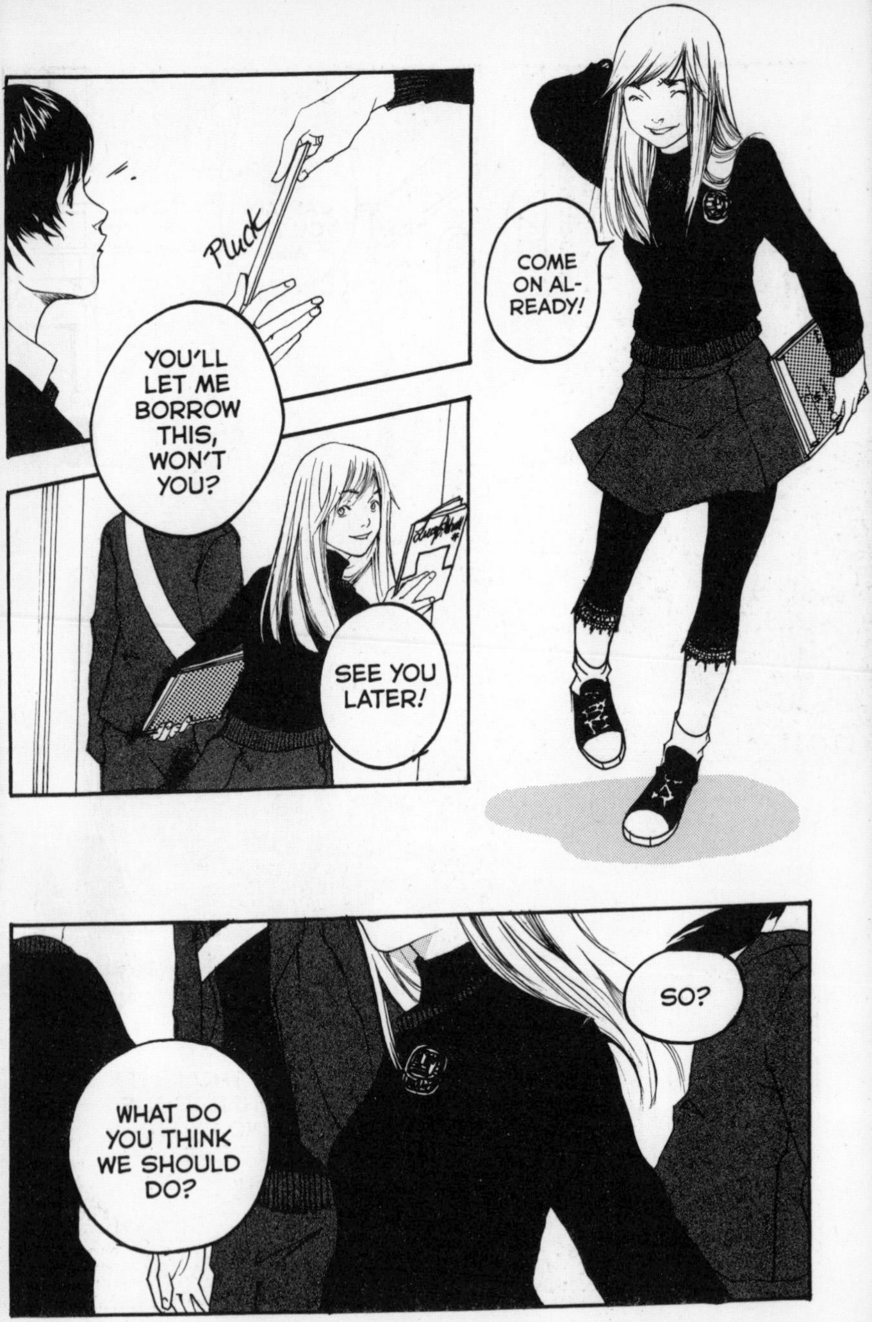
COME ON AL-READY!
PLUCK
YOU'LL LET ME BORROW THIS, WON'T YOU?
SEE YOU LATER!
SO?
WHAT DO YOU THINK WE SHOULD DO?

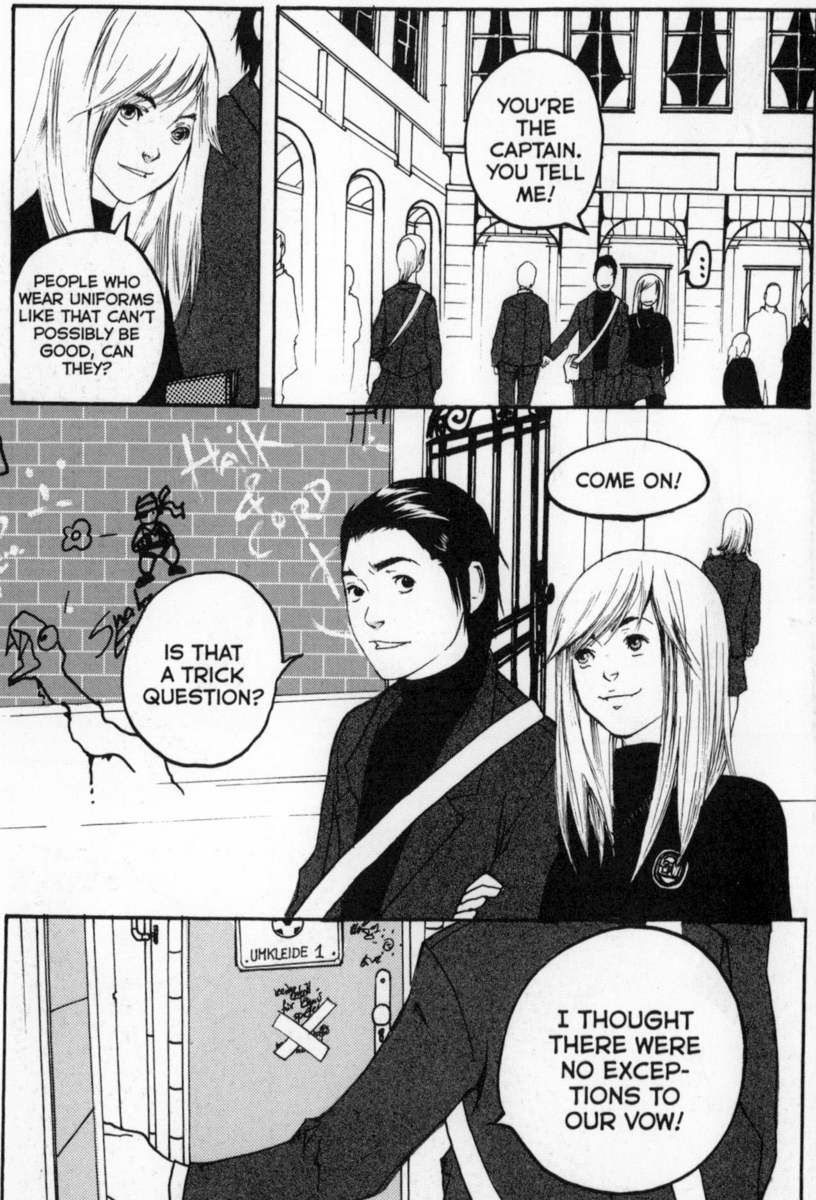
YOU'RE THE CAPTAIN. YOU TELL ME!
...
PEOPLE WHO WEAR UNIFORMS LIKE THAT CAN'T POSSIBLY BE GOOD, CAN THEY?
COME ON!
IS THAT A TRICK QUESTION?
UMKLEIDE 1
I THOUGHT THERE WERE NO EXCEP- TIONS TO OUR VOW!

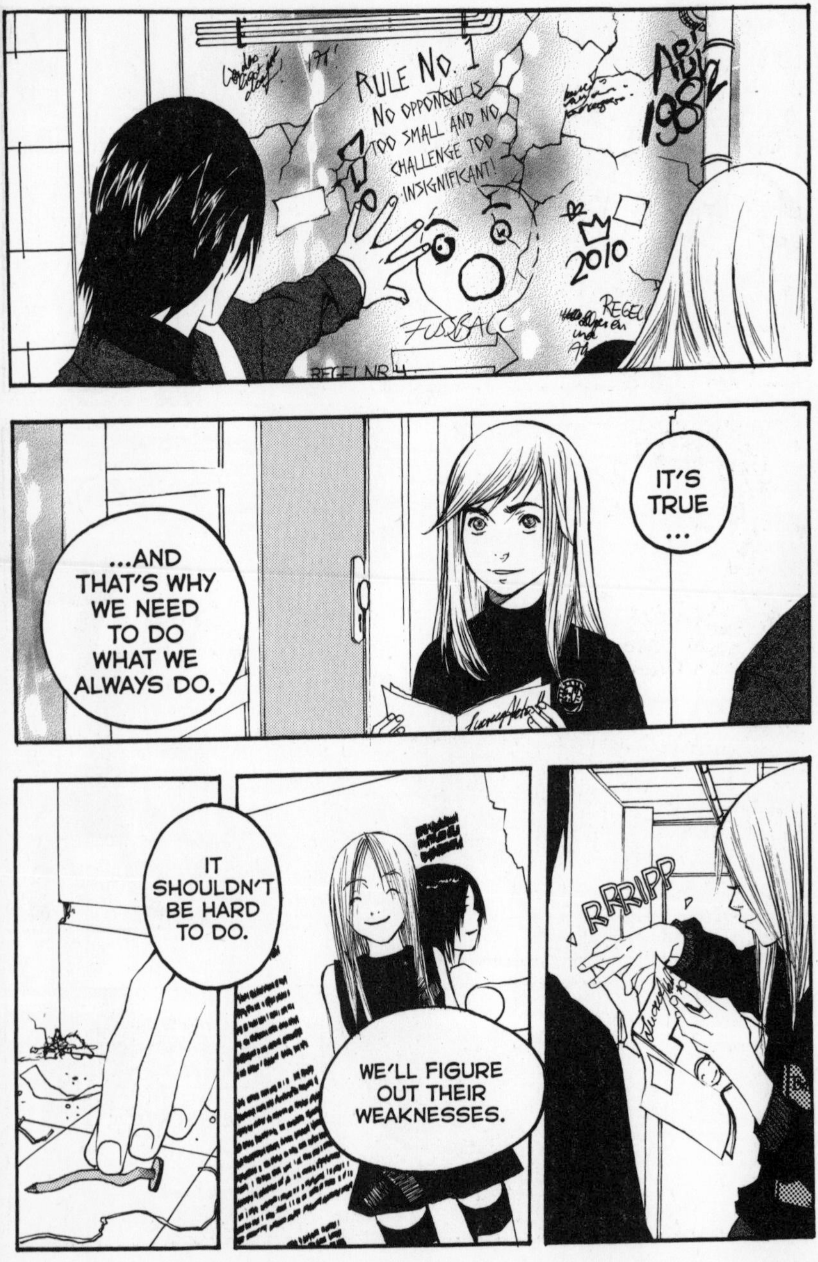
RULE NO. 1
NO OPPONENT IS TOO SMALL AND NO CHALLENGE TOO INSIGNIFICANT!
2010
FUSSBALL
IT'S TRUE ...
...AND THAT'S WHY WE NEED TO DO WHAT WE ALWAYS DO.
RRRIPP
WE'LL FIGURE OUT THEIR WEAKNESSES.
IT SHOULDN'T BE HARD TO DO.

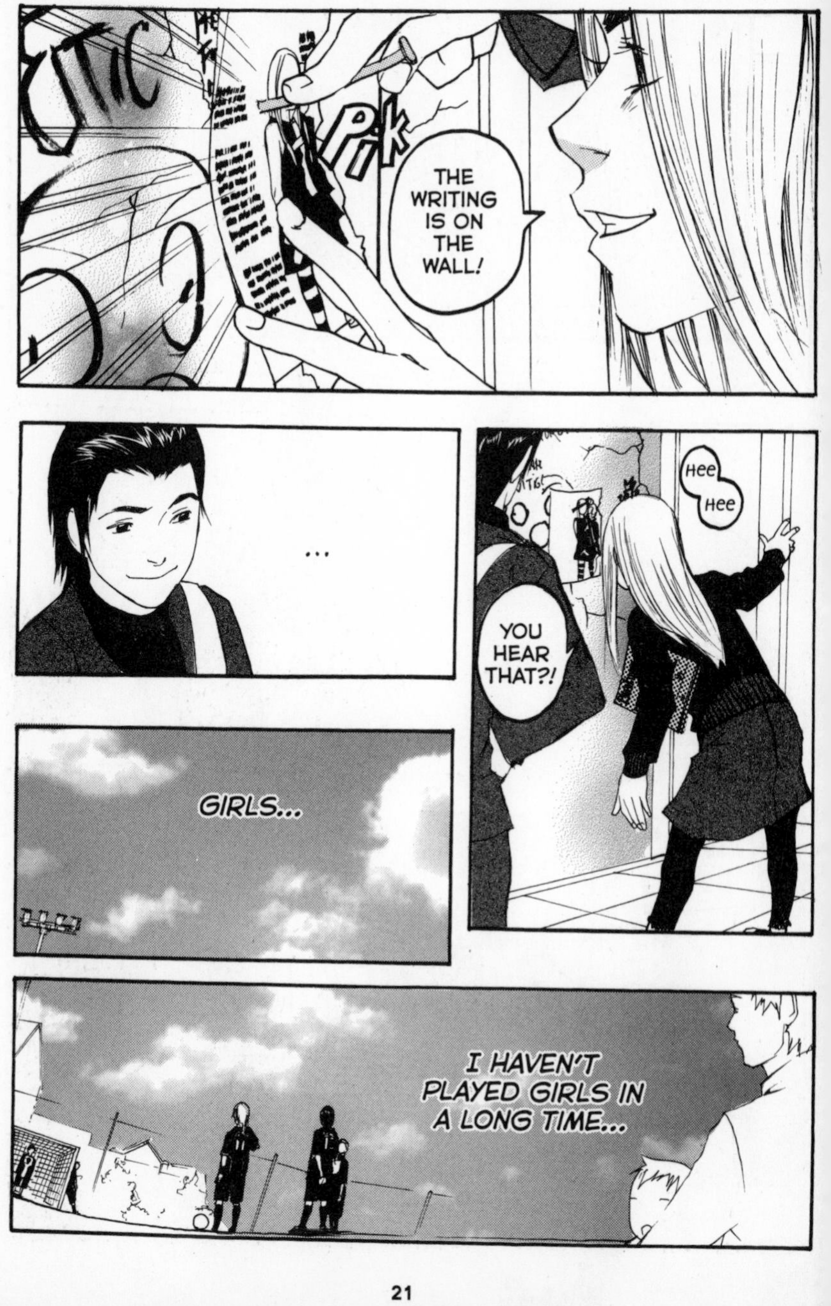
THE WRITING IS ON THE WALL!
Pik
Hee Hee
YOU HEAR THAT?!
...
GIRLS...
I HAVEN'T PLAYED GIRLS IN A LONG TIME...

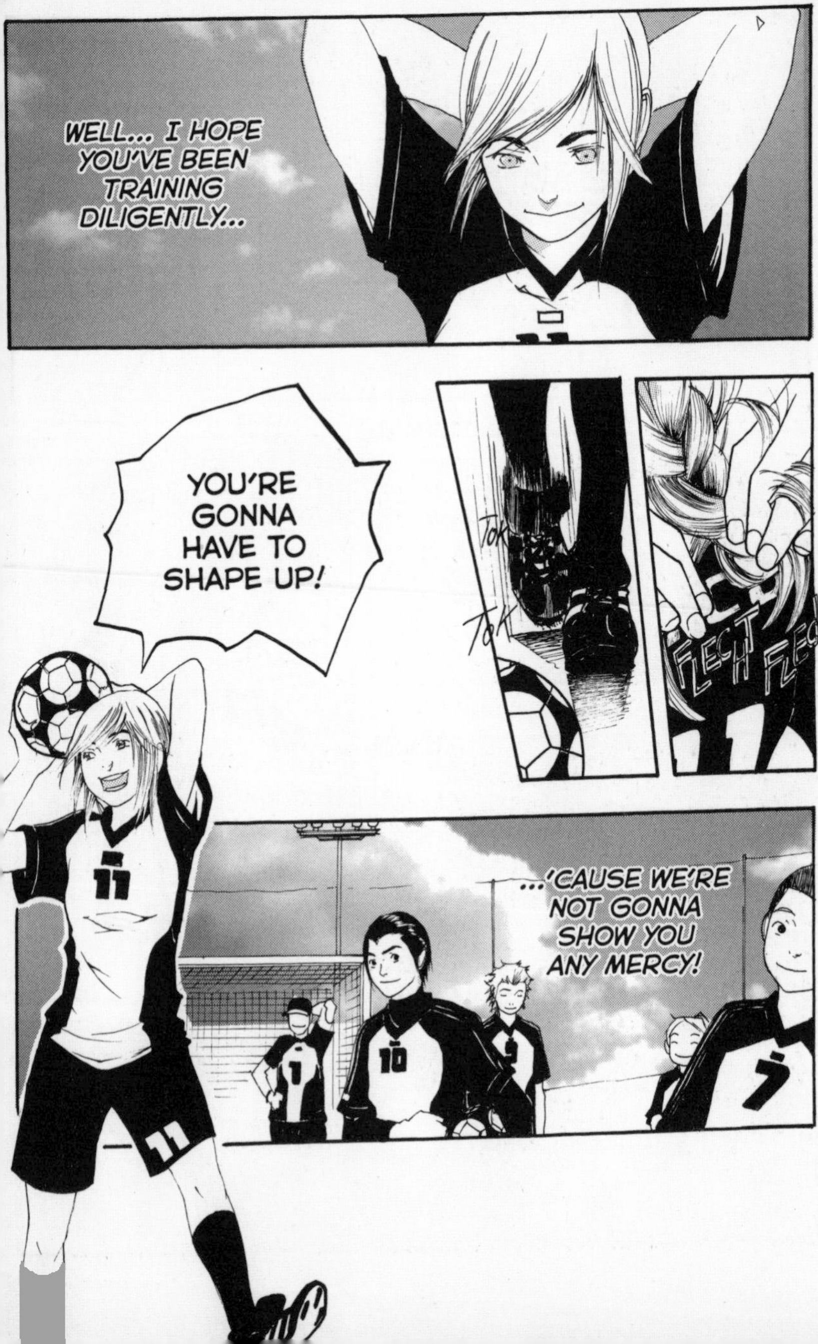
WELL... I HOPE YOU'VE BEEN TRAINING DILIGENTLY...
FLECHT FLECHT
Tok Tok
YOU'RE GONNA HAVE TO SHAPE UP!
...'CAUSE WE'RE NOT GONNA SHOW YOU ANY MERCY!

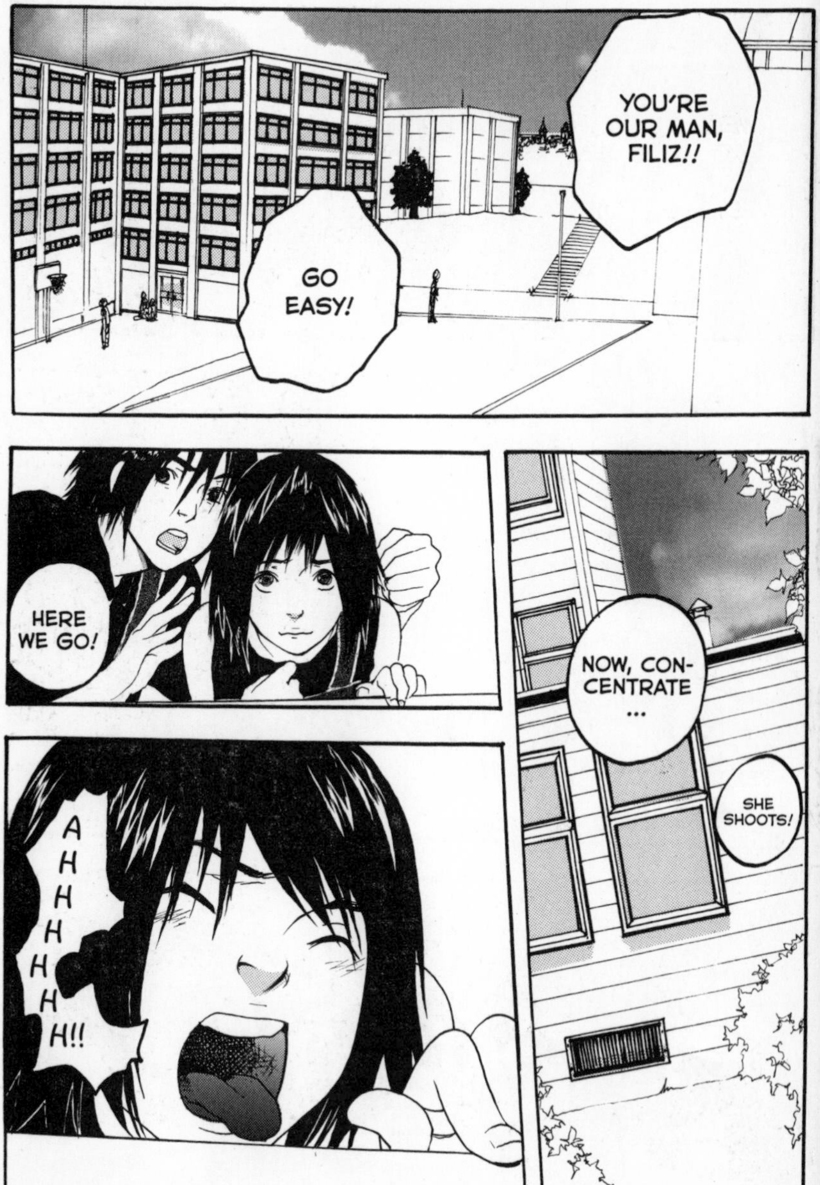
YOU'RE OUR MAN, FILIZ!!
GO EASY!
NOW, CONCENTRATE ...
SHE SHOOTS!
HERE WE GO!
AHHHHHHH!!

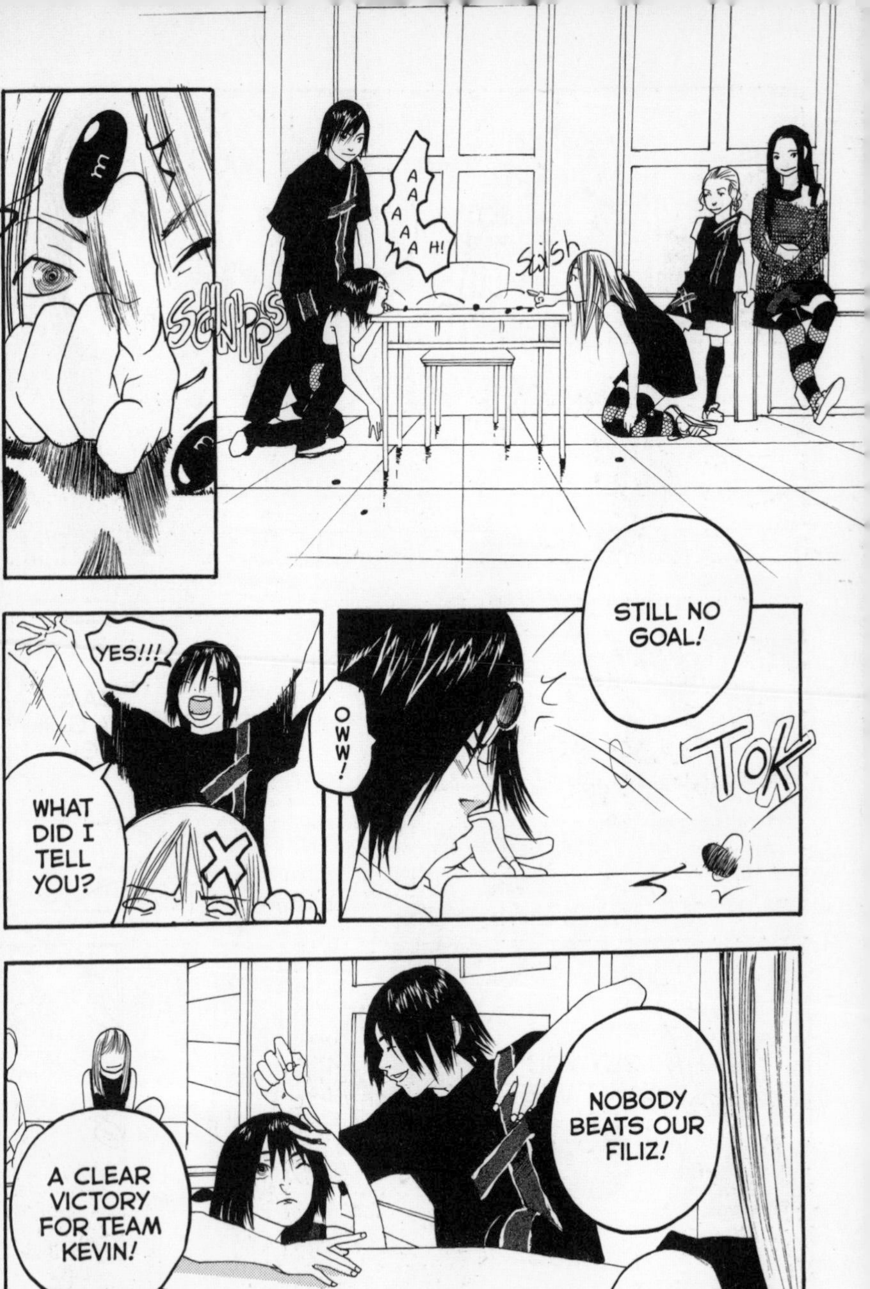
AAAAAH!
Swish
Schnipps
STILL NO GOAL!
TOK
OWW!
YES!!!
WHAT DID I TELL YOU?
NOBODY BEATS OUR FILIZ!
A CLEAR VICTORY FOR TEAM KEVIN!

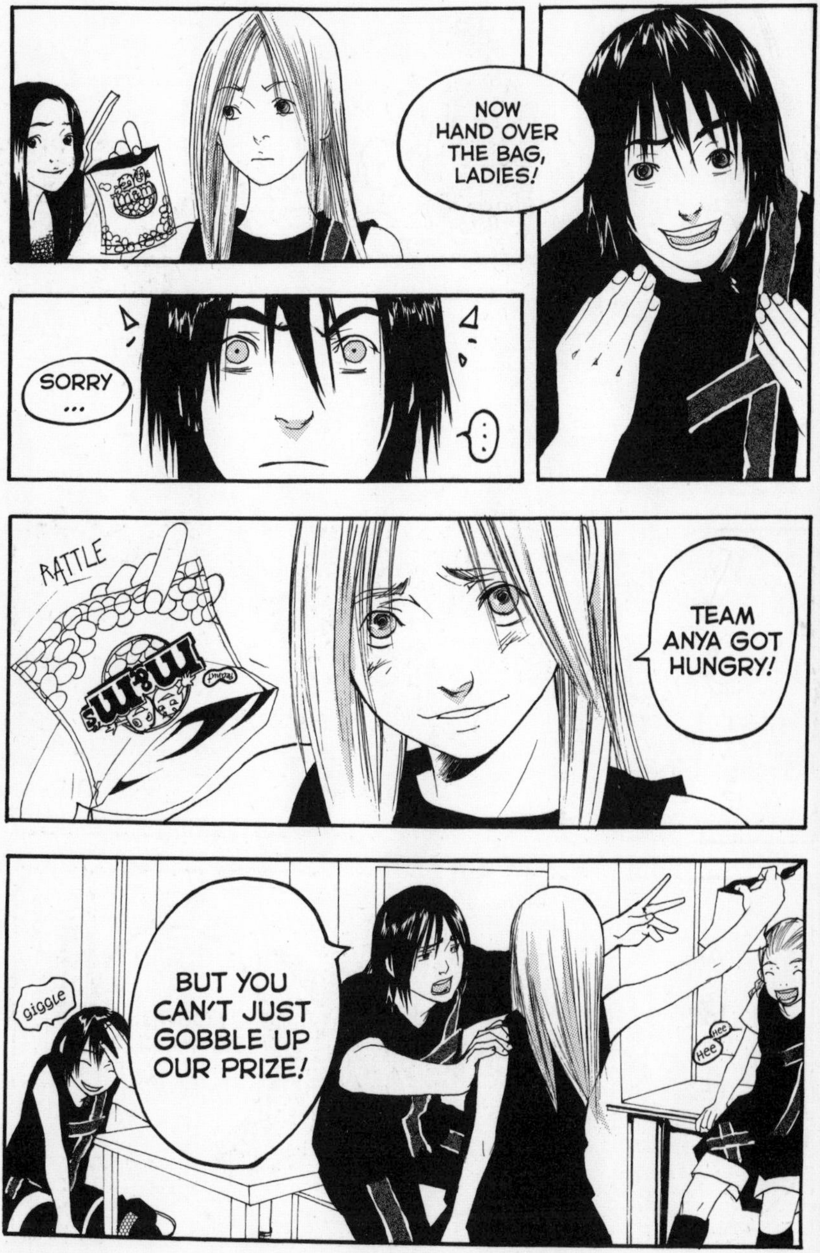
NOW HAND OVER THE BAG, LADIES!
SORRY ...
...
TEAM ANYA GOT HUNGRY!
RATTLE
Hee
Hee
BUT YOU CAN'T JUST GOBBLE UP OUR PRIZE!
giggle

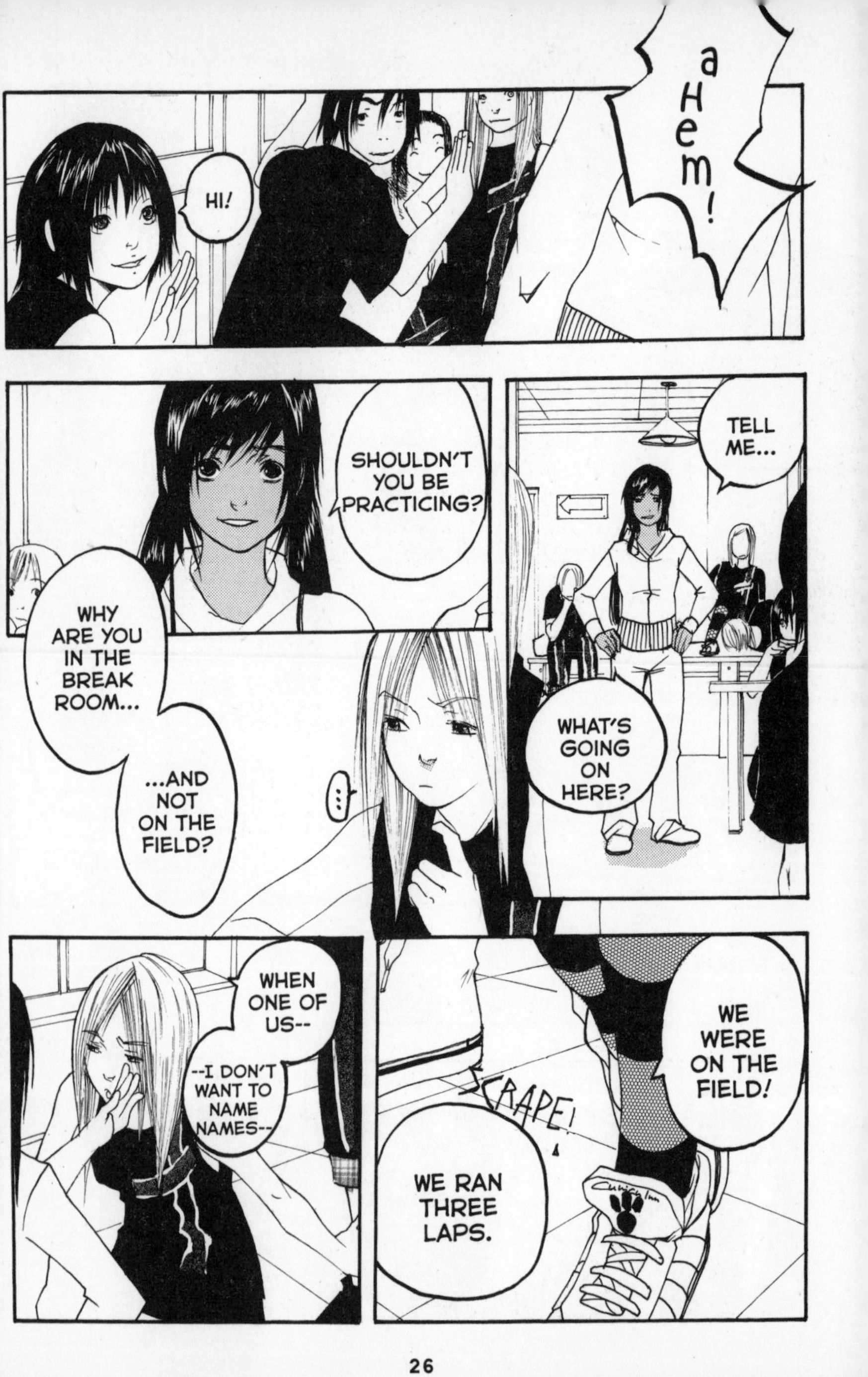
aHem!
HI!
TELL ME...
WHAT'S GOING ON HERE?
SHOULDN'T YOU BE PRACTICING?
WHY ARE YOU IN THE BREAK ROOM...
...AND NOT ON THE FIELD?
...
WE WERE ON THE FIELD!
SCRAPE!
WE RAN THREE LAPS.
WHEN ONE OF US--
--I DON'T WANT TO NAME NAMES--

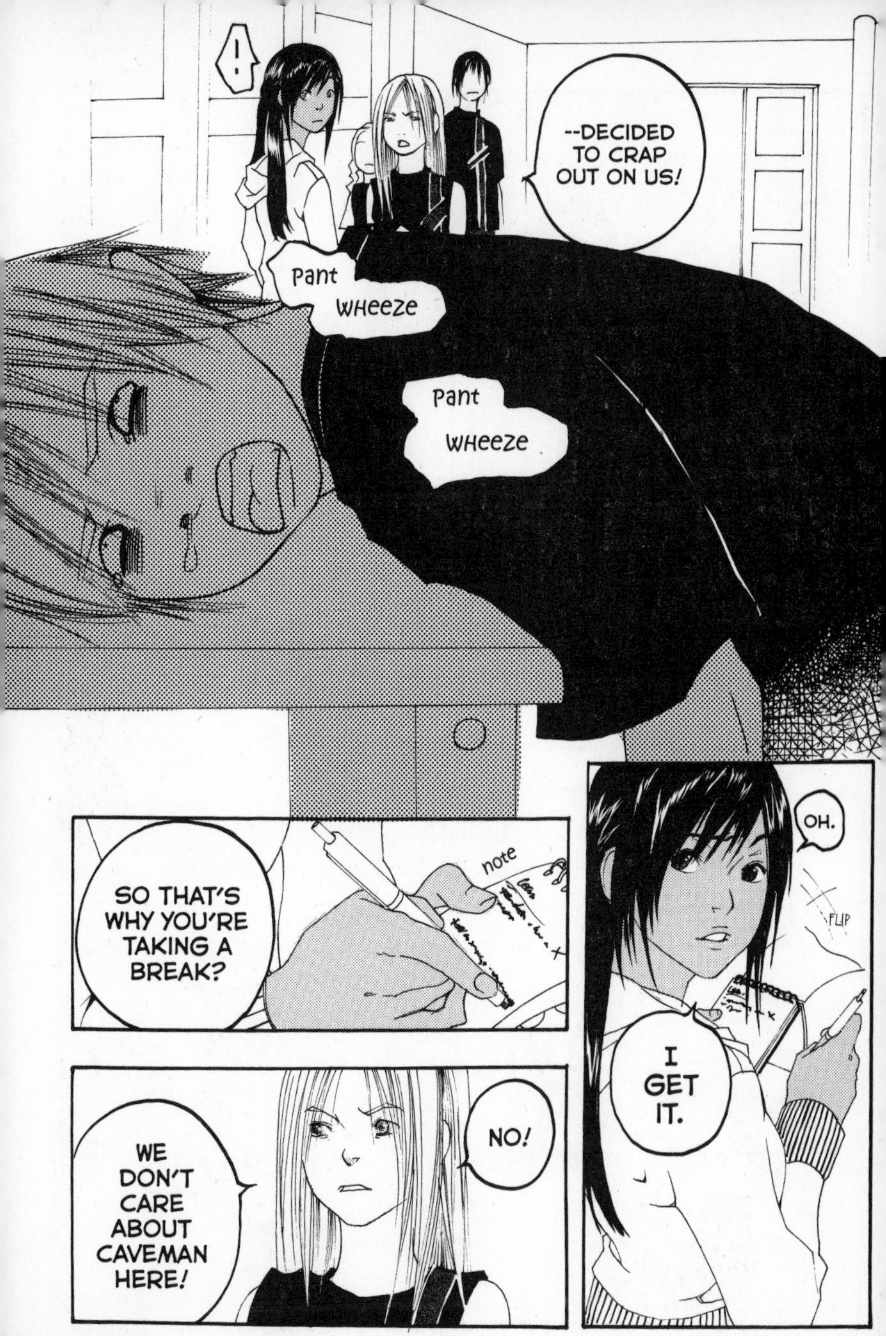
--DECIDED TO CRAP OUT ON US!
!
Pant WHEEZE
Pant WHEEZE
OH.
FLIP
I GET IT.
note
SO THAT'S WHY YOU'RE TAKING A BREAK?
NO!
WE DON'T CARE ABOUT CAVEMAN HERE!

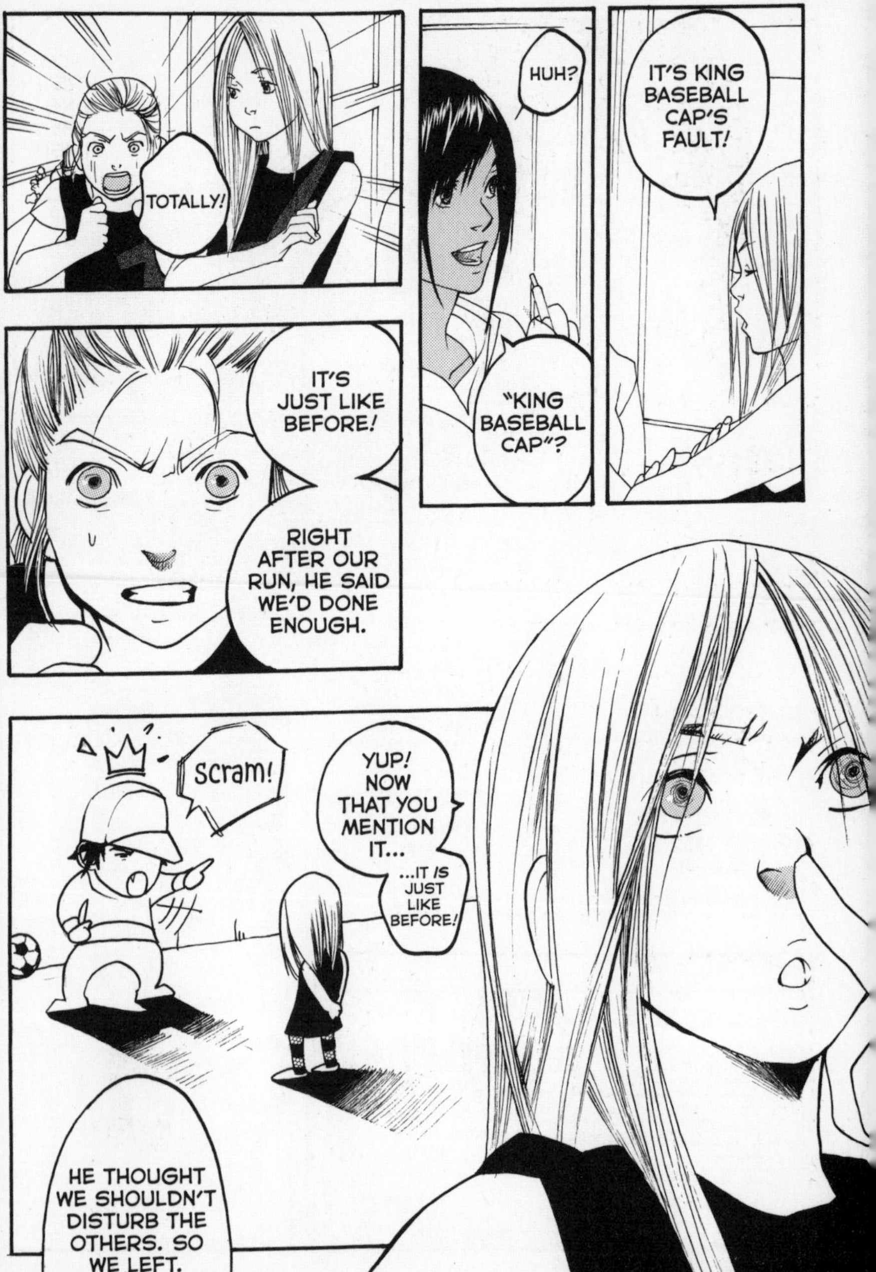
IT'S KING BASEBALL CAP'S FAULT!
HUH?
"KING BASEBALL CAP"?
TOTALLY!
IT'S JUST LIKE BEFORE!
RIGHT AFTER OUR RUN, HE SAID WE'D DONE ENOUGH.
YUP! NOW THAT YOU MENTION IT...
...IT *IS* JUST LIKE BEFORE!
Scram!
HE THOUGHT WE SHOULDN'T DISTURB THE OTHERS. SO WE LEFT.

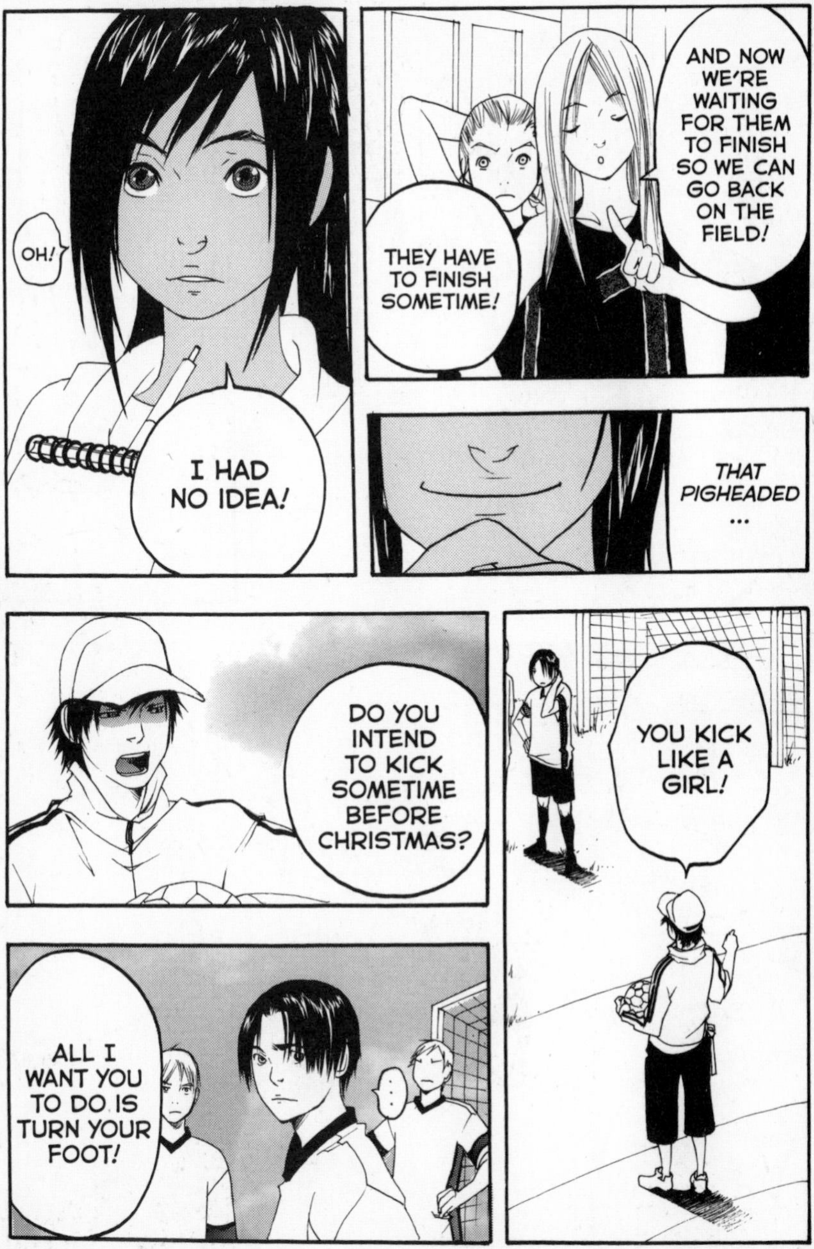
AND NOW WE'RE WAITING FOR THEM TO FINISH SO WE CAN GO BACK ON THE FIELD!
THEY HAVE TO FINISH SOMETIME!
THAT PIGHEADED ...
OH!
I HAD NO IDEA!
YOU KICK LIKE A GIRL!
DO YOU INTEND TO KICK SOMETIME BEFORE CHRISTMAS?
...
ALL I WANT YOU TO DO IS TURN YOUR FOOT!

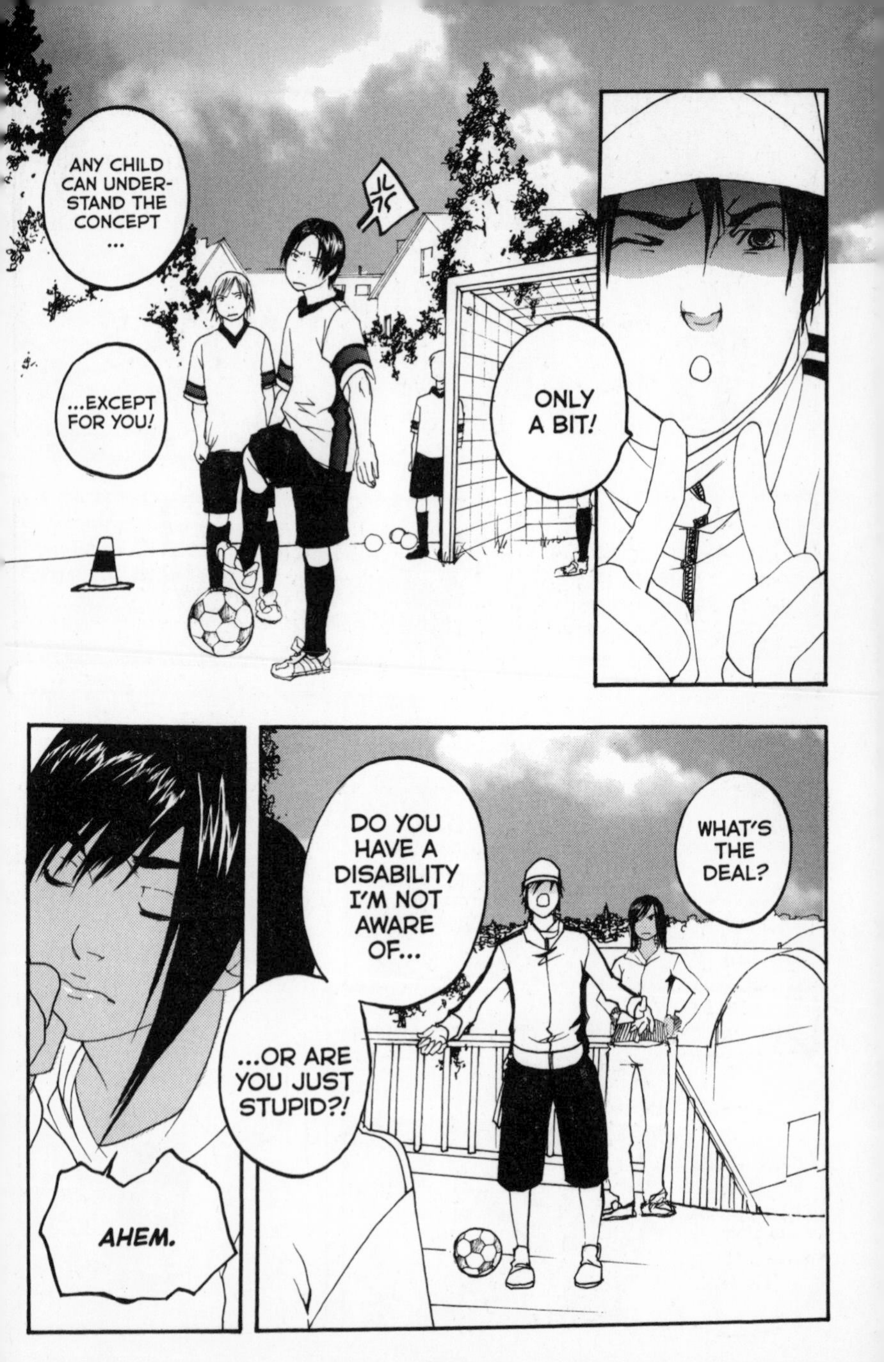
ONLY A BIT!
ANY CHILD CAN UNDERSTAND THE CONCEPT ...
...EXCEPT FOR YOU!
WHAT'S THE DEAL?
DO YOU HAVE A DISABILITY I'M NOT AWARE OF...
...OR ARE YOU JUST STUPID?!
AHEM.

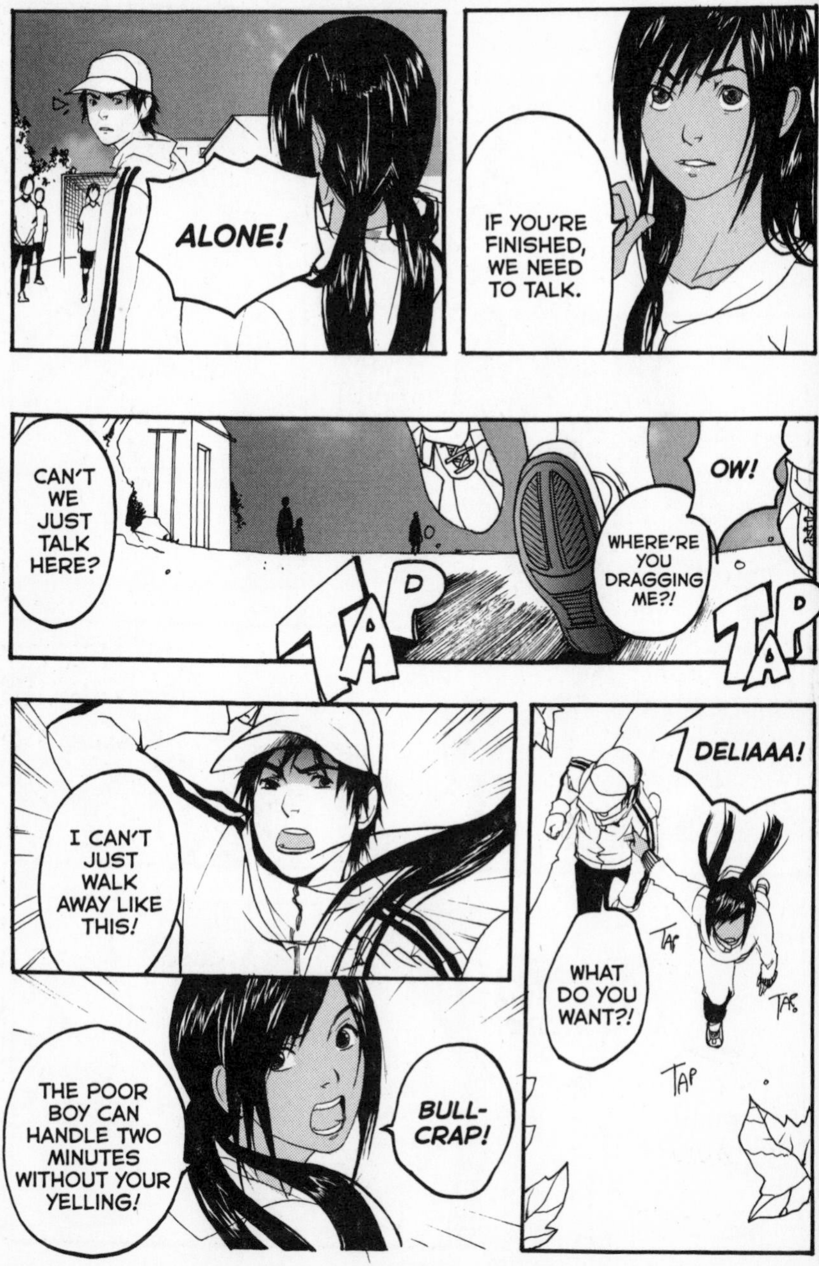
IF YOU'RE FINISHED, WE NEED TO TALK.
ALONE!
OW!
WHERE'RE YOU DRAGGING ME?!
TAP
CAN'T WE JUST TALK HERE?
TAP
DELIAAA!
WHAT DO YOU WANT?!
TAP
TAP
TAP
I CAN'T JUST WALK AWAY LIKE THIS!
BULL-CRAP!
THE POOR BOY CAN HANDLE TWO MINUTES WITHOUT YOUR YELLING!

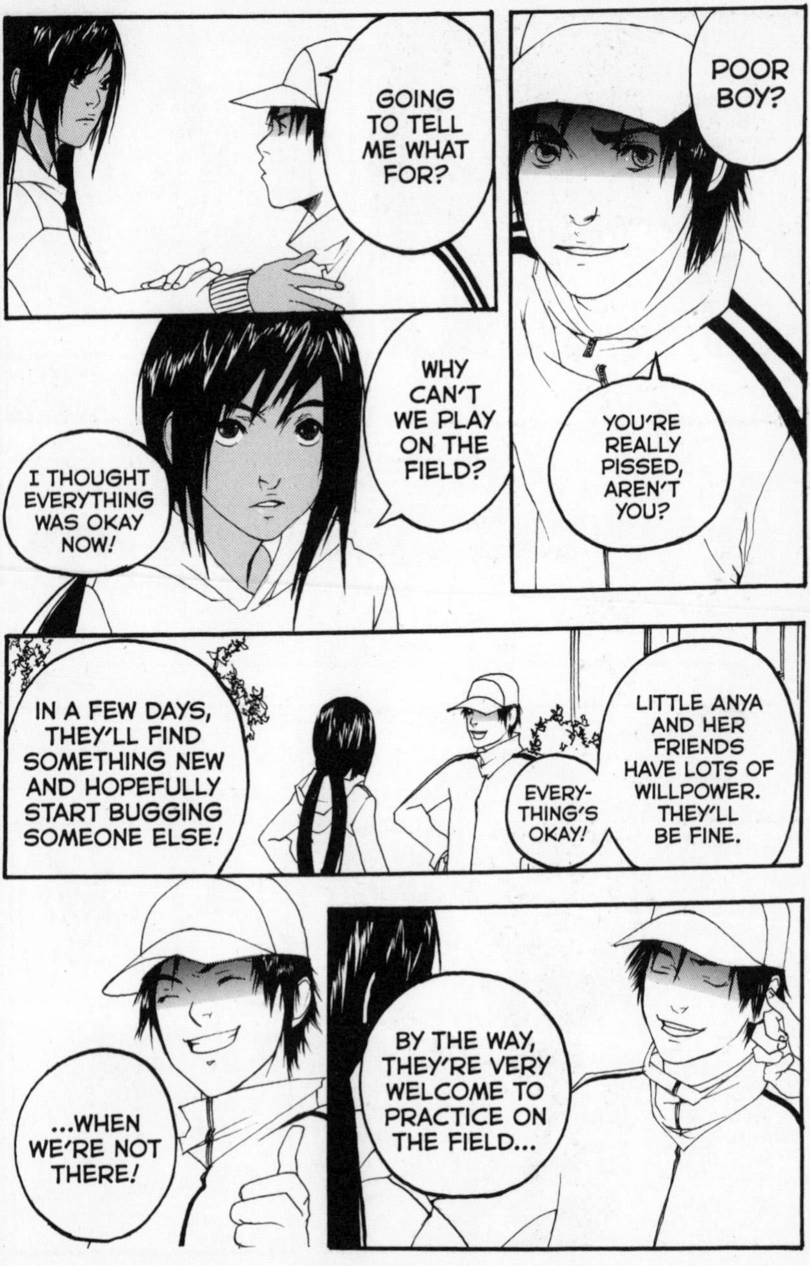
POOR BOY?
YOU'RE REALLY PISSED, AREN'T YOU?
GOING TO TELL ME WHAT FOR?
WHY CAN'T WE PLAY ON THE FIELD?
I THOUGHT EVERYTHING WAS OKAY NOW!
LITTLE ANYA AND HER FRIENDS HAVE LOTS OF WILLPOWER. THEY'LL BE FINE.
EVERY-THING'S OKAY!
IN A FEW DAYS, THEY'LL FIND SOMETHING NEW AND HOPEFULLY START BUGGING SOMEONE ELSE!
BY THE WAY, THEY'RE VERY WELCOME TO PRACTICE ON THE FIELD...
...WHEN WE'RE NOT THERE!

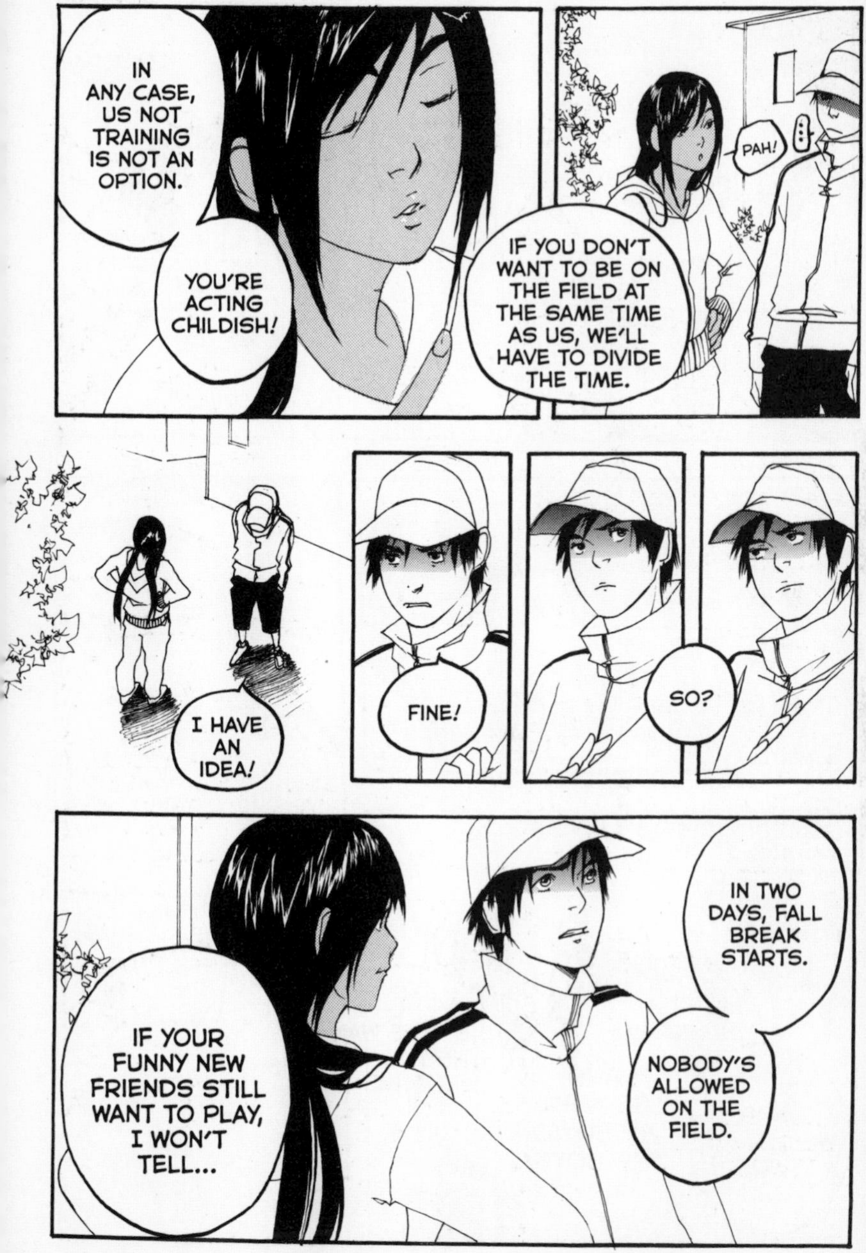
...
PAH!
IF YOU DON'T WANT TO BE ON THE FIELD AT THE SAME TIME AS US, WE'LL HAVE TO DIVIDE THE TIME.
IN ANY CASE, US NOT TRAINING IS NOT AN OPTION.
YOU'RE ACTING CHILDISH!
SO?
FINE!
I HAVE AN IDEA!
IN TWO DAYS, FALL BREAK STARTS.
NOBODY'S ALLOWED ON THE FIELD.
IF YOUR FUNNY NEW FRIENDS STILL WANT TO PLAY, I WON'T TELL...

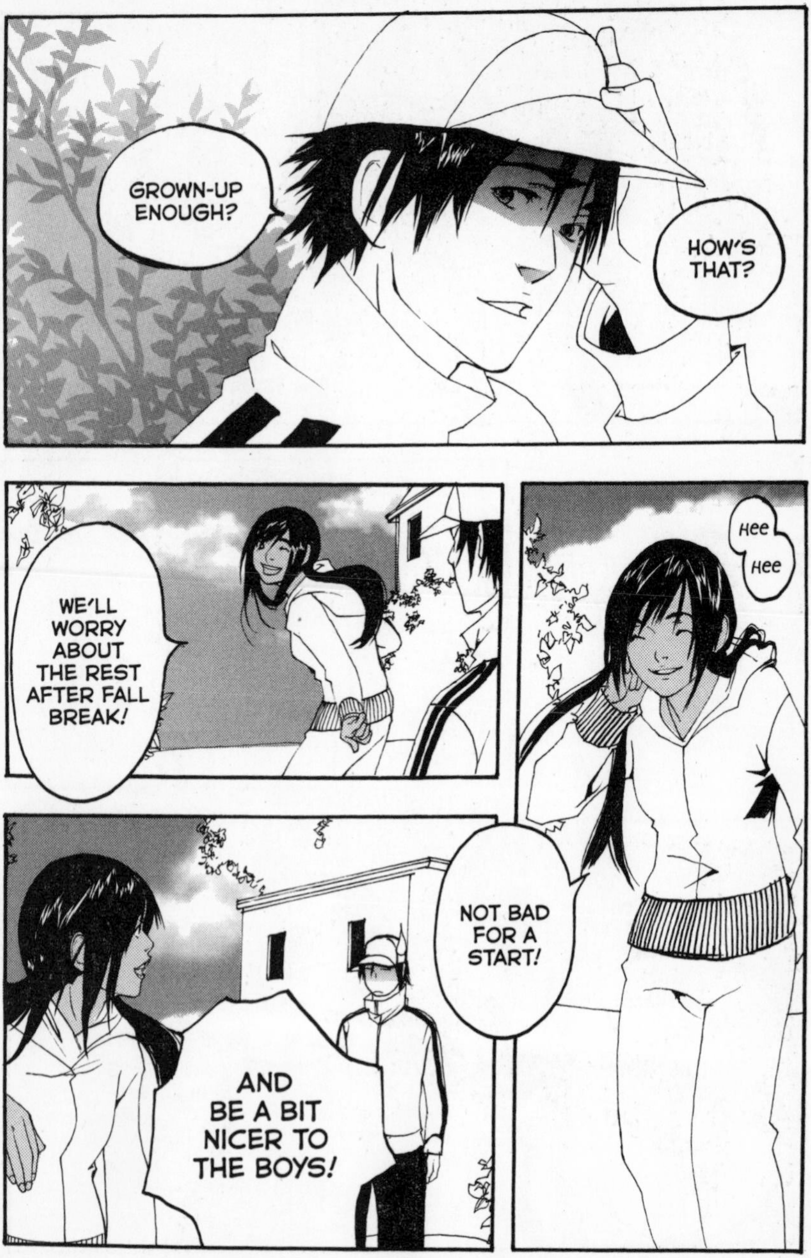
HOW'S THAT?
GROWN-UP ENOUGH?
Hee hee
NOT BAD FOR A START!
WE'LL WORRY ABOUT THE REST AFTER FALL BREAK!
AND BE A BIT NICER TO THE BOYS!

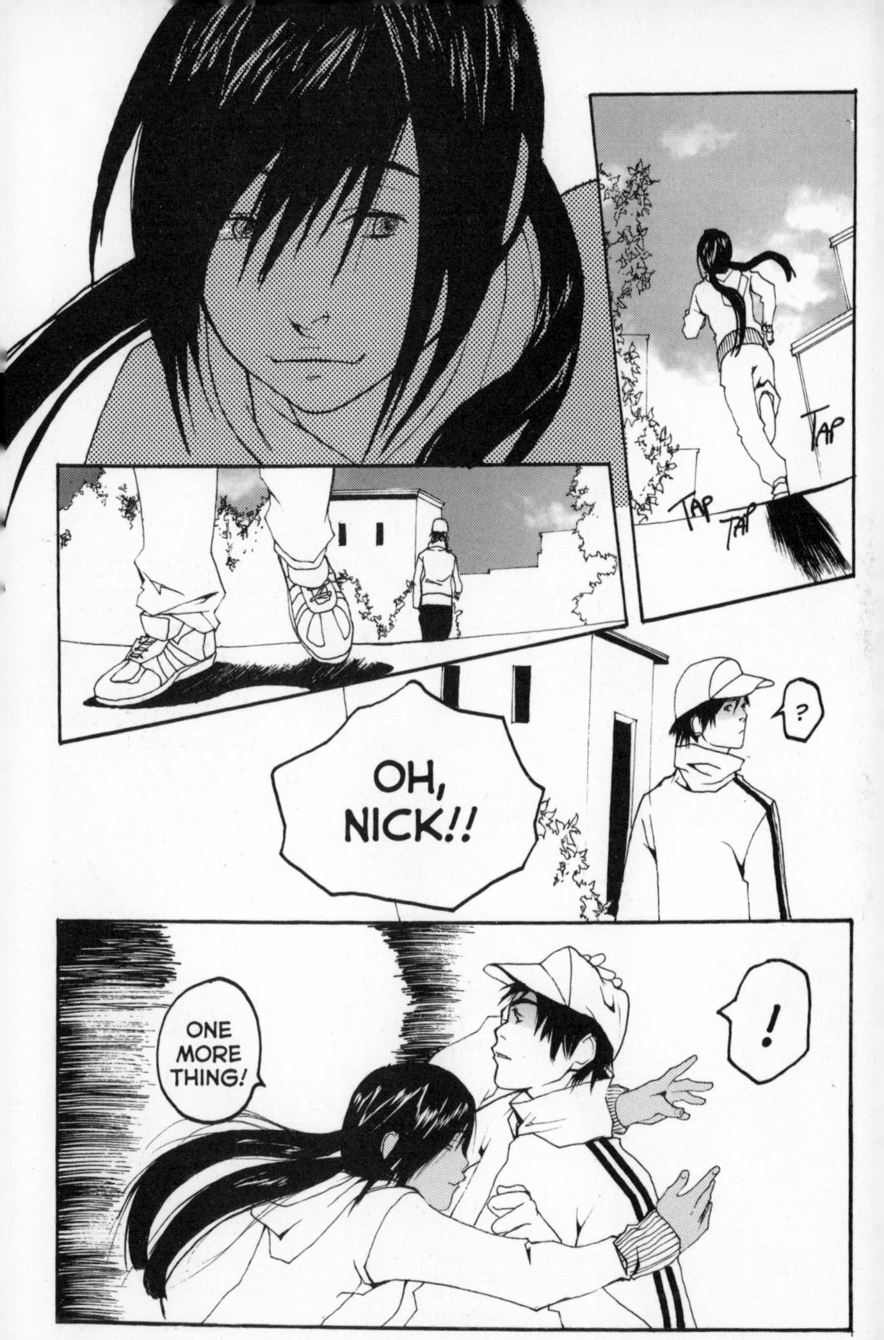
TAP
TAP
TAP
?
OH, NICK!!
!
ONE MORE THING!

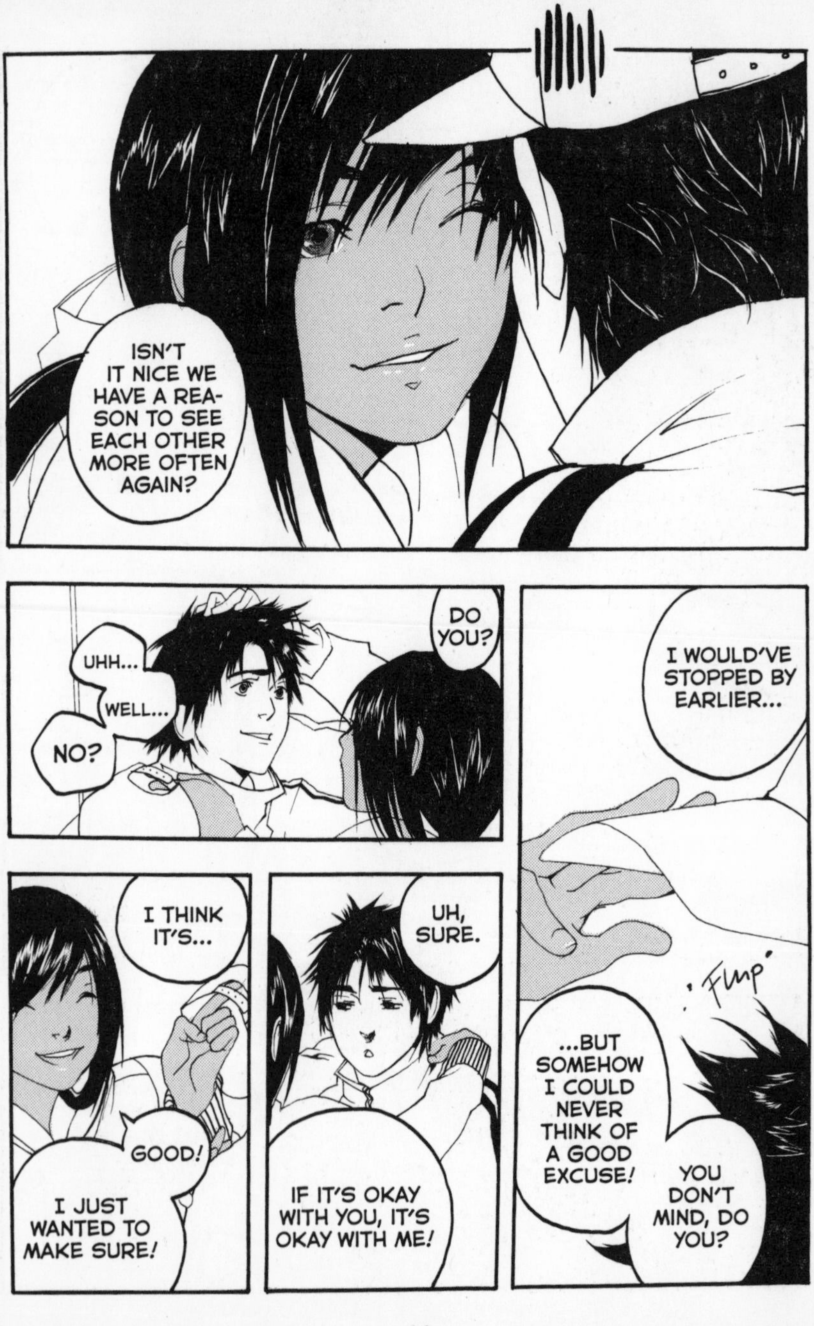
ISN'T IT NICE WE HAVE A REA- SON TO SEE EACH OTHER MORE OFTEN AGAIN?
I WOULD'VE STOPPED BY EARLIER...
...BUT SOMEHOW I COULD NEVER THINK OF A GOOD EXCUSE!
FLMP
YOU DON'T MIND, DO YOU?
DO YOU?
UHH...
WELL...
NO?
UH, SURE.
IF IT'S OKAY WITH YOU, IT'S OKAY WITH ME!
I THINK IT'S...
GOOD!
I JUST WANTED TO MAKE SURE!

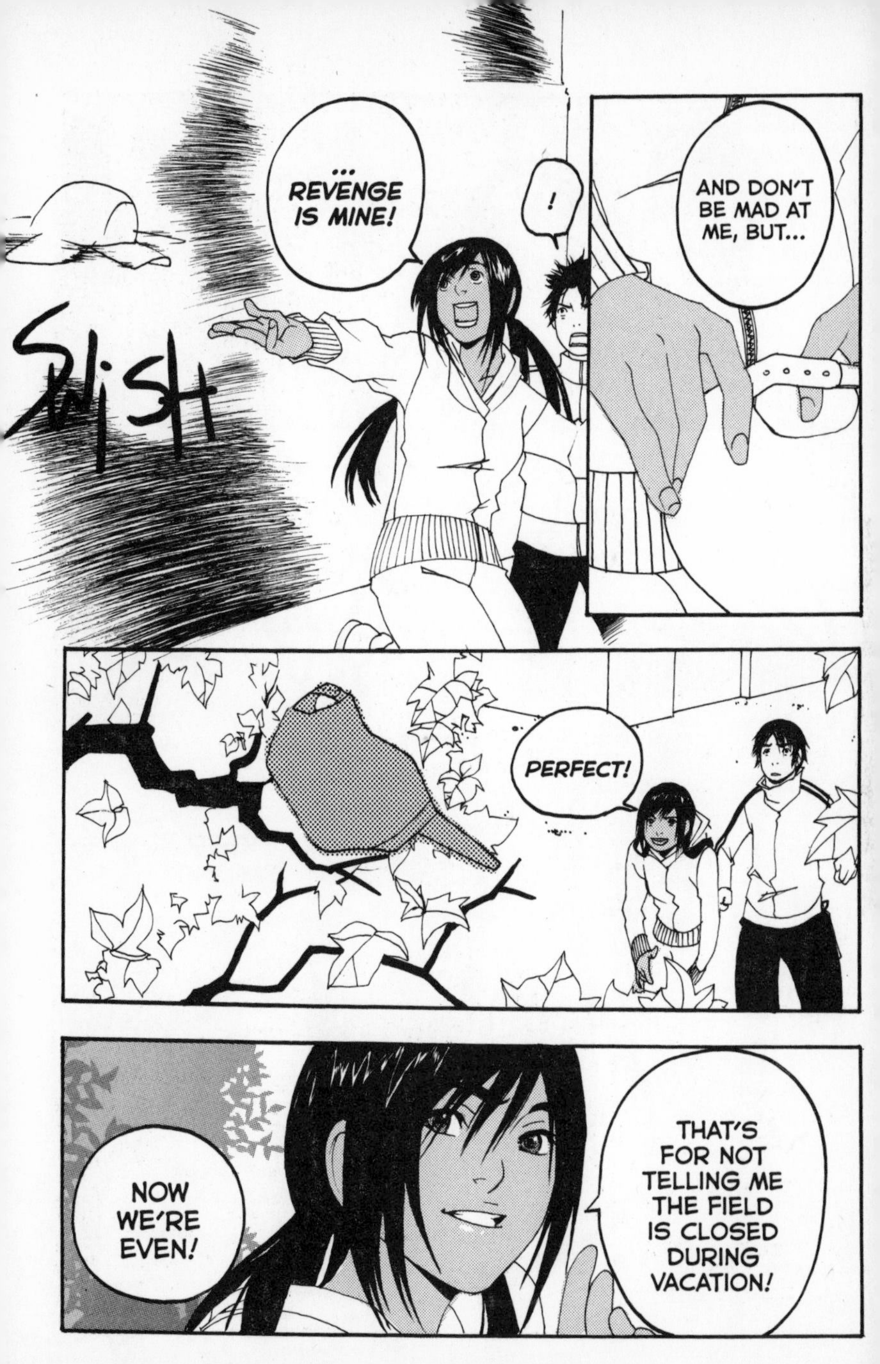
AND DON'T BE MAD AT ME, BUT...
...REVENGE IS MINE!
!
SWISH
PERFECT!
THAT'S FOR NOT TELLING ME THE FIELD IS CLOSED DURING VACATION!
NOW WE'RE EVEN!

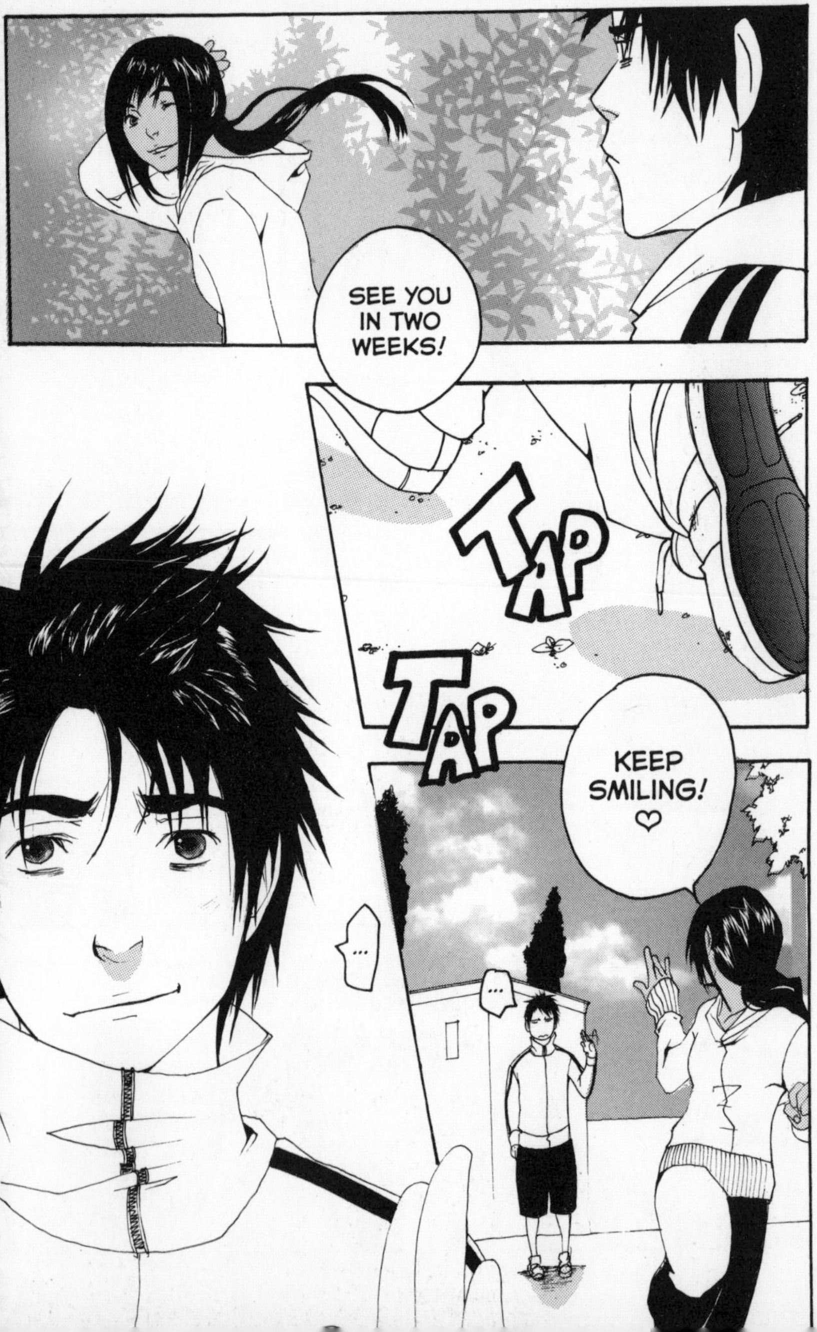
SEE YOU IN TWO WEEKS!
TAP
TAP
KEEP SMILING! ♡
...
...

14

VACATION BEGINS

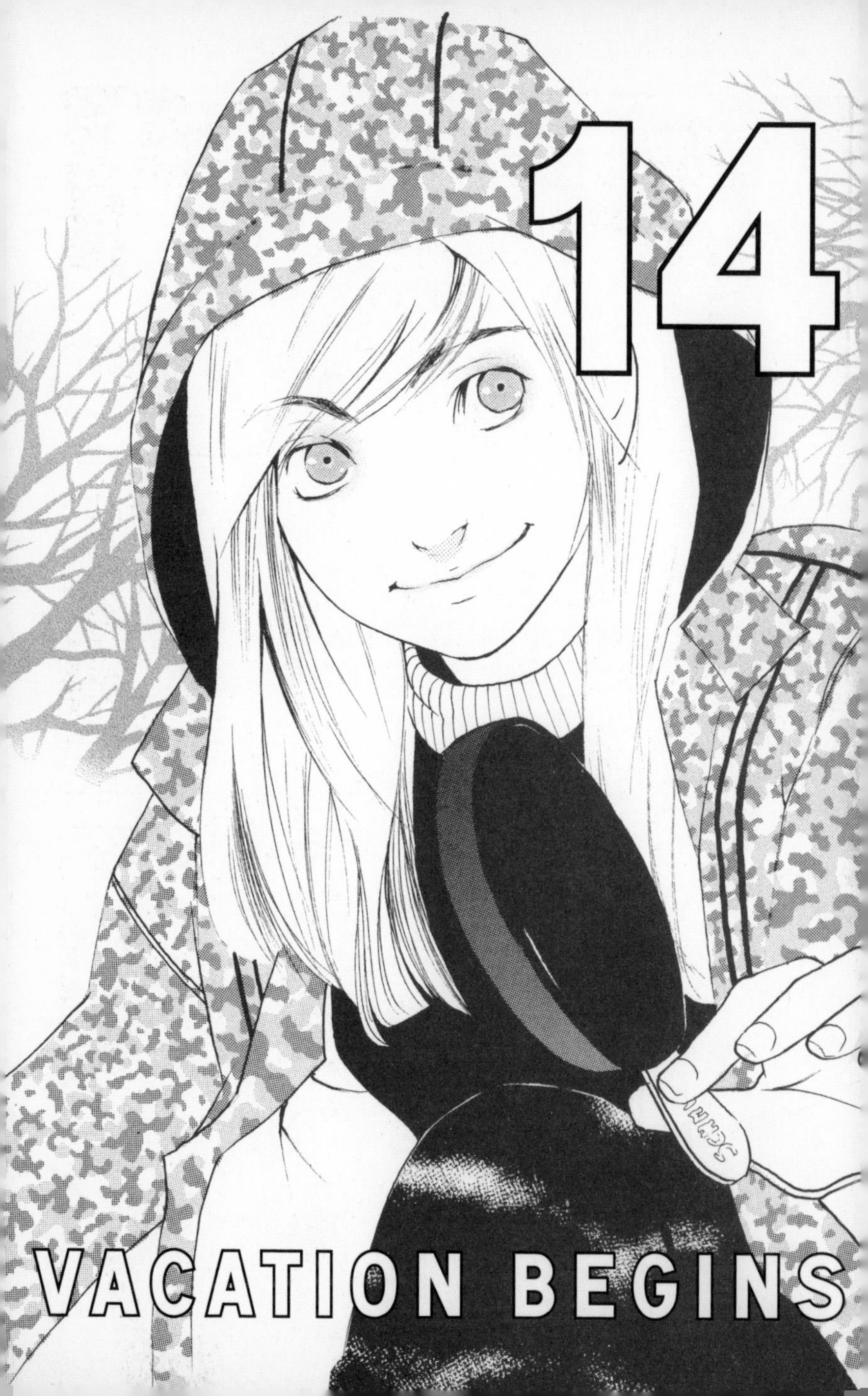

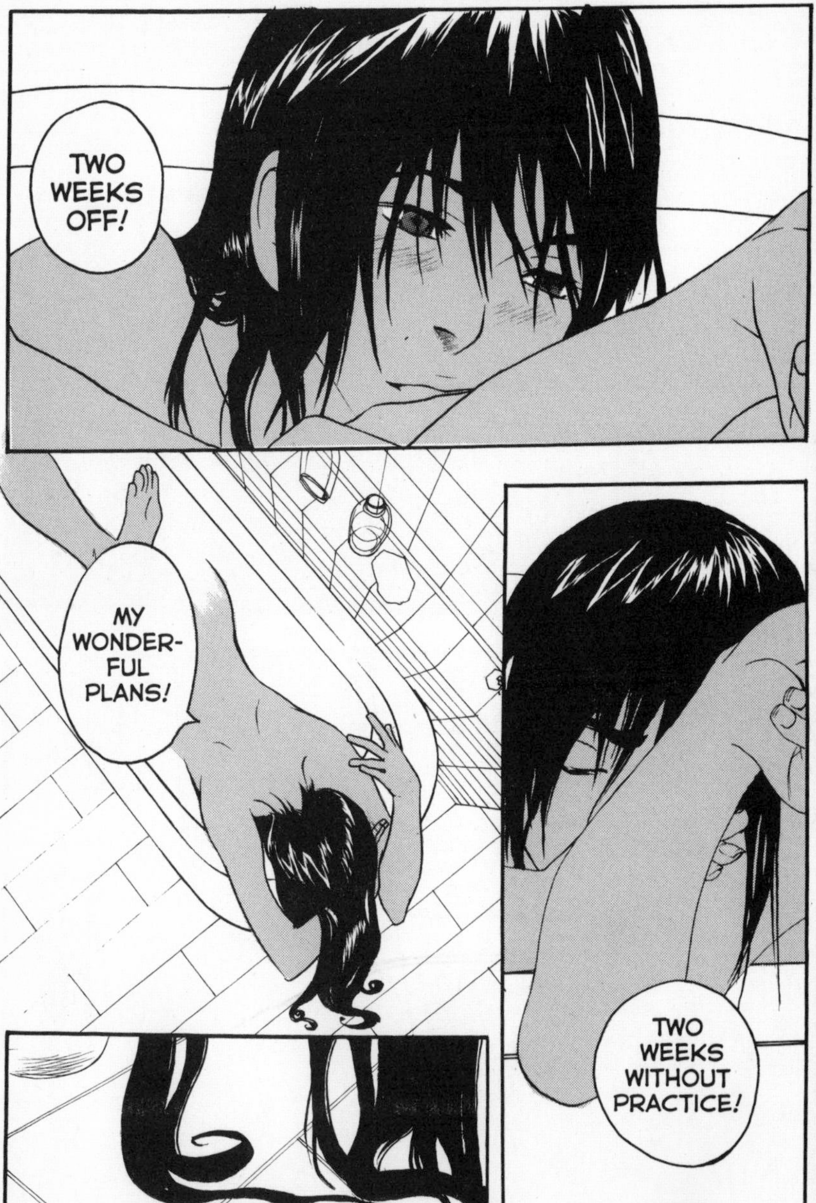
TWO WEEKS OFF!
TWO WEEKS WITHOUT PRACTICE!
MY WONDER-FUL PLANS!

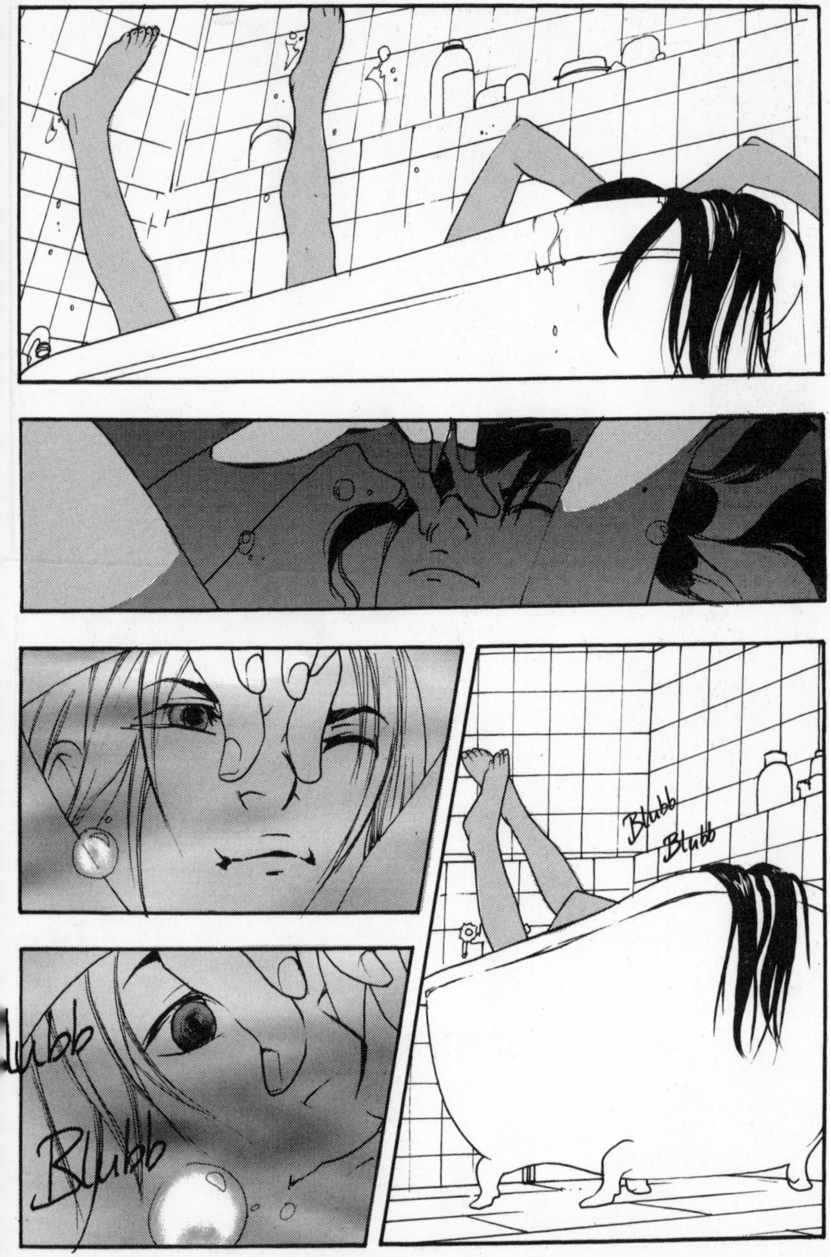
Blubb
Blubb
Blubb

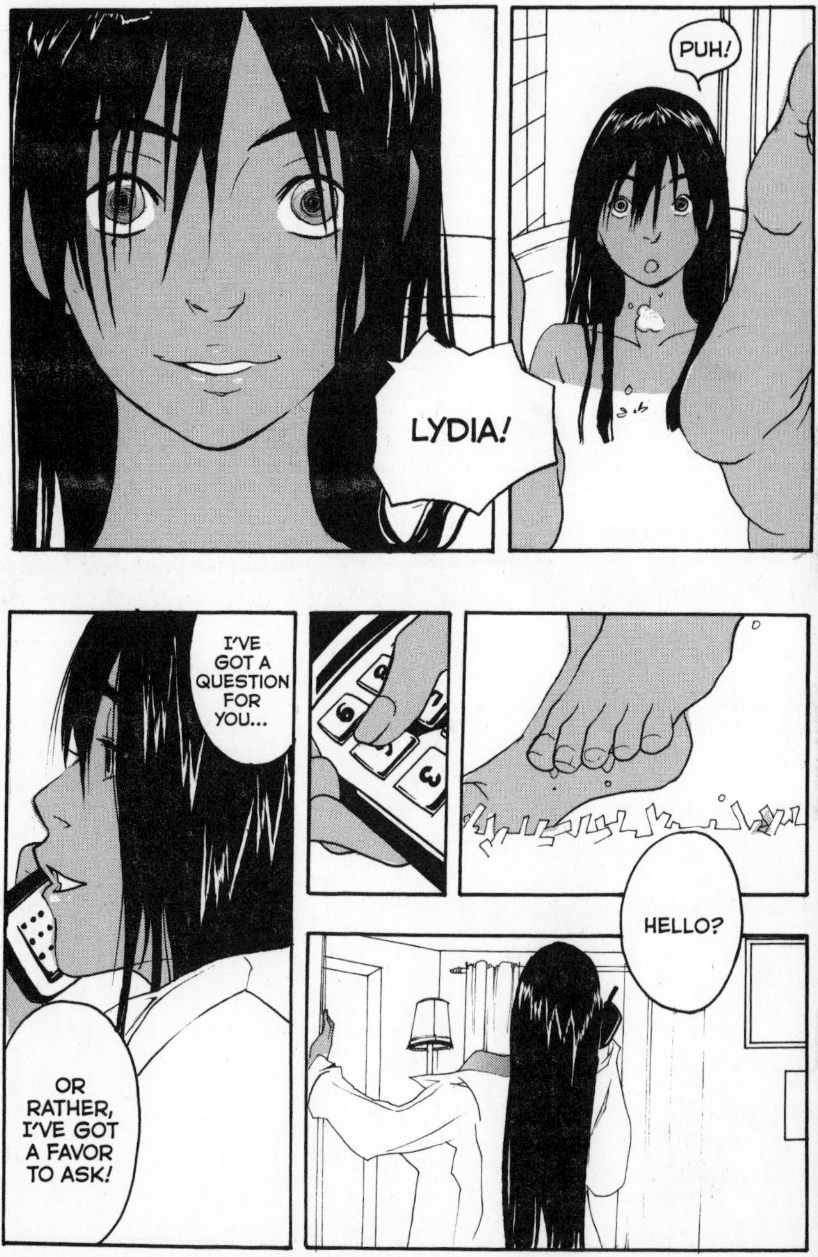
PUH!
LYDIA!
HELLO?
I'VE GOT A QUESTION FOR YOU...
OR RATHER, I'VE GOT A FAVOR TO ASK!

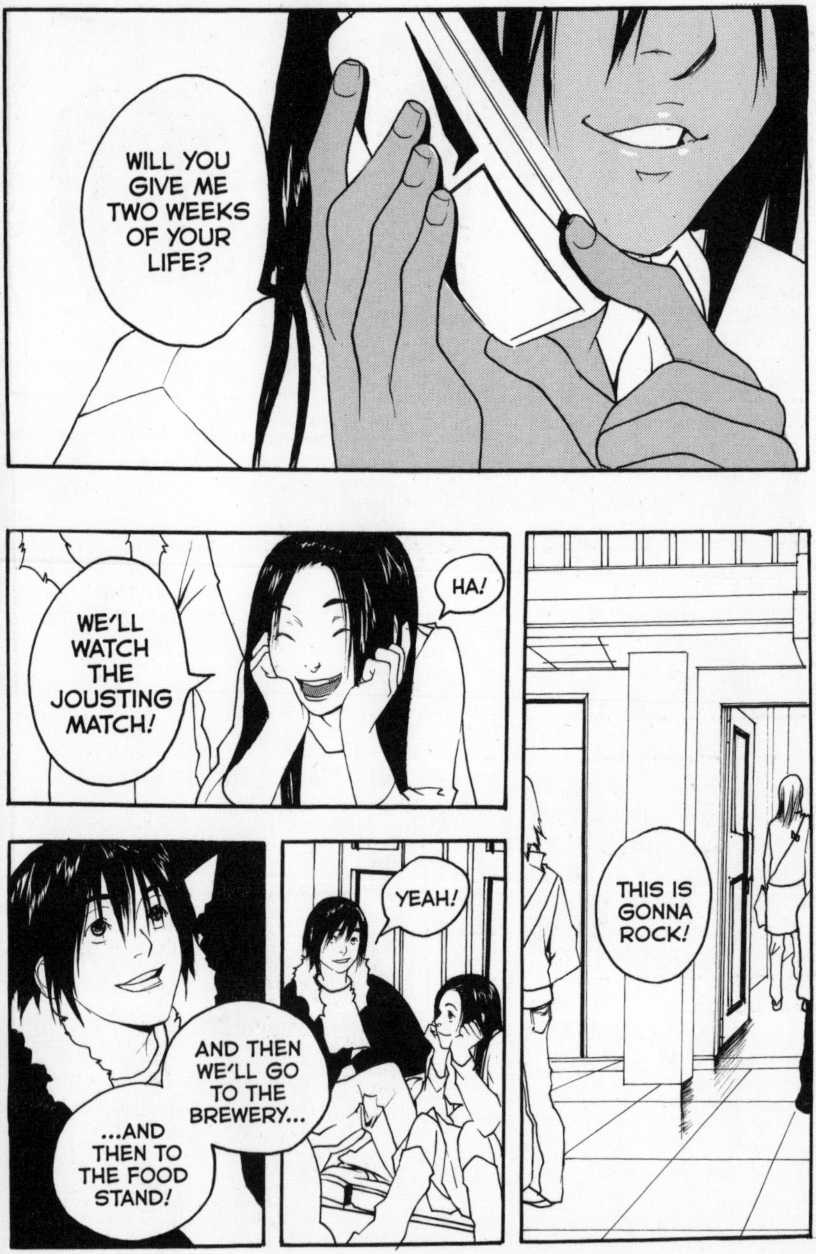
WILL YOU GIVE ME TWO WEEKS OF YOUR LIFE?
THIS IS GONNA ROCK!
HA!
WE'LL WATCH THE JOUSTING MATCH!
YEAH!
AND THEN WE'LL GO TO THE BREWERY...
...AND THEN TO THE FOOD STAND!

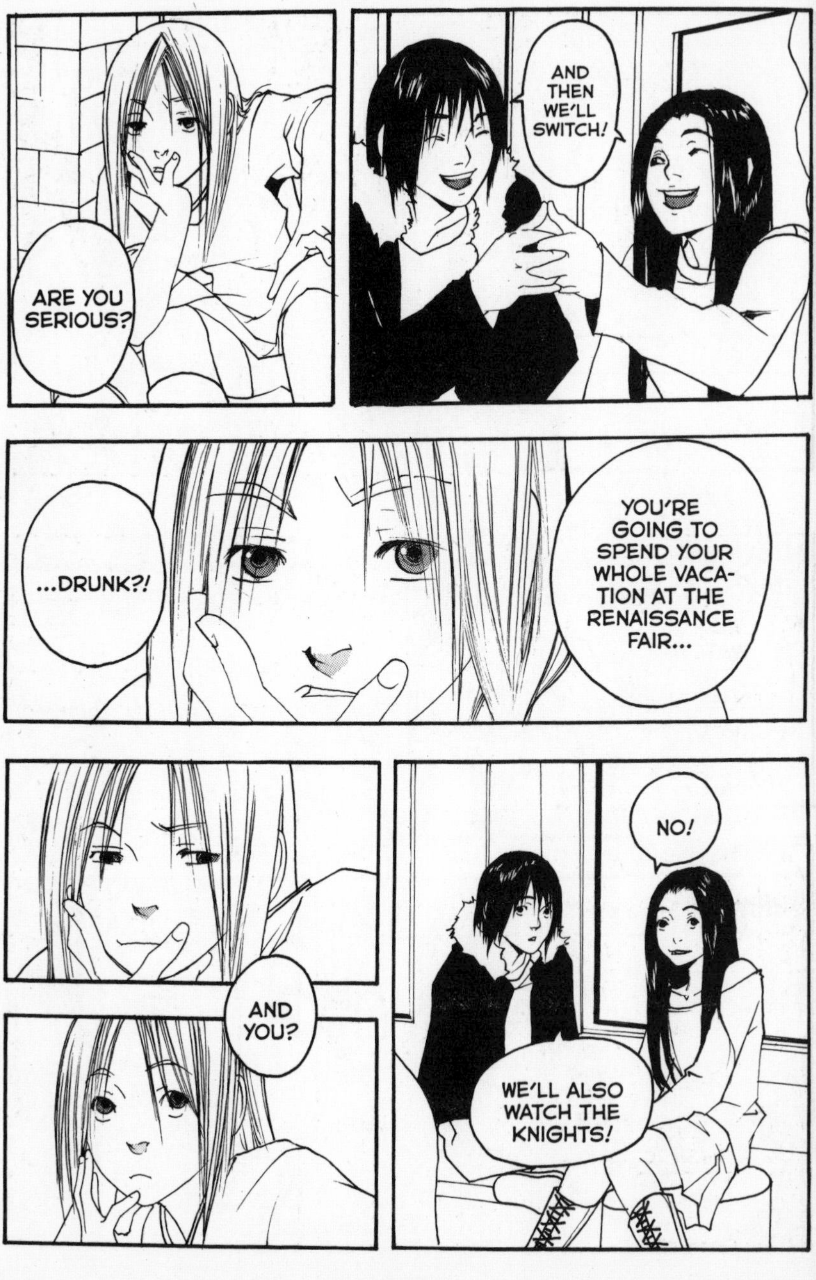
AND THEN WE'LL SWITCH!
ARE YOU SERIOUS?
YOU'RE GOING TO SPEND YOUR WHOLE VACA-TION AT THE RENAISSANCE FAIR...
...DRUNK?!
NO!
WE'LL ALSO WATCH THE KNIGHTS!
AND YOU?

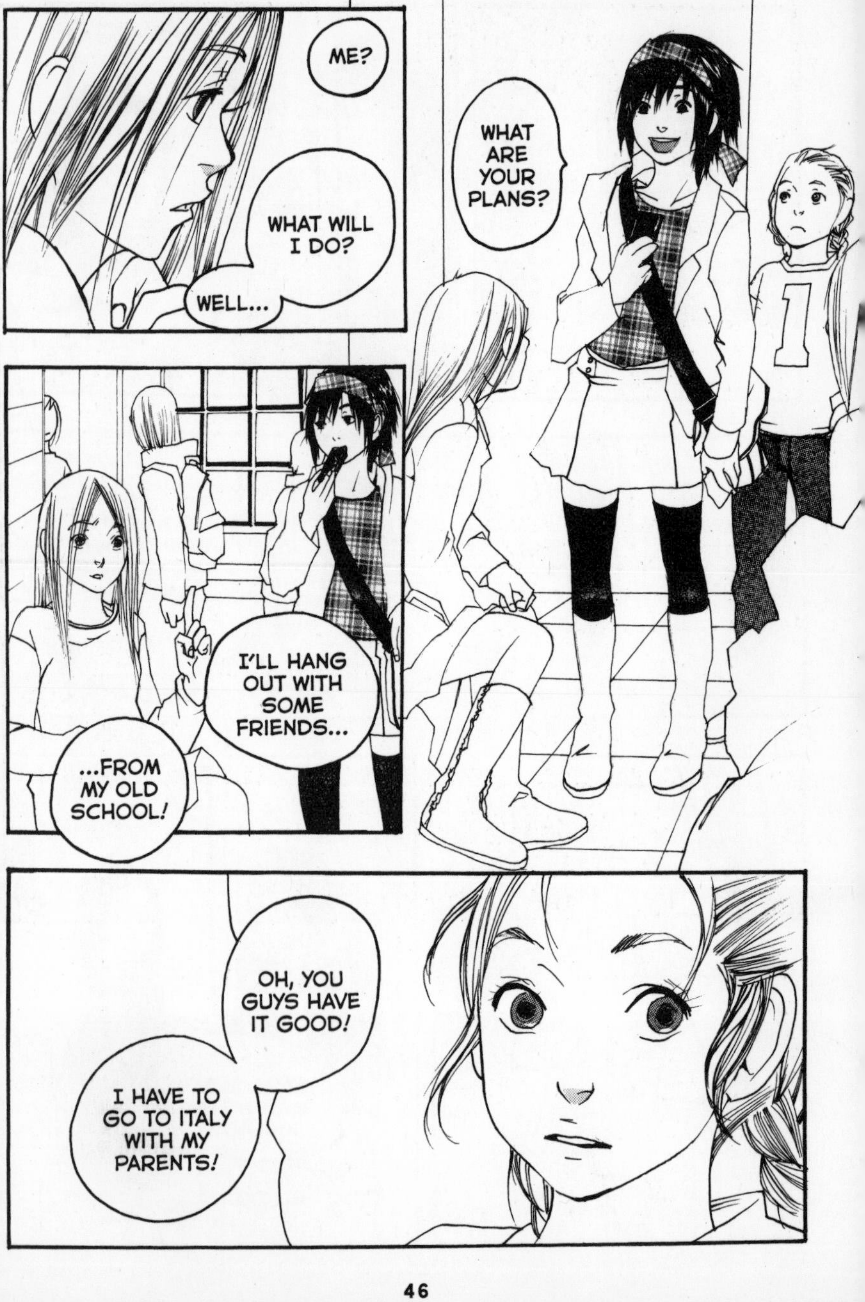
WHAT ARE YOUR PLANS?
ME?
WHAT WILL I DO?
WELL...
I'LL HANG OUT WITH SOME FRIENDS...
...FROM MY OLD SCHOOL!
OH, YOU GUYS HAVE IT GOOD!
I HAVE TO GO TO ITALY WITH MY PARENTS!

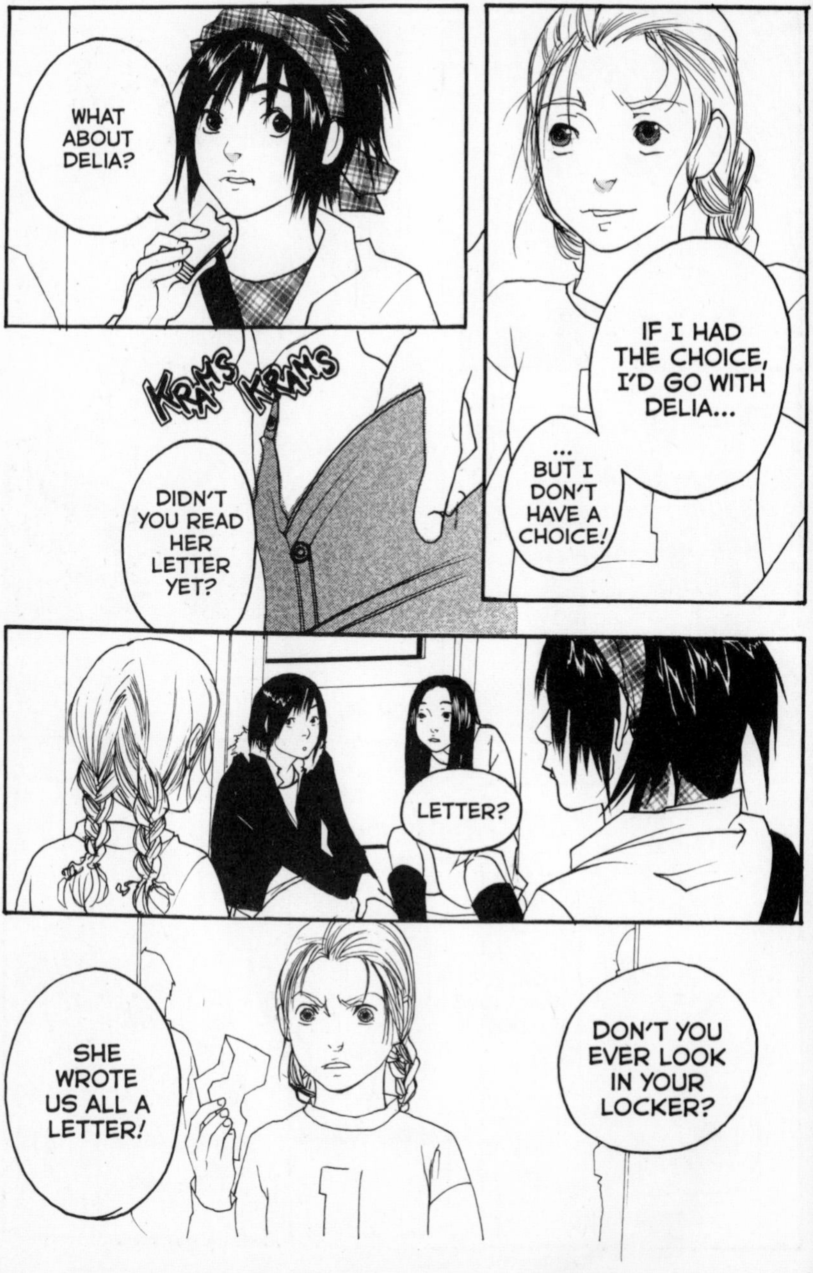
IF I HAD THE CHOICE, I'D GO WITH DELIA...
... BUT I DON'T HAVE A CHOICE!
WHAT ABOUT DELIA?
KRAMS KRAMS
DIDN'T YOU READ HER LETTER YET?
LETTER?
DON'T YOU EVER LOOK IN YOUR LOCKER?
SHE WROTE US ALL A LETTER!

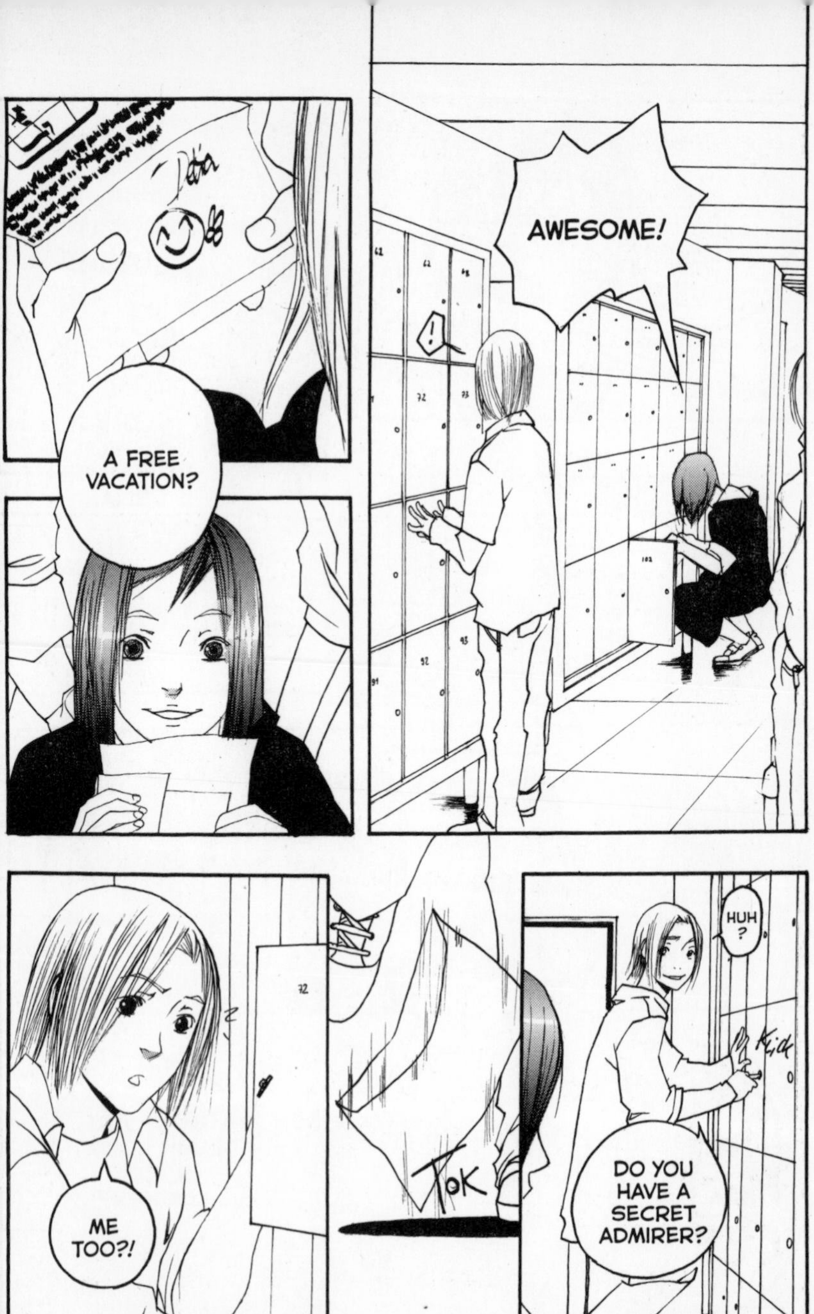
!
AWESOME!
A FREE VACATION?
HUH?
Kick
DO YOU HAVE A SECRET ADMIRER?
TOK
ME TOO?!

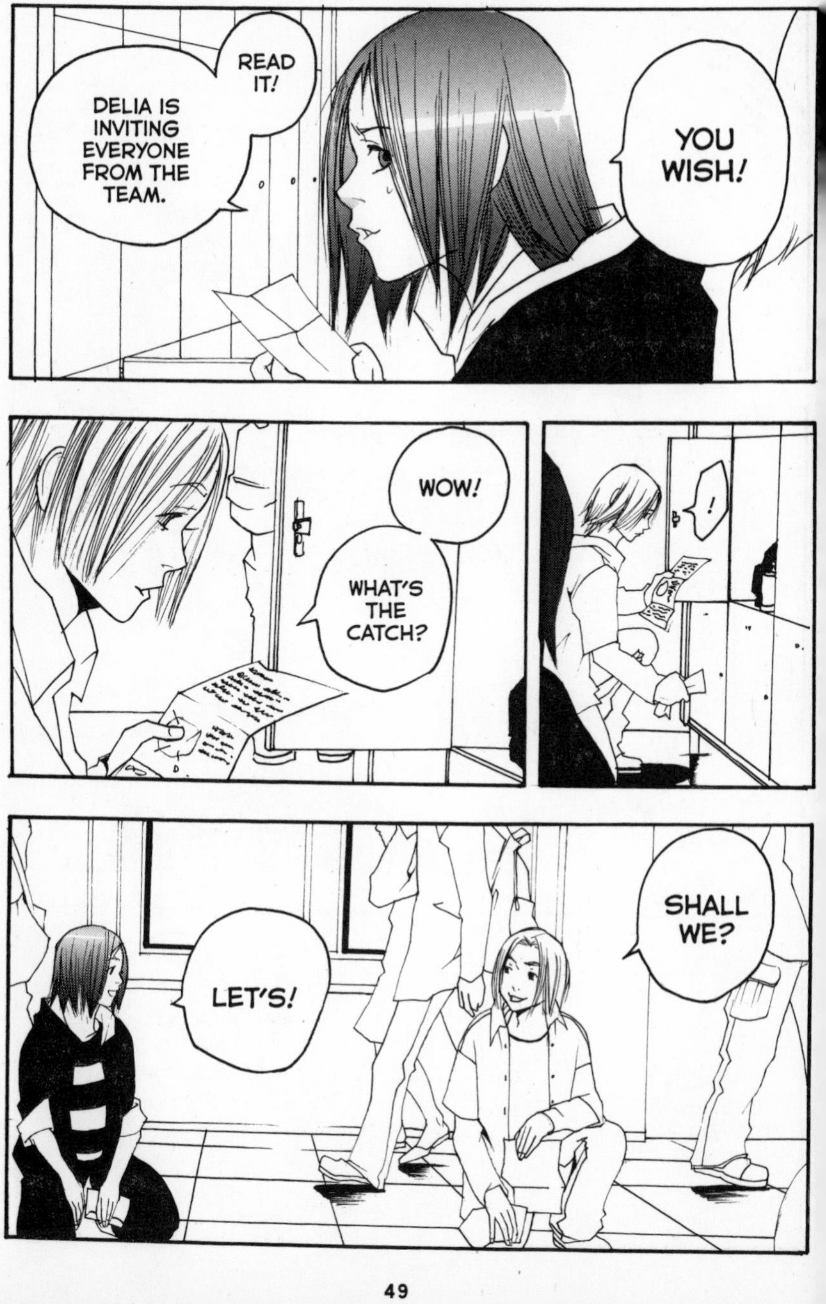
YOU WISH!
READ IT!
DELIA IS INVITING EVERYONE FROM THE TEAM.
!
WOW!
WHAT'S THE CATCH?
SHALL WE?
LET'S!

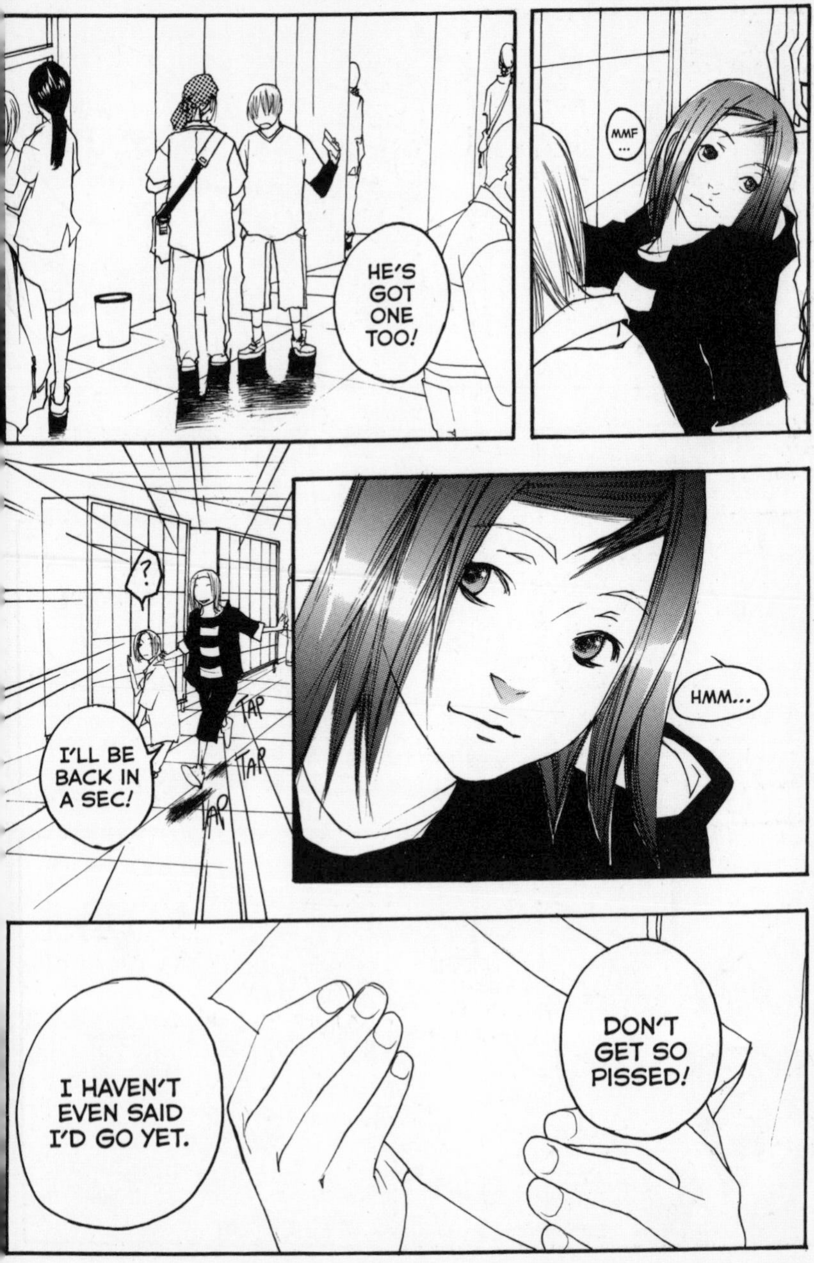
MMF...
HE'S GOT ONE TOO!
HMM...
?
I'LL BE BACK IN A SEC!
TAP
TAP
TAP
DON'T GET SO PISSED!
I HAVEN'T EVEN SAID I'D GO YET.

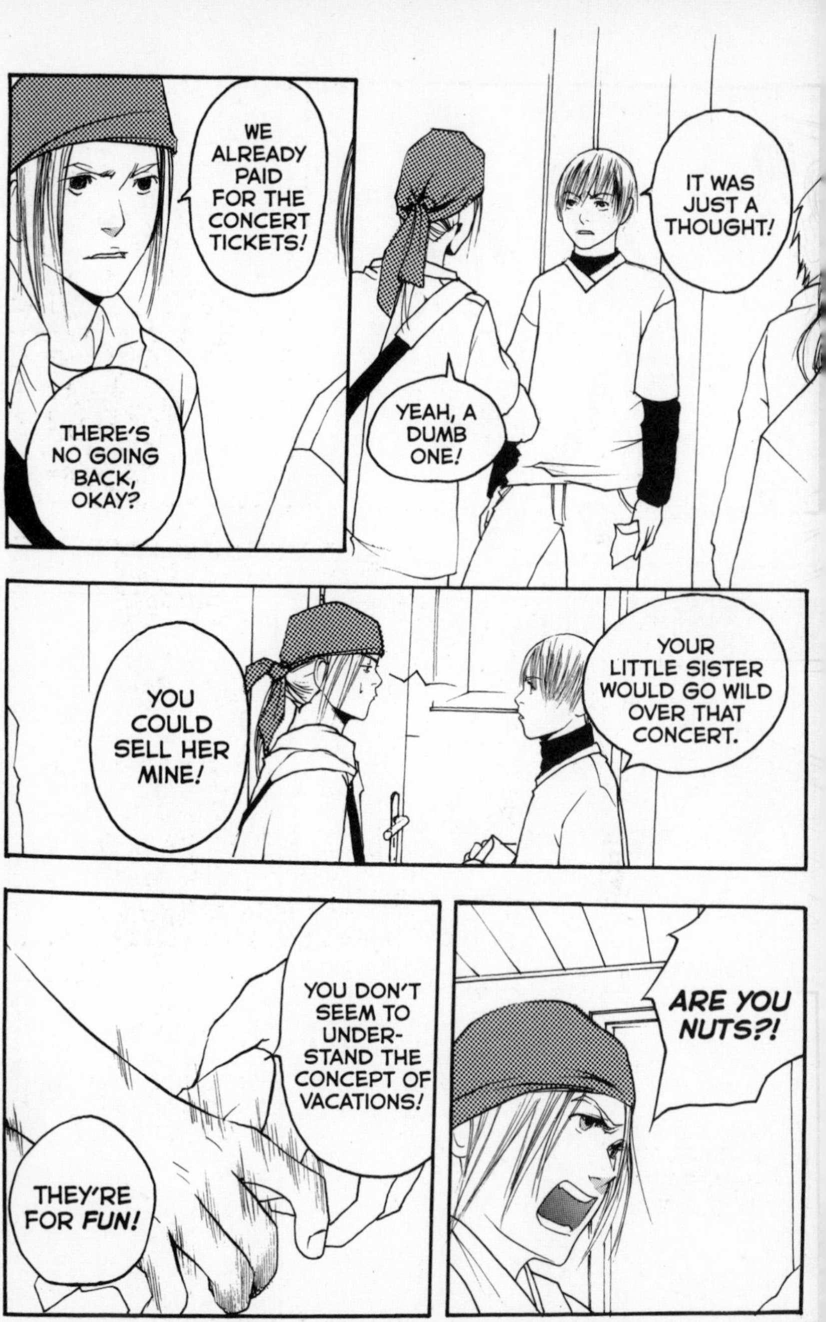
IT WAS JUST A THOUGHT!
YEAH, A DUMB ONE!
WE ALREADY PAID FOR THE CONCERT TICKETS!
THERE'S NO GOING BACK, OKAY?
YOUR LITTLE SISTER WOULD GO WILD OVER THAT CONCERT.
YOU COULD SELL HER MINE!
ARE YOU NUTS?!
YOU DON'T SEEM TO UNDER-STAND THE CONCEPT OF VACATIONS!
THEY'RE FOR *FUN*!

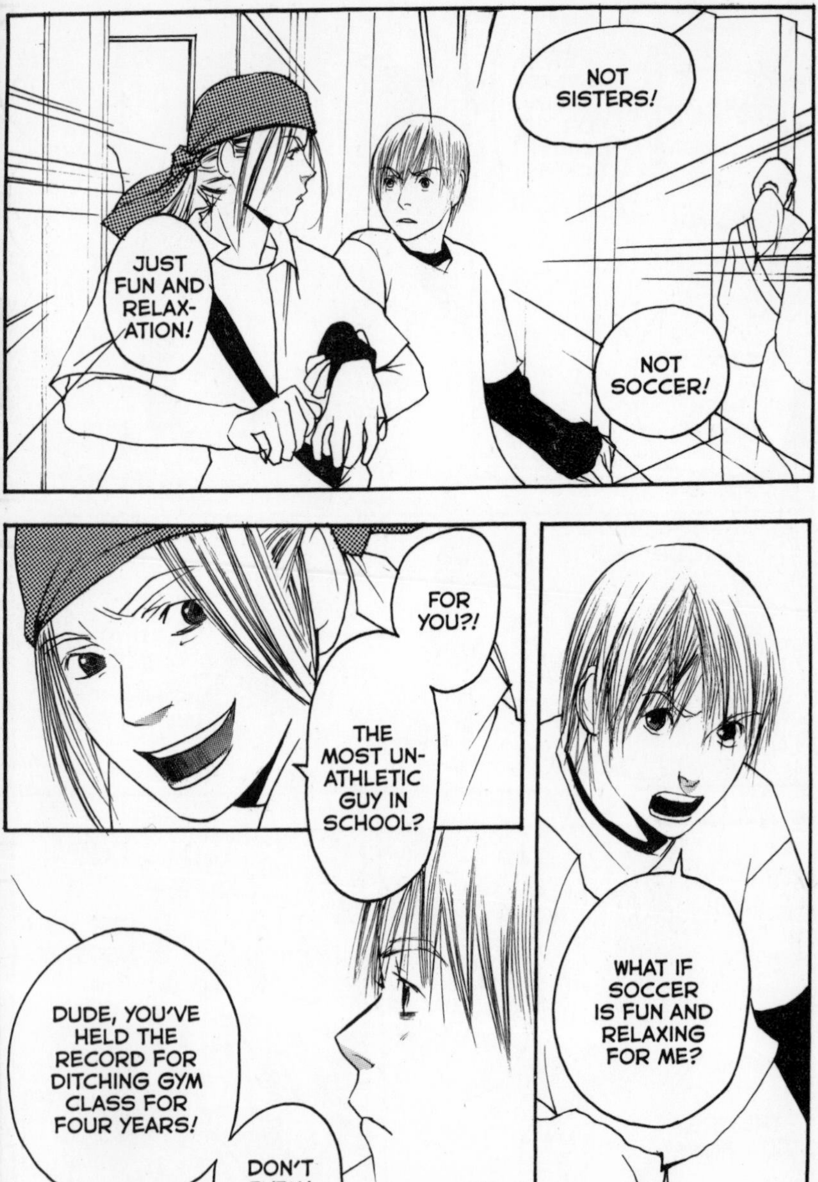
NOT SISTERS!
NOT SOCCER!
JUST FUN AND RELAXATION!
WHAT IF SOCCER IS FUN AND RELAXING FOR ME?
FOR YOU?!
THE MOST UNATHLETIC GUY IN SCHOOL?
DUDE, YOU'VE HELD THE RECORD FOR DITCHING GYM CLASS FOR FOUR YEARS!
DON'T EVEN!

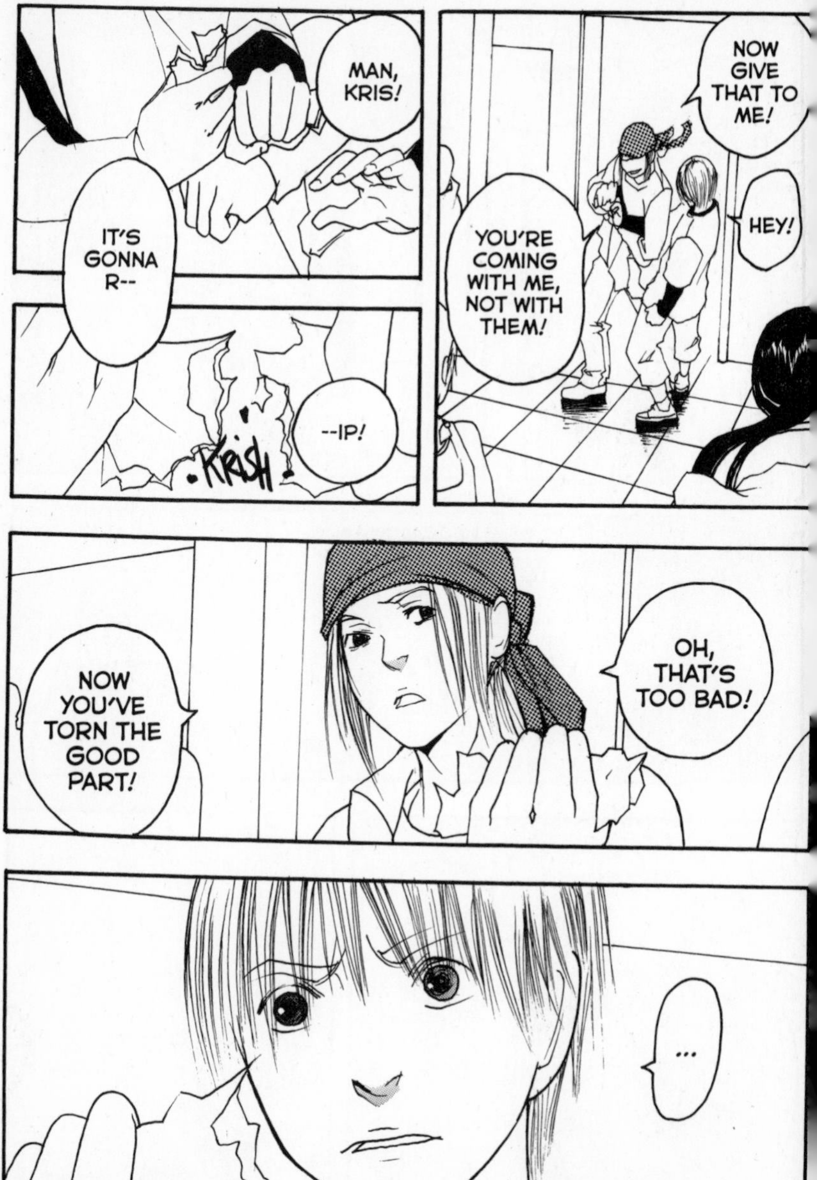
NOW GIVE THAT TO ME!
HEY!
YOU'RE COMING WITH ME, NOT WITH THEM!
MAN, KRIS!
IT'S GONNA R--
--IP!
KRISH
OH, THAT'S TOO BAD!
NOW YOU'VE TORN THE GOOD PART!
...

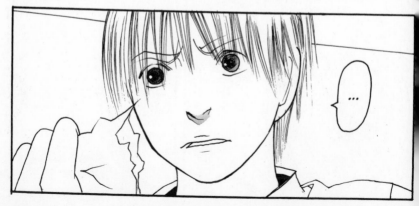

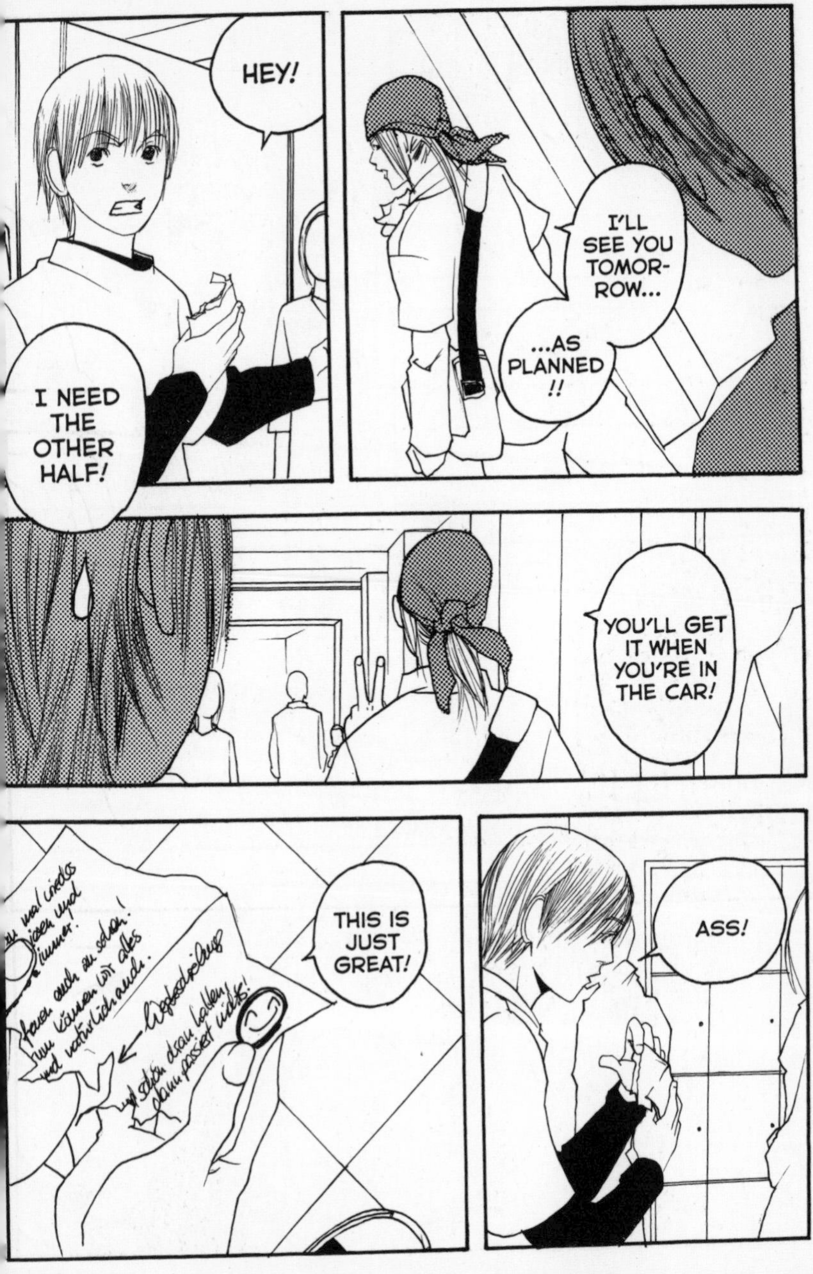
I'LL SEE YOU TOMOR-ROW...
...AS PLANNED !!
HEY!
I NEED THE OTHER HALF!
YOU'LL GET IT WHEN YOU'RE IN THE CAR!
ASS!
THIS IS JUST GREAT!

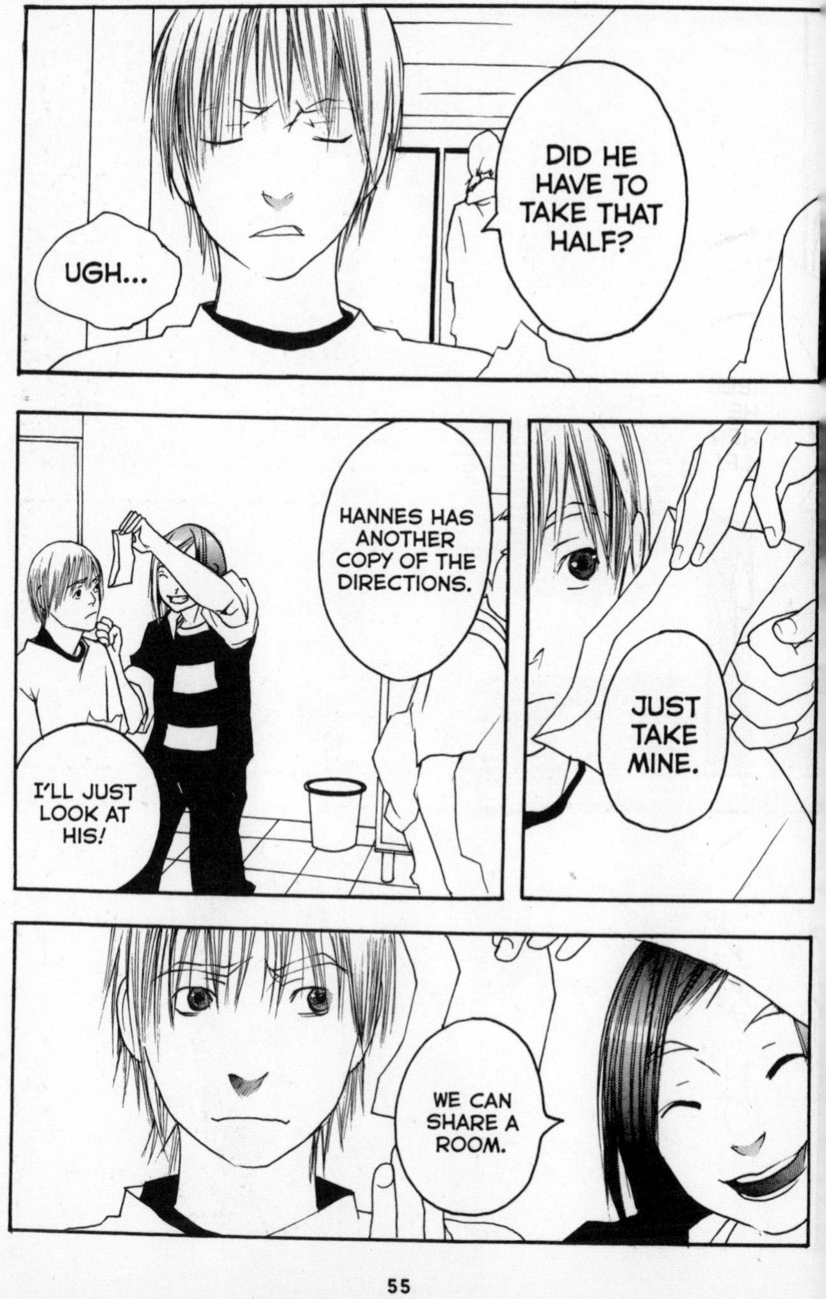
DID HE HAVE TO TAKE THAT HALF?
UGH...
JUST TAKE MINE.
HANNES HAS ANOTHER COPY OF THE DIRECTIONS.
I'LL JUST LOOK AT HIS!
WE CAN SHARE A ROOM.

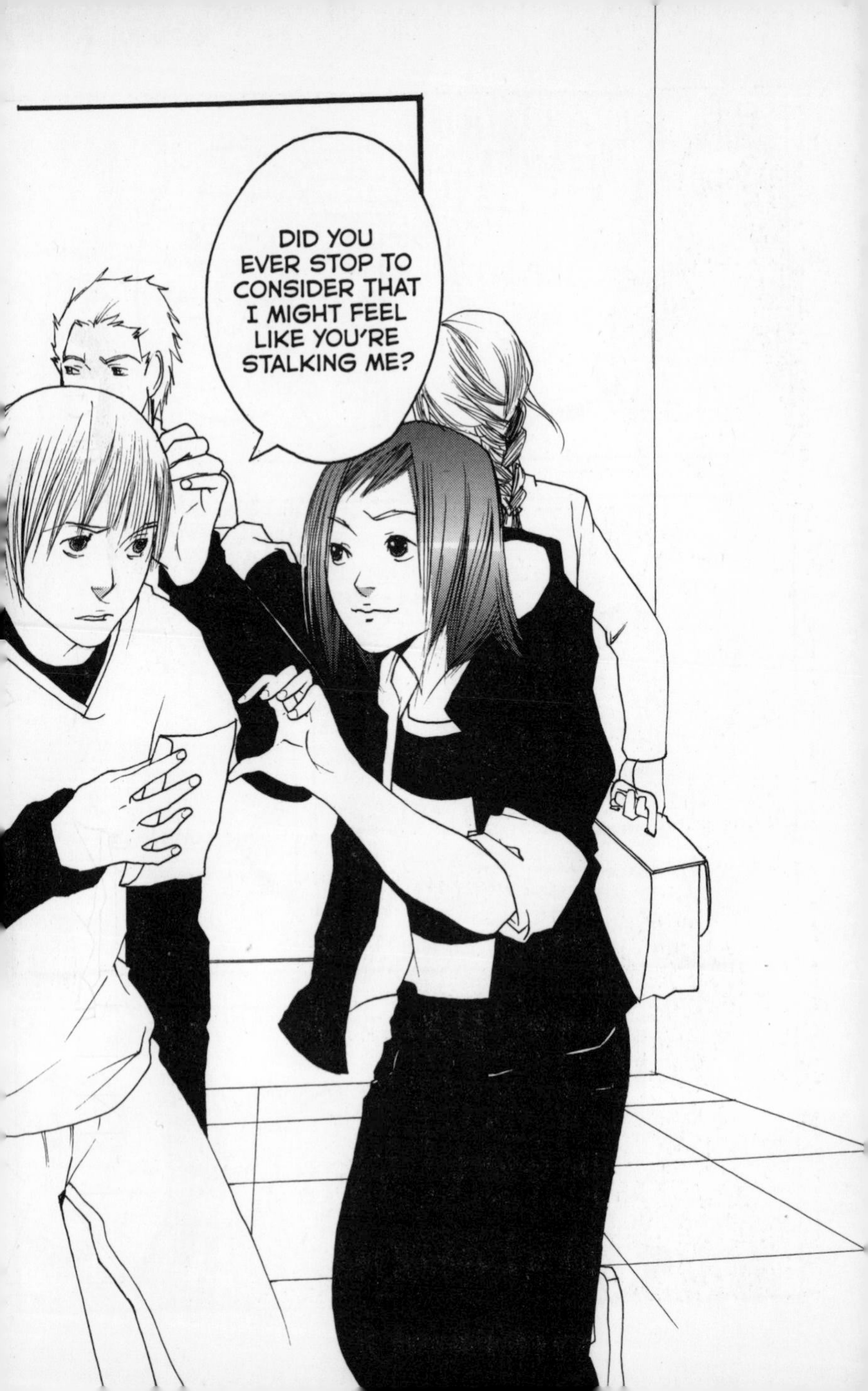
DID YOU EVER STOP TO CONSIDER THAT I MIGHT FEEL LIKE YOU'RE STALKING ME?

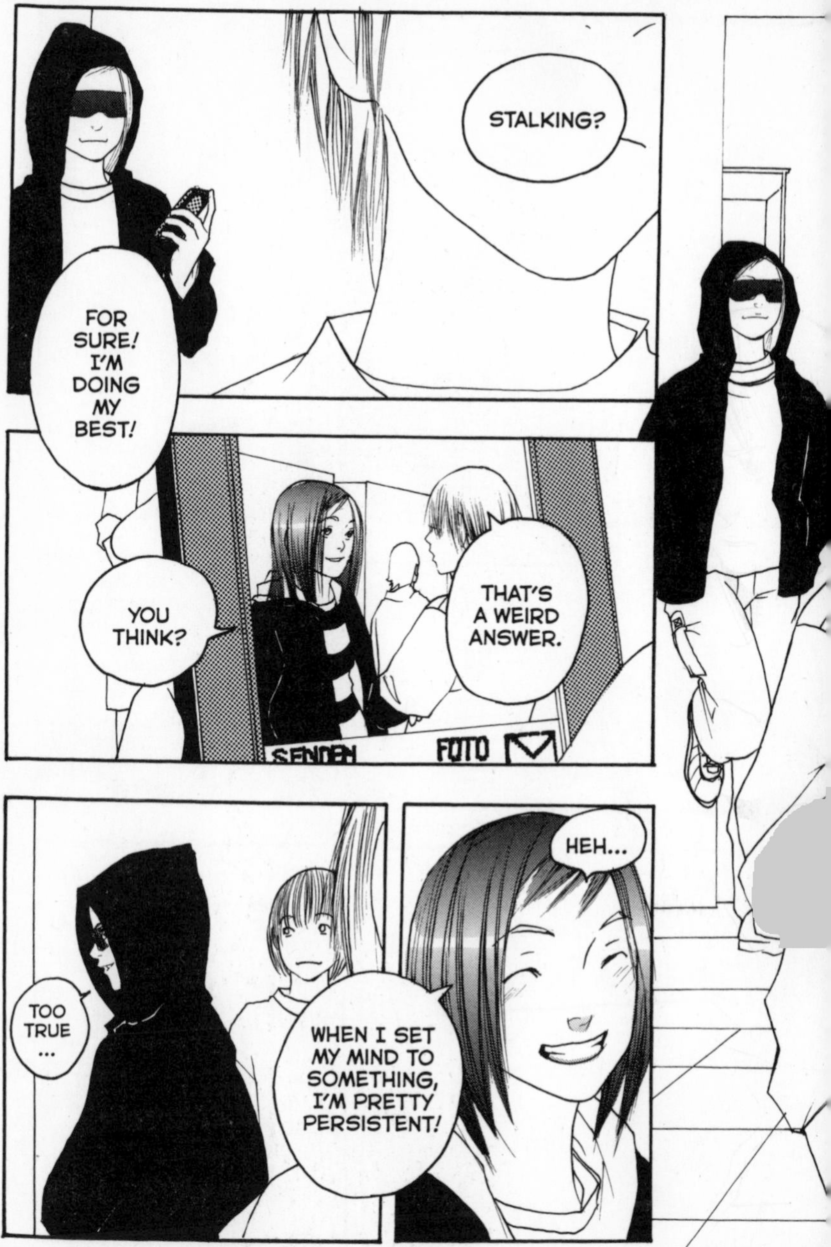
STALKING?
FOR SURE! I'M DOING MY BEST!
THAT'S A WEIRD ANSWER.
YOU THINK?
SENDEN
FOTO
HEH...
WHEN I SET MY MIND TO SOMETHING, I'M PRETTY PERSISTENT!
TOO TRUE ...

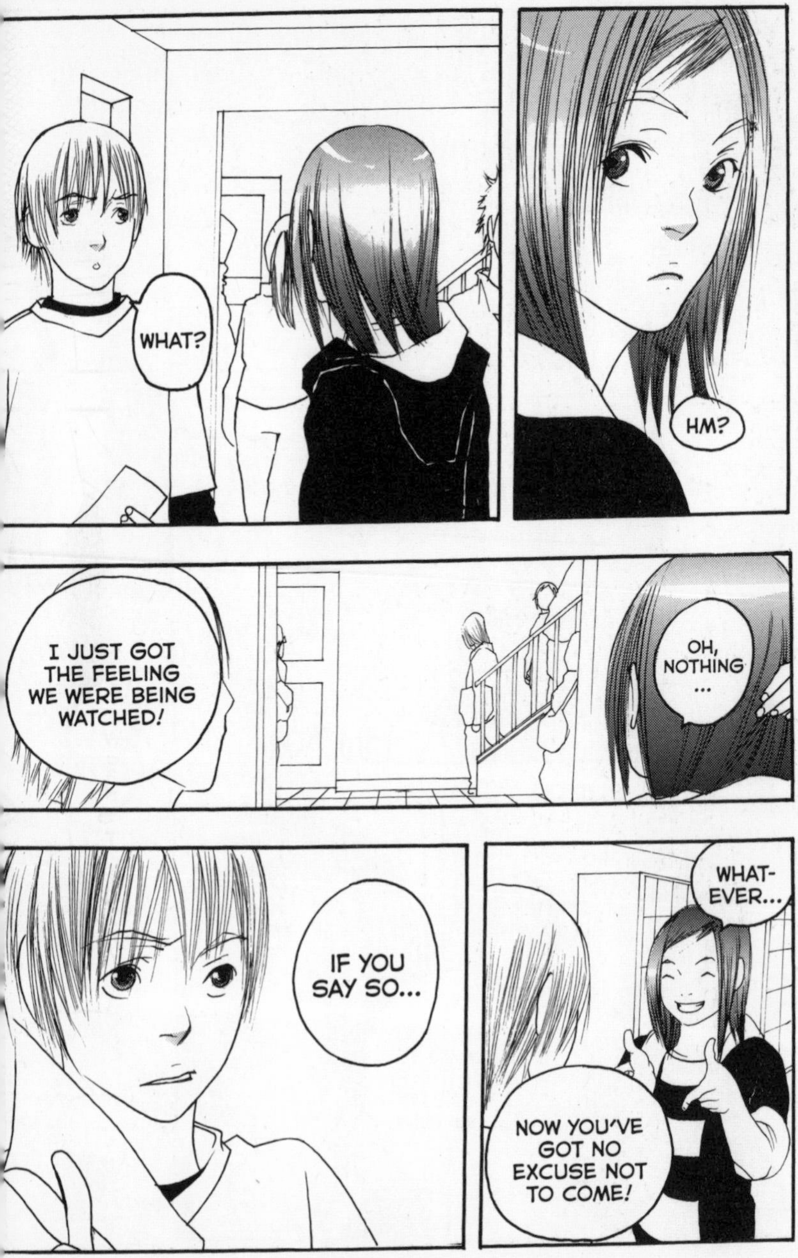
HM?
WHAT?
OH, NOTHING ...
I JUST GOT THE FEELING WE WERE BEING WATCHED!
WHAT-EVER...
NOW YOU'VE GOT NO EXCUSE NOT TO COME!
IF YOU SAY SO...

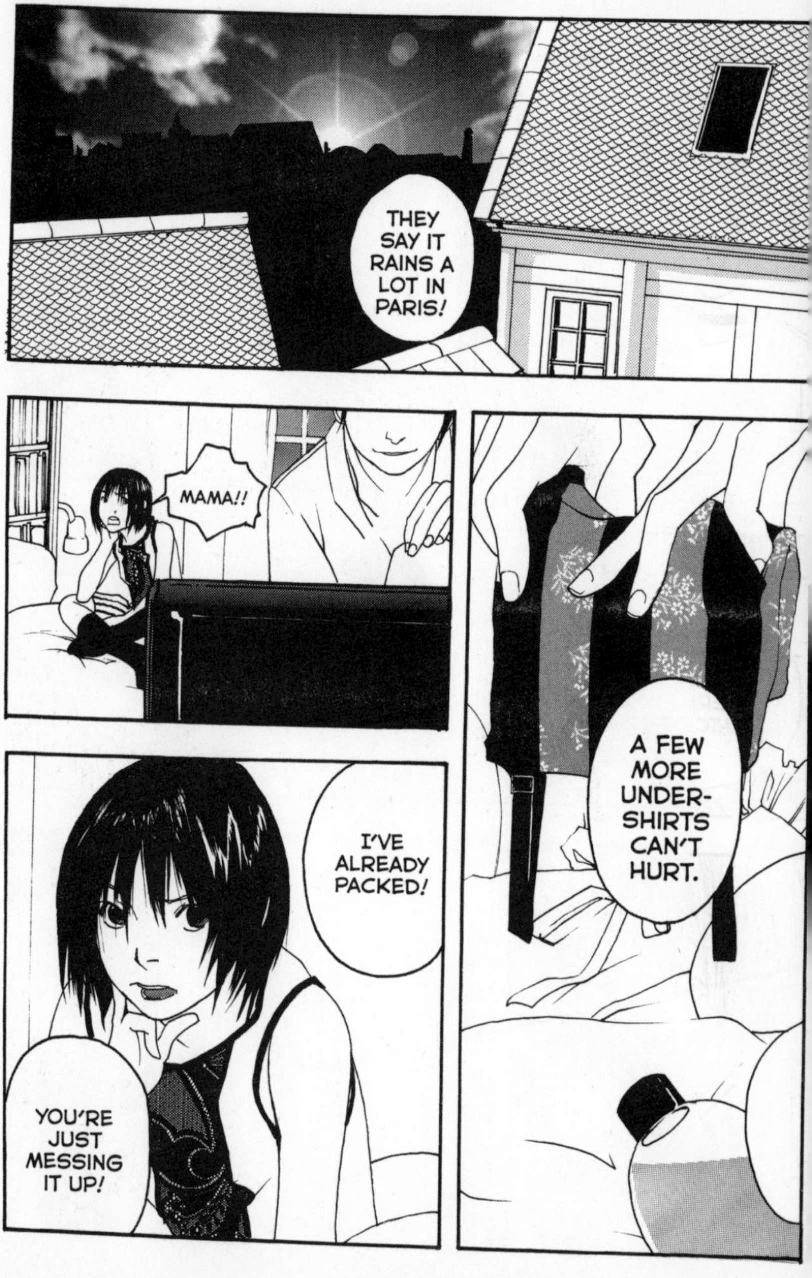
THEY SAY IT RAINS A LOT IN PARIS!
A FEW MORE UNDER-SHIRTS CAN'T HURT.
MAMA!!
I'VE ALREADY PACKED!
YOU'RE JUST MESSING IT UP!

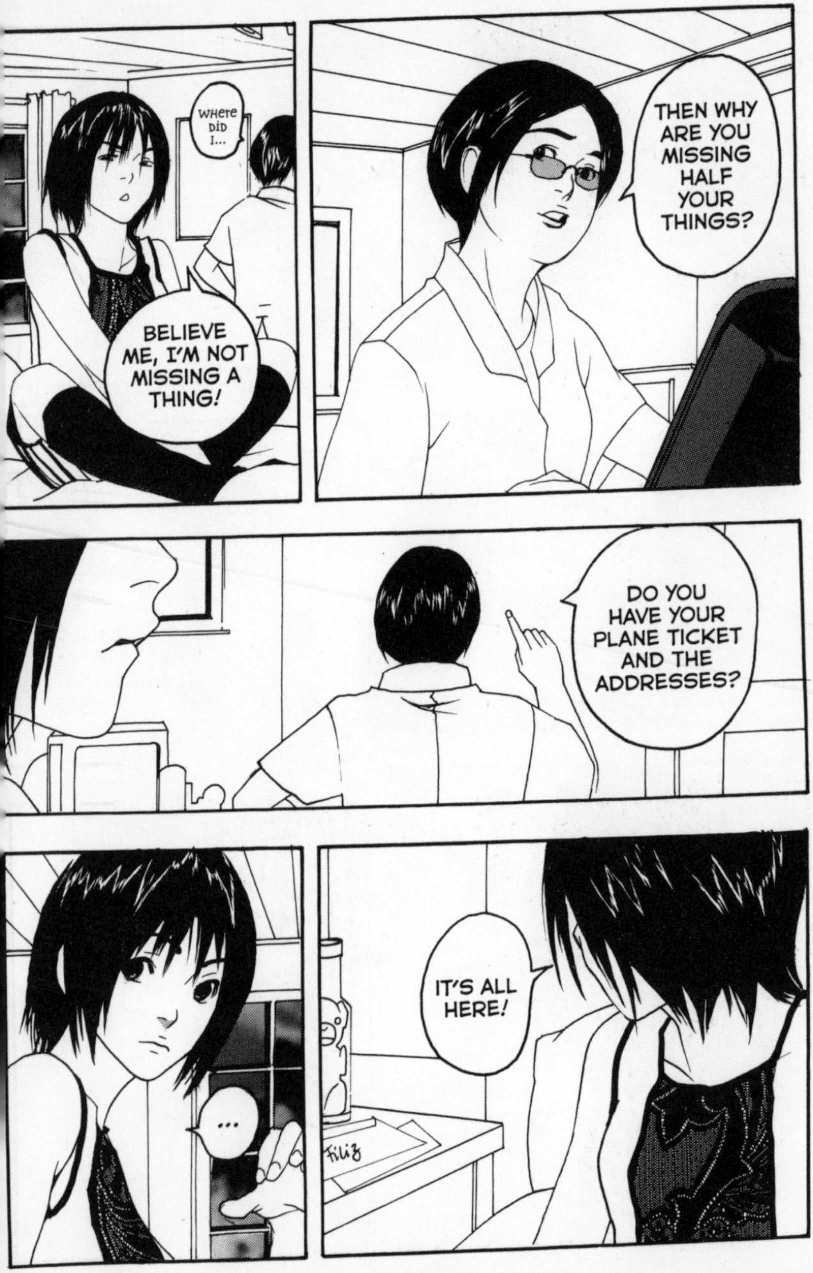
THEN WHY ARE YOU MISSING HALF YOUR THINGS?
WHere DID I...
BELIEVE ME, I'M NOT MISSING A THING!
DO YOU HAVE YOUR PLANE TICKET AND THE ADDRESSES?
IT'S ALL HERE!
...

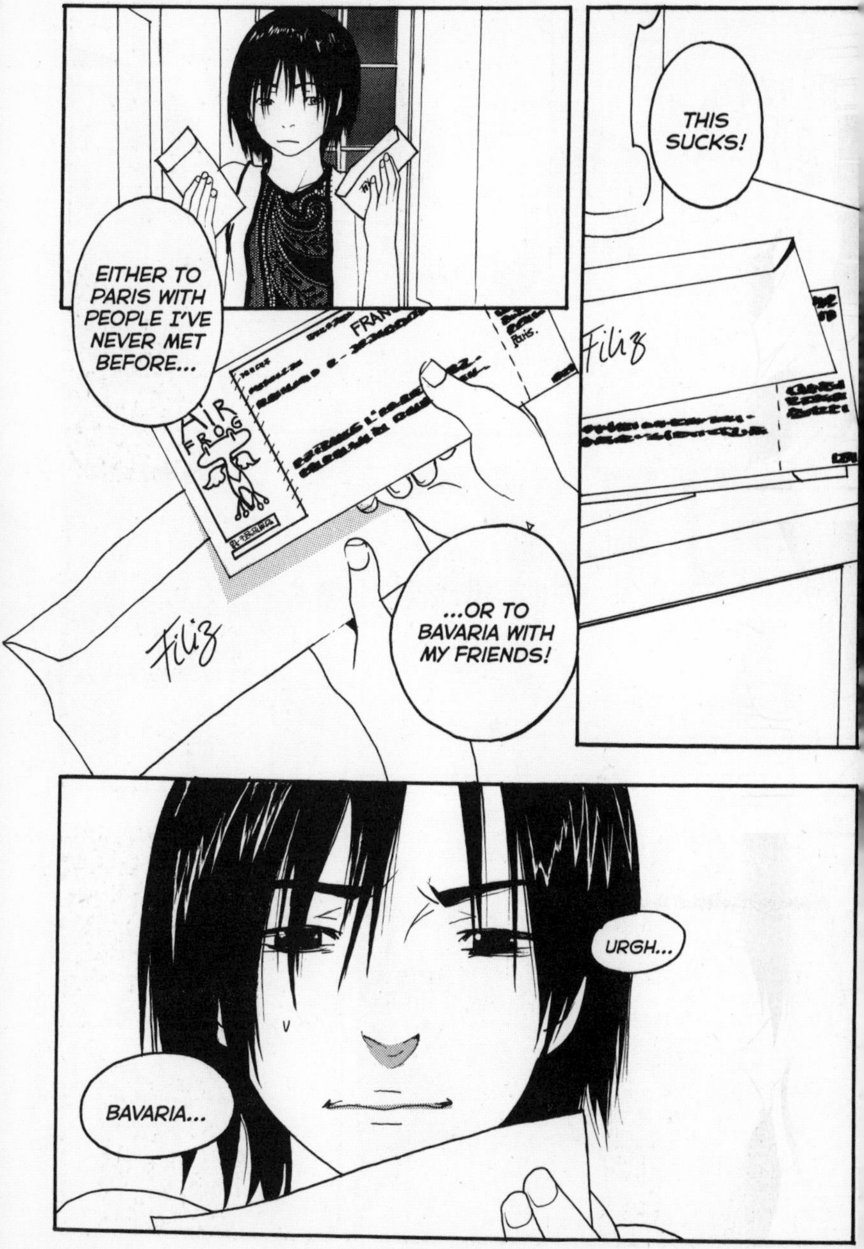
THIS SUCKS!
EITHER TO PARIS WITH PEOPLE I'VE NEVER MET BEFORE...
...OR TO BAVARIA WITH MY FRIENDS!
URGH...
BAVARIA...

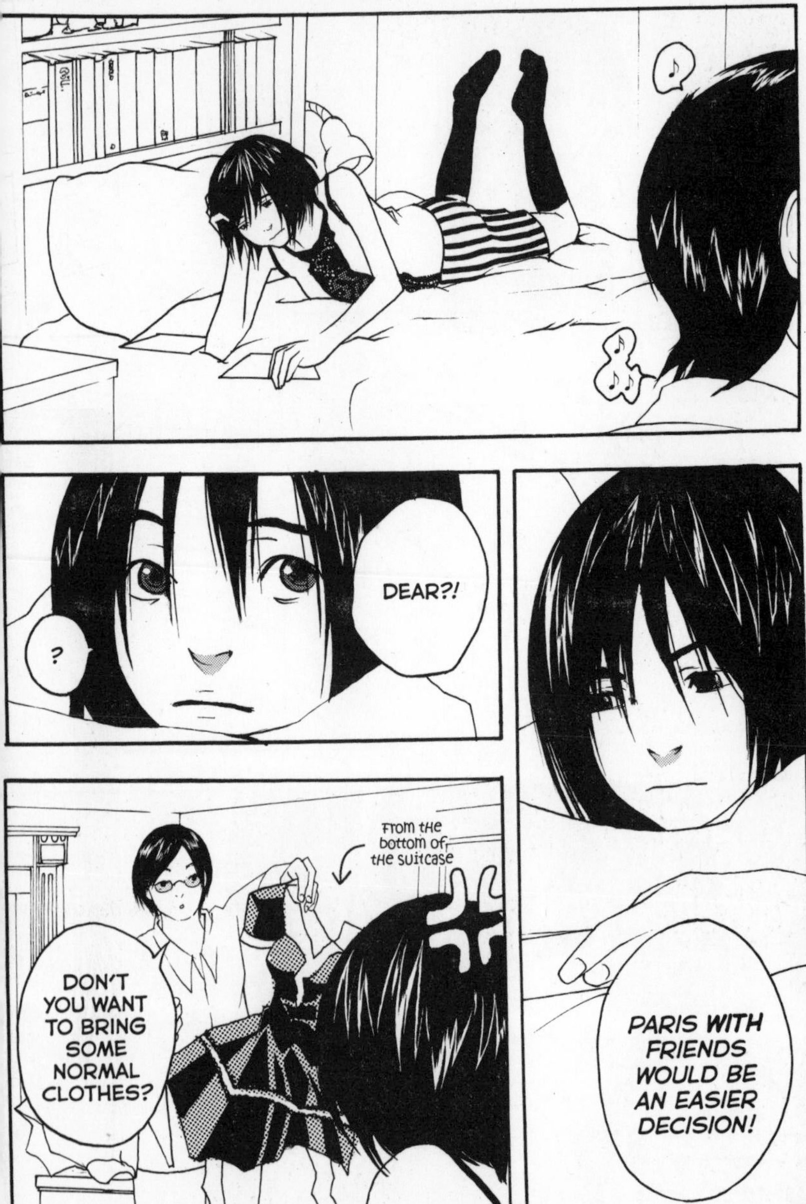
♪
♪♪
PARIS WITH FRIENDS WOULD BE AN EASIER DECISION!
DEAR?!
?
From the bottom of the suitcase
DON'T YOU WANT TO BRING SOME NORMAL CLOTHES?

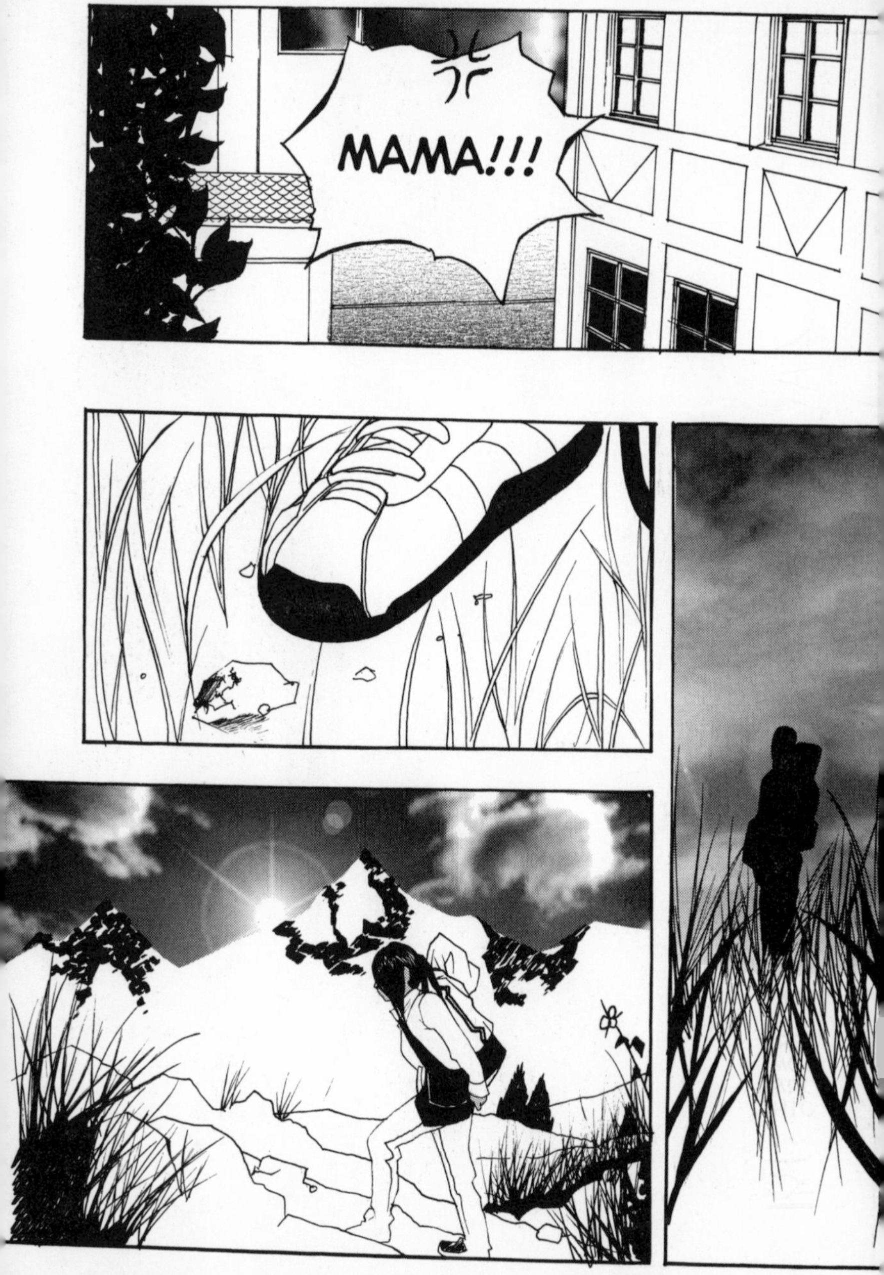
MAMA!!!

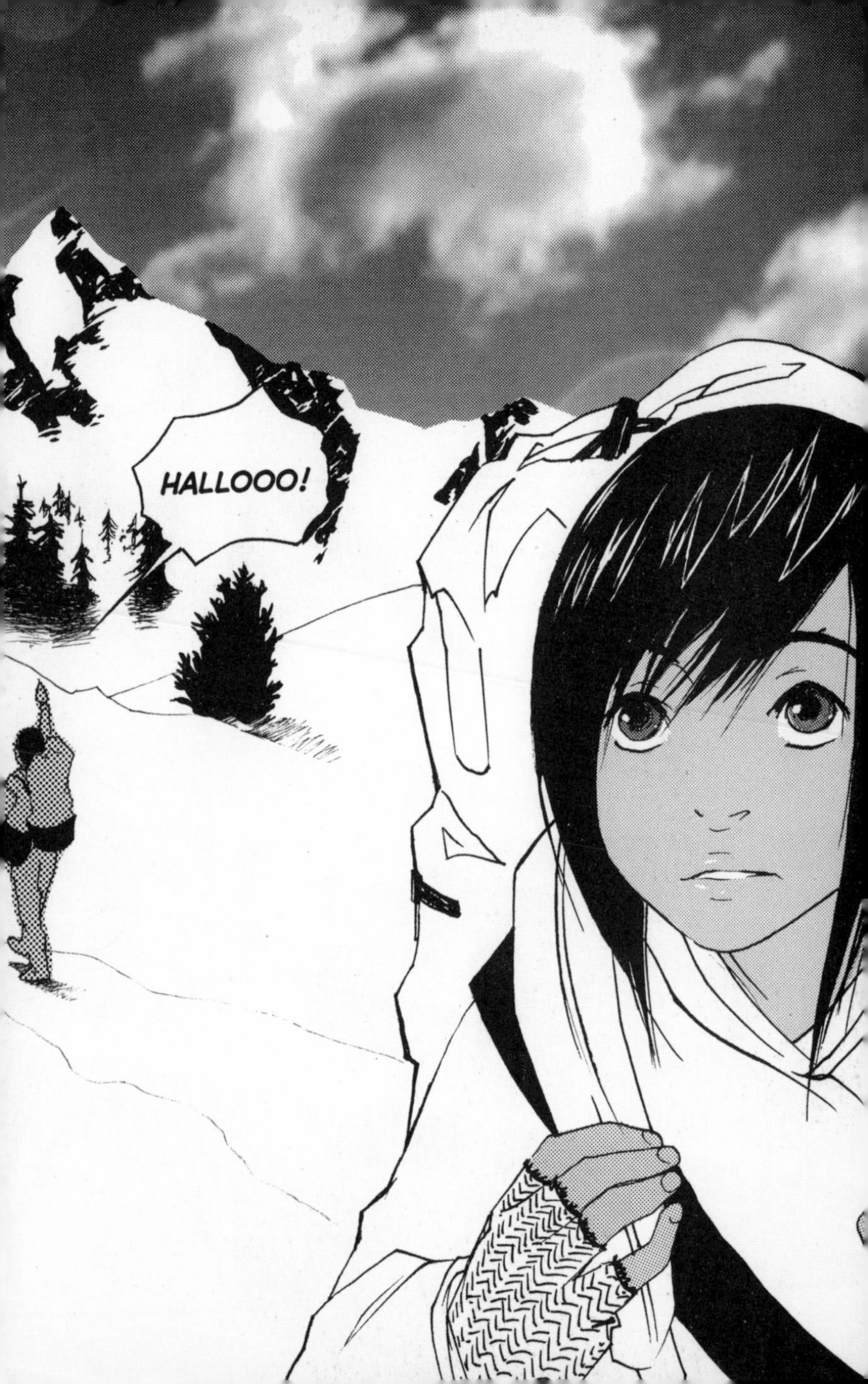
HALLOOO!

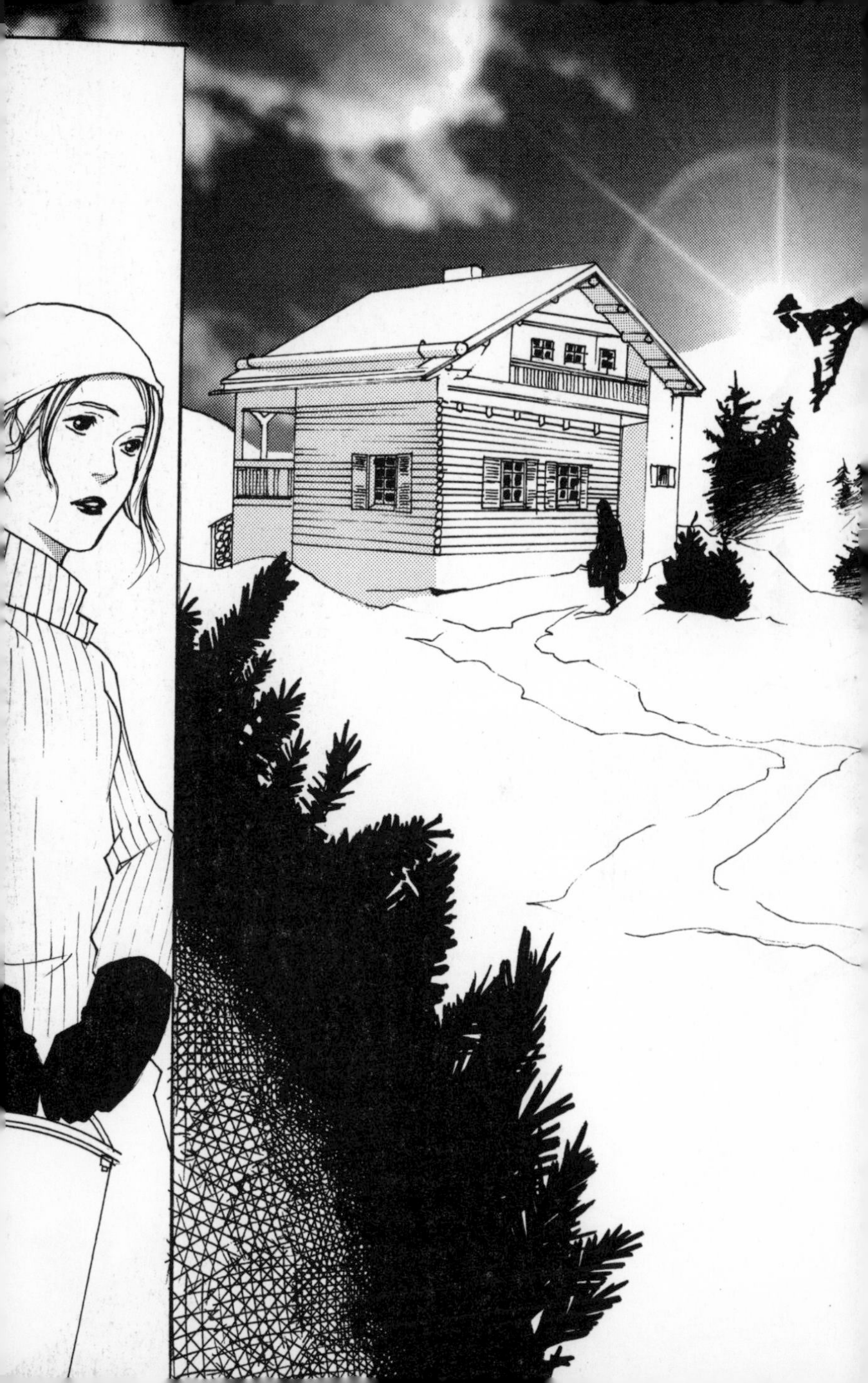

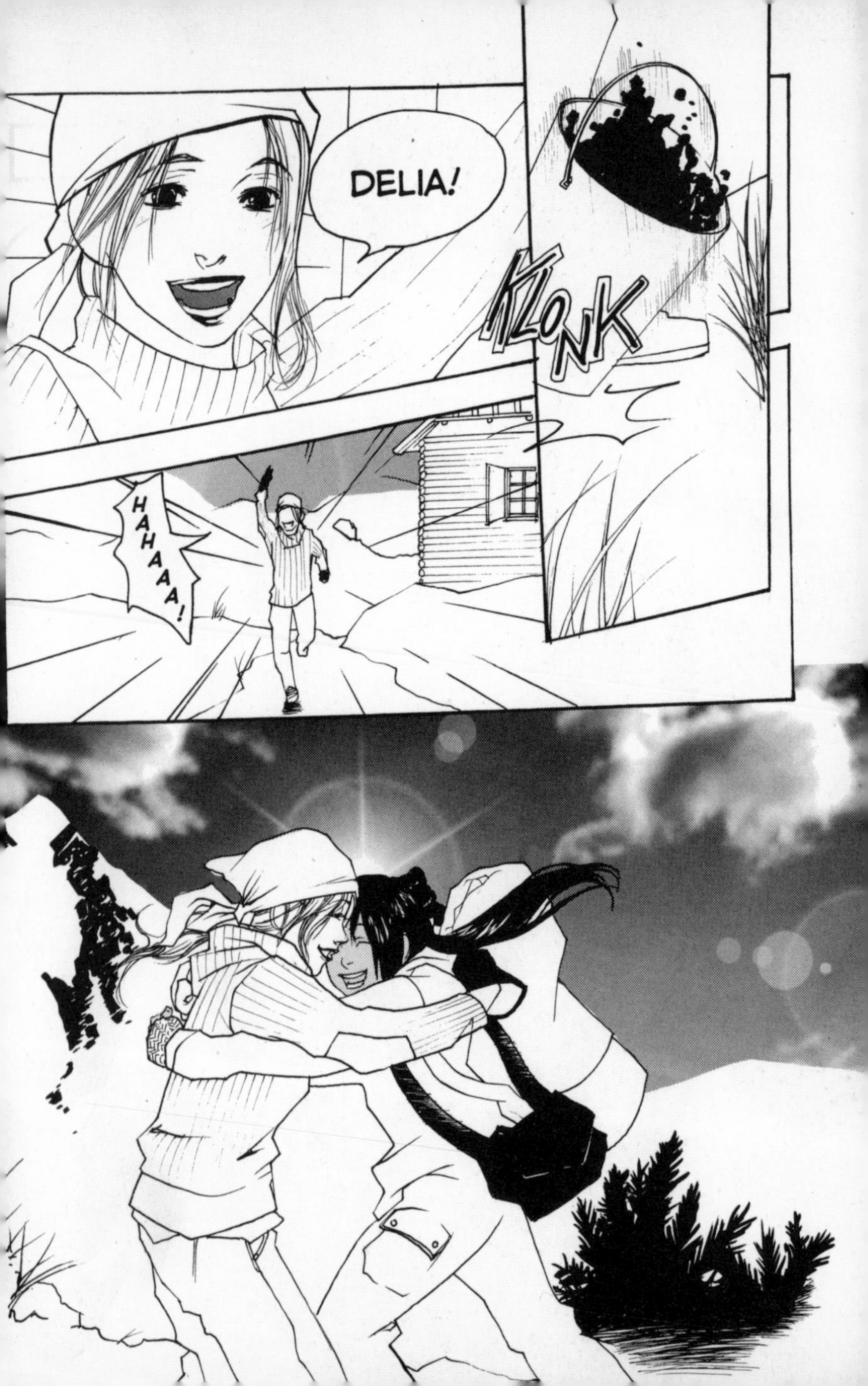
KLONK
DELIA!
HAHAAAA!

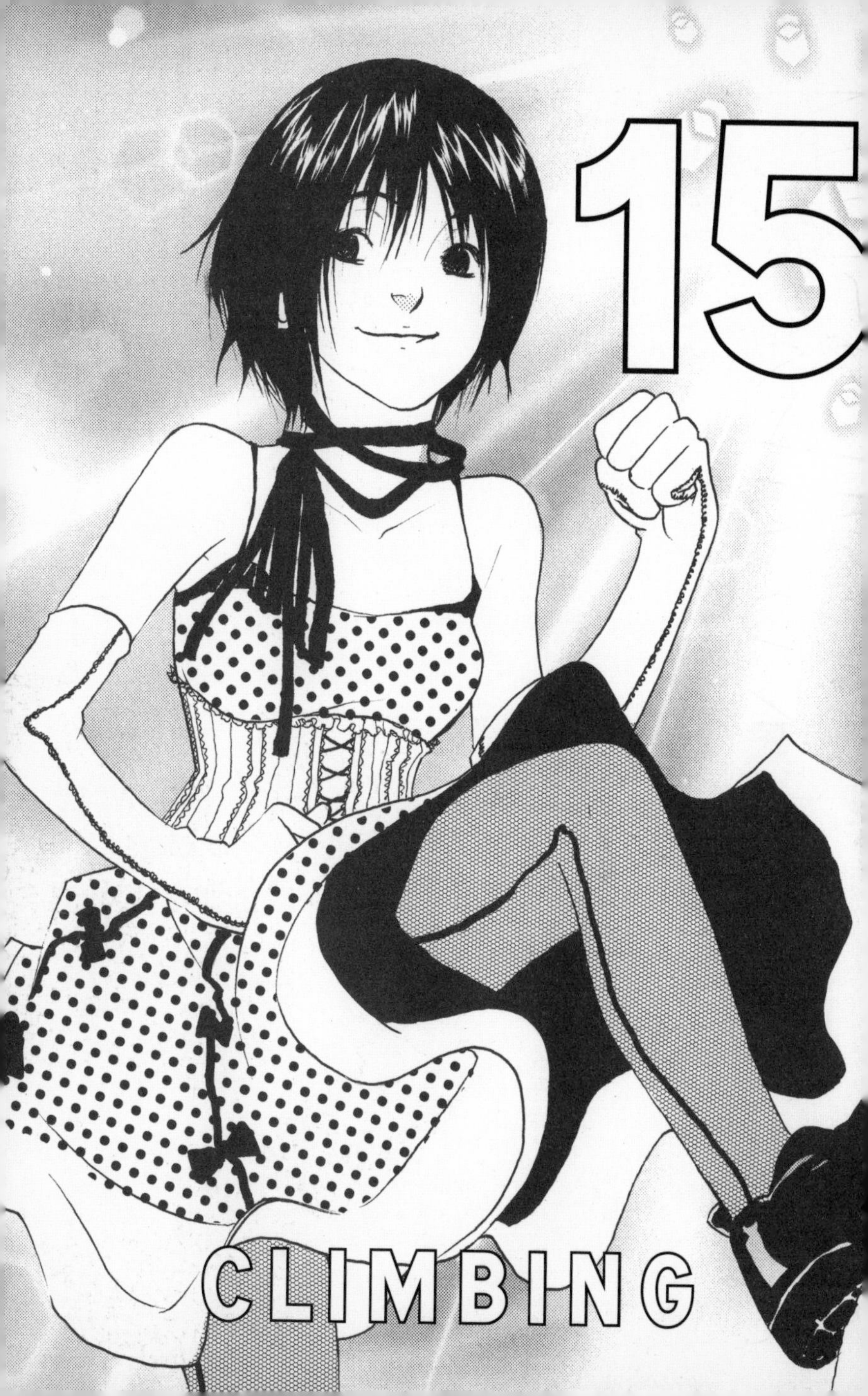
15
CLIMBING

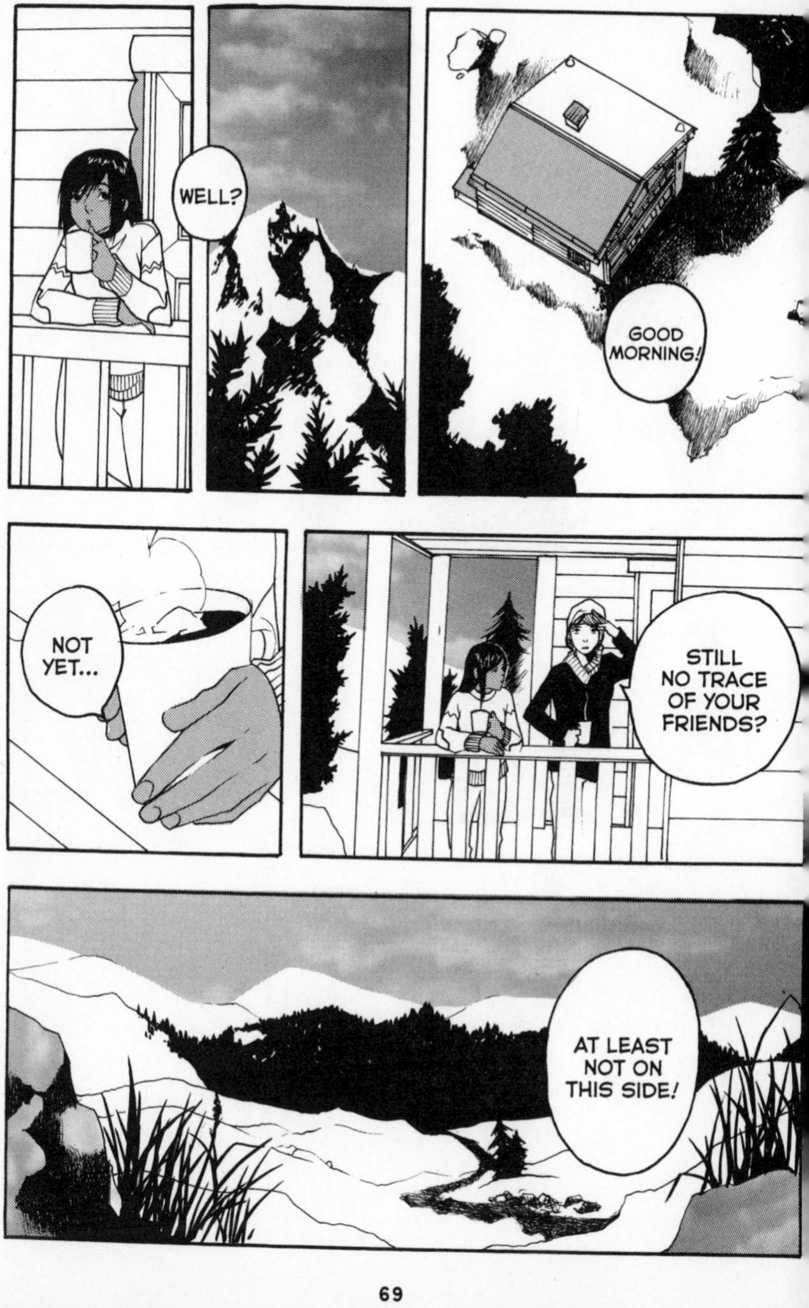
GOOD MORNING!
WELL?
STILL NO TRACE OF YOUR FRIENDS?
NOT YET...
AT LEAST NOT ON THIS SIDE!

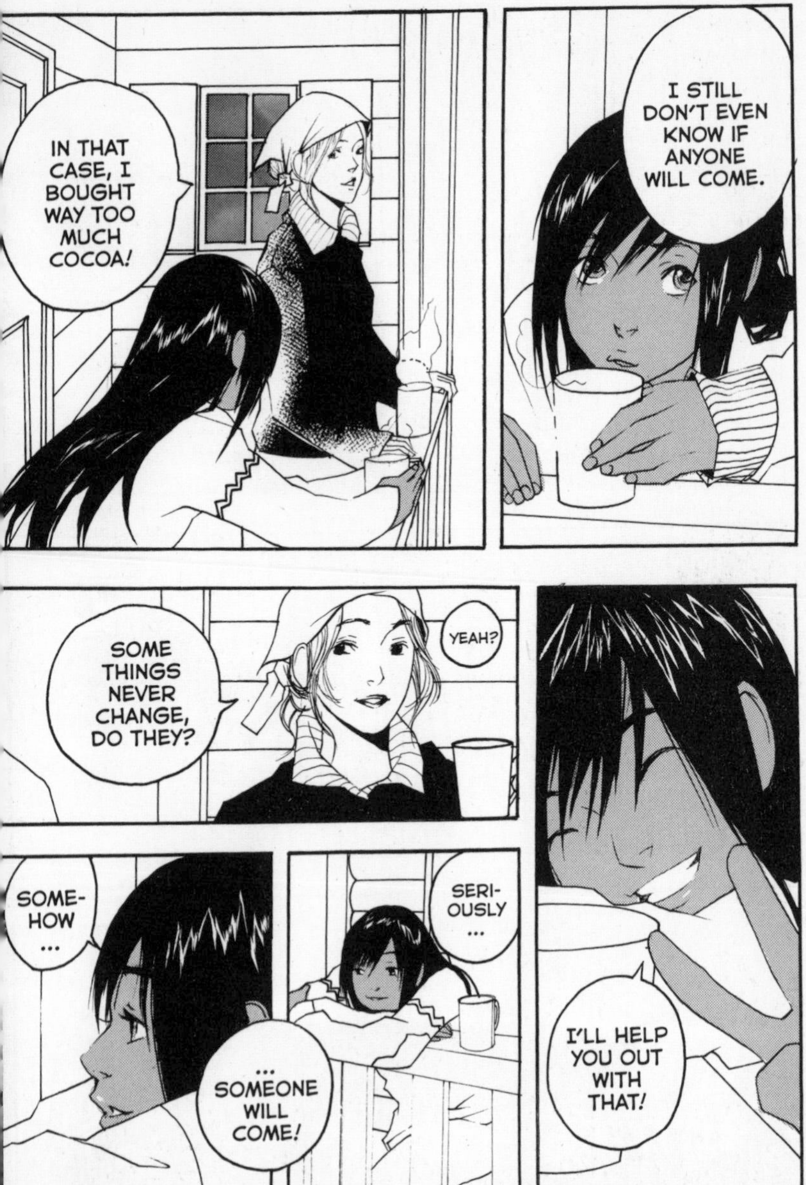
I STILL DON'T EVEN KNOW IF ANYONE WILL COME.
IN THAT CASE, I BOUGHT WAY TOO MUCH COCOA!
I'LL HELP YOU OUT WITH THAT!
YEAH?
SOME THINGS NEVER CHANGE, DO THEY?
SERI-OUSLY ...
... SOMEONE WILL COME!
SOME-HOW ...

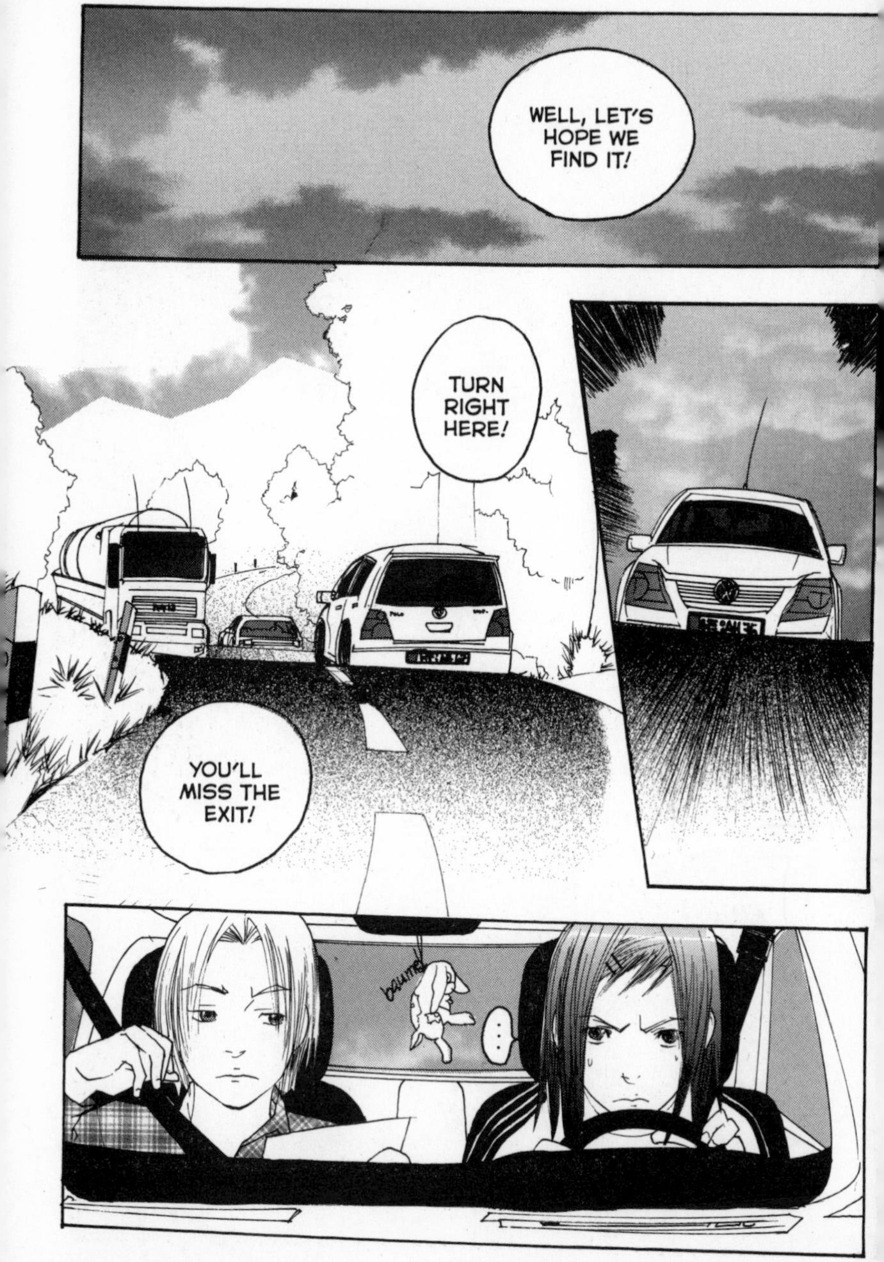
WELL, LET'S HOPE WE FIND IT!
TURN RIGHT HERE!
YOU'LL MISS THE EXIT!
...

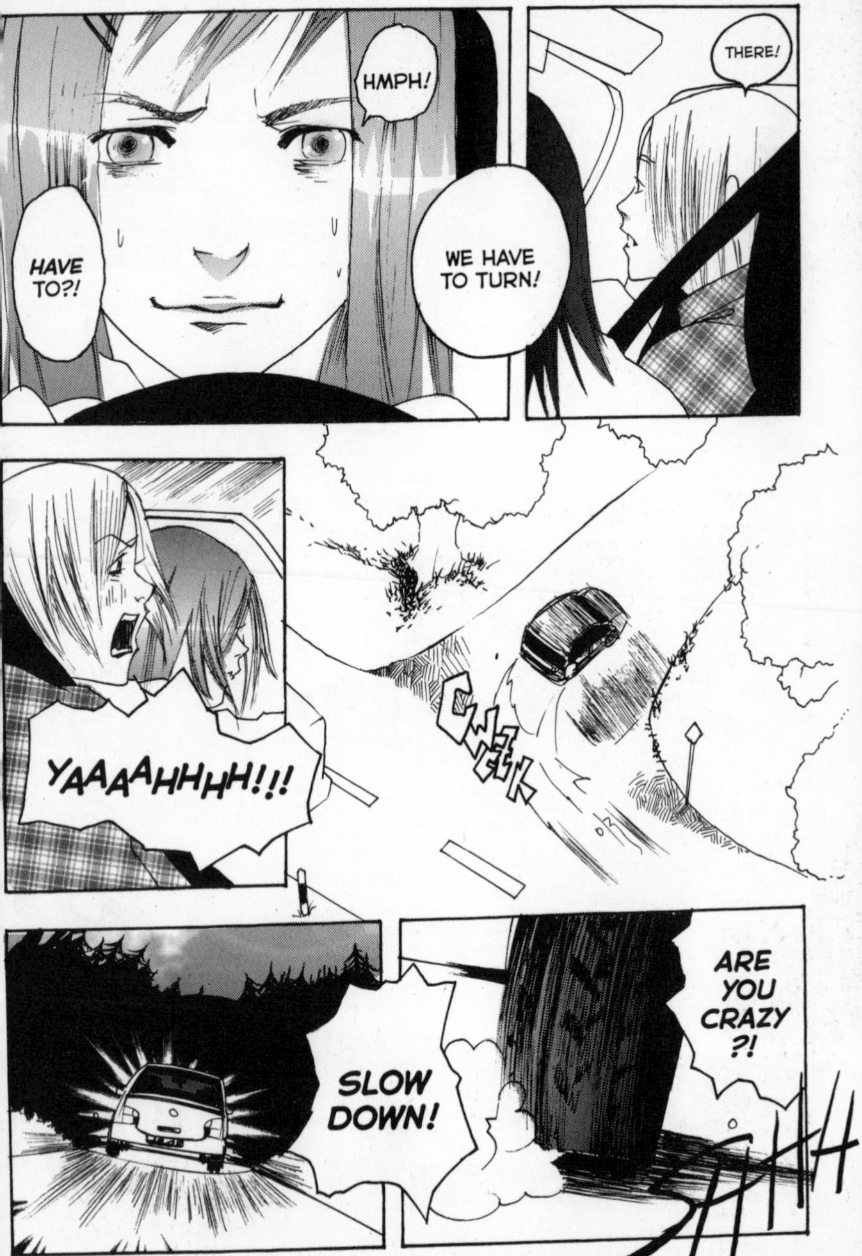
THERE!
WE HAVE TO TURN!
HMPH!
HAVE TO?!
YAAAAHHHH!!!
ARE YOU CRAZY ?!
SLOW DOWN!

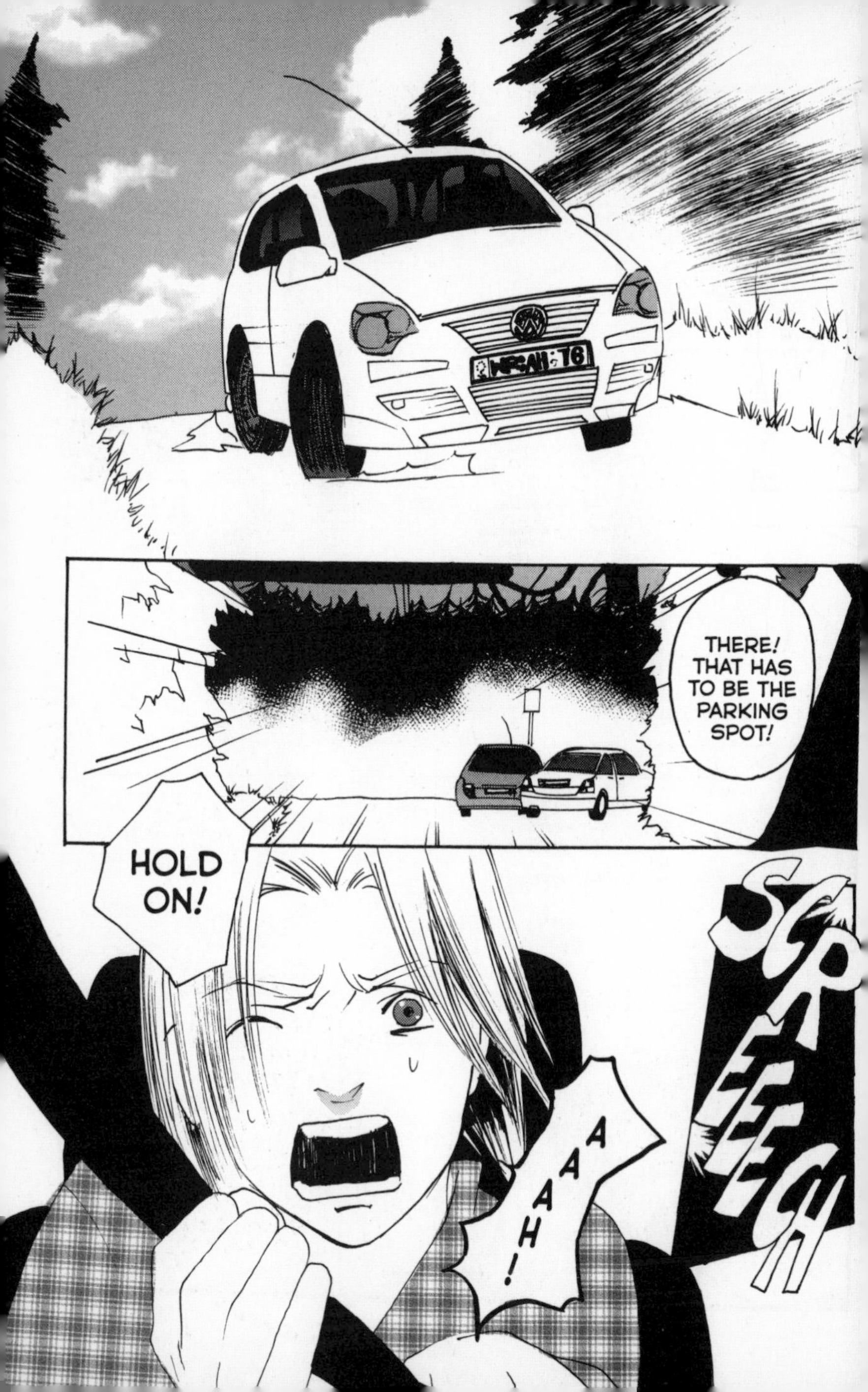

THERE! THAT HAS TO BE THE PARKING SPOT!
SCREEEECH
AAAAH!
HOLD ON!

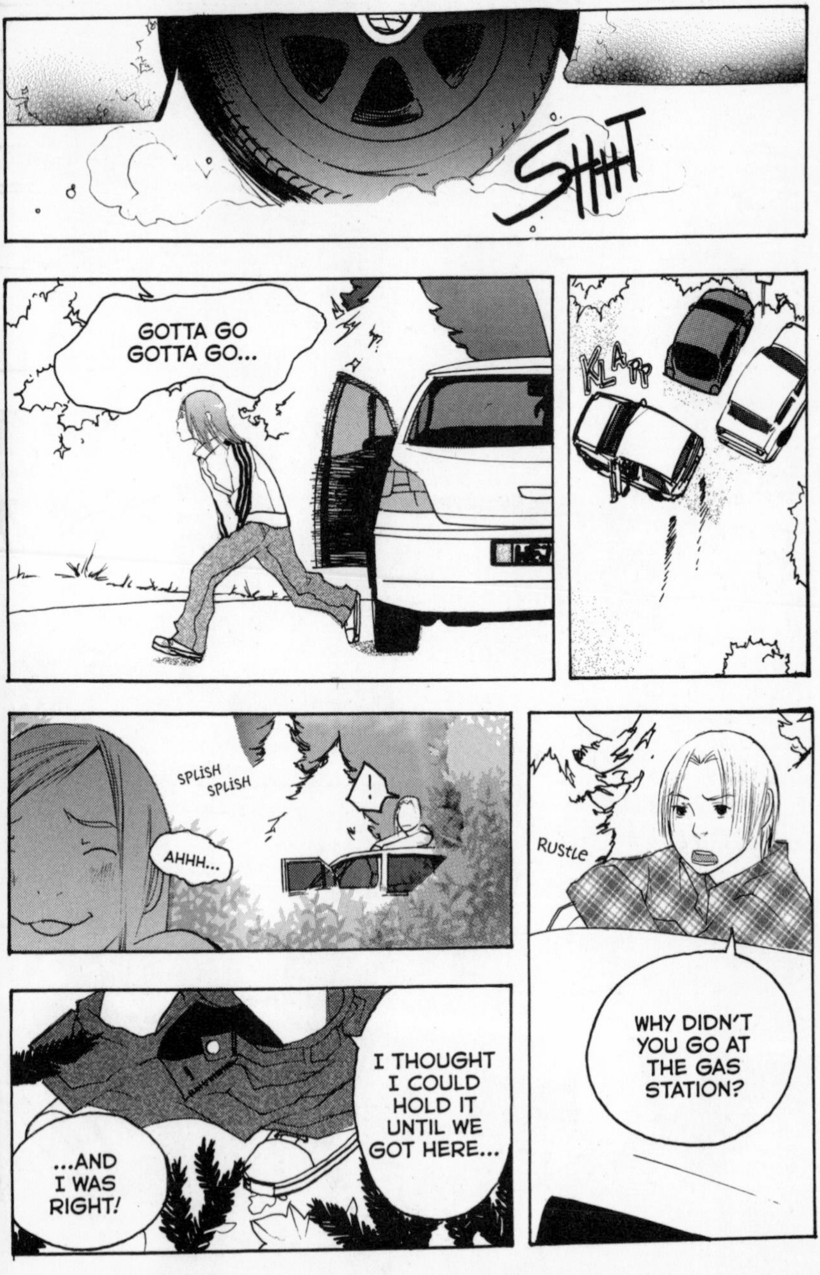
SHHT
KLAPP
GOTTA GO GOTTA GO...
RUSTLE
WHY DIDN'T YOU GO AT THE GAS STATION?
SPLISH SPLISH
!
AHHH...
I THOUGHT I COULD HOLD IT UNTIL WE GOT HERE...
...AND I WAS RIGHT!

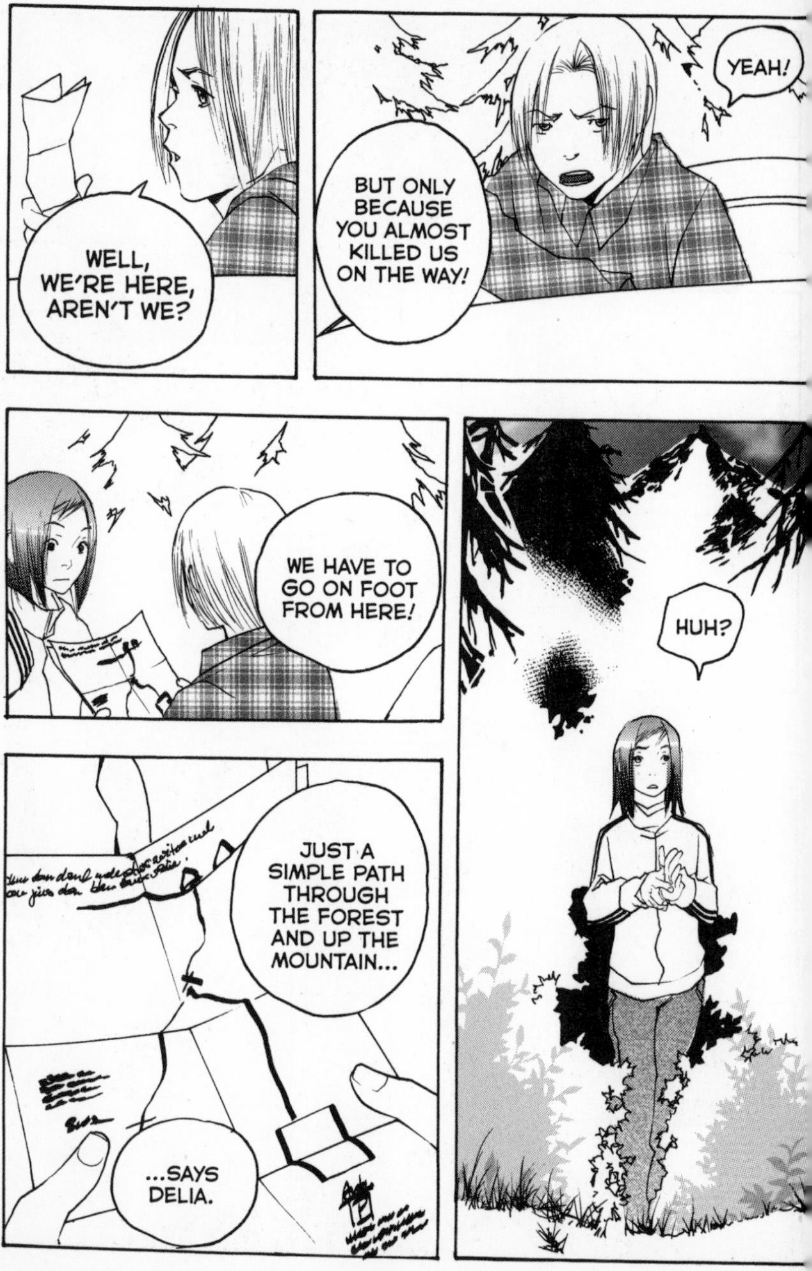
YEAH!
BUT ONLY BECAUSE YOU ALMOST KILLED US ON THE WAY!
WELL, WE'RE HERE, AREN'T WE?
HUH?
WE HAVE TO GO ON FOOT FROM HERE!
JUST A SIMPLE PATH THROUGH THE FOREST AND UP THE MOUNTAIN...
...SAYS DELIA.

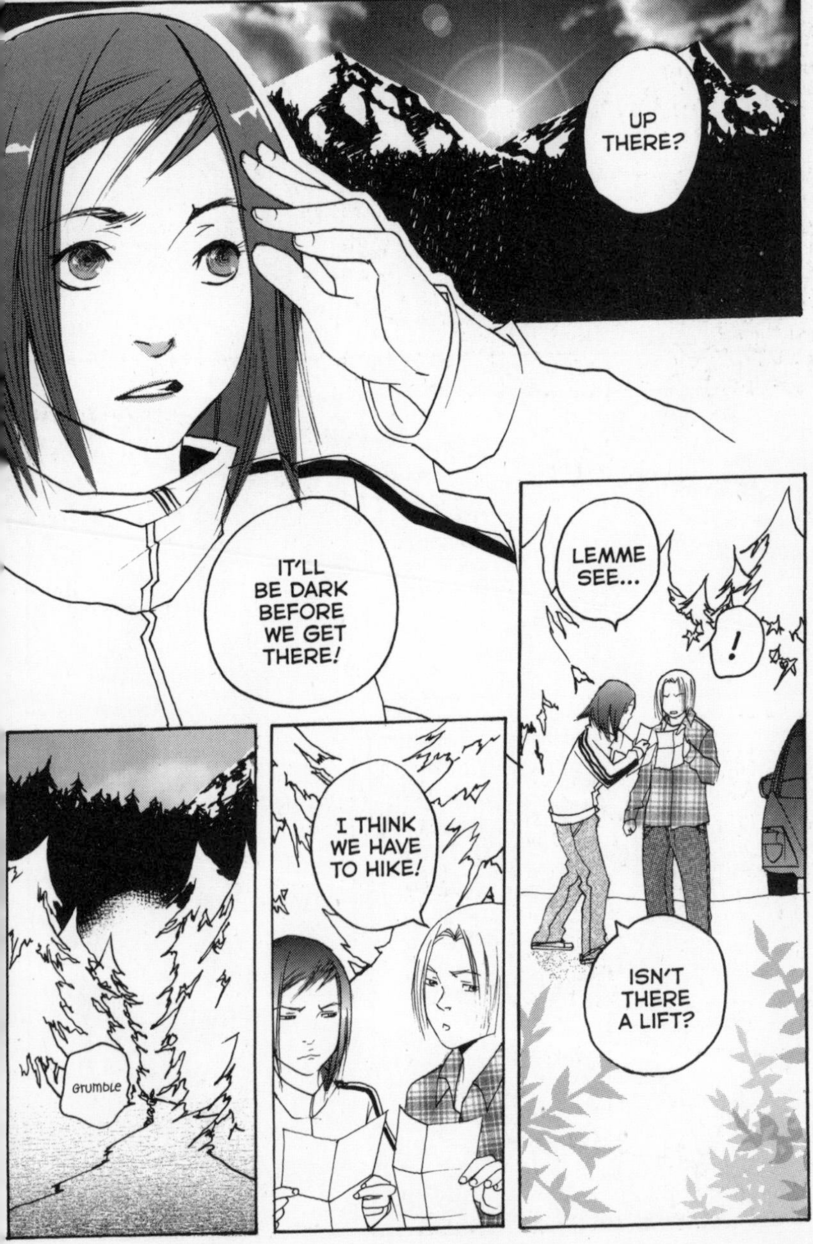
UP THERE?
IT'LL BE DARK BEFORE WE GET THERE!
LEMME SEE...
!
ISN'T THERE A LIFT?
I THINK WE HAVE TO HIKE!
GRUMBLE

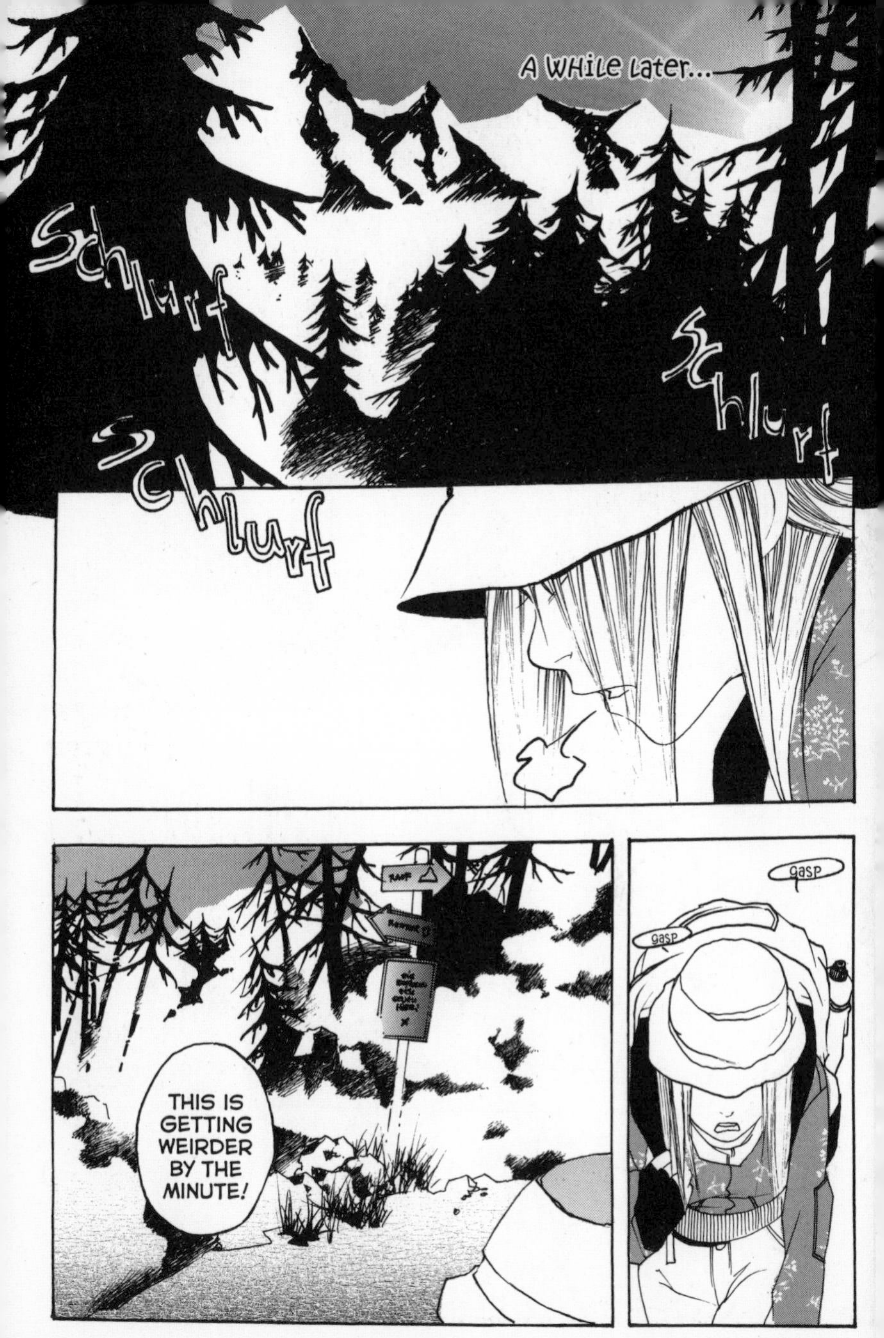
A WHILE later...
Schlurf
Schlurf
Schlurf
gasp
gasp
THIS IS GETTING WEIRDER BY THE MINUTE!

DOOT
DOOT
DOOT
DOOT

DOOT

DOOT

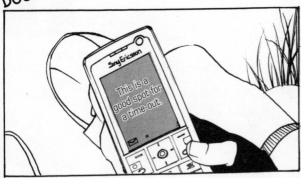

This is a good spot for a time-out.

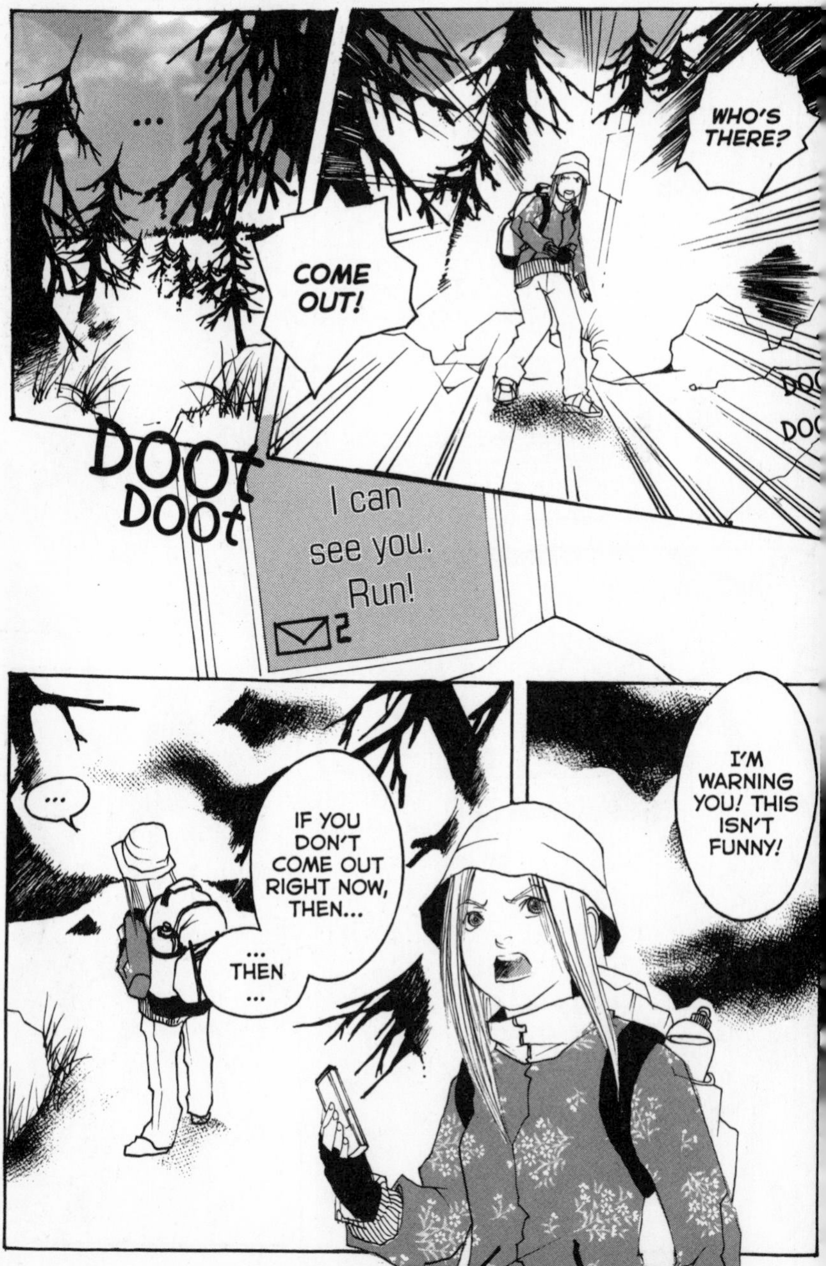
WHO'S THERE?
COME OUT!
...
DOOT DOOT
I can see you. Run!
2
I'M WARNING YOU! THIS ISN'T FUNNY!
IF YOU DON'T COME OUT RIGHT NOW, THEN...
...THEN...
...

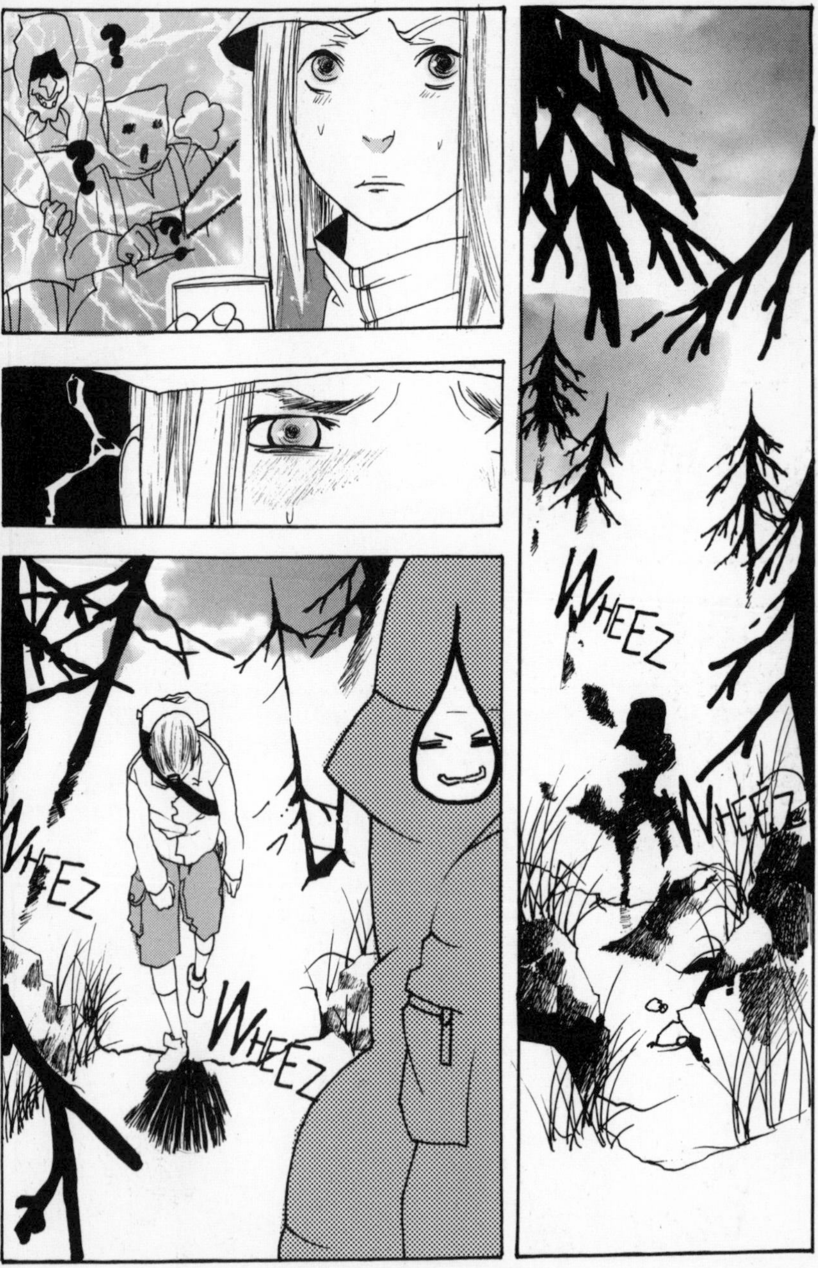
WHEEZ
WHEEZ
WHEEZ
WHEEZ

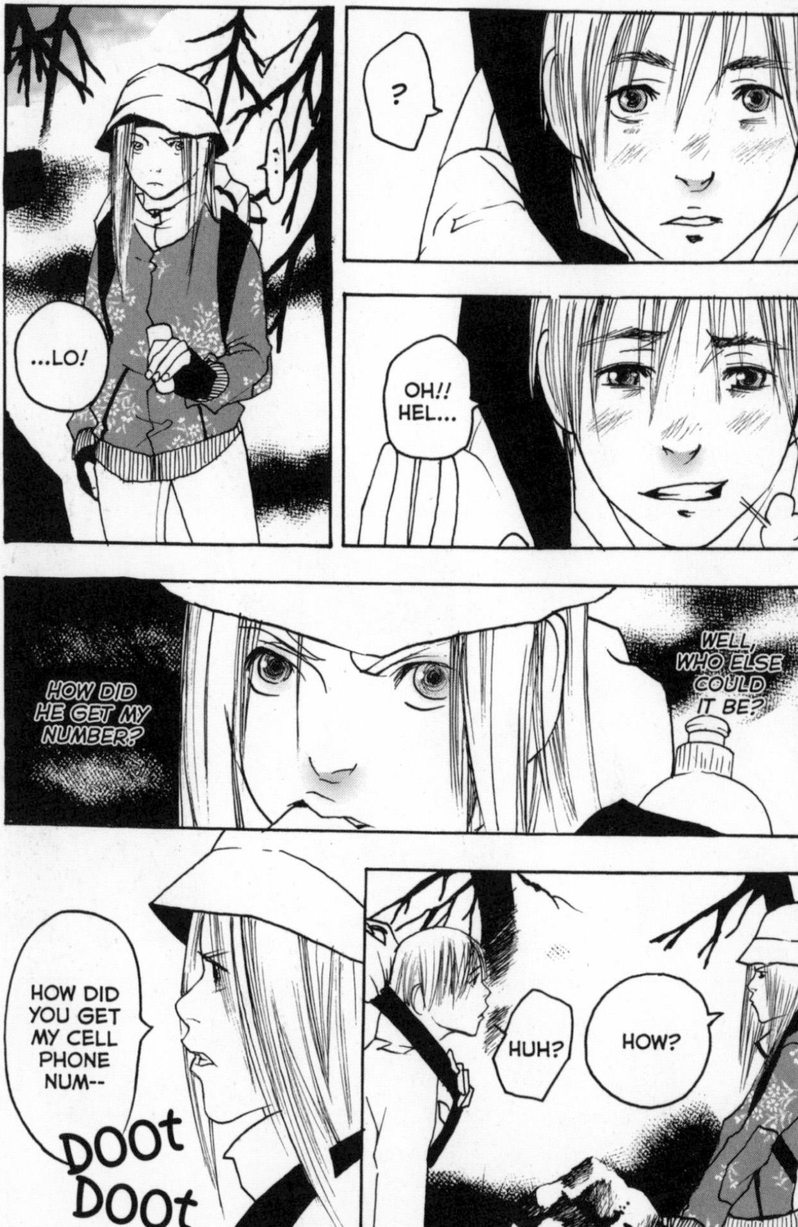
?
OH!! HEL...
...
...LO!
WELL, WHO ELSE COULD IT BE?
HOW DID HE GET MY NUMBER?
HOW?
HUH?
HOW DID YOU GET MY CELL PHONE NUM--
DOOT DOOT

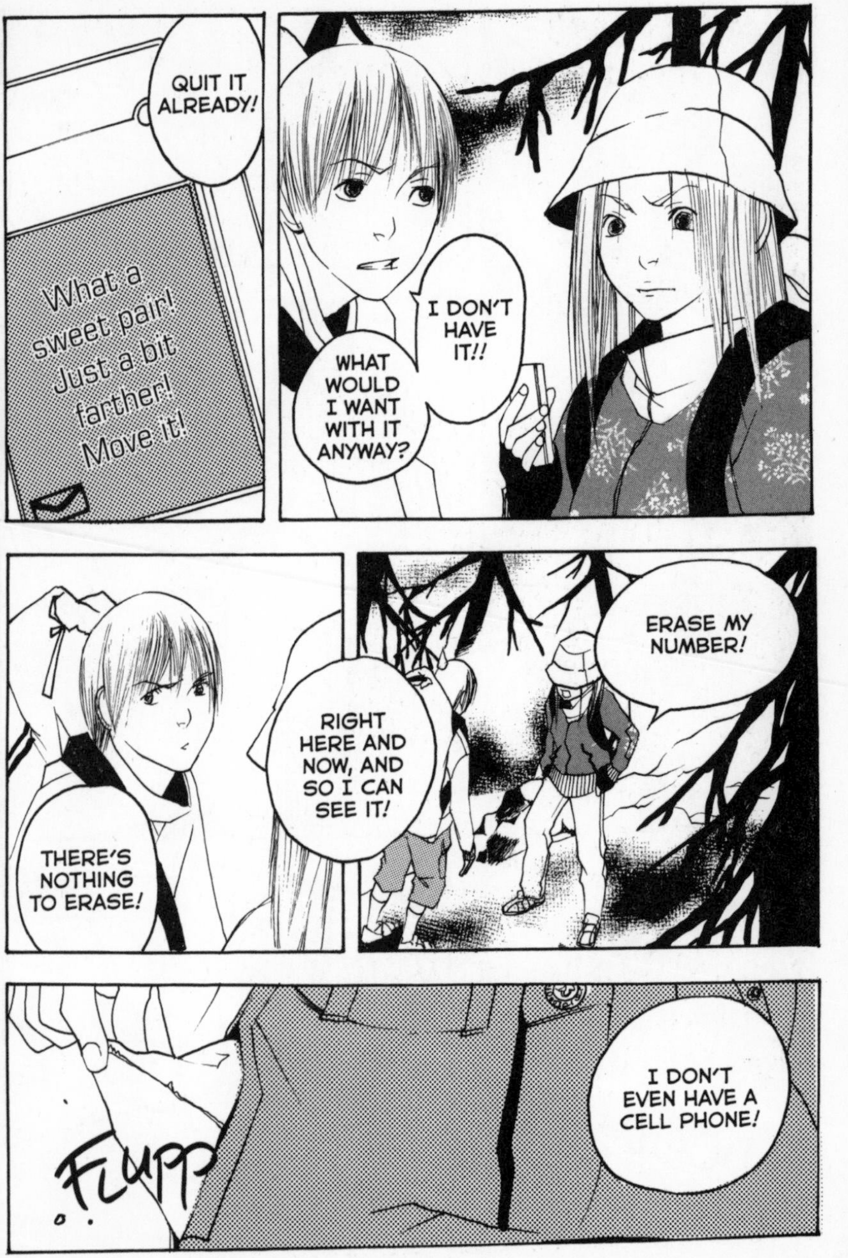
I DON'T HAVE IT!!
WHAT WOULD I WANT WITH IT ANYWAY?
QUIT IT ALREADY!
What a sweet pair! Just a bit farther! Move it!
ERASE MY NUMBER!
RIGHT HERE AND NOW, AND SO I CAN SEE IT!
THERE'S NOTHING TO ERASE!
I DON'T EVEN HAVE A CELL PHONE!
FLUPP

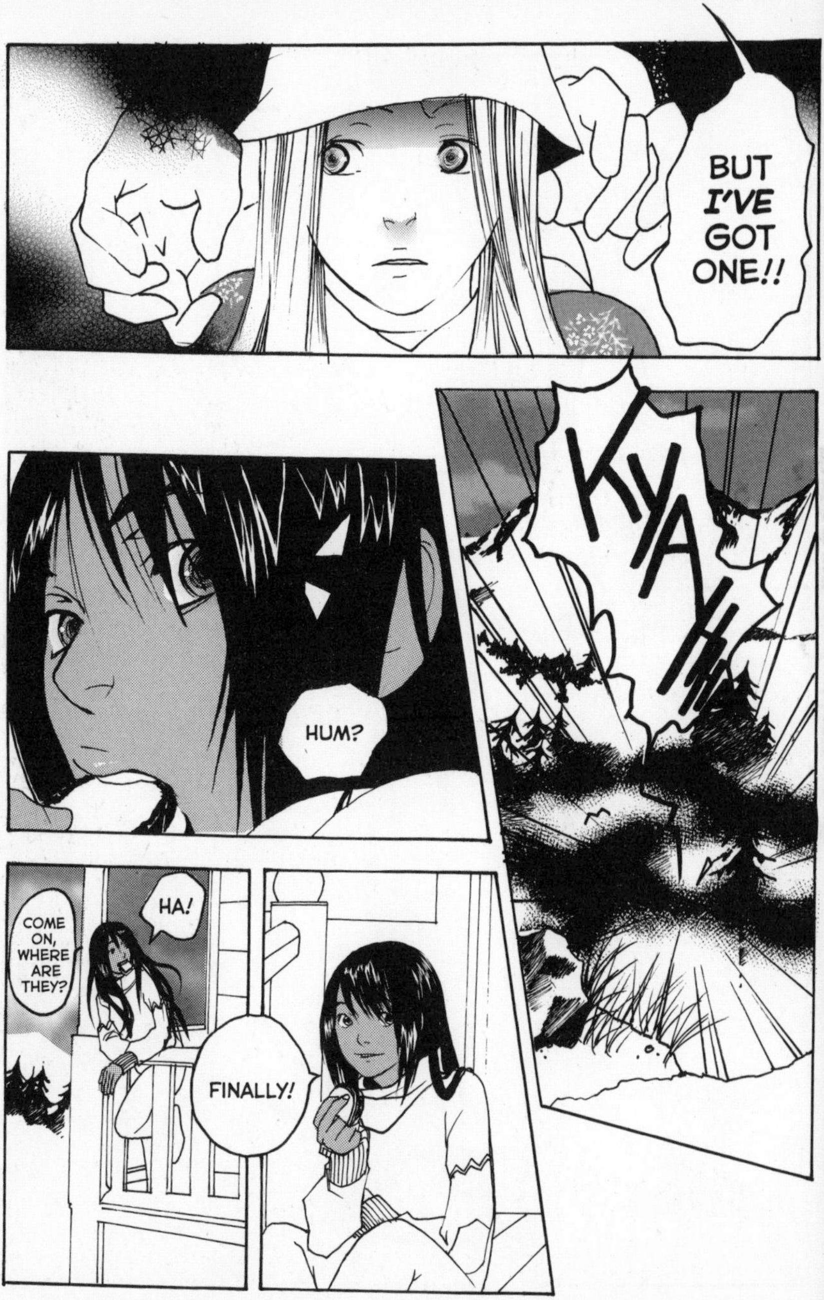
BUT I'VE GOT ONE!!
KYAHHH
HUM?
FINALLY!
HA!
COME ON, WHERE ARE THEY?

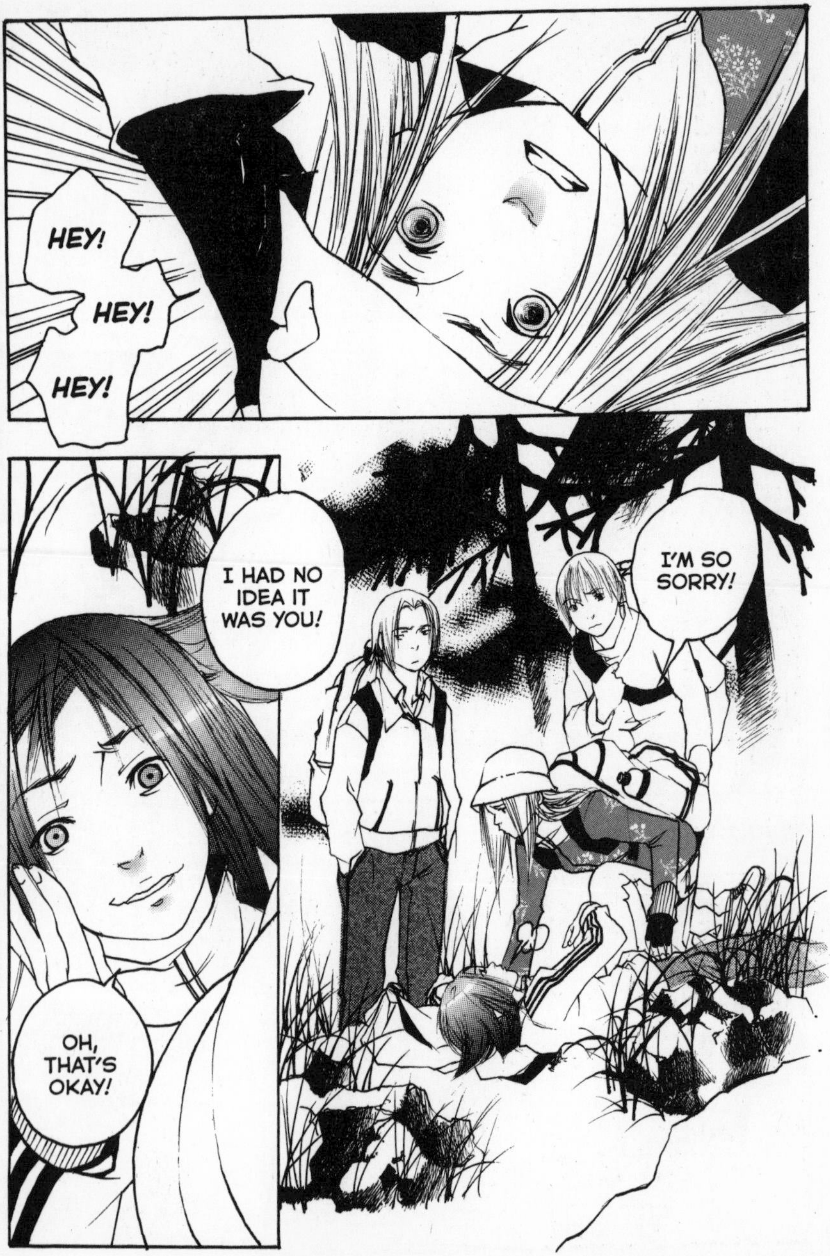
HEY!
HEY!
HEY!
I'M SO SORRY!
I HAD NO IDEA IT WAS YOU!
OH, THAT'S OKAY!

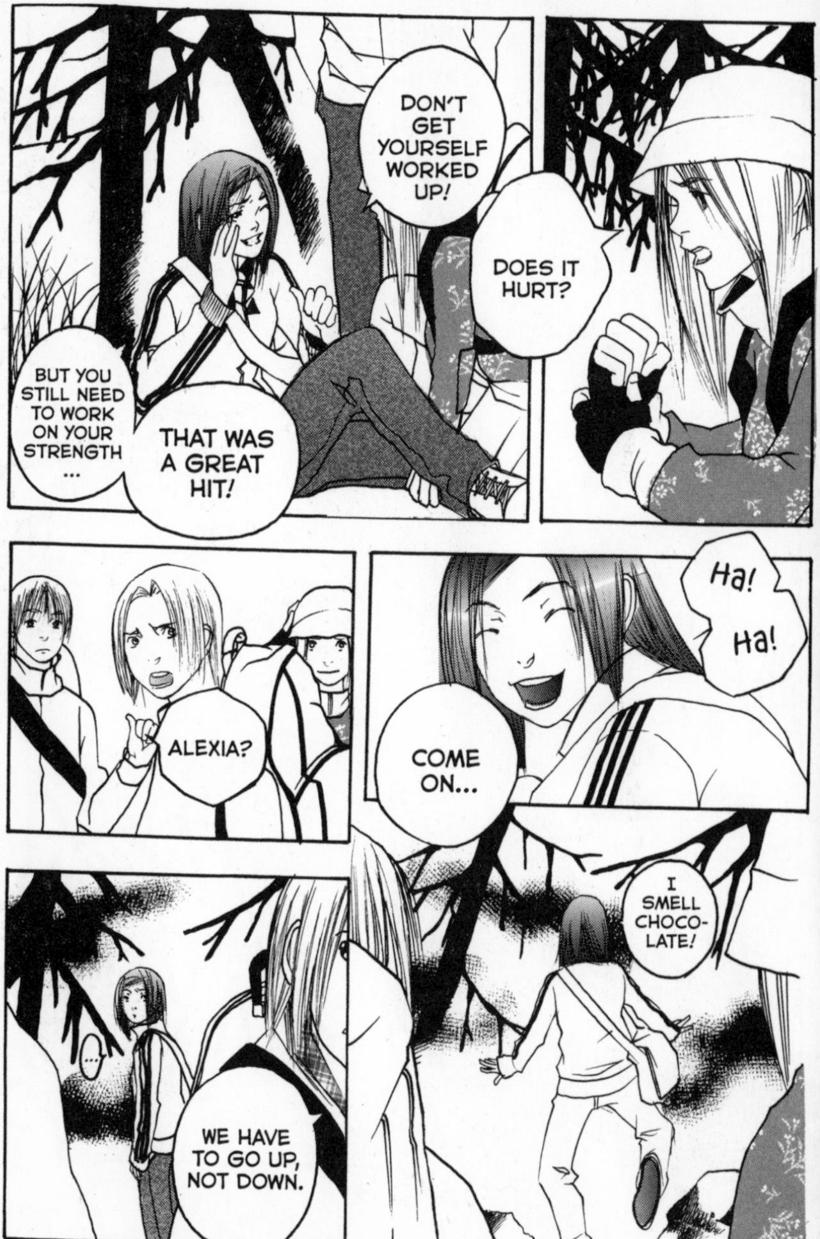
DOES IT HURT?
DON'T GET YOURSELF WORKED UP!
THAT WAS A GREAT HIT!
BUT YOU STILL NEED TO WORK ON YOUR STRENGTH ...
Ha! Ha!
COME ON...
ALEXIA?
I SMELL CHOCO-LATE!
...
WE HAVE TO GO UP, NOT DOWN.

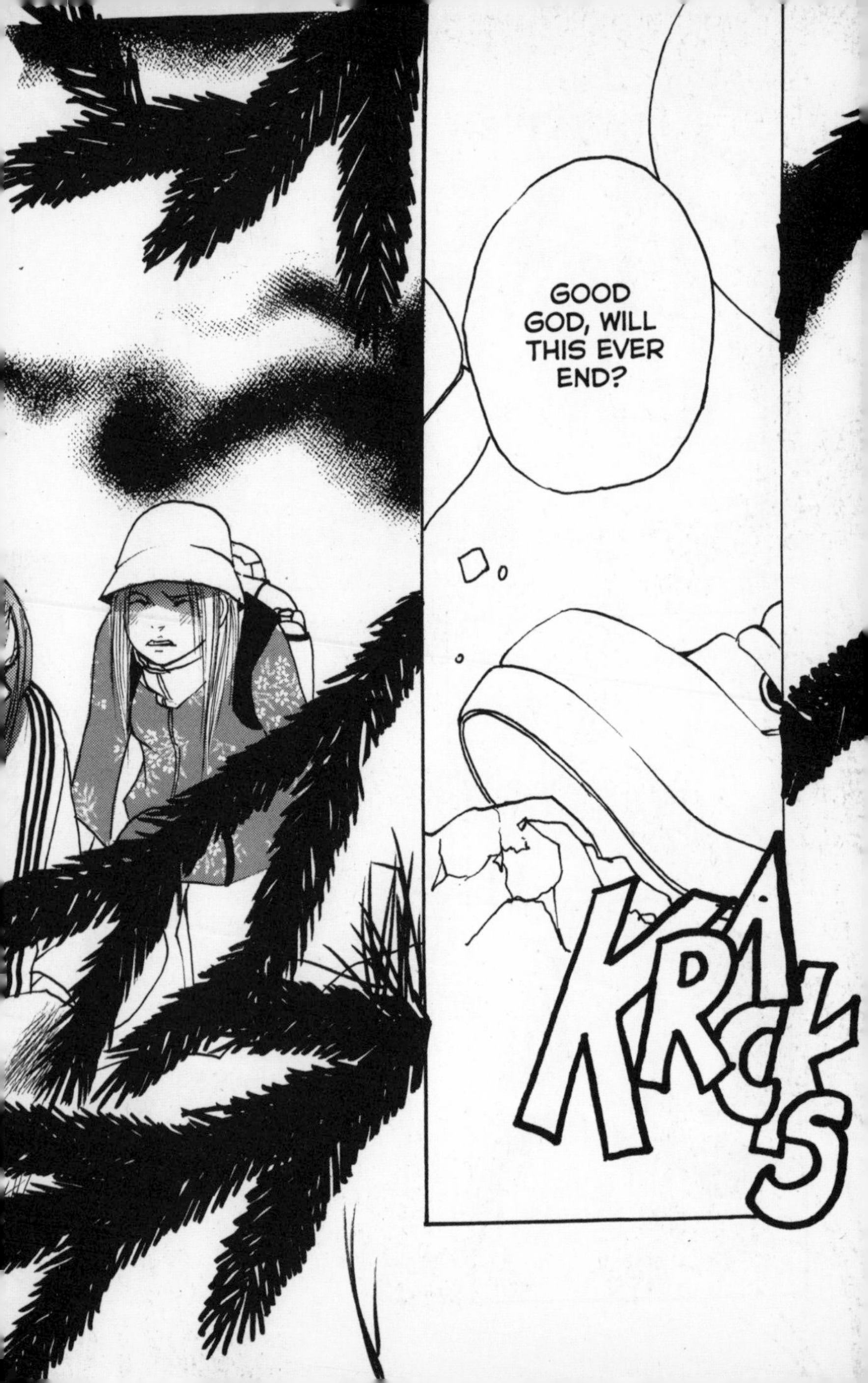
GOOD GOD, WILL THIS EVER END?
KRACKS

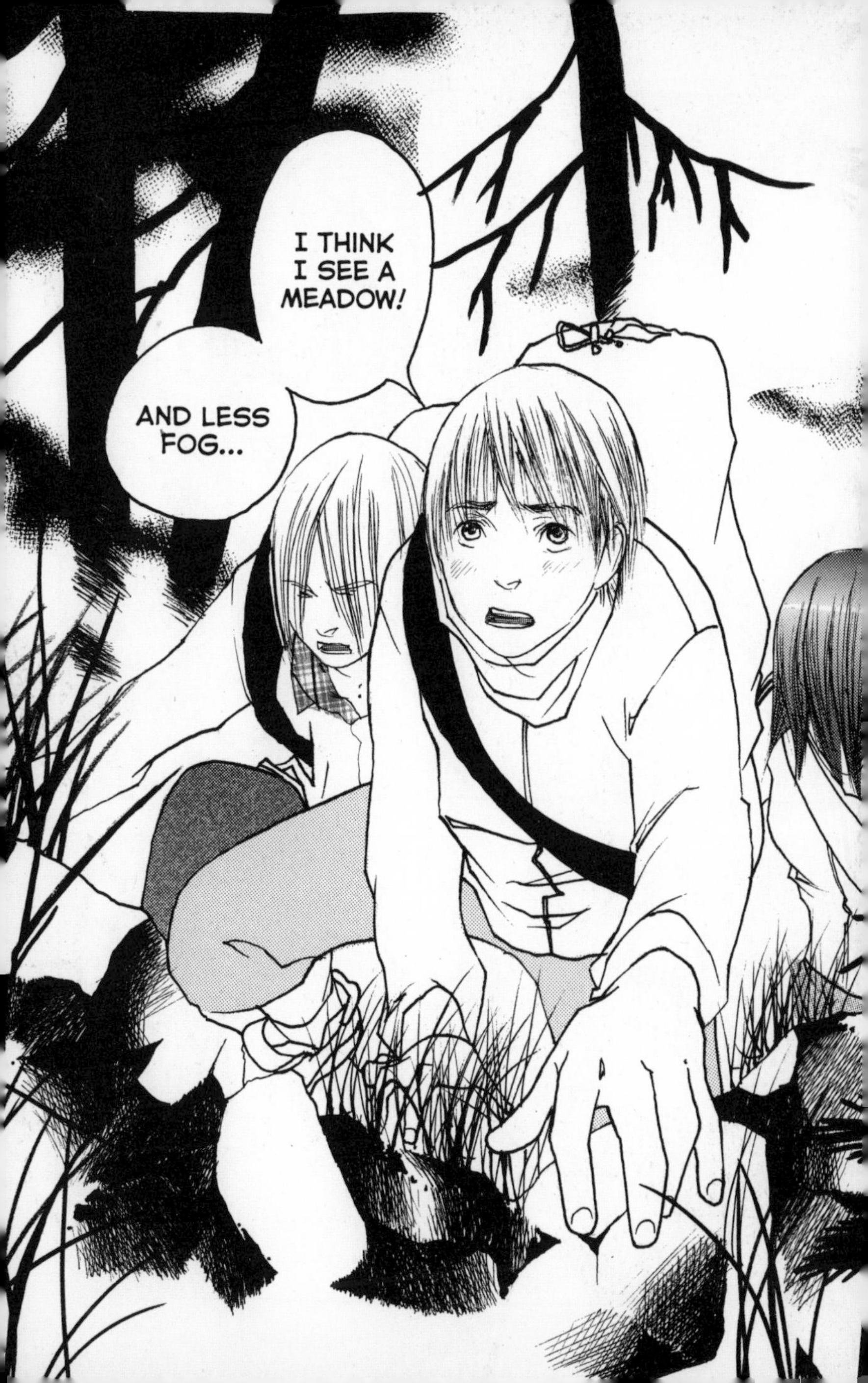
I THINK I SEE A MEADOW!
AND LESS FOG...

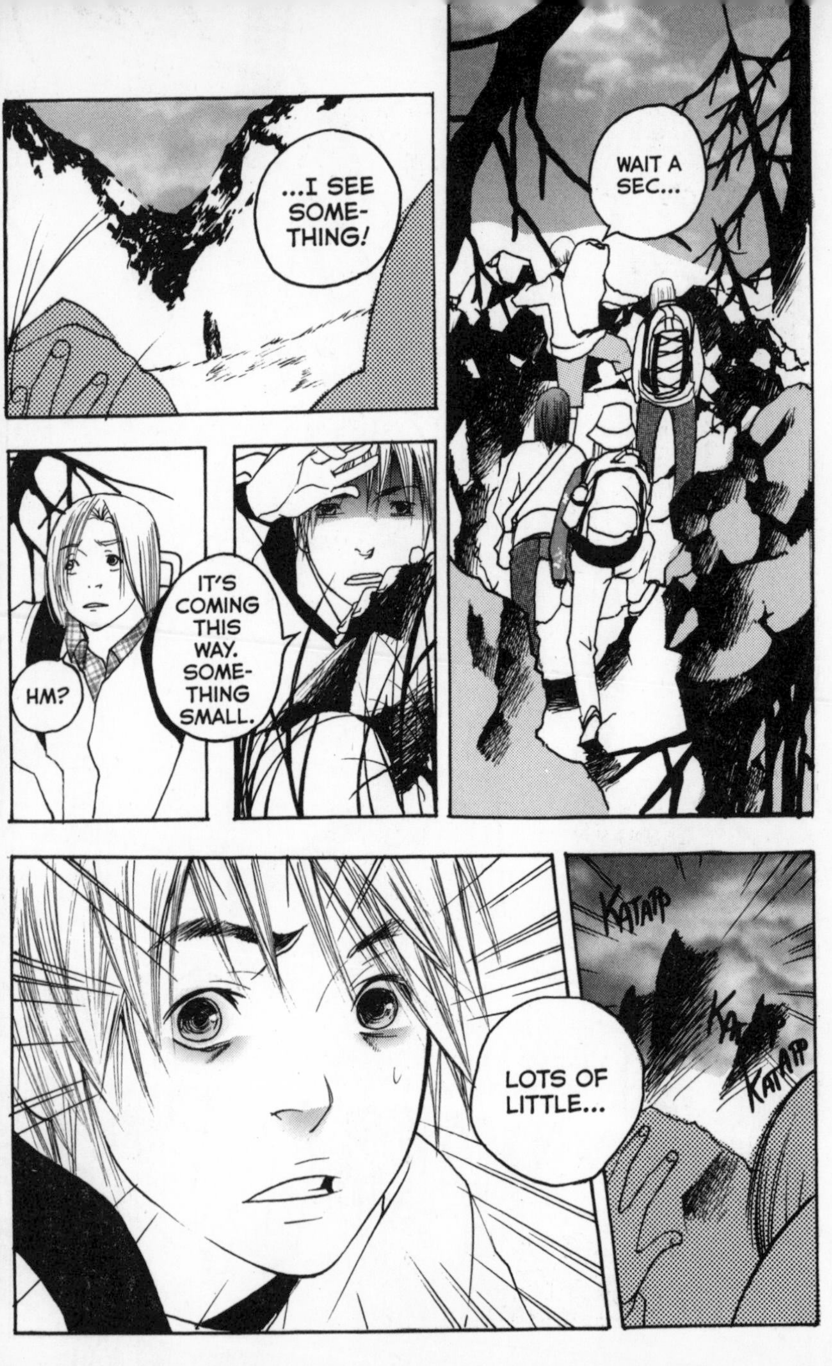
WAIT A SEC...
...I SEE SOMETHING!
IT'S COMING THIS WAY. SOMETHING SMALL.
HM?
KATAPP
KATAPP
LOTS OF LITTLE...

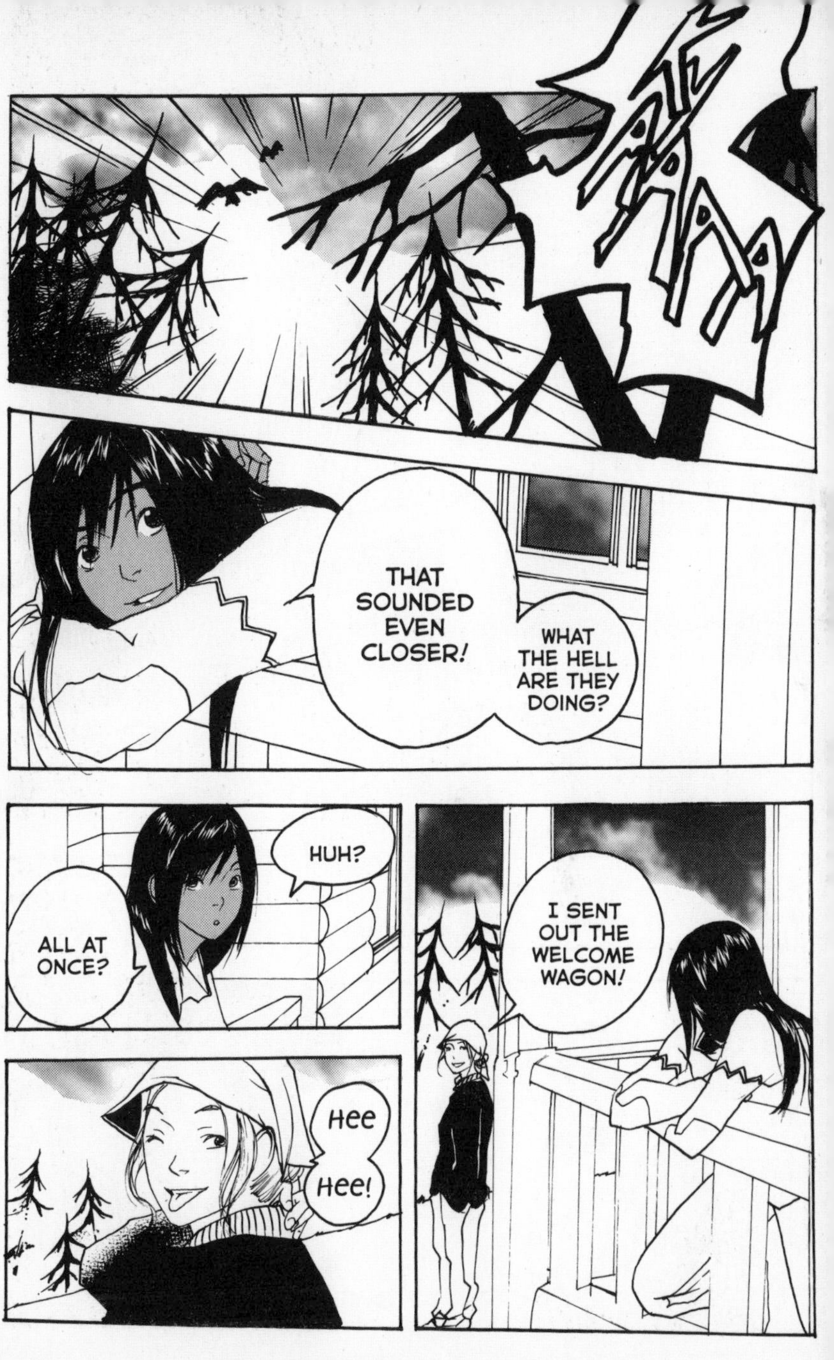
THAT SOUNDED EVEN CLOSER!
WHAT THE HELL ARE THEY DOING?
I SENT OUT THE WELCOME WAGON!
HUH?
ALL AT ONCE?
Hee
Hee!

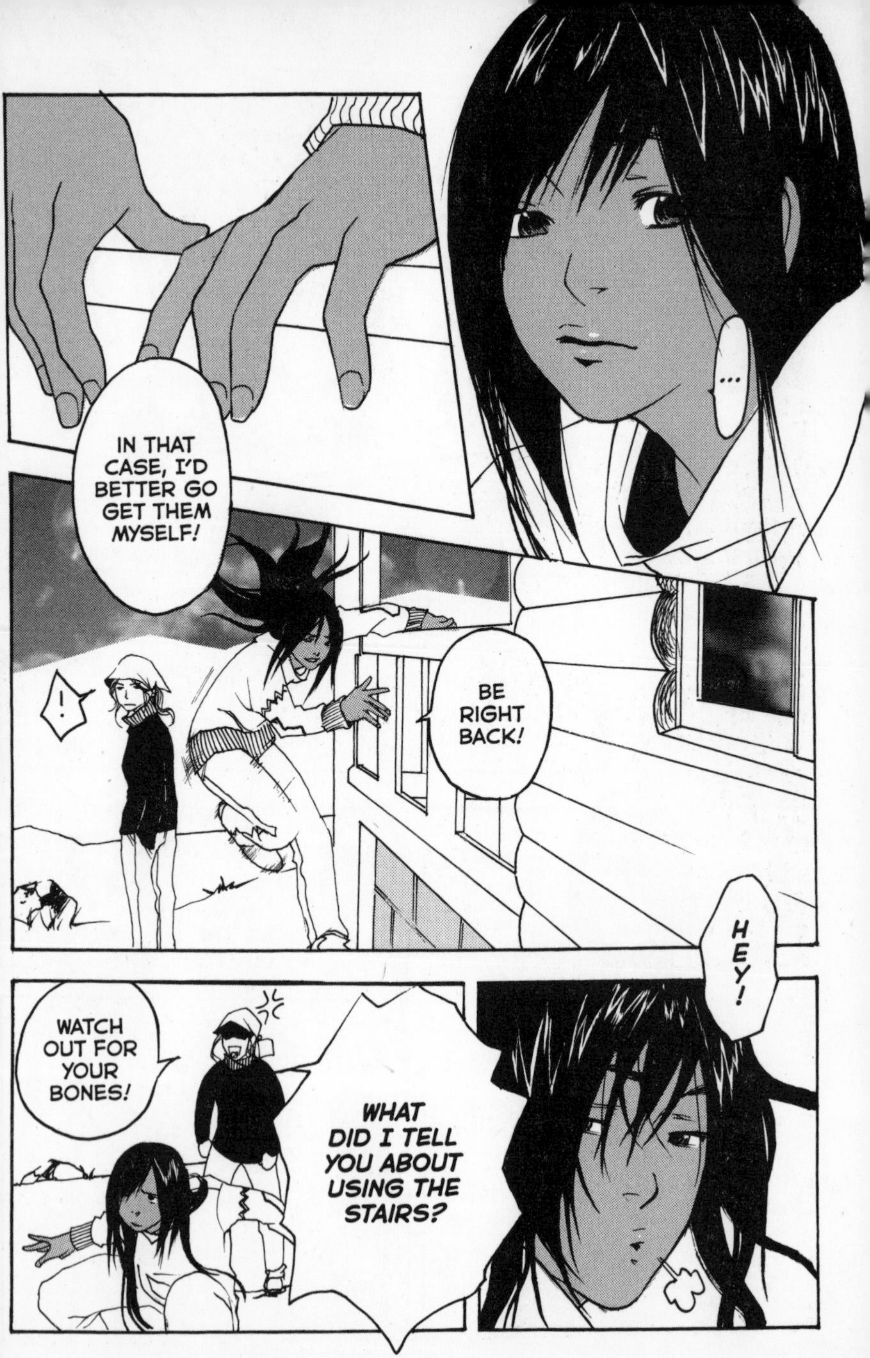
...
IN THAT CASE, I'D BETTER GO GET THEM MYSELF!
BE RIGHT BACK!
!
HEY!
WHAT DID I TELL YOU ABOUT USING THE STAIRS?
WATCH OUT FOR YOUR BONES!

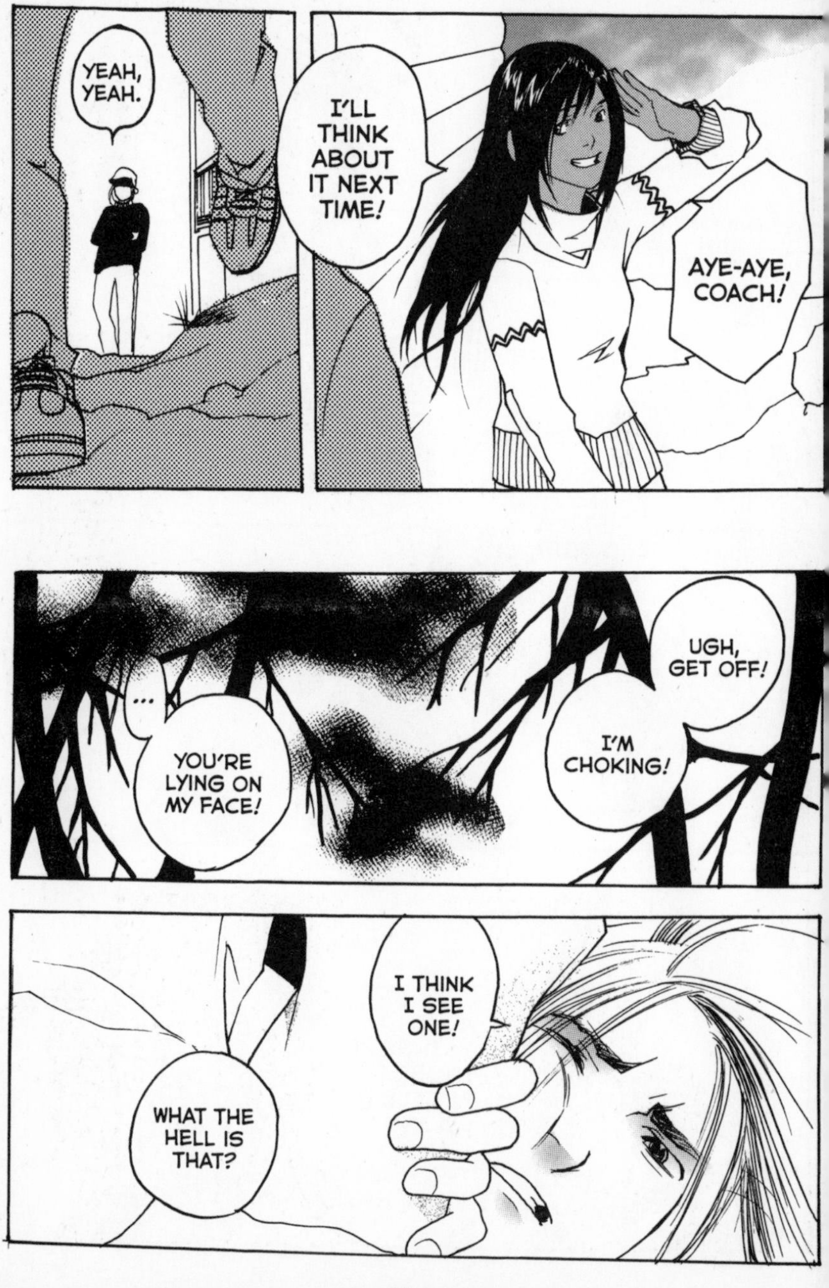
AYE-AYE, COACH!
I'LL THINK ABOUT IT NEXT TIME!
YEAH, YEAH.
UGH, GET OFF!
I'M CHOKING!
...
YOU'RE LYING ON MY FACE!
I THINK I SEE ONE!
WHAT THE HELL IS THAT?

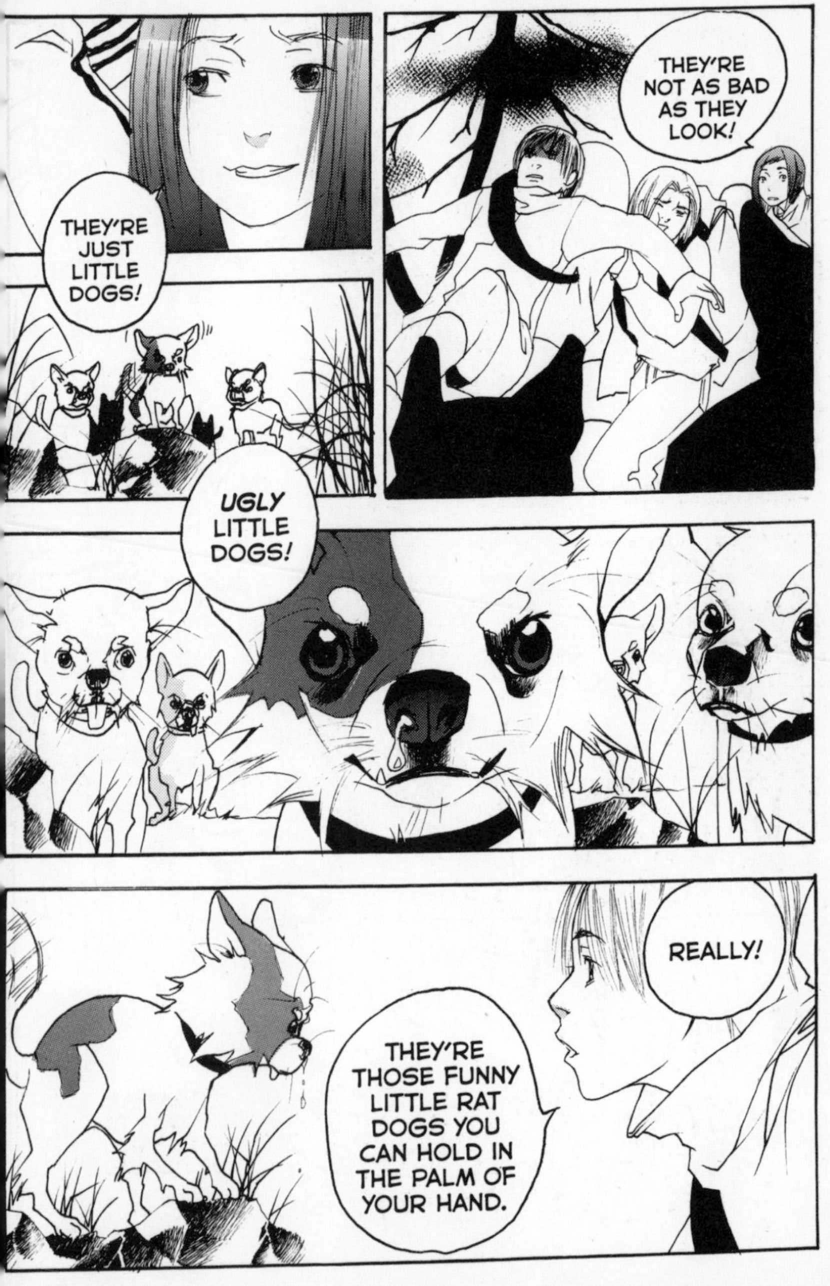
THEY'RE NOT AS BAD AS THEY LOOK!
THEY'RE JUST LITTLE DOGS!
UGLY LITTLE DOGS!
REALLY!
THEY'RE THOSE FUNNY LITTLE RAT DOGS YOU CAN HOLD IN THE PALM OF YOUR HAND.

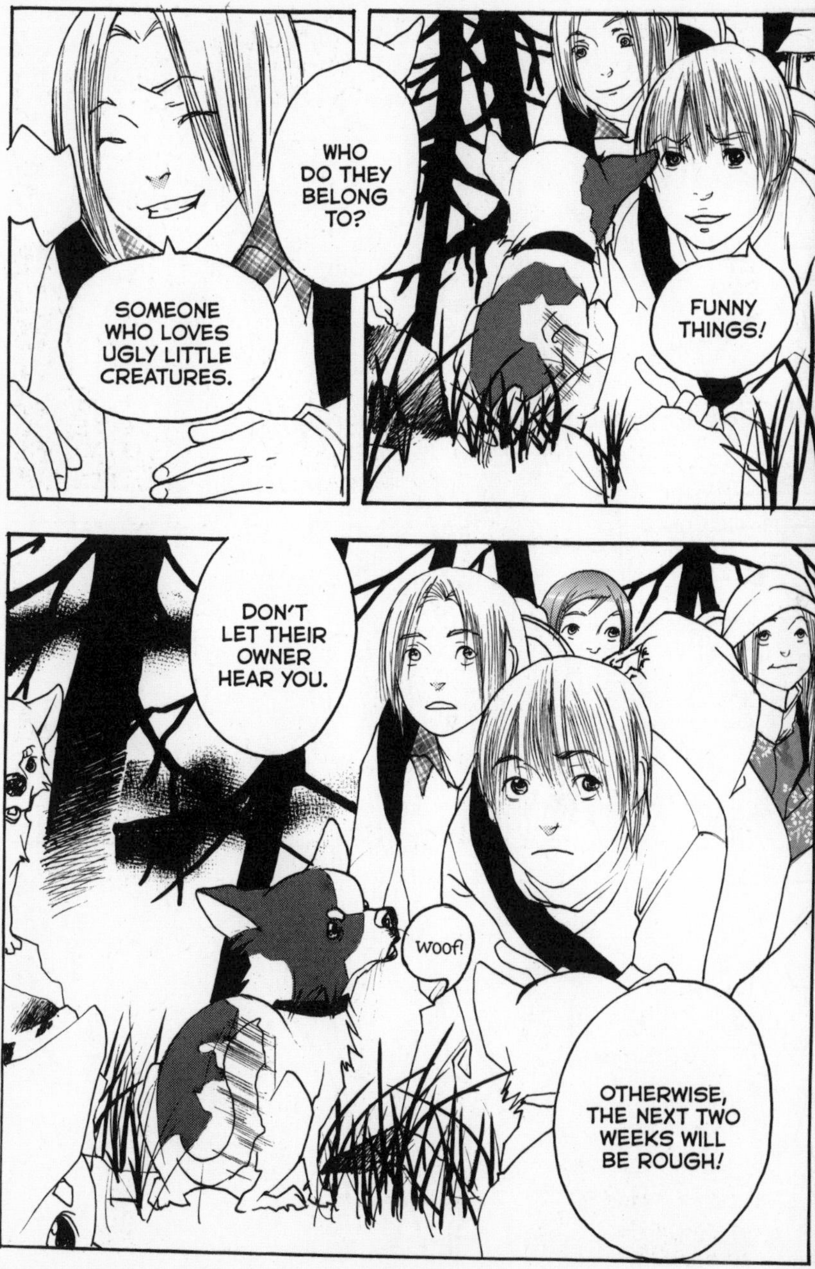
FUNNY THINGS!
WHO DO THEY BELONG TO?
SOMEONE WHO LOVES UGLY LITTLE CREATURES.
DON'T LET THEIR OWNER HEAR YOU.
woof!
OTHERWISE, THE NEXT TWO WEEKS WILL BE ROUGH!

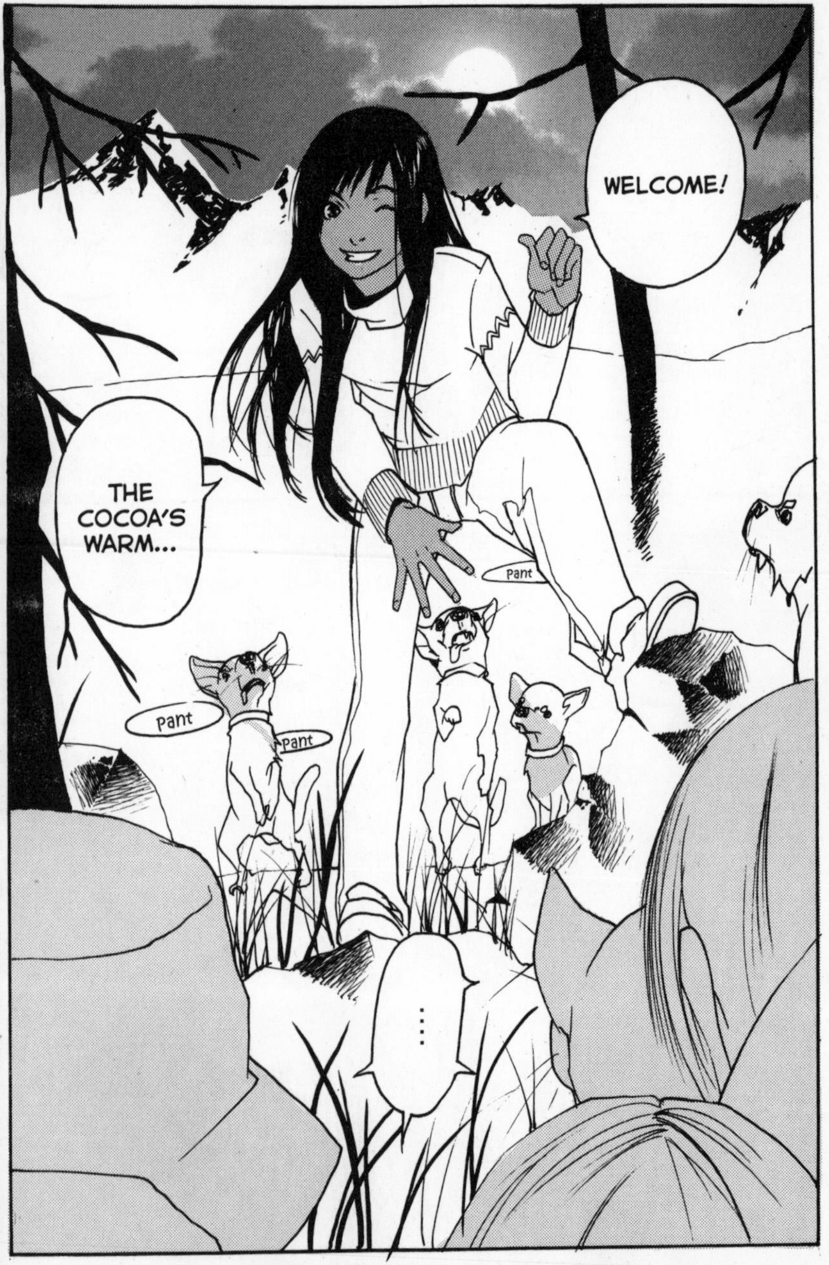
WELCOME!
THE COCOA'S WARM...
Pant
Pant
Pant
....

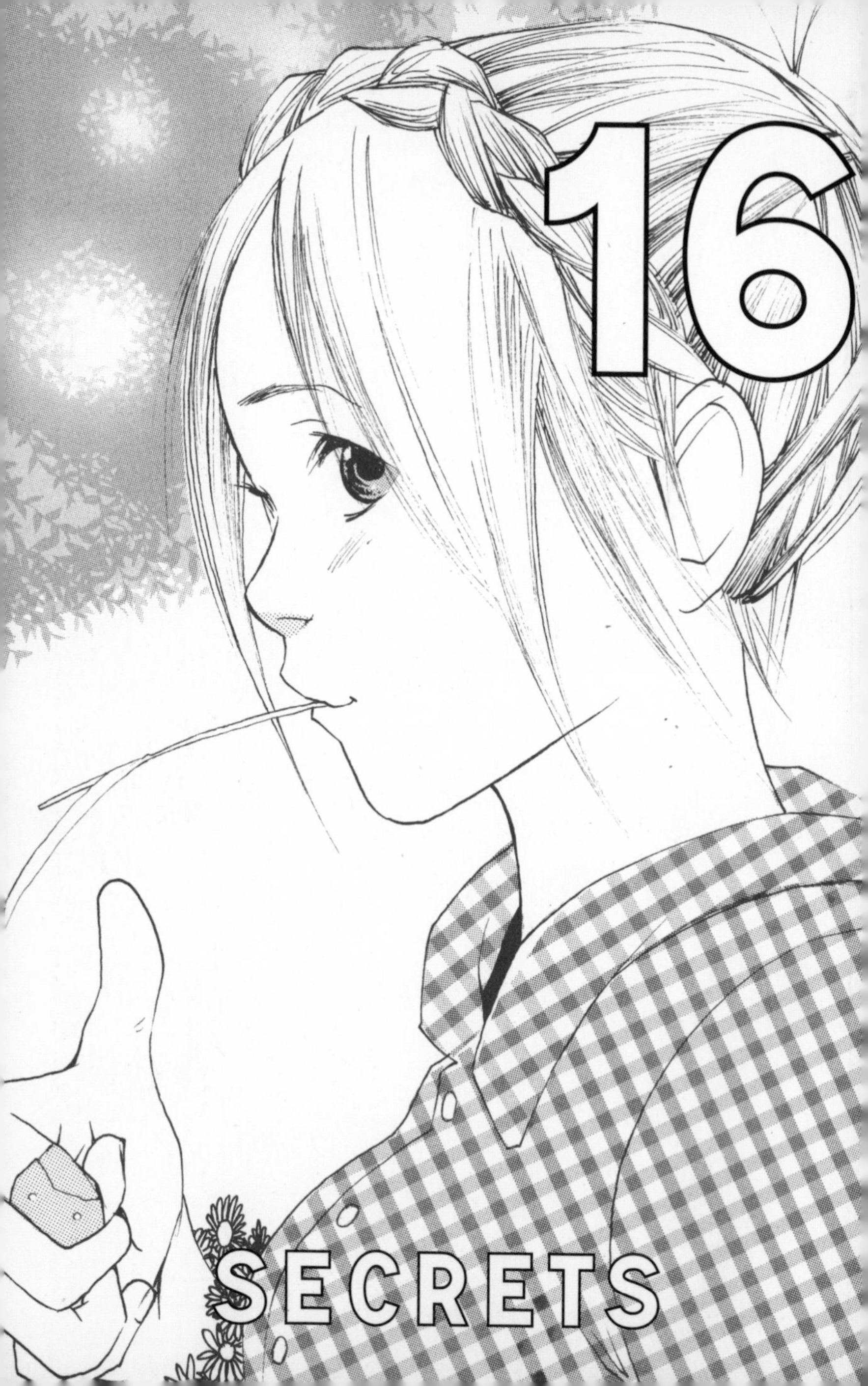
16
SECRETS

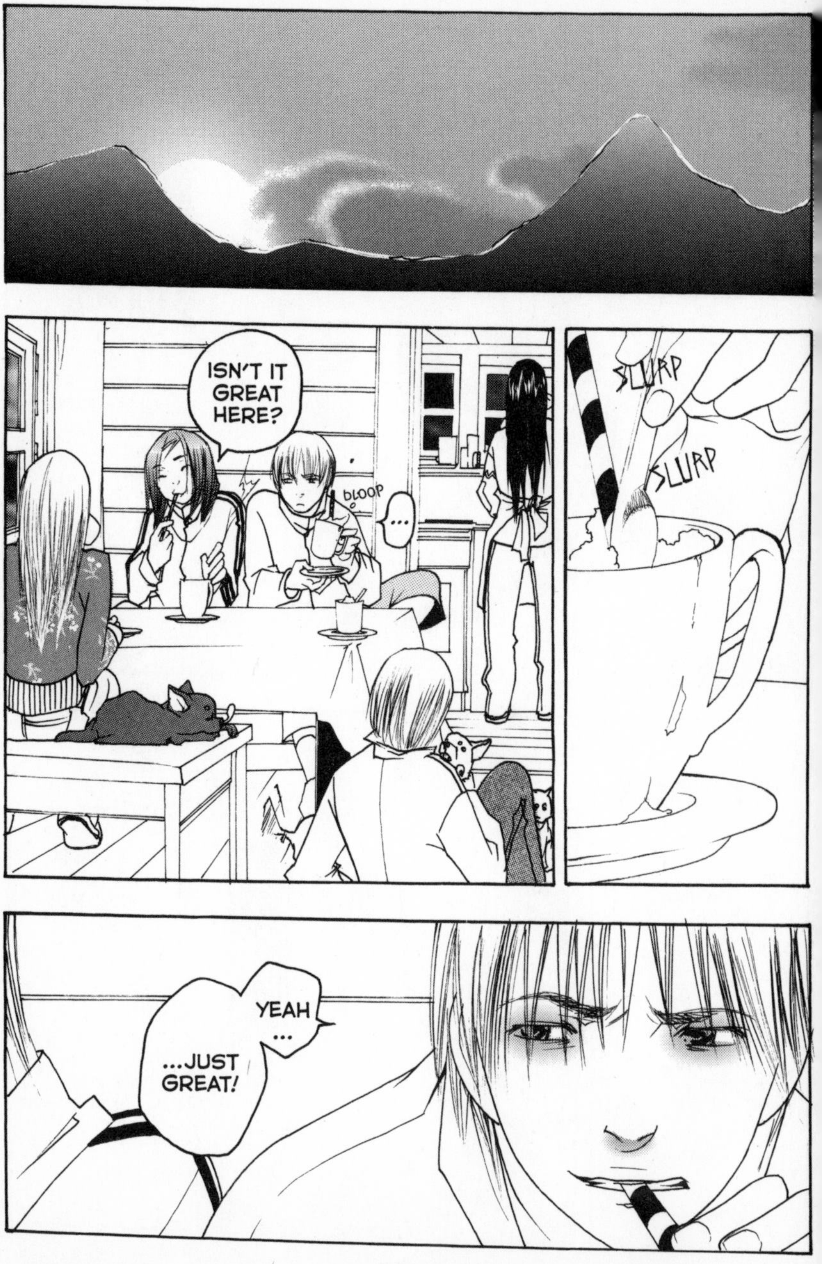
SLURP
SLURP
ISN'T IT GREAT HERE?
BLOOP
...
YEAH ...
...JUST GREAT!

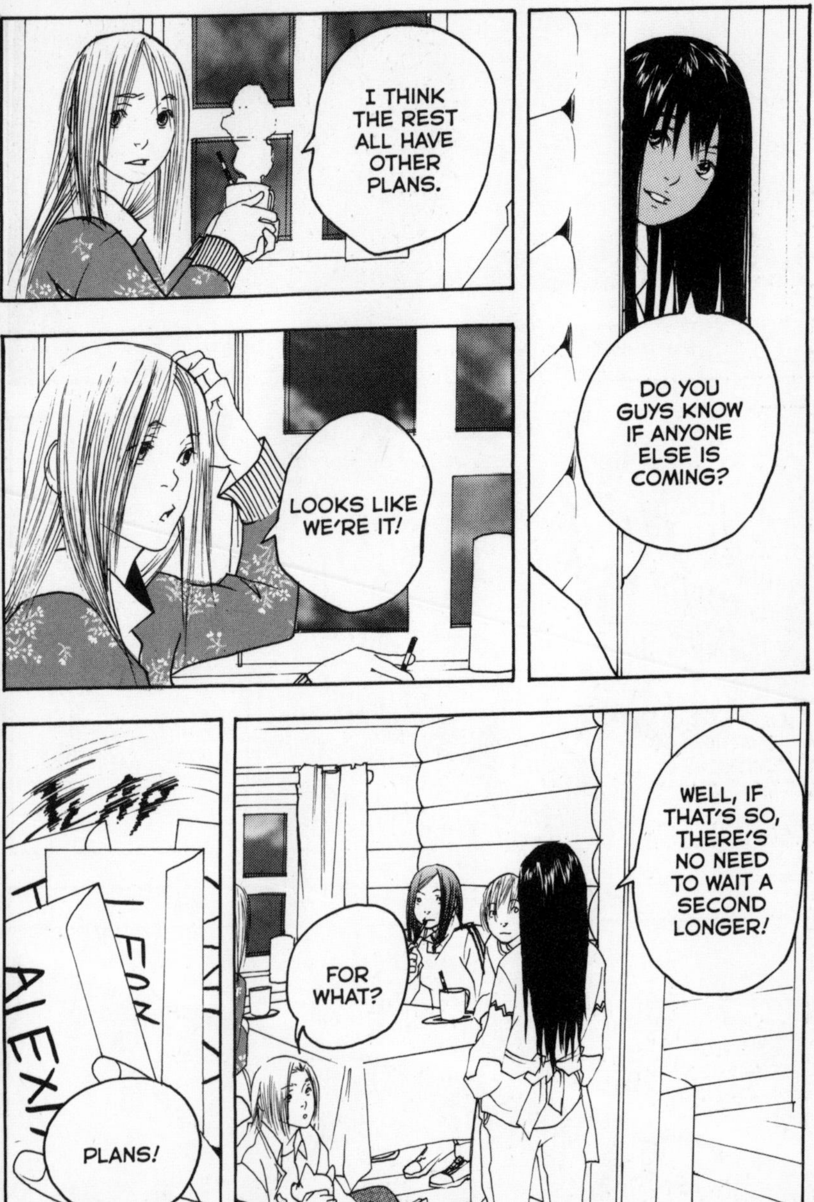
DO YOU GUYS KNOW IF ANYONE ELSE IS COMING?
I THINK THE REST ALL HAVE OTHER PLANS.
LOOKS LIKE WE'RE IT!
WELL, IF THAT'S SO, THERE'S NO NEED TO WAIT A SECOND LONGER!
FOR WHAT?
FLAP
PLANS!

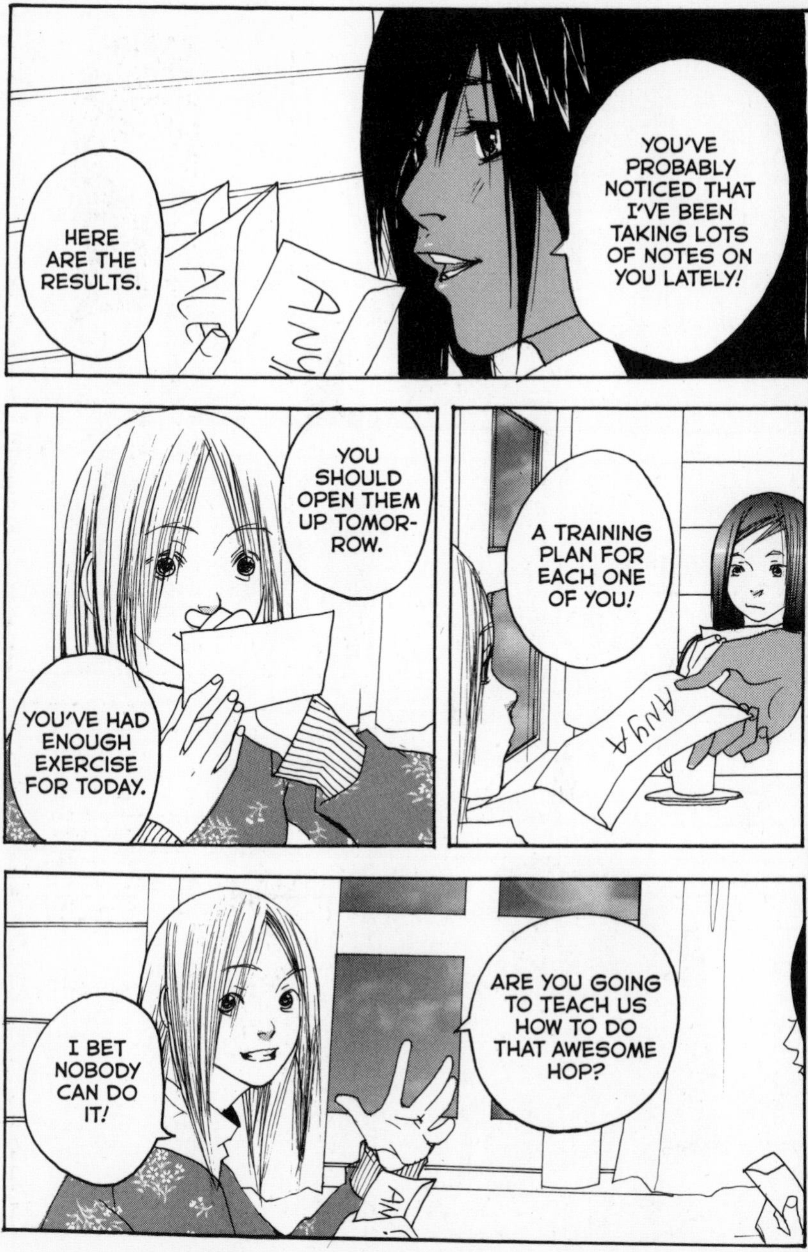
YOU'VE PROBABLY NOTICED THAT I'VE BEEN TAKING LOTS OF NOTES ON YOU LATELY!
HERE ARE THE RESULTS.
A TRAINING PLAN FOR EACH ONE OF YOU!
ANYA
YOU SHOULD OPEN THEM UP TOMOR-ROW.
YOU'VE HAD ENOUGH EXERCISE FOR TODAY.
ARE YOU GOING TO TEACH US HOW TO DO THAT AWESOME HOP?
I BET NOBODY CAN DO IT!

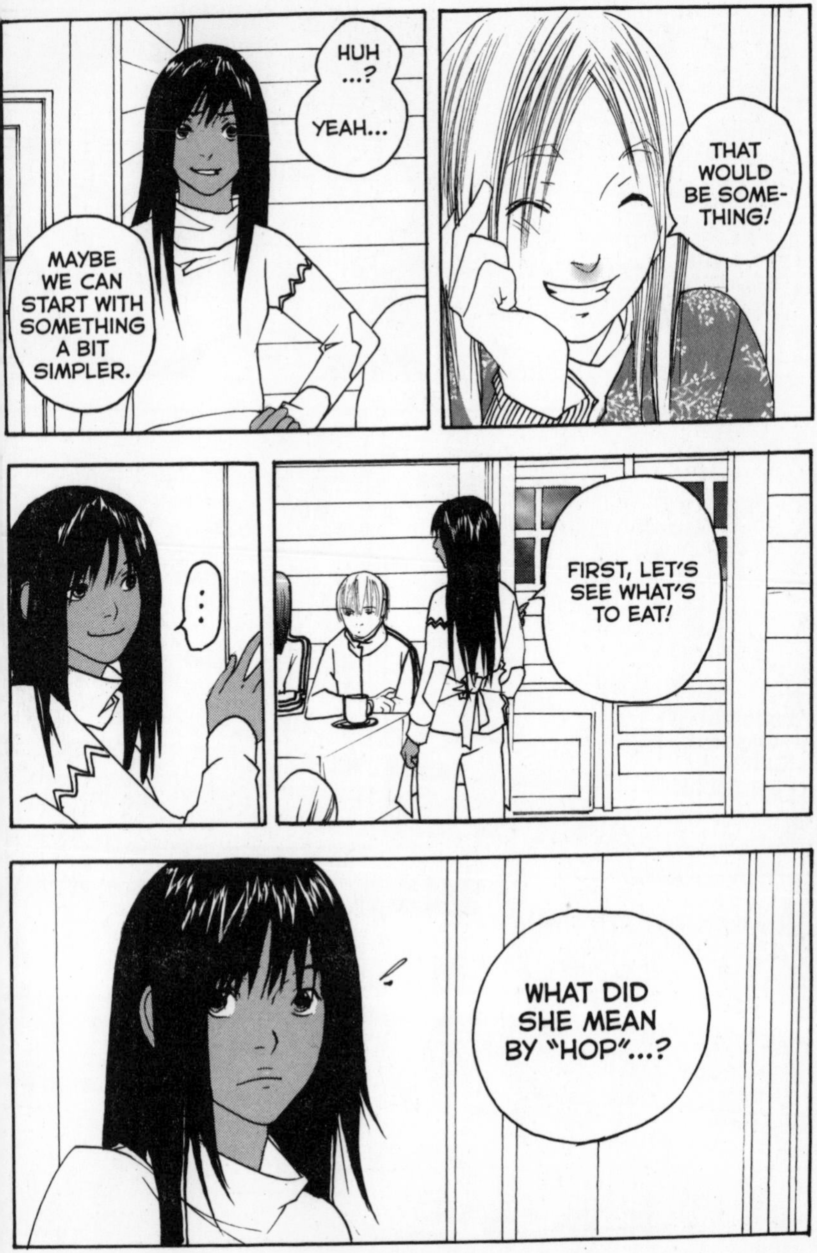
THAT WOULD BE SOME-THING!
HUH ...? YEAH...
MAYBE WE CAN START WITH SOMETHING A BIT SIMPLER.
FIRST, LET'S SEE WHAT'S TO EAT!
...
WHAT DID SHE MEAN BY "HOP"...?

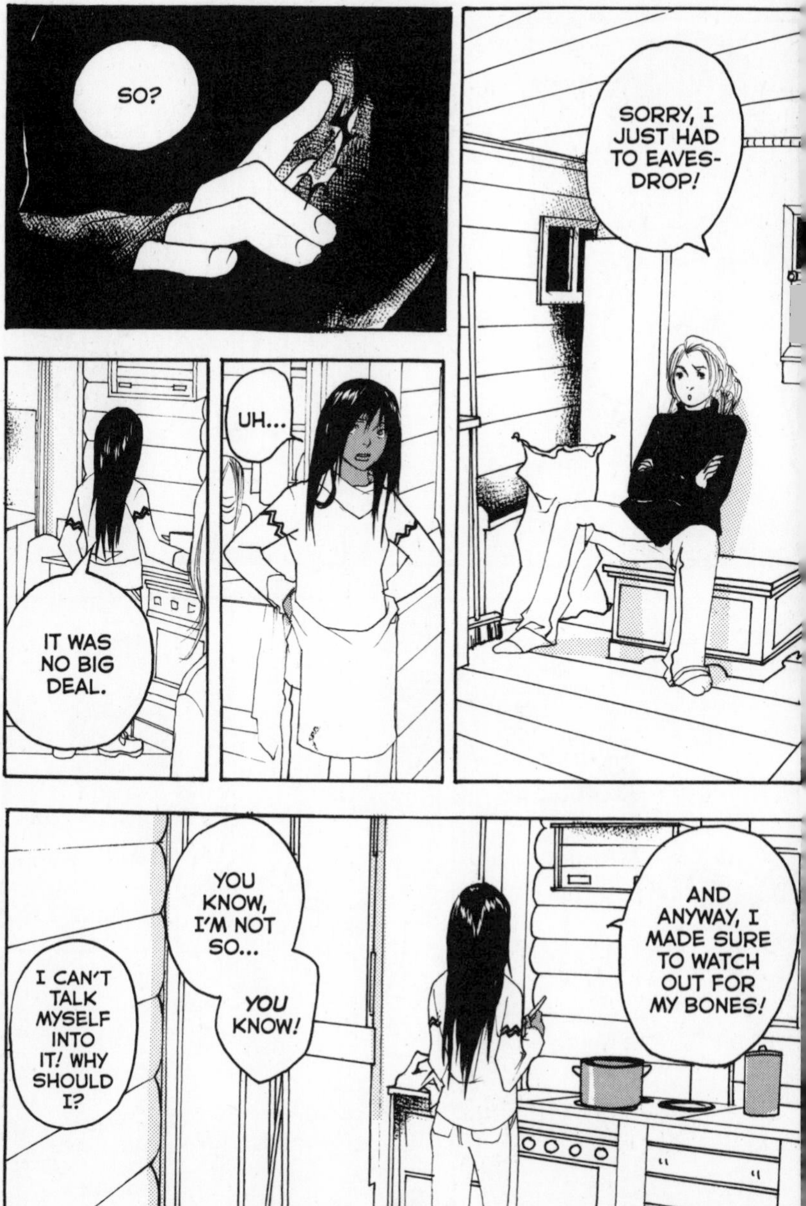
SORRY, I JUST HAD TO EAVES-DROP!
SO?
UH...
IT WAS NO BIG DEAL.
AND ANYWAY, I MADE SURE TO WATCH OUT FOR MY BONES!
YOU KNOW, I'M NOT SO...
YOU KNOW!
I CAN'T TALK MYSELF INTO IT! WHY SHOULD I?

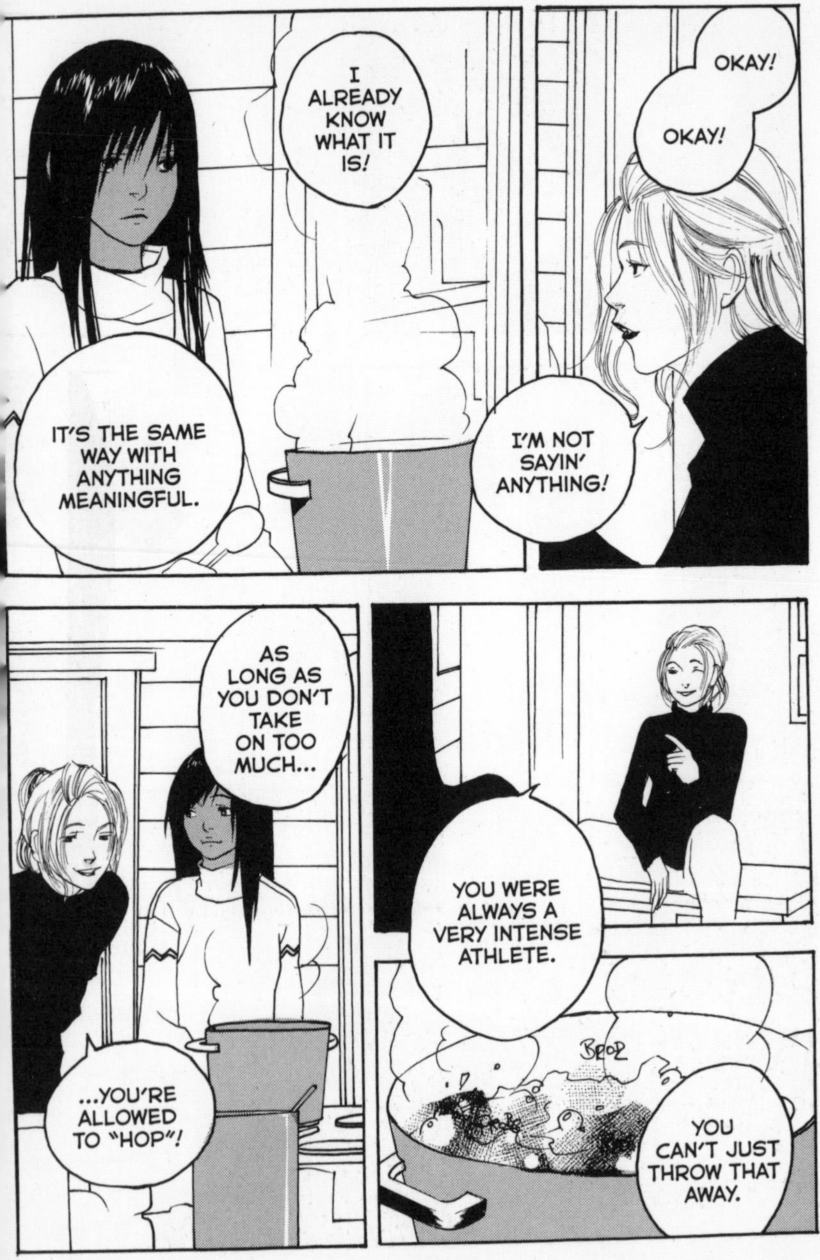
OKAY!
OKAY!
I'M NOT SAYIN' ANYTHING!
I ALREADY KNOW WHAT IT IS!
IT'S THE SAME WAY WITH ANYTHING MEANINGFUL.
YOU WERE ALWAYS A VERY INTENSE ATHLETE.
BROP
YOU CAN'T JUST THROW THAT AWAY.
AS LONG AS YOU DON'T TAKE ON TOO MUCH...
...YOU'RE ALLOWED TO "HOP"!

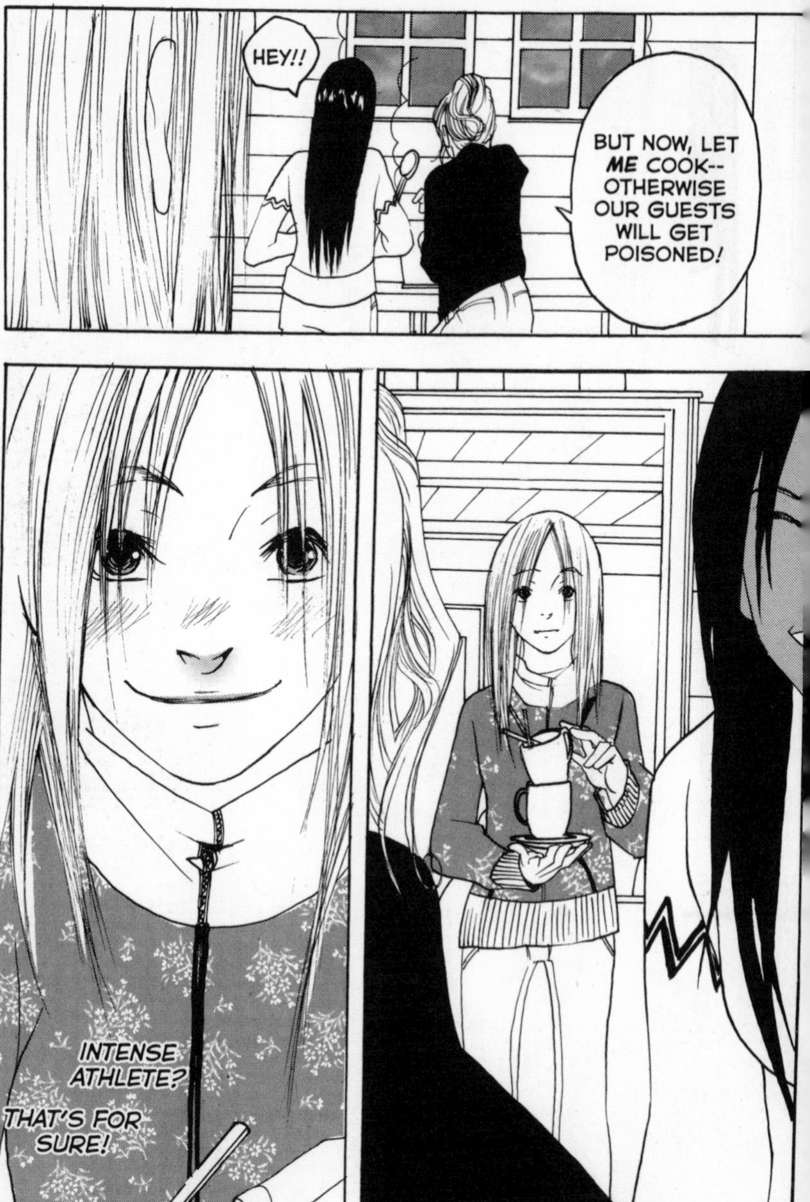
BUT NOW, LET *ME* COOK-- OTHERWISE OUR GUESTS WILL GET POISONED!
HEY!!
INTENSE ATHLETE?
THAT'S FOR SURE!

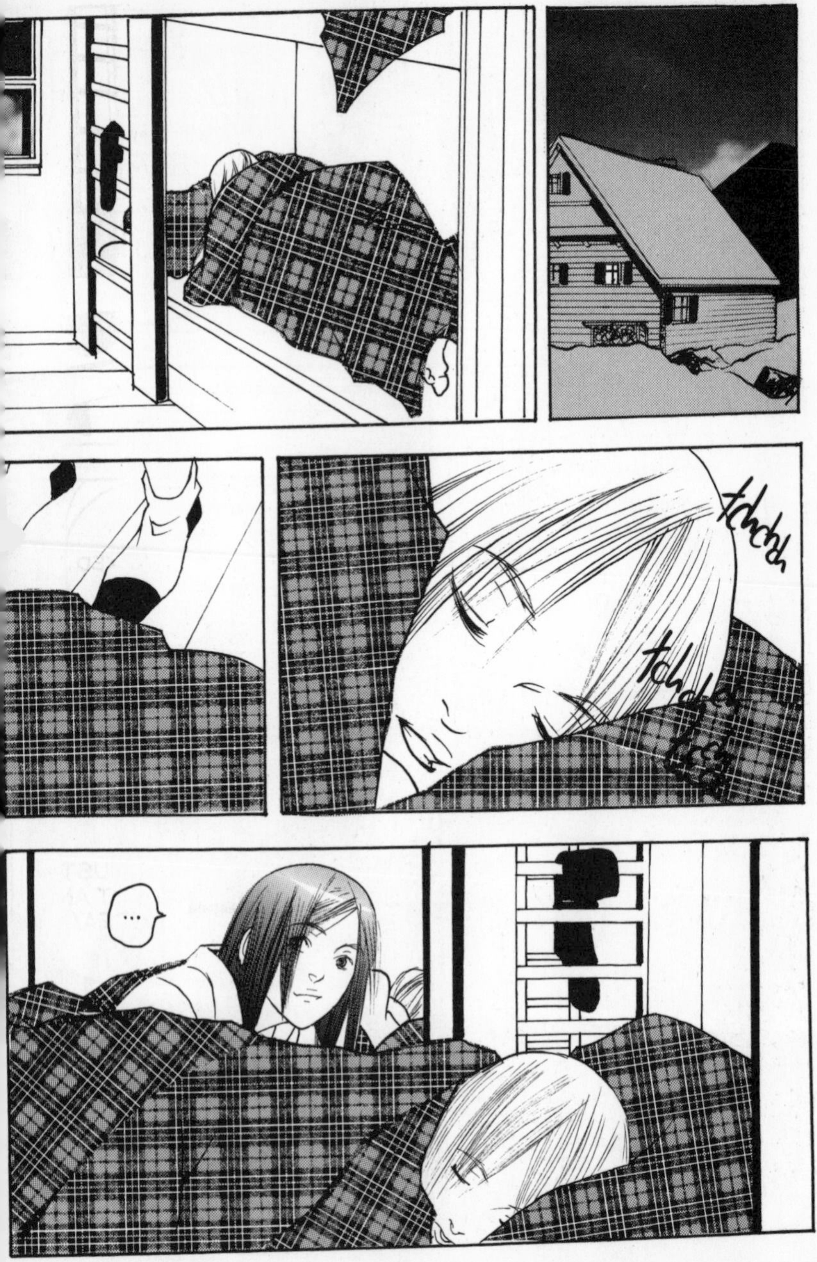
tchchch
...

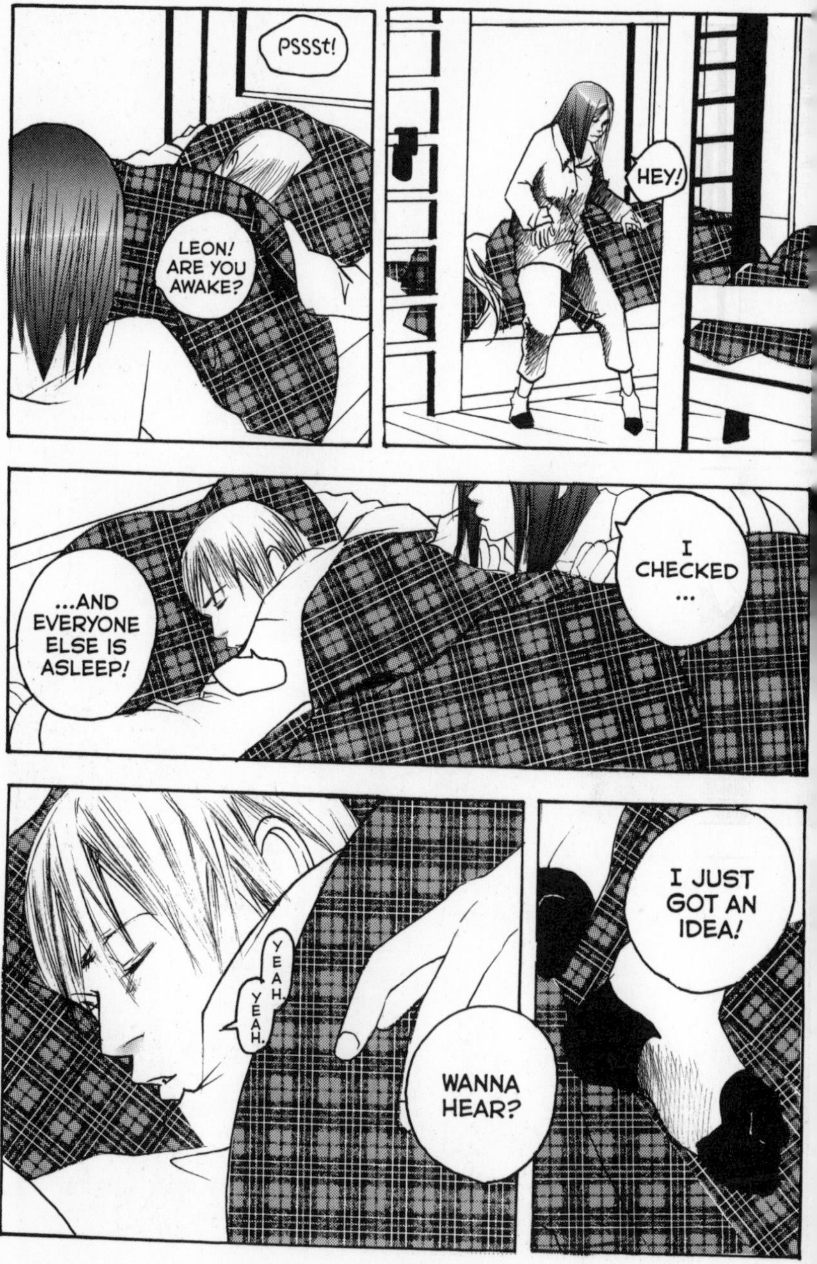
HEY!
PSSSt!
LEON! ARE YOU AWAKE?
I CHECKED ...
...AND EVERYONE ELSE IS ASLEEP!
I JUST GOT AN IDEA!
WANNA HEAR?
YEAH.
YEAH.

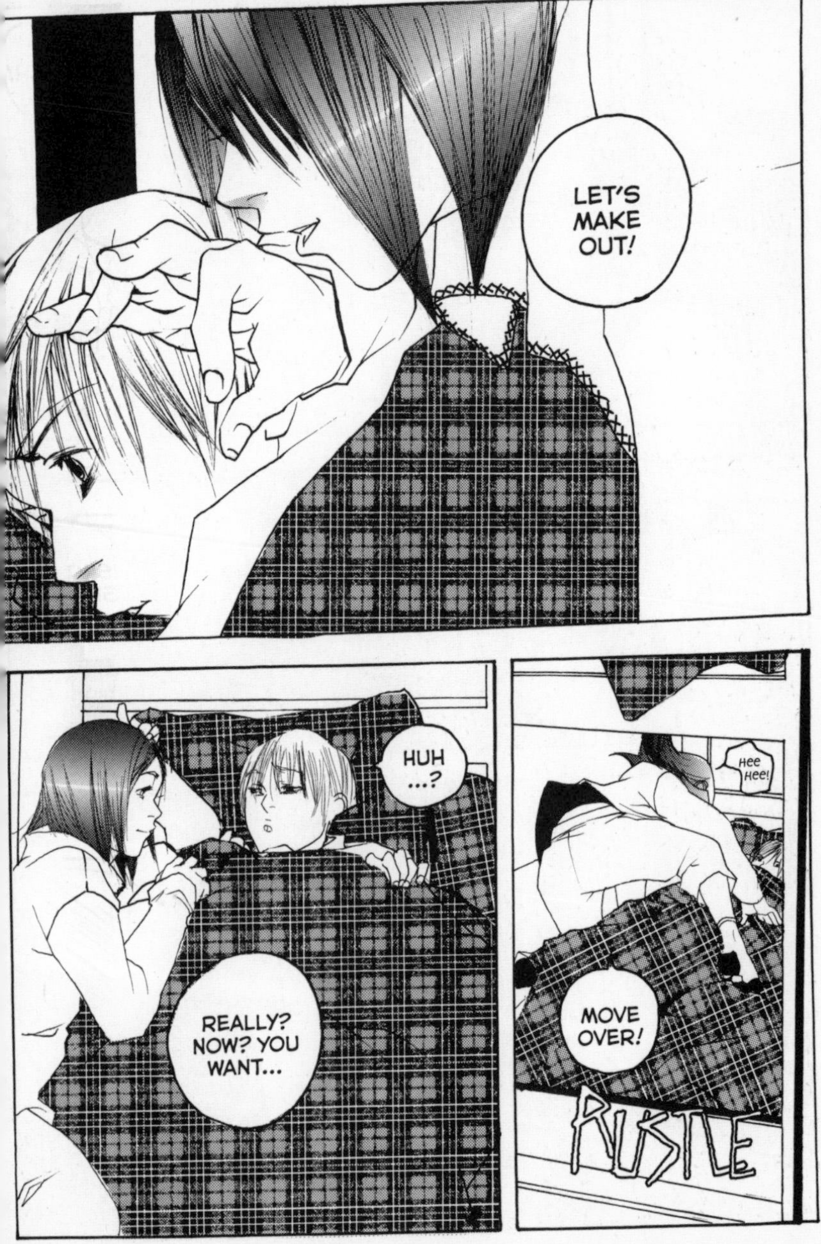
LET'S MAKE OUT!
Hee hee!
MOVE OVER!
RUSTLE
HUH ...?
REALLY? NOW? YOU WANT...

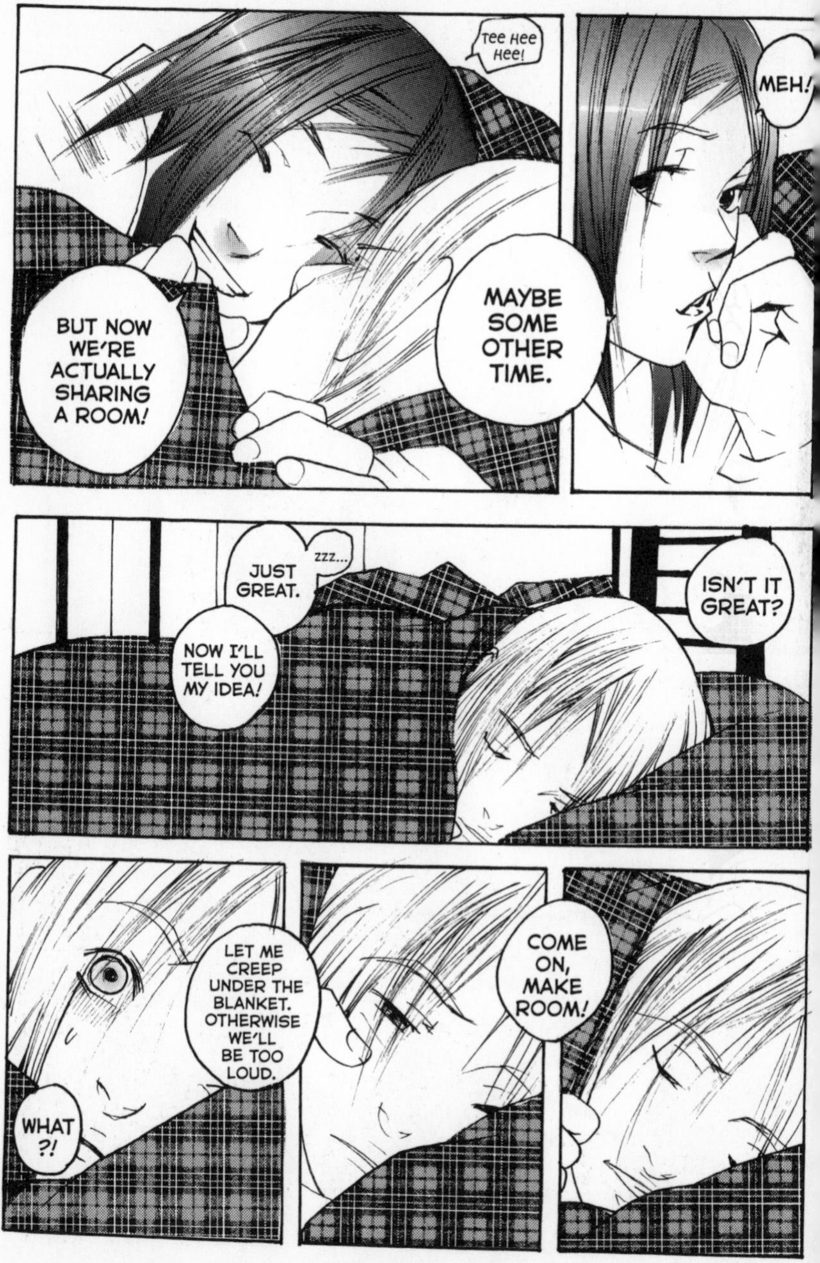
MEH!
MAYBE SOME OTHER TIME.
TEE HEE HEE!
BUT NOW WE'RE ACTUALLY SHARING A ROOM!
ISN'T IT GREAT?
JUST GREAT.
zzz...
NOW I'LL TELL YOU MY IDEA!
COME ON, MAKE ROOM!
LET ME CREEP UNDER THE BLANKET. OTHERWISE WE'LL BE TOO LOUD.
WHAT ?!

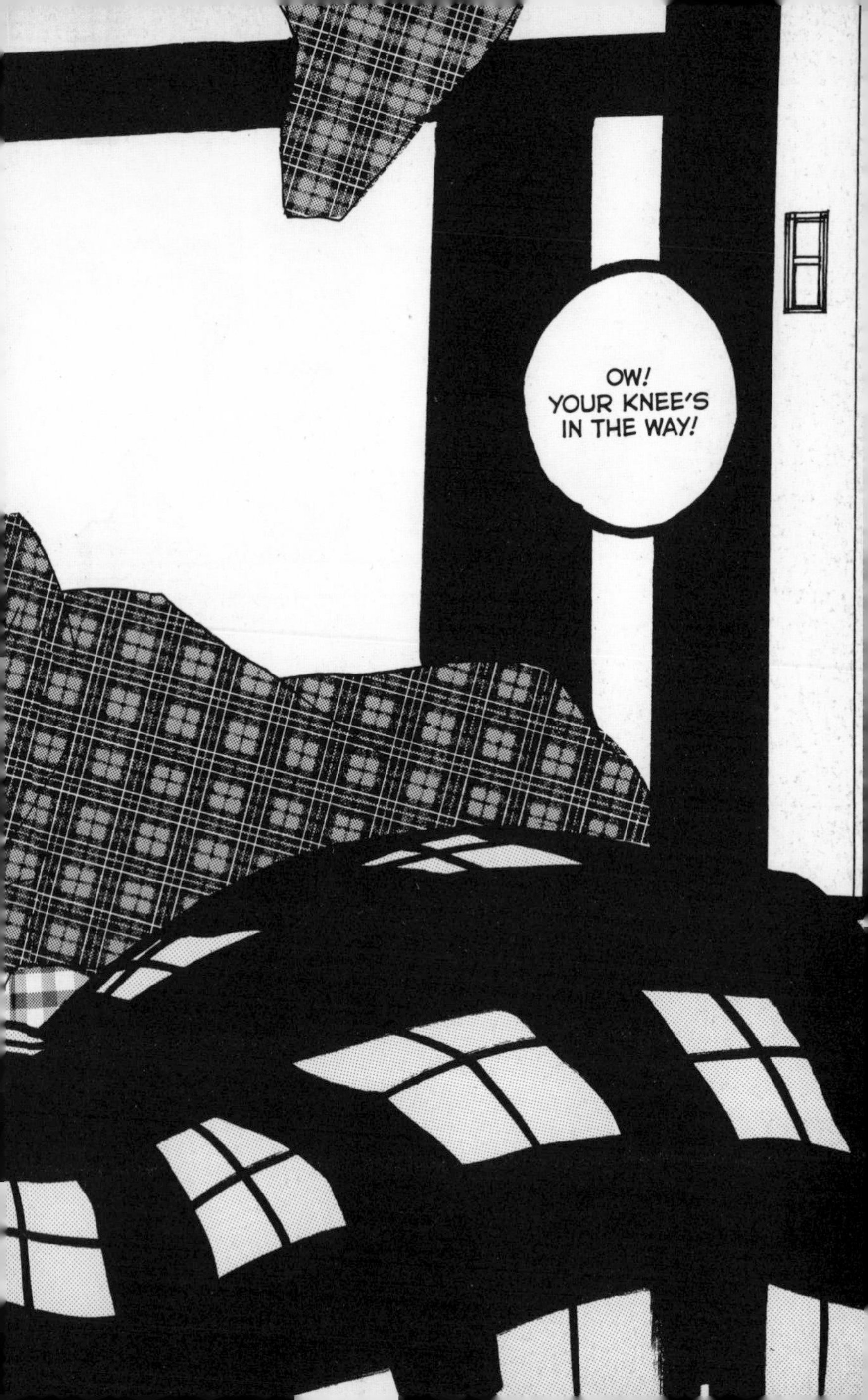
OW! YOUR KNEE'S IN THE WAY!

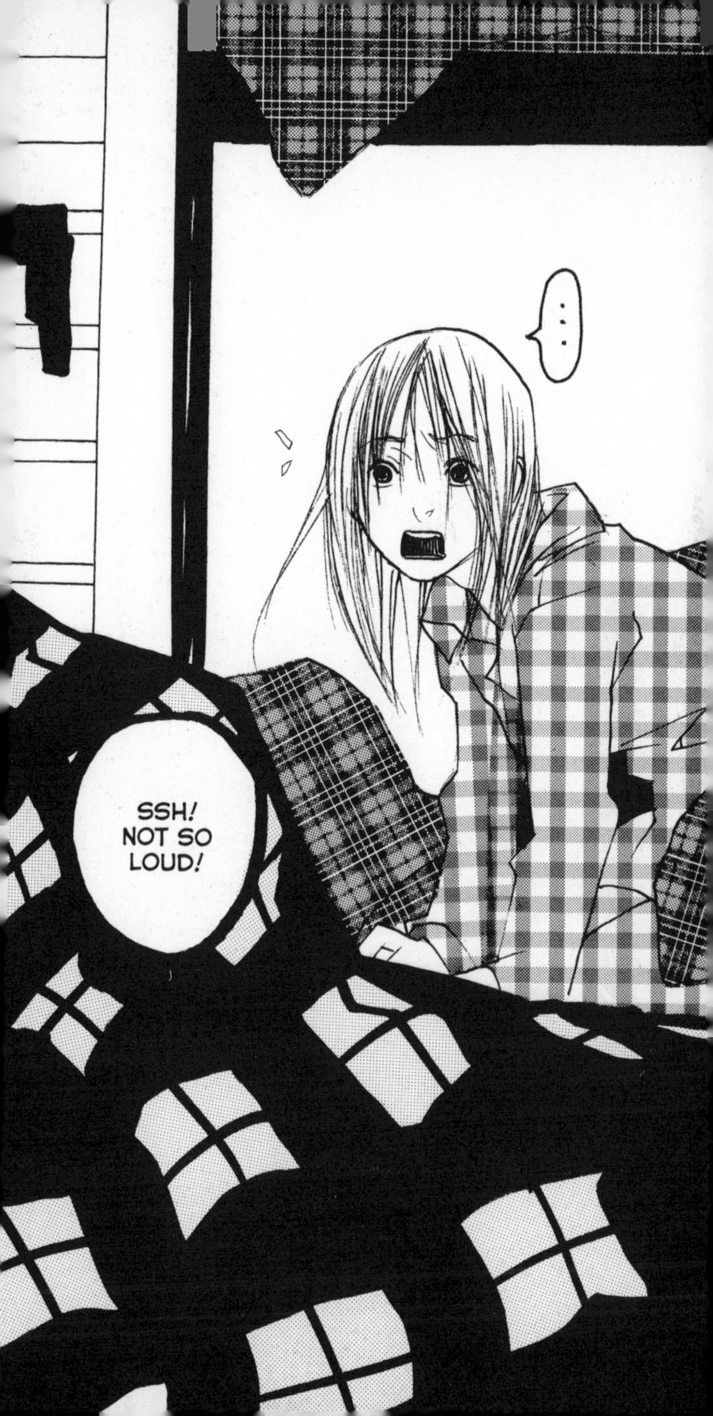
...
SSH! NOT SO LOUD!

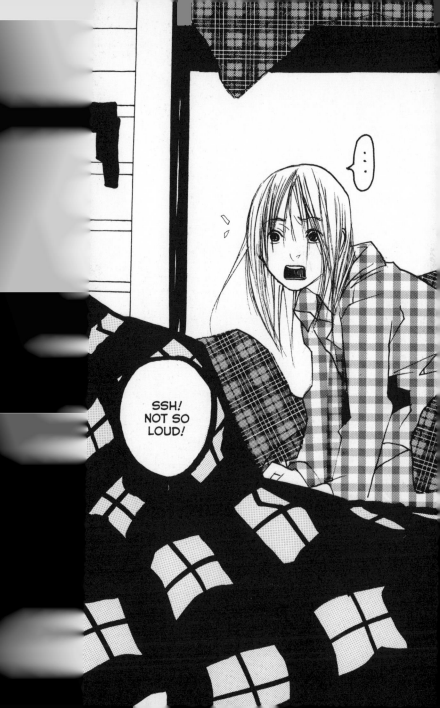

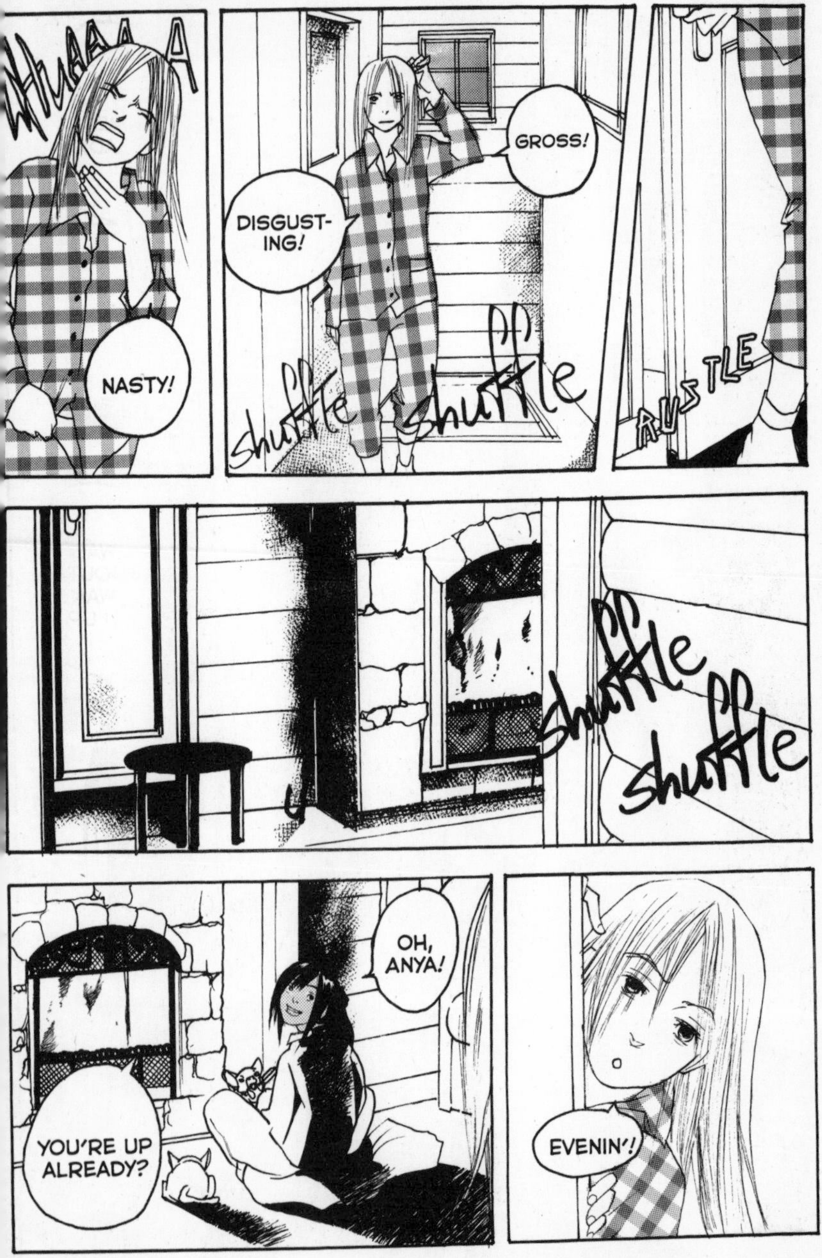
RUSTLE
GROSS!
DISGUST-ING!
shuffle
shuffle
WHAAAA
NASTY!
shuffle
shuffle
EVENIN'!
OH, ANYA!
YOU'RE UP ALREADY?

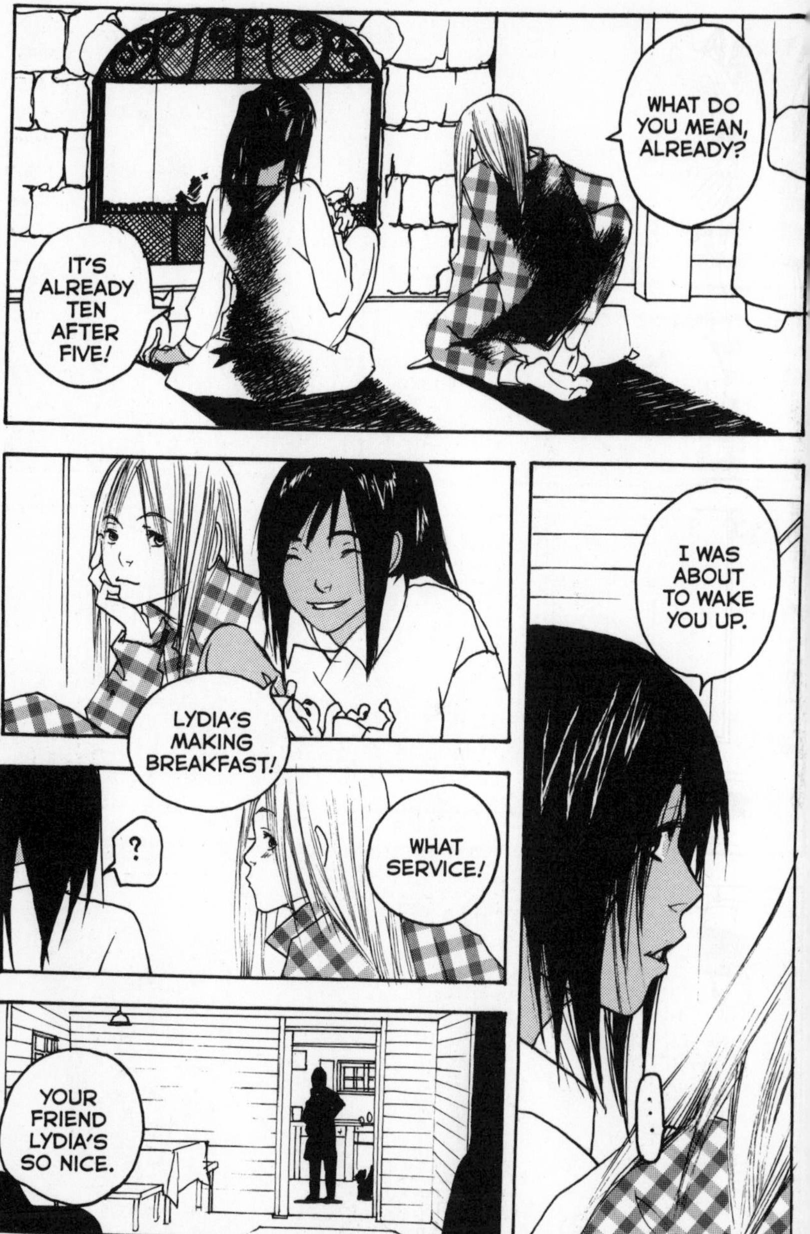
WHAT DO YOU MEAN, ALREADY?
IT'S ALREADY TEN AFTER FIVE!
I WAS ABOUT TO WAKE YOU UP.
...
LYDIA'S MAKING BREAKFAST!
WHAT SERVICE!
?
YOUR FRIEND LYDIA'S SO NICE.

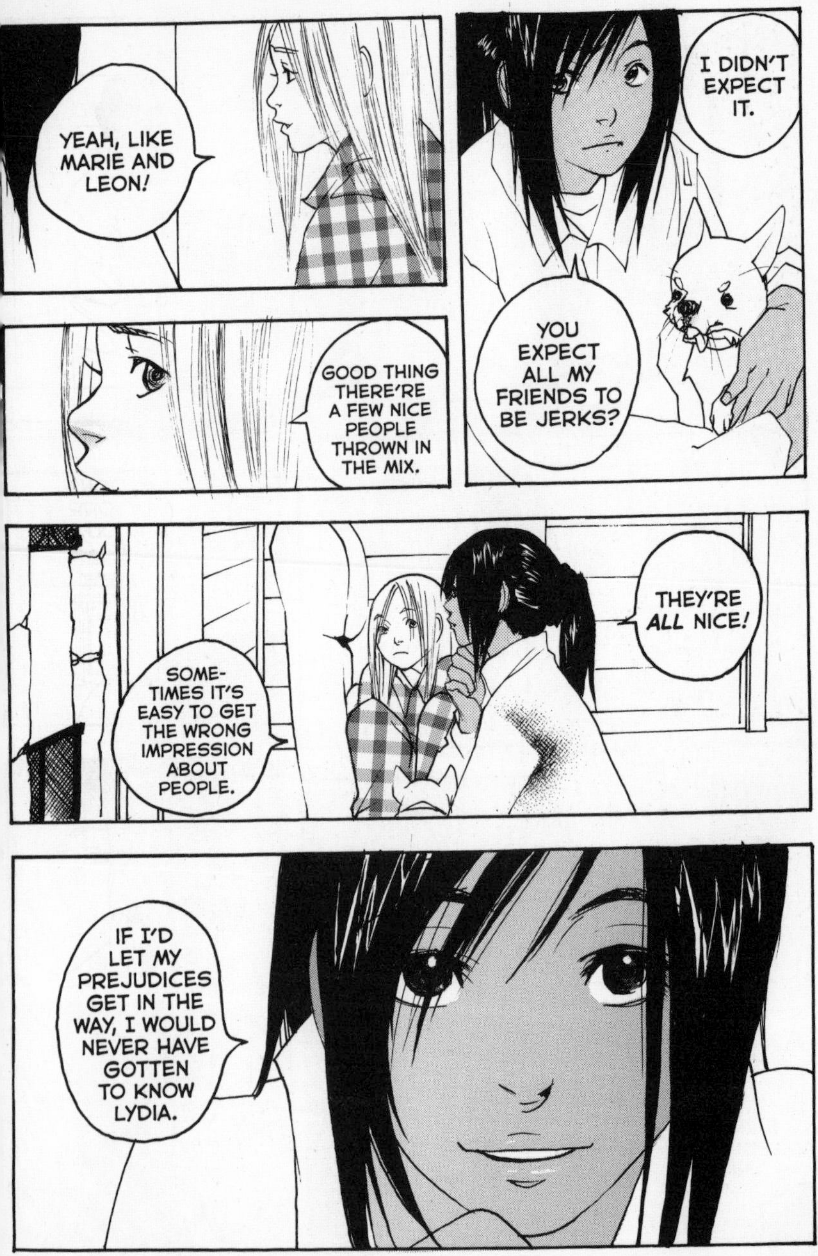
I DIDN'T EXPECT IT.
YOU EXPECT ALL MY FRIENDS TO BE JERKS?
YEAH, LIKE MARIE AND LEON!
GOOD THING THERE'RE A FEW NICE PEOPLE THROWN IN THE MIX.
THEY'RE *ALL* NICE!
SOME-TIMES IT'S EASY TO GET THE WRONG IMPRESSION ABOUT PEOPLE.
IF I'D LET MY PREJUDICES GET IN THE WAY, I WOULD NEVER HAVE GOTTEN TO KNOW LYDIA.

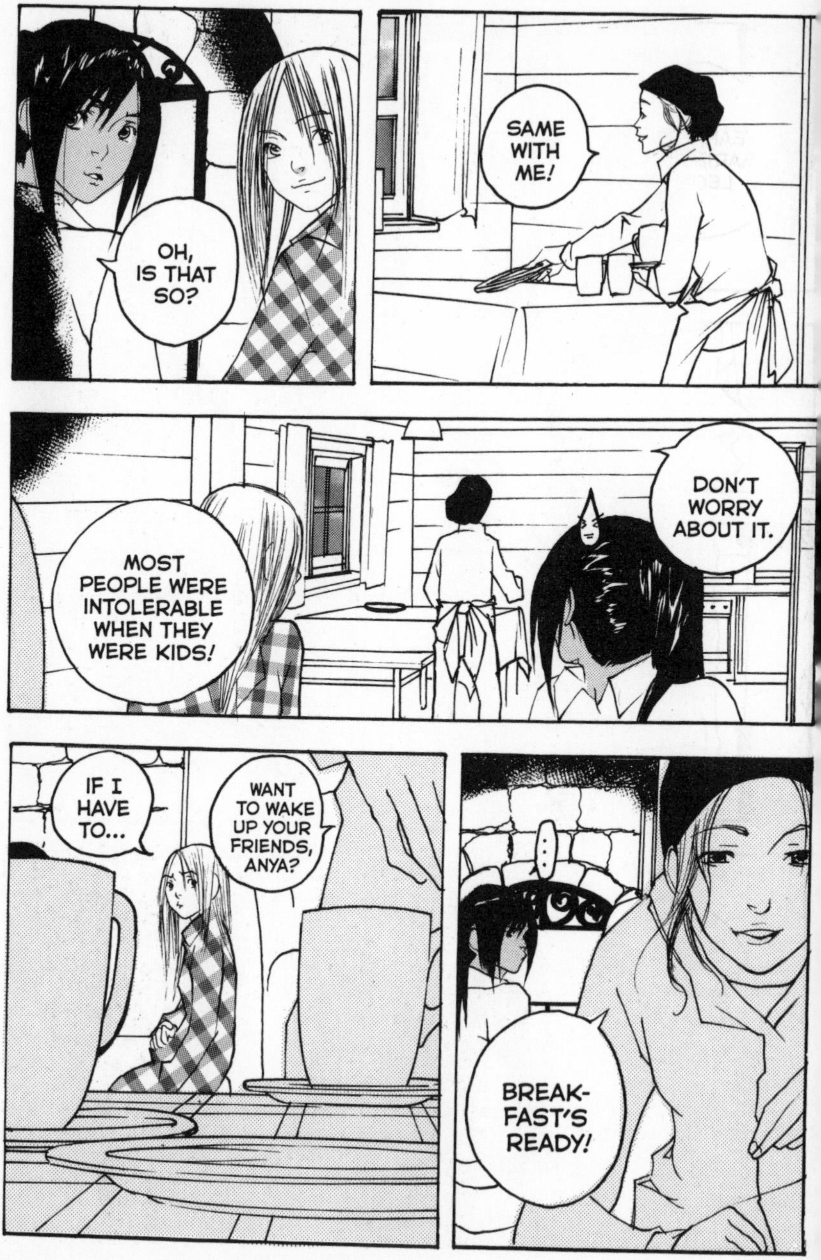
SAME WITH ME!
OH, IS THAT SO?
DON'T WORRY ABOUT IT.
MOST PEOPLE WERE INTOLERABLE WHEN THEY WERE KIDS!
...
BREAK-FAST'S READY!
WANT TO WAKE UP YOUR FRIENDS, ANYA?
IF I HAVE TO...

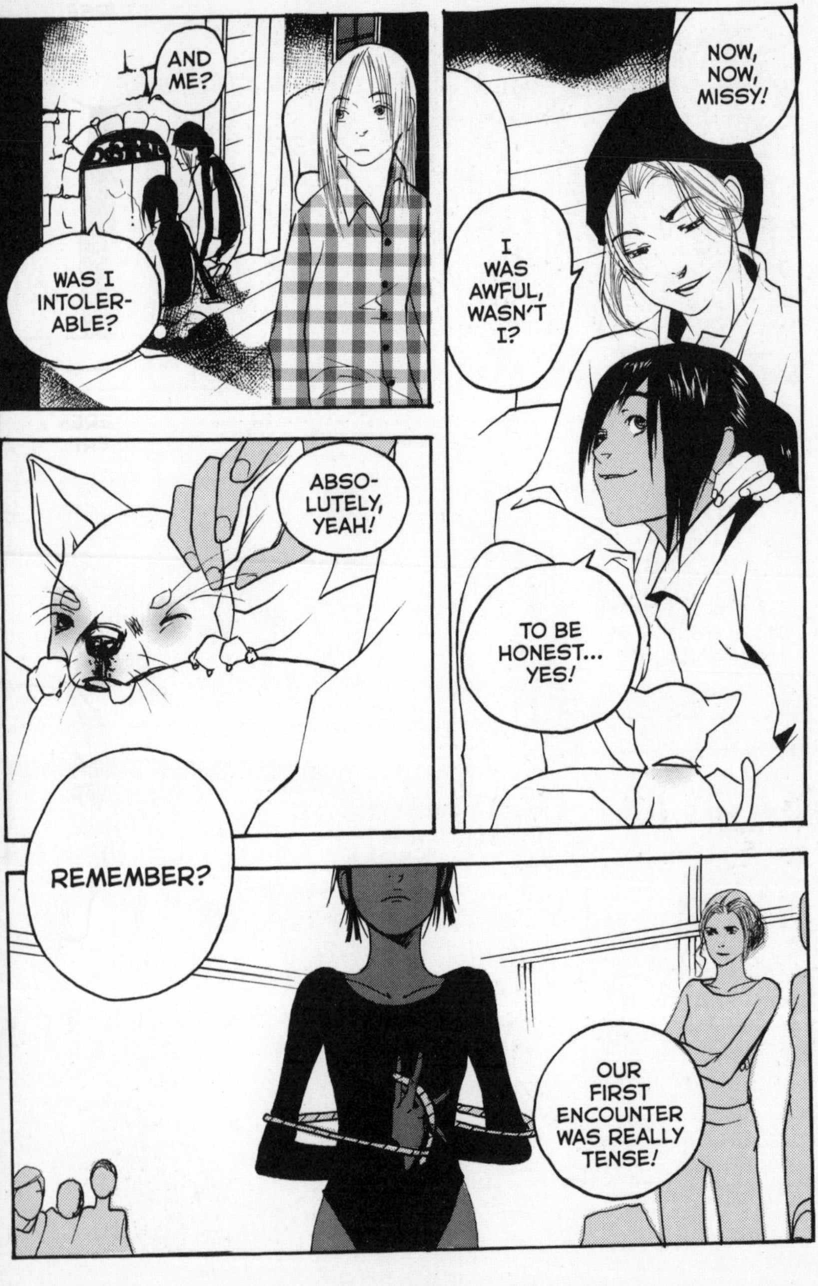
NOW, NOW, MISSY!
I WAS AWFUL, WASN'T I?
TO BE HONEST... YES!
AND ME?
WAS I INTOLERABLE?
ABSOLUTELY, YEAH!
REMEMBER?
OUR FIRST ENCOUNTER WAS REALLY TENSE!

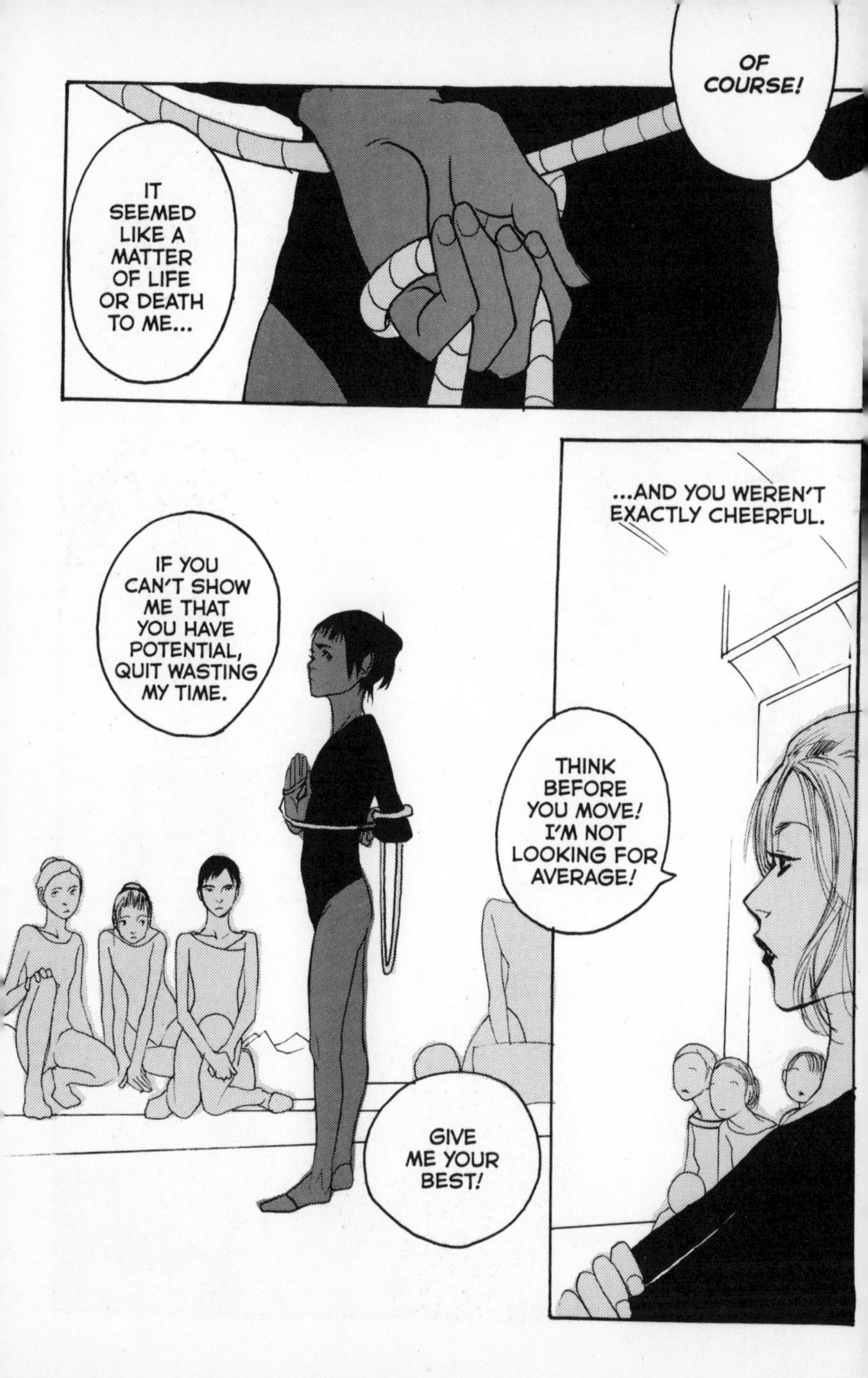
OF COURSE!
IT SEEMED LIKE A MATTER OF LIFE OR DEATH TO ME...
...AND YOU WEREN'T EXACTLY CHEERFUL.
THINK BEFORE YOU MOVE! I'M NOT LOOKING FOR AVERAGE!
IF YOU CAN'T SHOW ME THAT YOU HAVE POTENTIAL, QUIT WASTING MY TIME.
GIVE ME YOUR BEST!

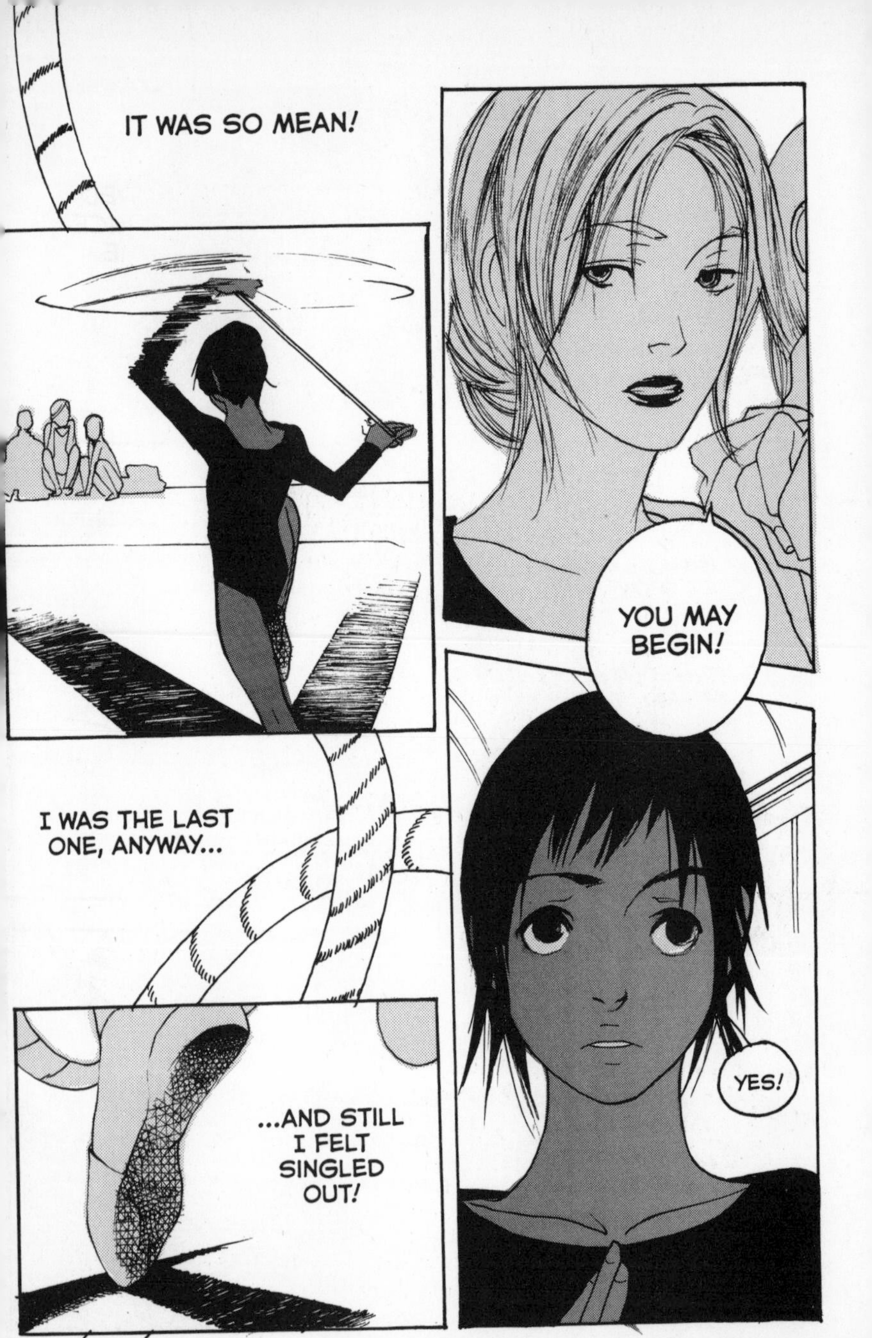
YOU MAY BEGIN!
YES!
IT WAS SO MEAN!
I WAS THE LAST ONE, ANYWAY...
...AND STILL I FELT SINGLED OUT!

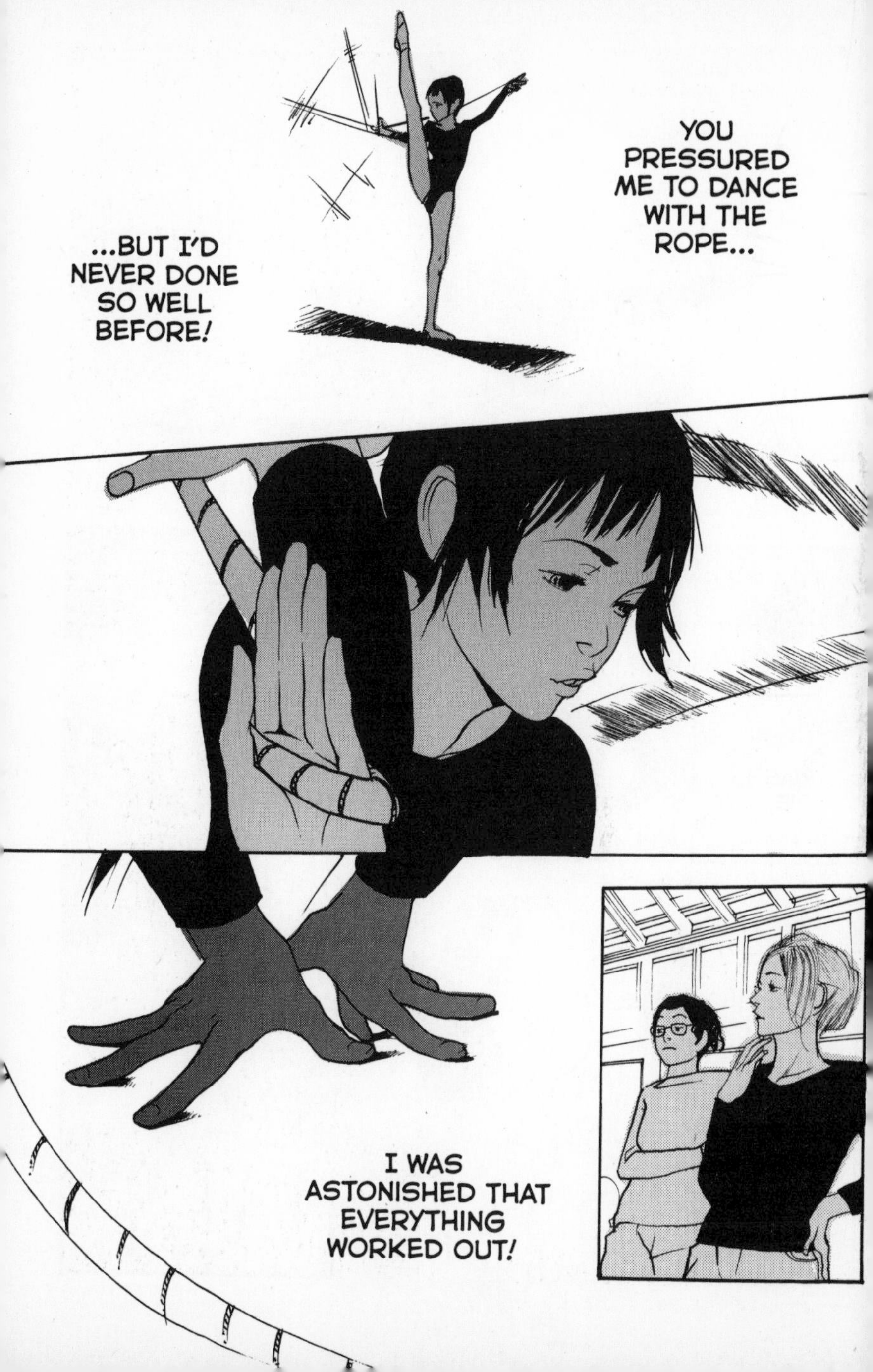
YOU PRESSURED ME TO DANCE WITH THE ROPE...
...BUT I'D NEVER DONE SO WELL BEFORE!
I WAS ASTONISHED THAT EVERYTHING WORKED OUT!

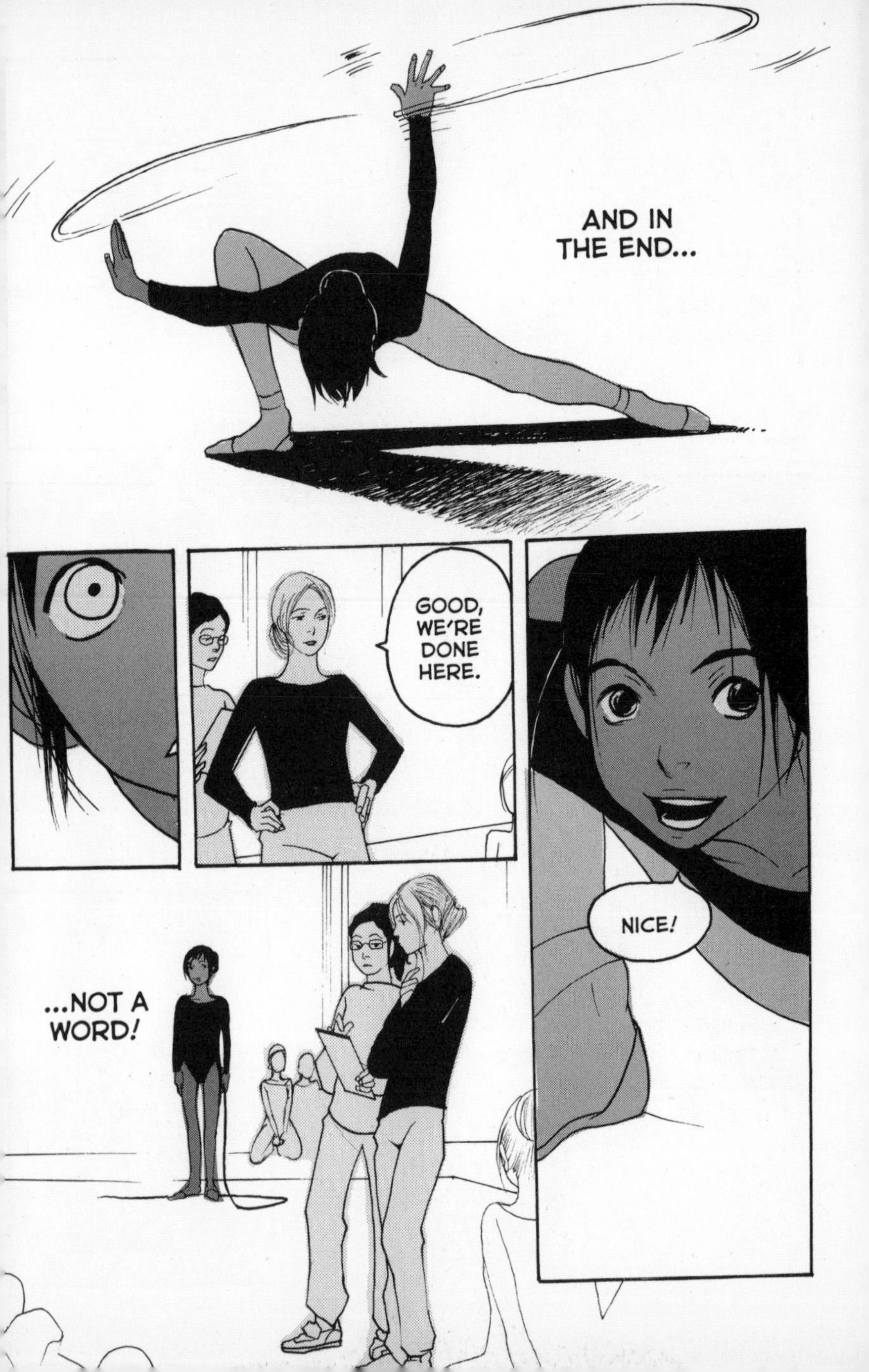
AND IN THE END...
NICE!
GOOD, WE'RE DONE HERE.
...NOT A WORD!

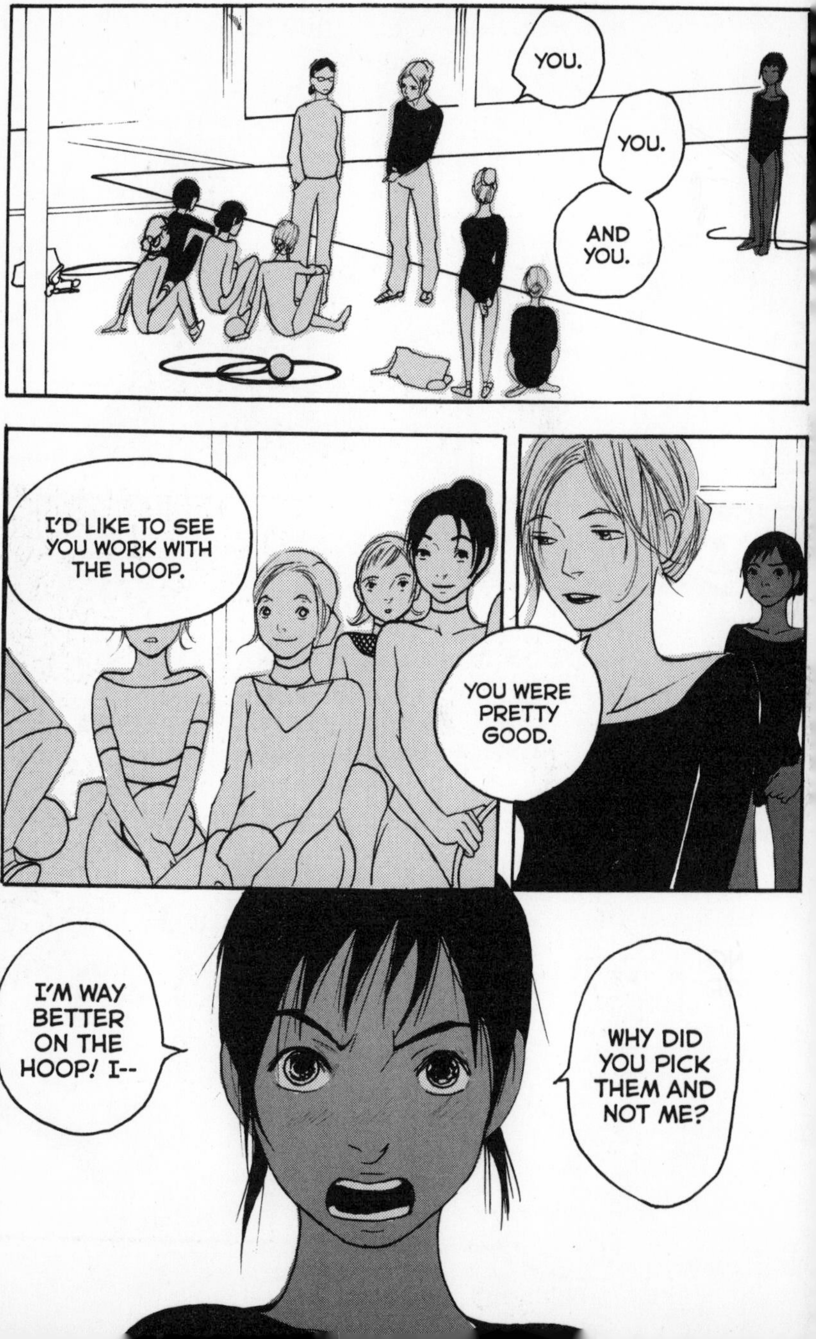
YOU.
YOU.
AND YOU.
YOU WERE PRETTY GOOD.
I'D LIKE TO SEE YOU WORK WITH THE HOOP.
WHY DID YOU PICK THEM AND NOT ME?
I'M WAY BETTER ON THE HOOP! I--

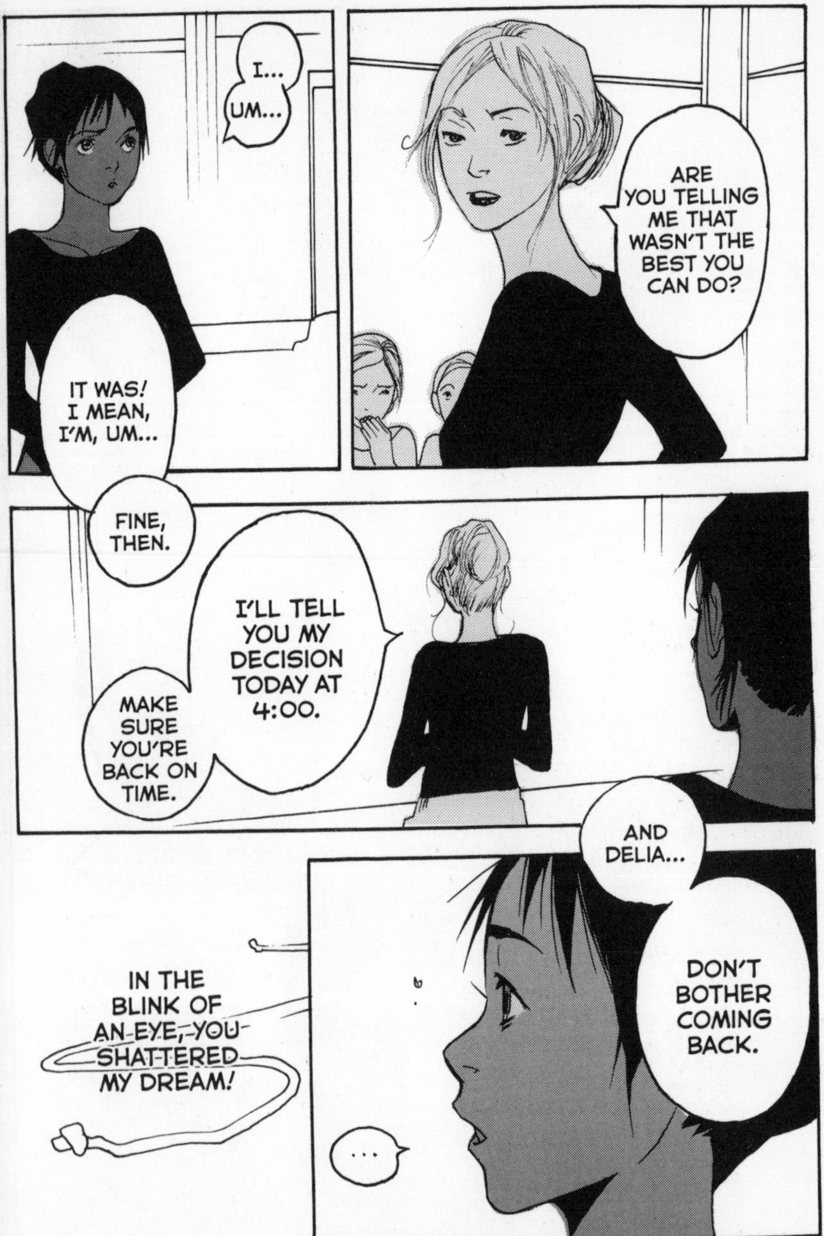
ARE YOU TELLING ME THAT WASN'T THE BEST YOU CAN DO?
I...
UM...
IT WAS! I MEAN, I'M, UM...
FINE, THEN.
I'LL TELL YOU MY DECISION TODAY AT 4:00.
MAKE SURE YOU'RE BACK ON TIME.
AND DELIA...
DON'T BOTHER COMING BACK.
IN THE BLINK OF AN EYE, YOU SHATTERED MY DREAM!
...

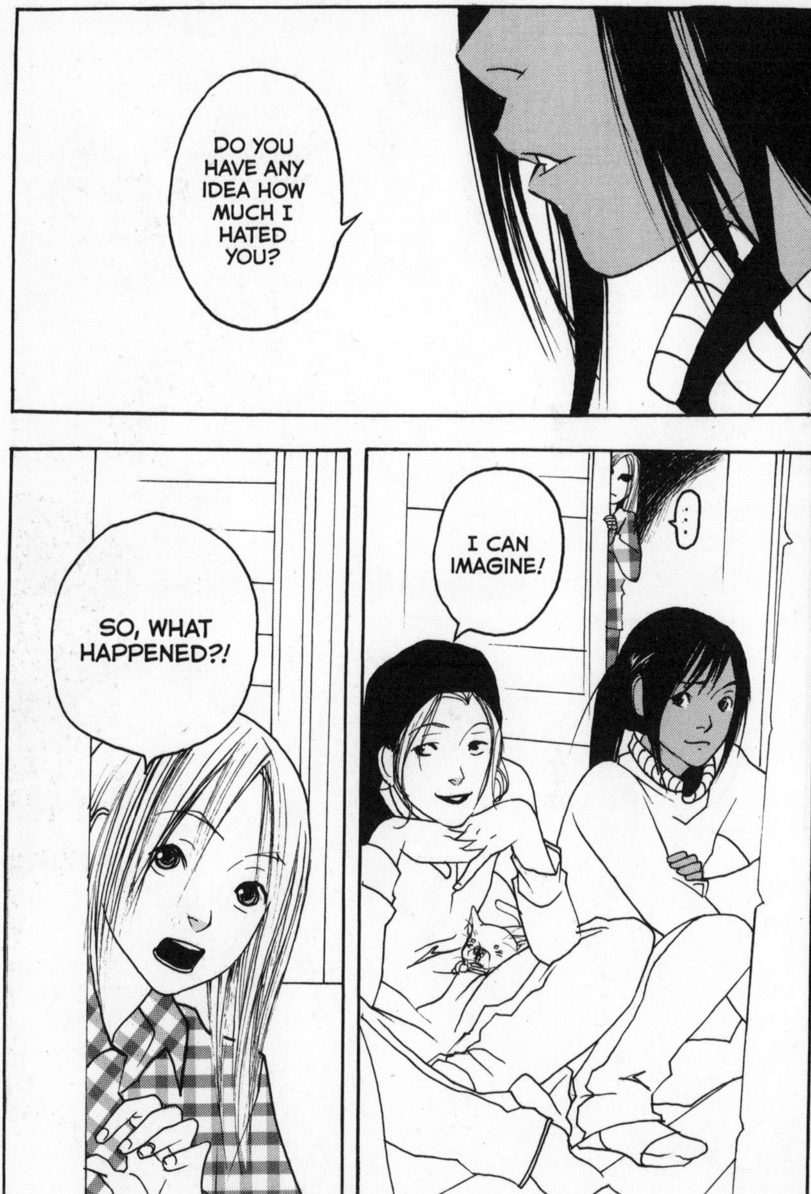
DO YOU HAVE ANY IDEA HOW MUCH I HATED YOU?
...
I CAN IMAGINE!
SO, WHAT HAPPENED?!

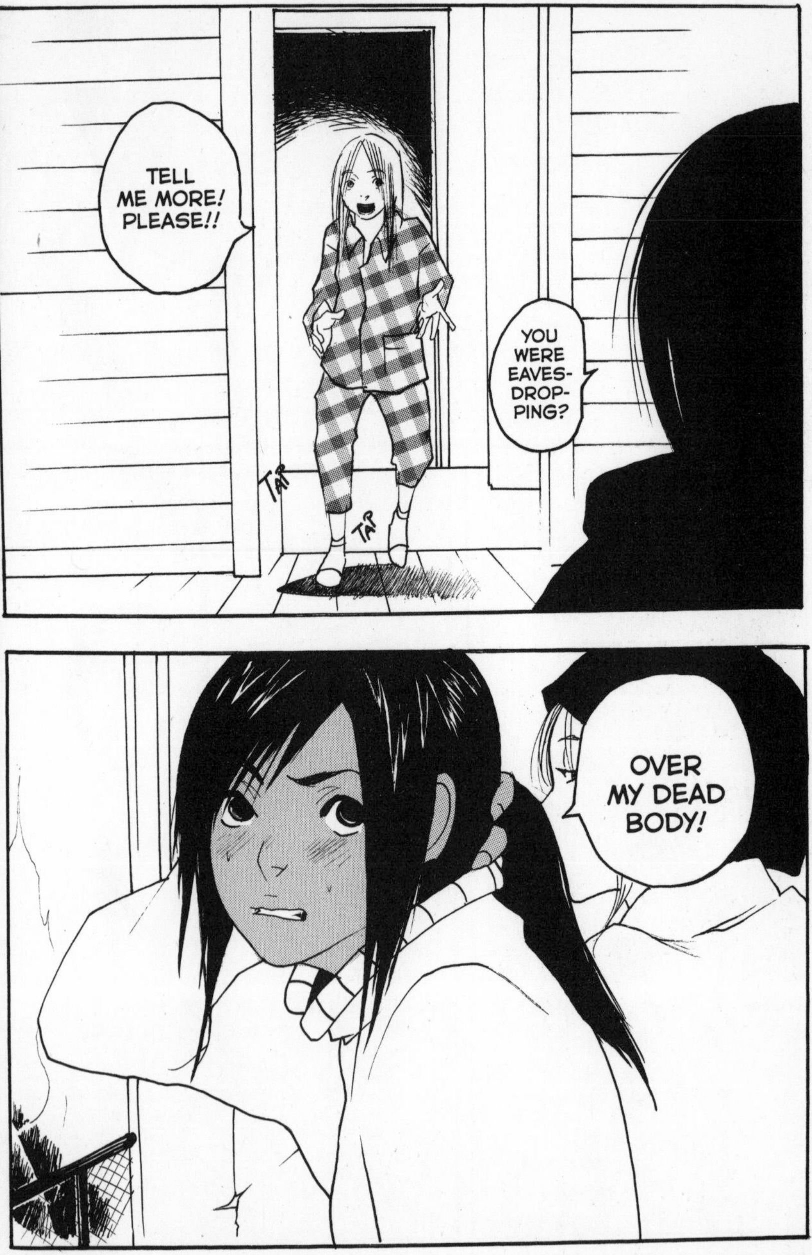
YOU WERE EAVES-DROPPING?
TELL ME MORE! PLEASE!!
TAP
TAP
OVER MY DEAD BODY!

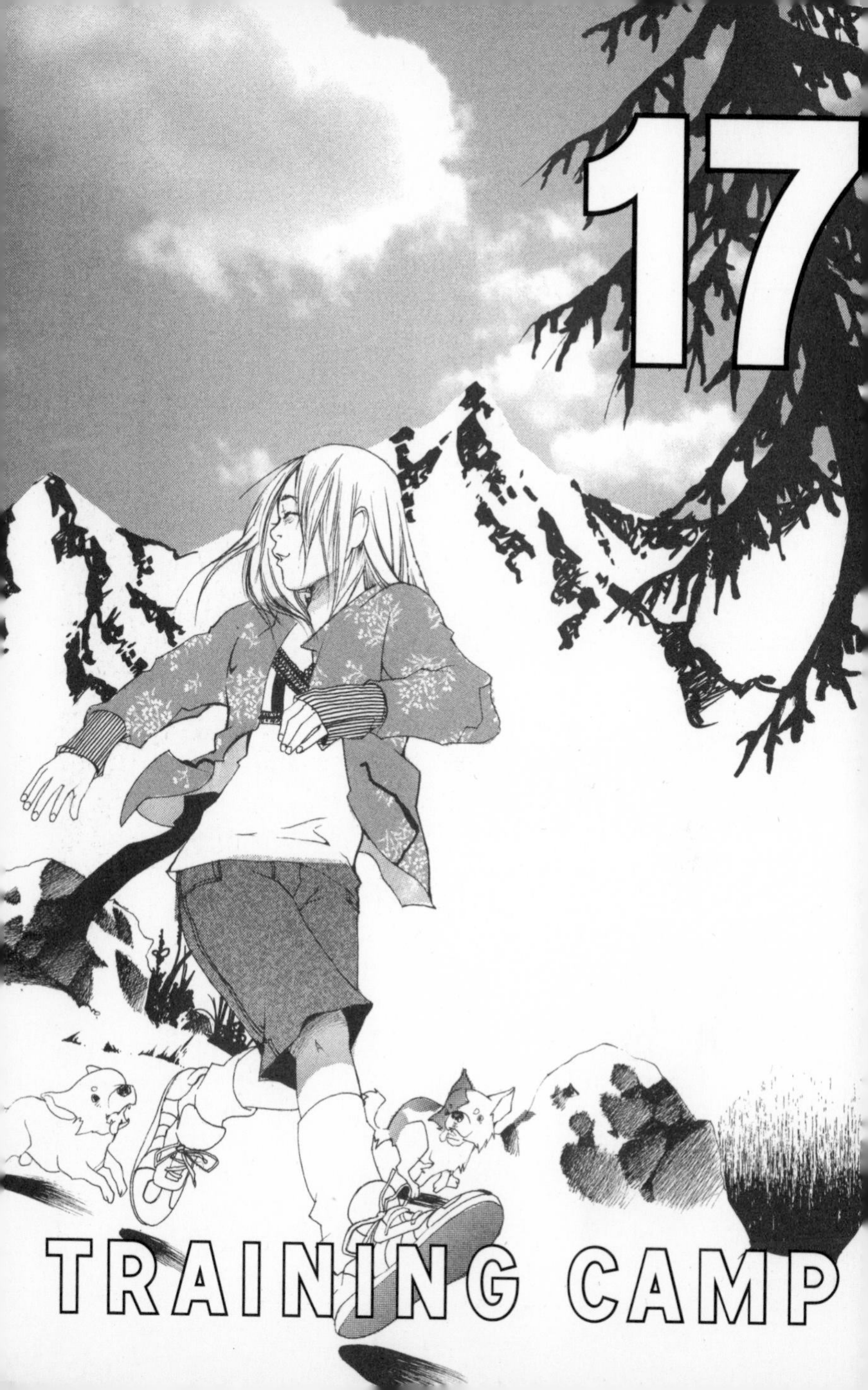
17
TRAINING CAMP

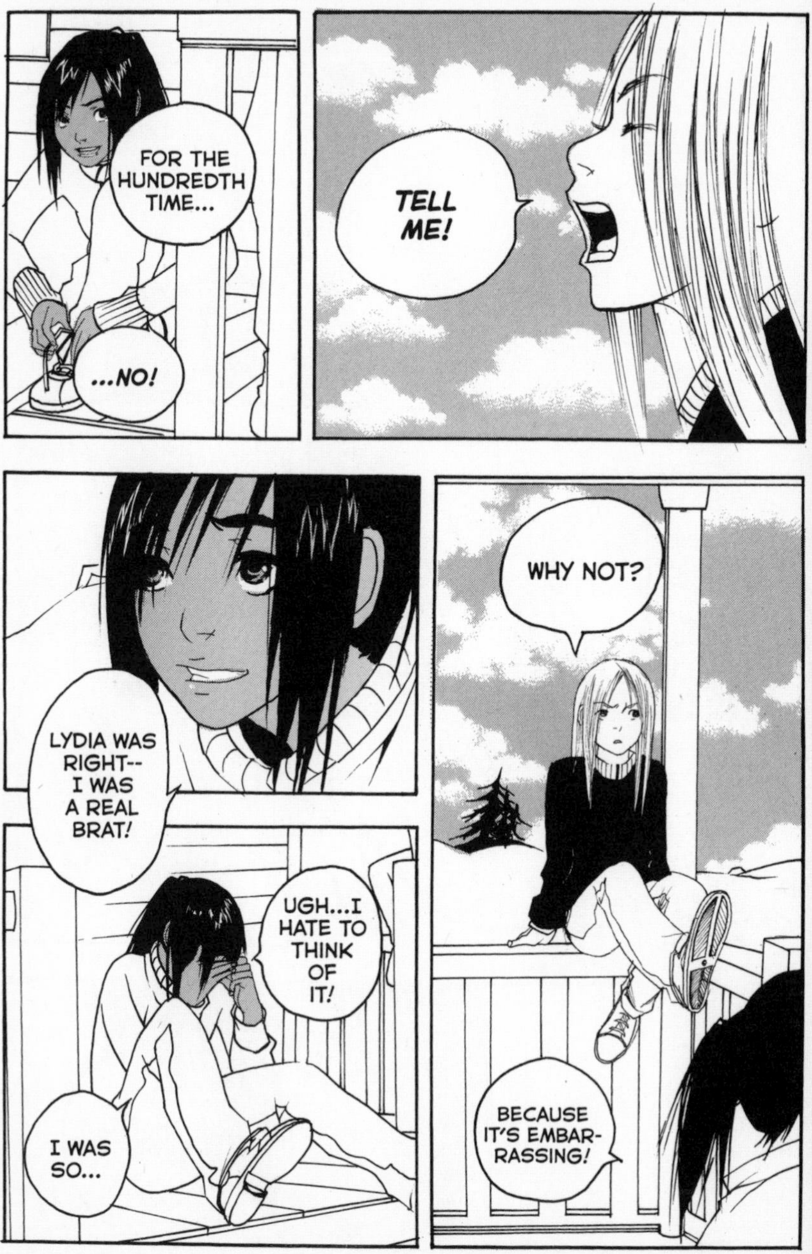
TELL ME!
FOR THE HUNDREDTH TIME...
...NO!
WHY NOT?
BECAUSE IT'S EMBARRASSING!
LYDIA WAS RIGHT-- I WAS A REAL BRAT!
UGH...I HATE TO THINK OF IT!
I WAS SO...

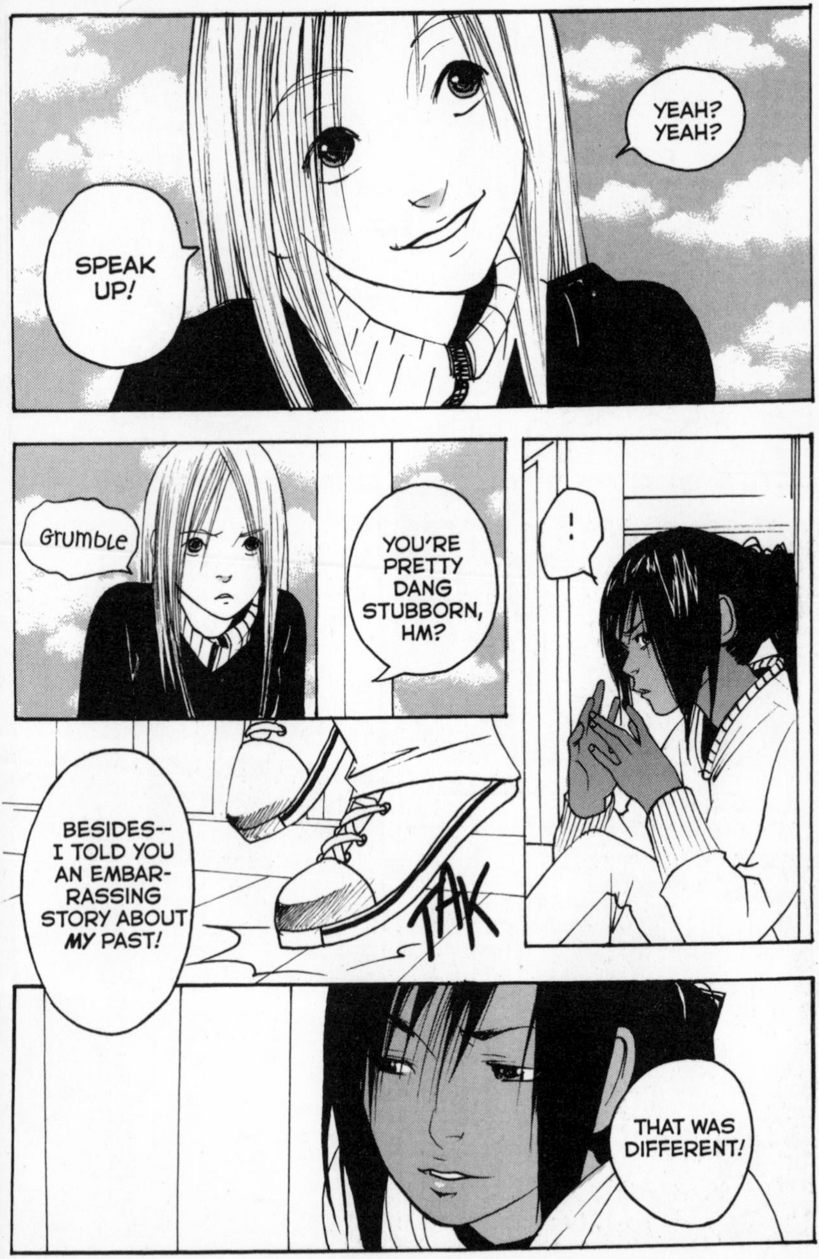
YEAH? YEAH?
SPEAK UP!
!
YOU'RE PRETTY DANG STUBBORN, HM?
Grumble
TAK
BESIDES-- I TOLD YOU AN EMBAR-RASSING STORY ABOUT *MY* PAST!
THAT WAS DIFFERENT!

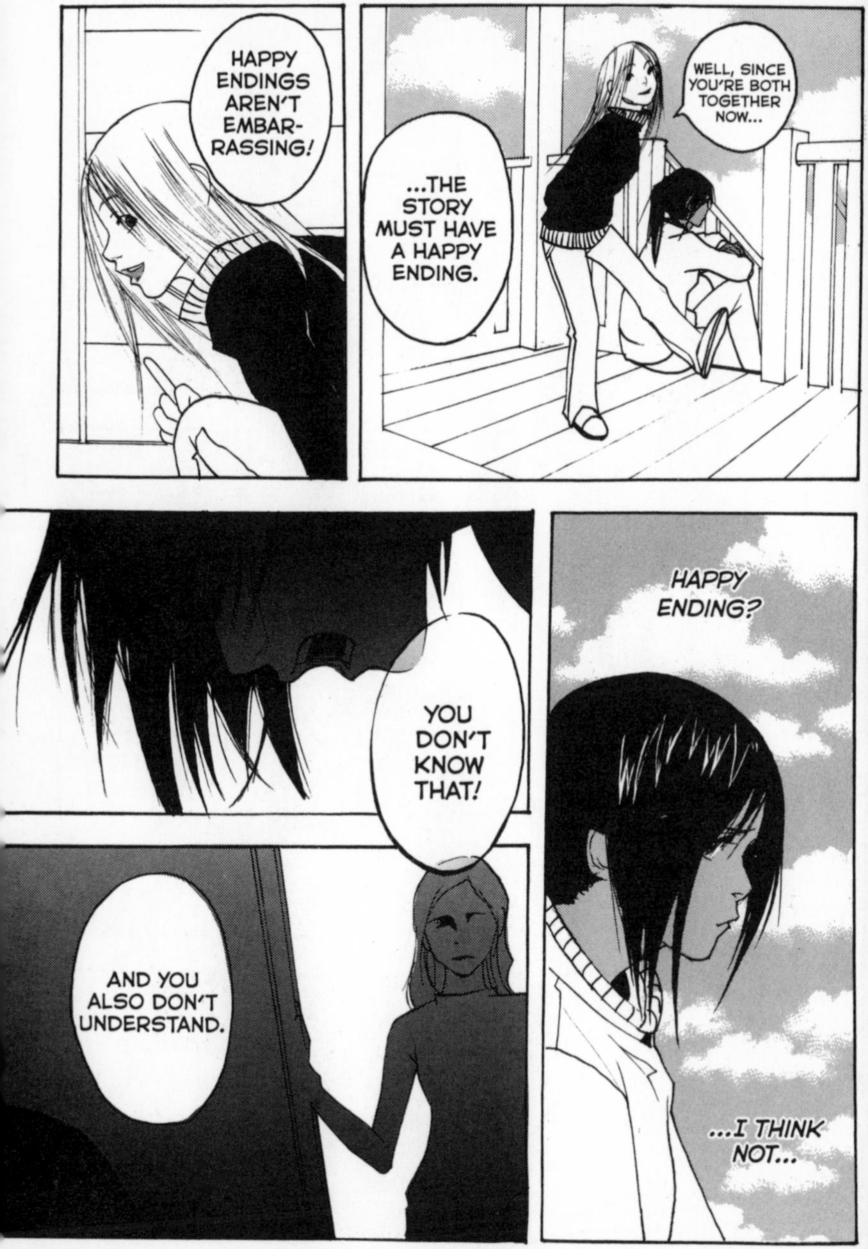
WELL, SINCE YOU'RE BOTH TOGETHER NOW...
...THE STORY MUST HAVE A HAPPY ENDING.
HAPPY ENDINGS AREN'T EMBARRASSING!
HAPPY ENDING?
...I THINK NOT...
YOU DON'T KNOW THAT!
AND YOU ALSO DON'T UNDERSTAND.

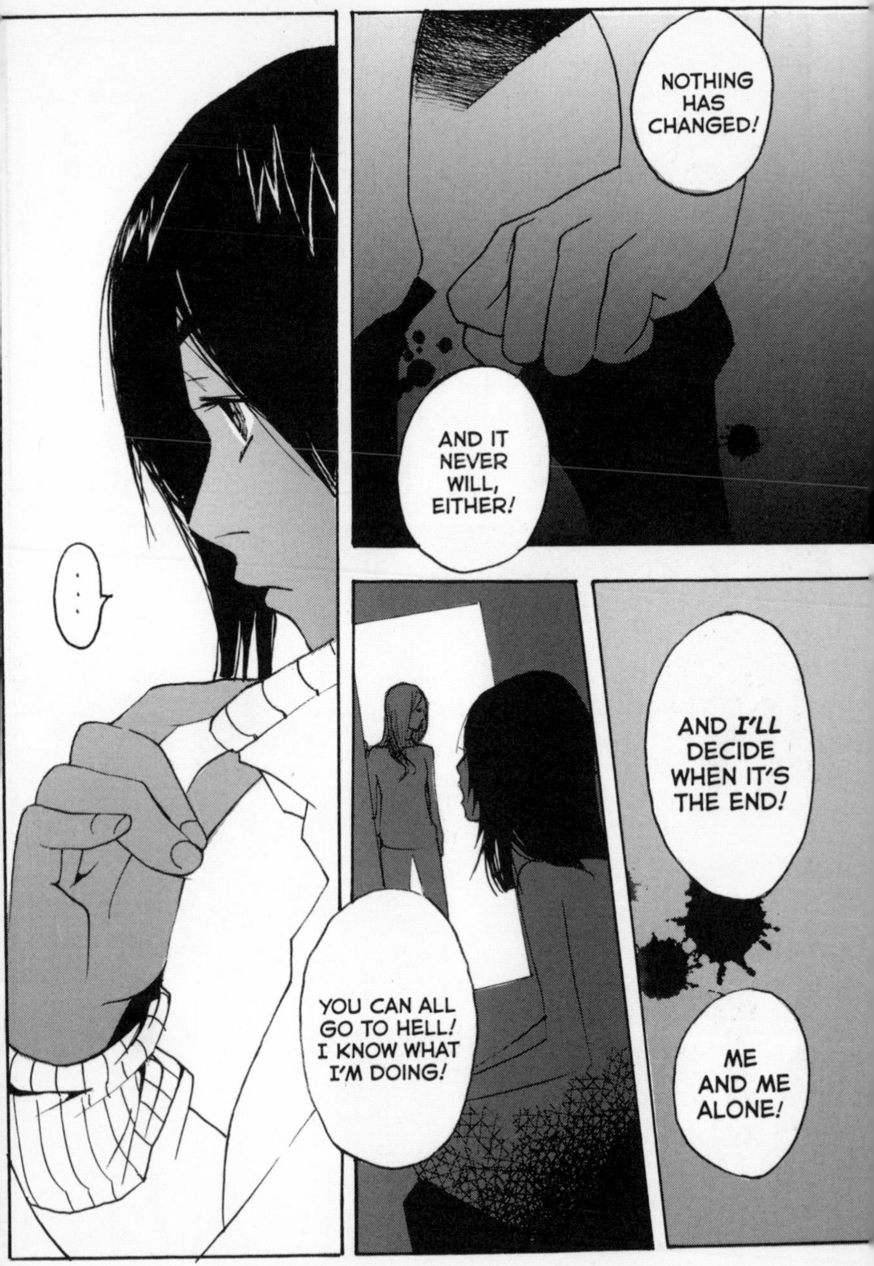
NOTHING HAS CHANGED!
AND IT NEVER WILL, EITHER!
AND *I'LL* DECIDE WHEN IT'S THE END!
ME AND ME ALONE!
YOU CAN ALL GO TO HELL! I KNOW WHAT I'M DOING!
...

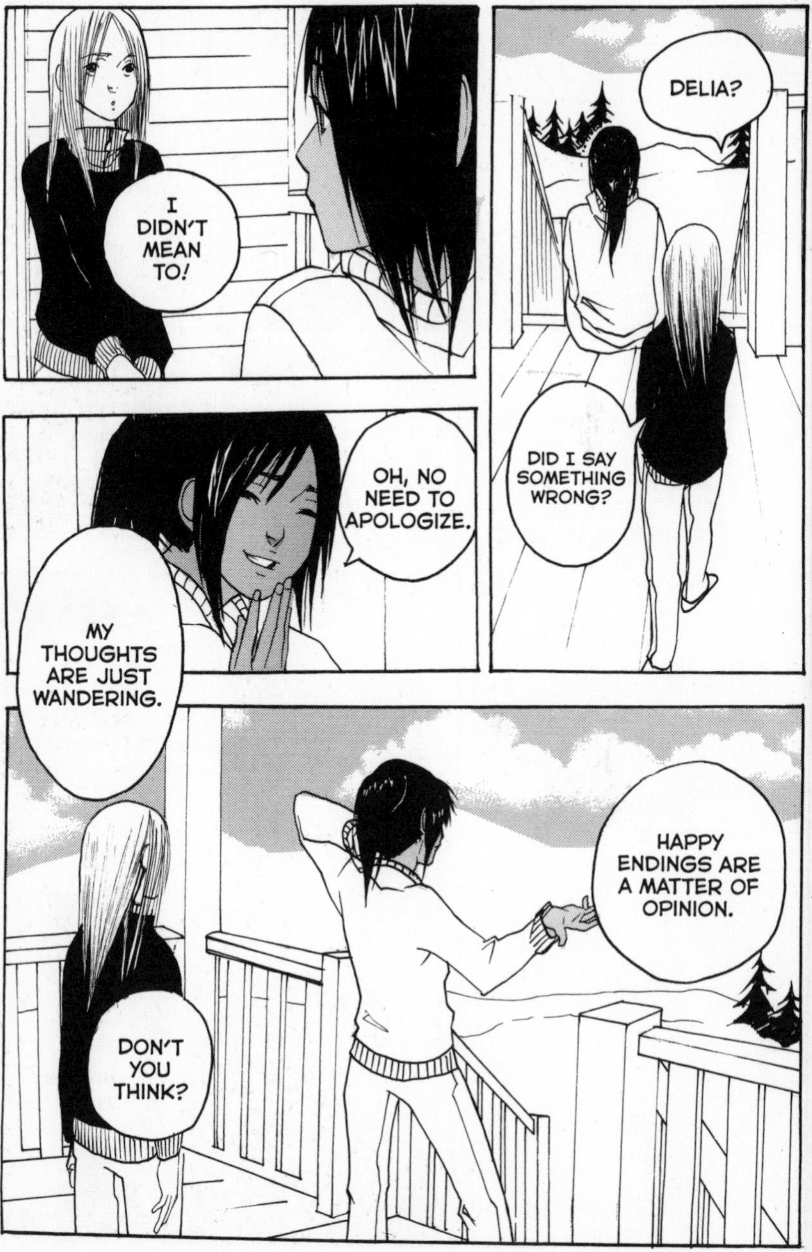
DELIA?
DID I SAY SOMETHING WRONG?
I DIDN'T MEAN TO!
OH, NO NEED TO APOLOGIZE.
MY THOUGHTS ARE JUST WANDERING.
HAPPY ENDINGS ARE A MATTER OF OPINION.
DON'T YOU THINK?

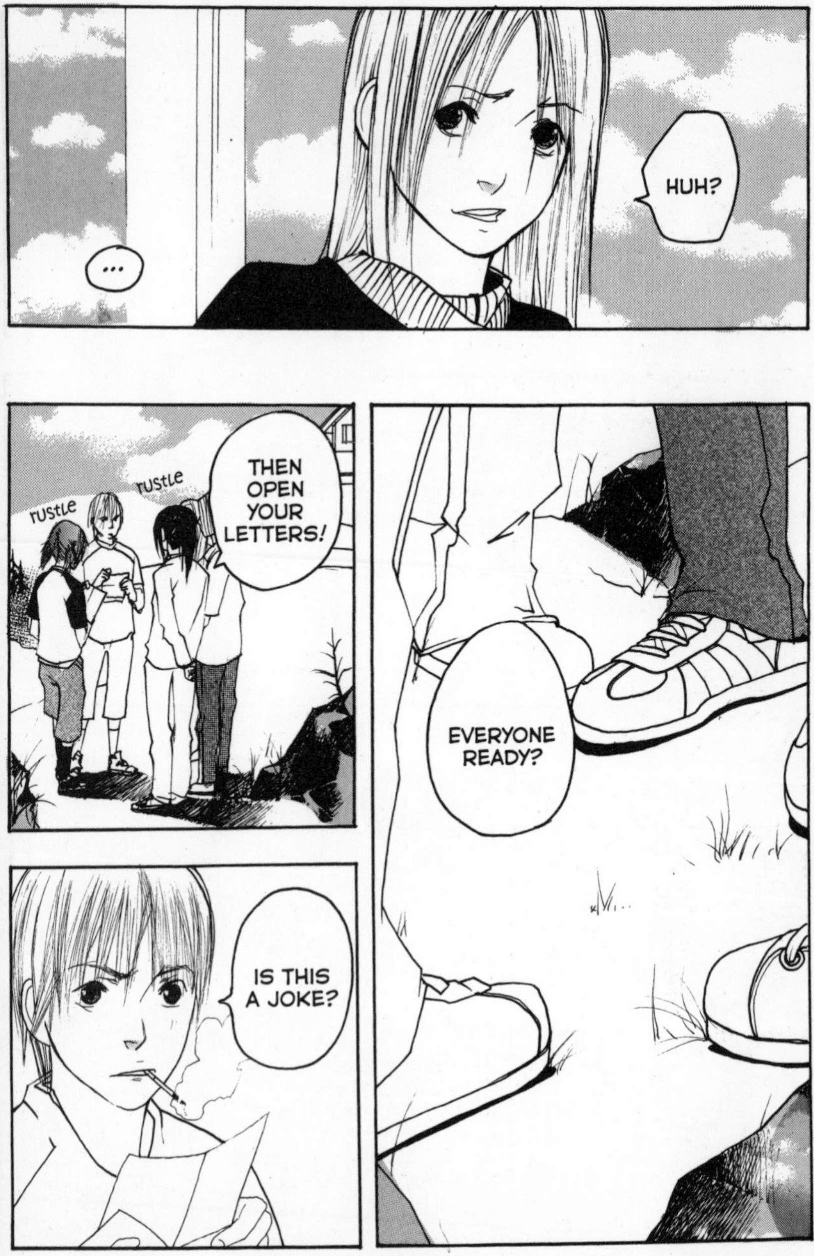
HUH?
...
EVERYONE READY?
THEN OPEN YOUR LETTERS!
rustle
rustle
IS THIS A JOKE?

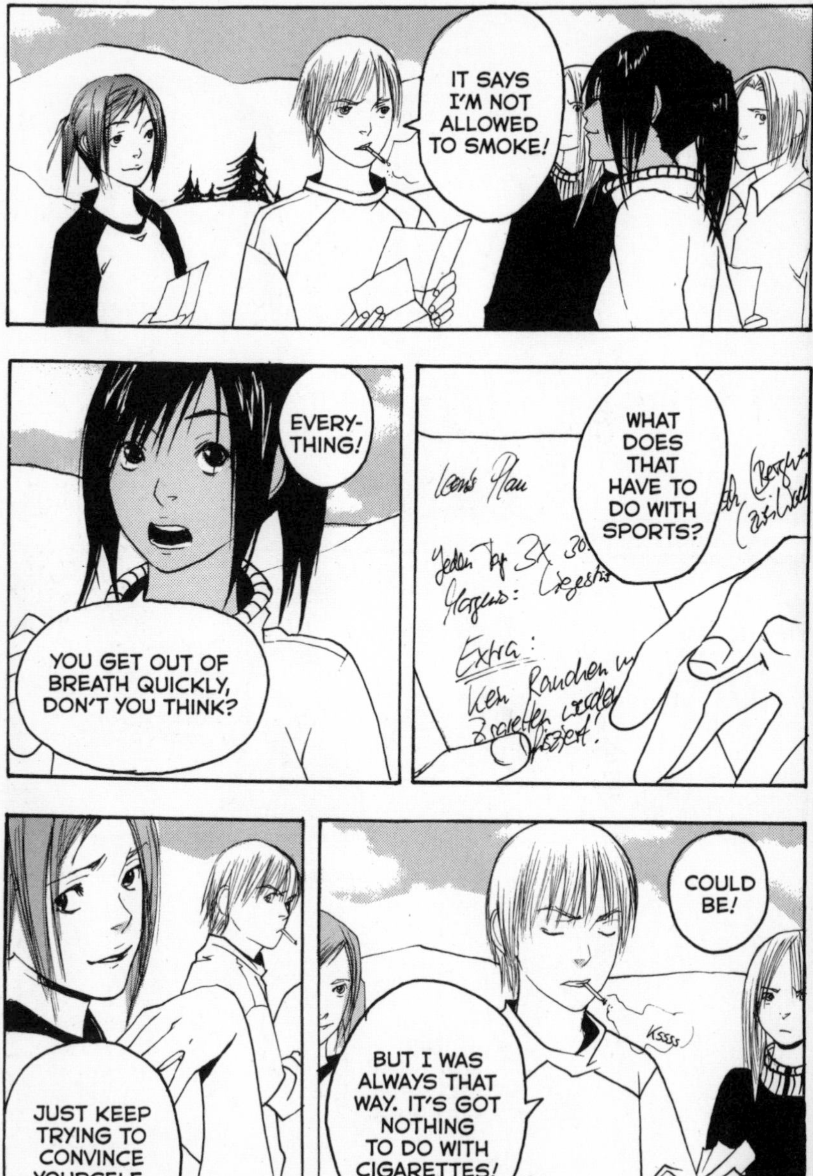
IT SAYS I'M NOT ALLOWED TO SMOKE!
WHAT DOES THAT HAVE TO DO WITH SPORTS?
EVERY-THING!
YOU GET OUT OF BREATH QUICKLY, DON'T YOU THINK?
COULD BE!
Kssss
BUT I WAS ALWAYS THAT WAY. IT'S GOT NOTHING TO DO WITH CIGARETTES!
JUST KEEP TRYING TO CONVINCE YOURSELF.

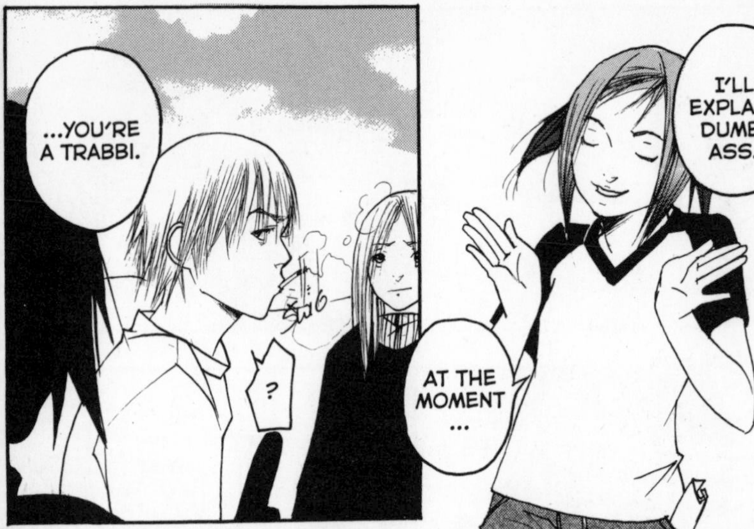
I'LL EXPLAIN, DUMB-ASS.
AT THE MOMENT ...
...YOU'RE A TRABBI.
?

*Trabbi: Trabant, a cheap East German car.

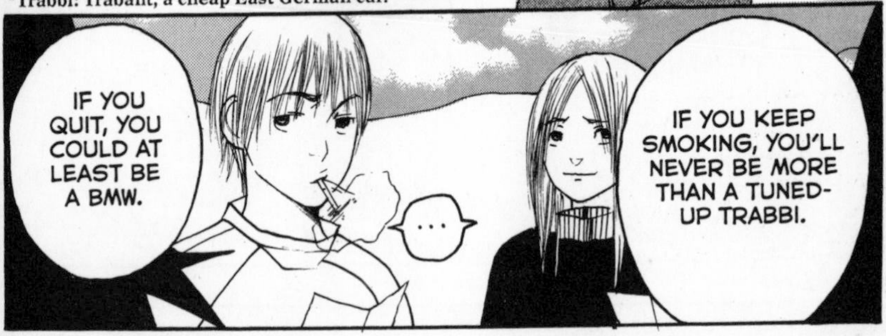
IF YOU KEEP SMOKING, YOU'LL NEVER BE MORE THAN A TUNED-UP TRABBI.
...
IF YOU QUIT, YOU COULD AT LEAST BE A BMW.

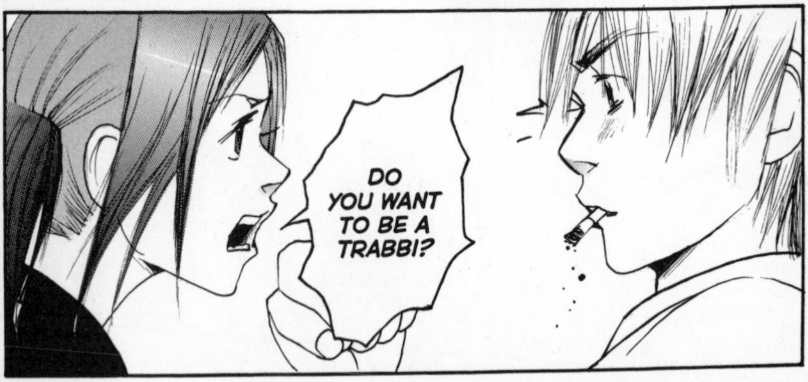
DO YOU WANT TO BE A TRABBI?

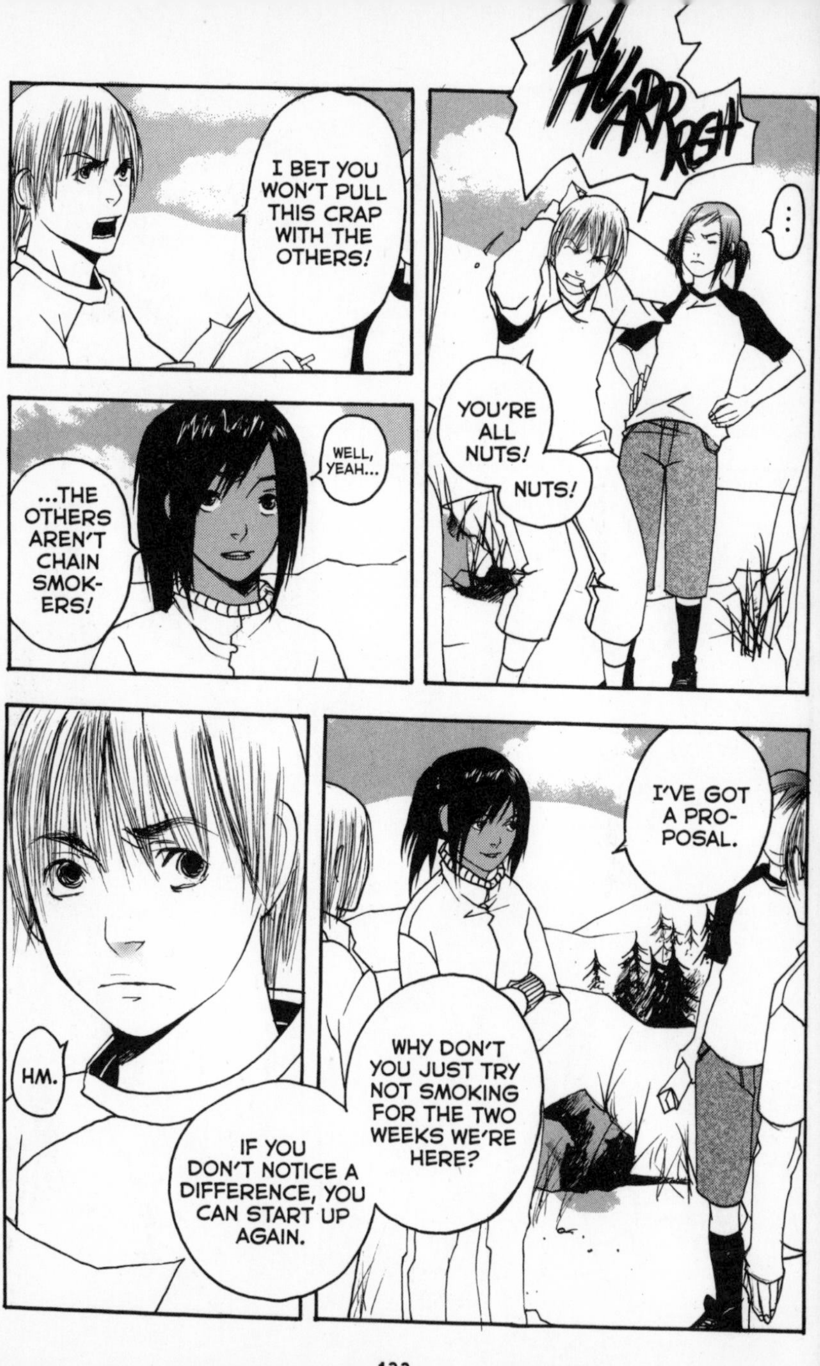
WHUARRRGH
...
YOU'RE ALL NUTS!
NUTS!
I BET YOU WON'T PULL THIS CRAP WITH THE OTHERS!
WELL, YEAH...
...THE OTHERS AREN'T CHAIN SMOK-ERS!
I'VE GOT A PRO-POSAL.
WHY DON'T YOU JUST TRY NOT SMOKING FOR THE TWO WEEKS WE'RE HERE?
HM.
IF YOU DON'T NOTICE A DIFFERENCE, YOU CAN START UP AGAIN.

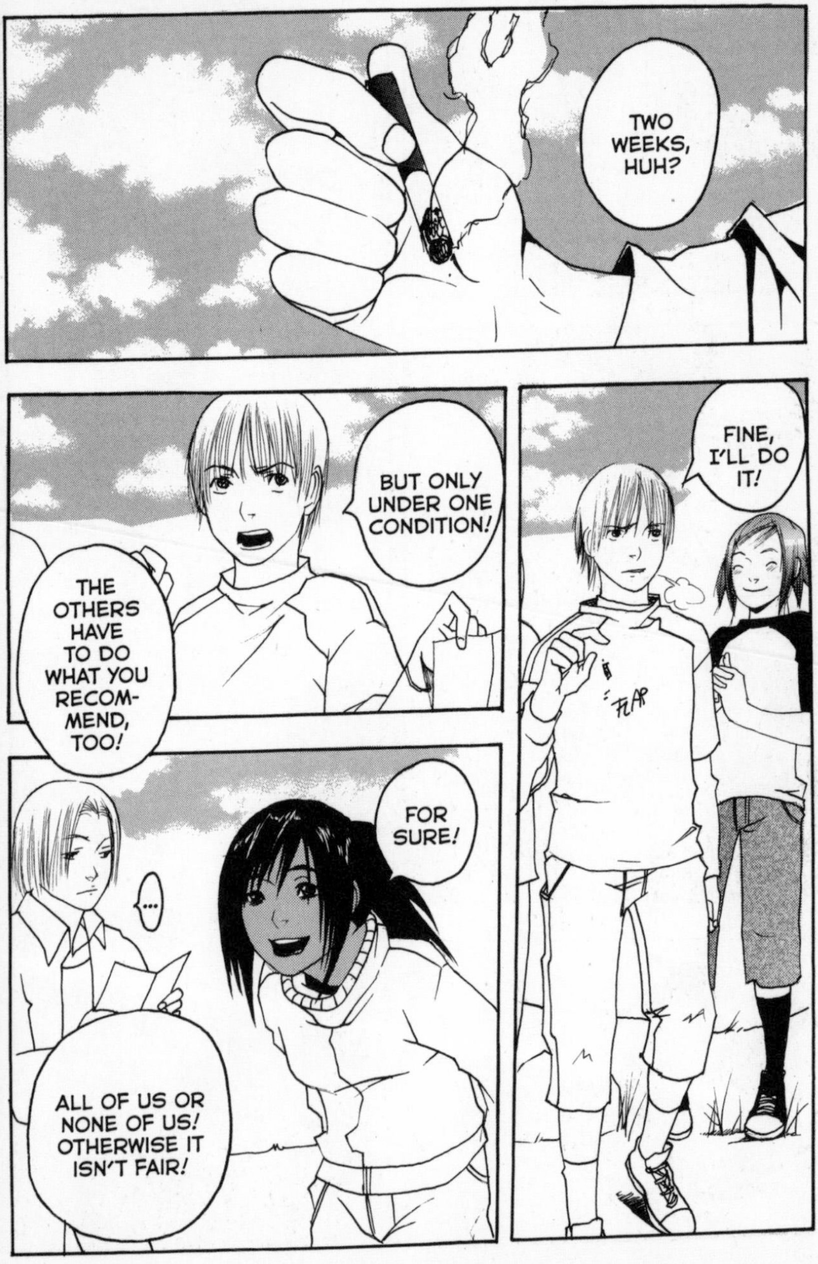
TWO WEEKS, HUH?
FINE, I'LL DO IT!
FLAP
BUT ONLY UNDER ONE CONDITION!
THE OTHERS HAVE TO DO WHAT YOU RECOMMEND, TOO!
FOR SURE!
...
ALL OF US OR NONE OF US! OTHERWISE IT ISN'T FAIR!

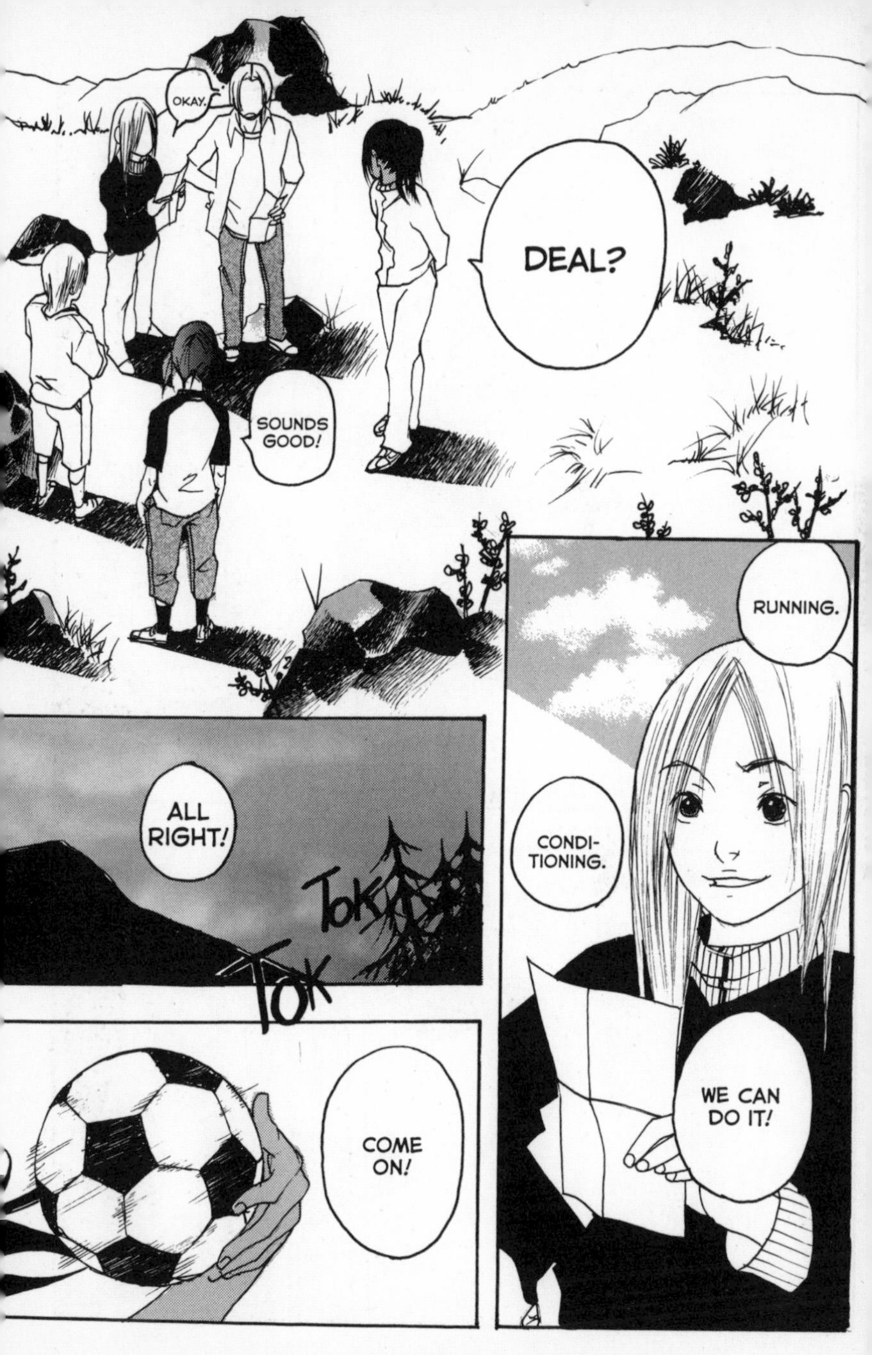
DEAL?
OKAY.
SOUNDS GOOD!
RUNNING.
CONDI-TIONING.
WE CAN DO IT!
ALL RIGHT!
TOK
TOK
COME ON!

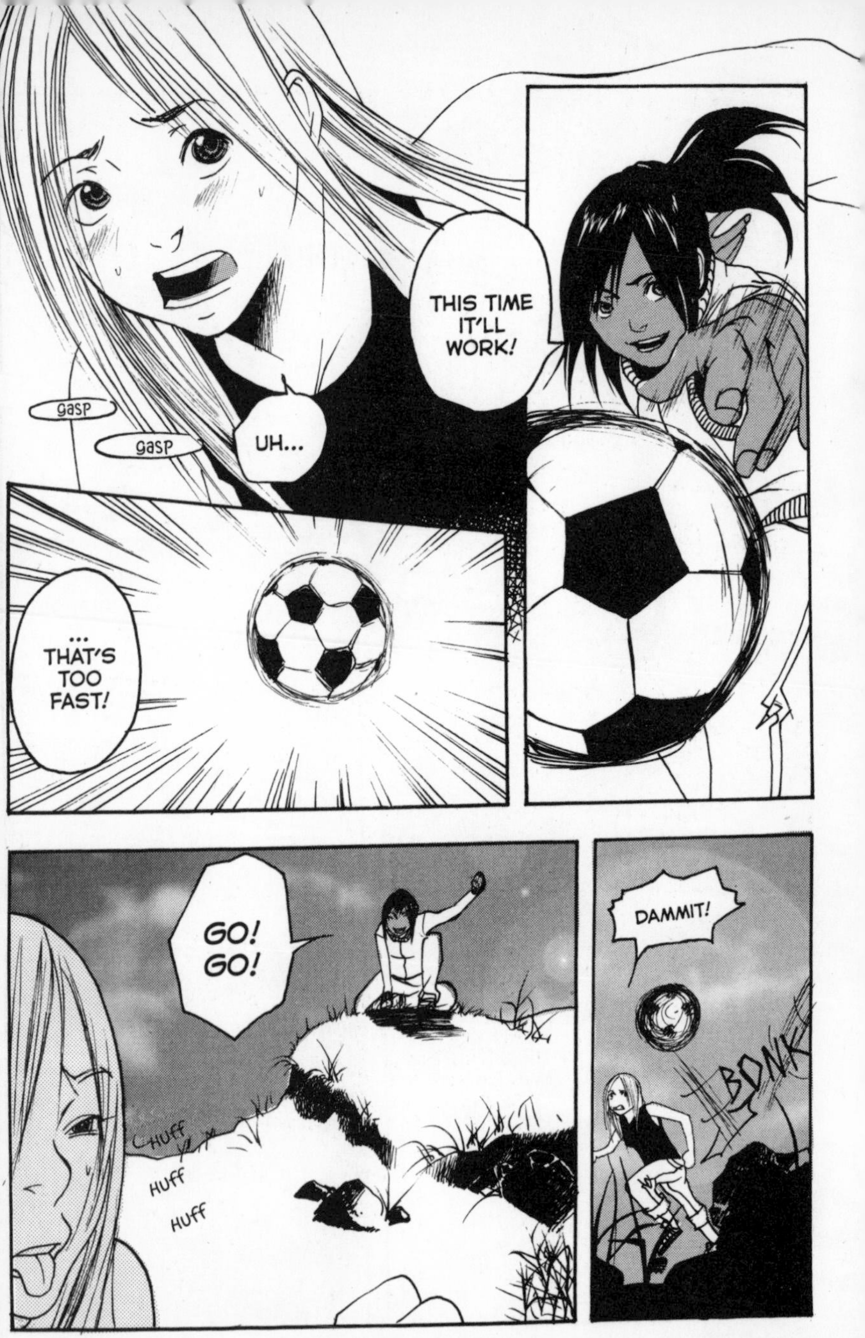
THIS TIME IT'LL WORK!
gasp
gasp
UH...
... THAT'S TOO FAST!
DAMMIT!
BONK
GO! GO!
HUFF
HUFF
HUFF

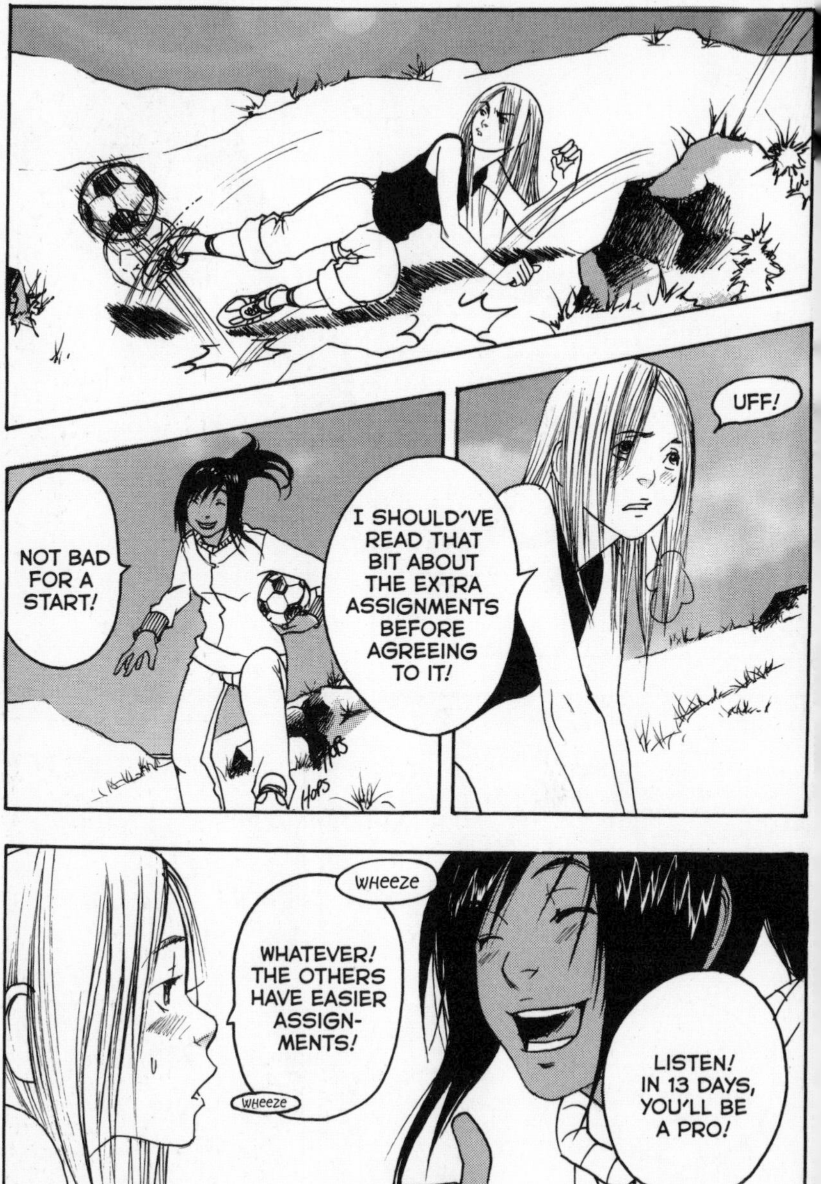
UFF!
I SHOULD'VE READ THAT BIT ABOUT THE EXTRA ASSIGNMENTS BEFORE AGREEING TO IT!
NOT BAD FOR A START!
HOPS
HOPS
LISTEN! IN 13 DAYS, YOU'LL BE A PRO!
WHEEZE
WHATEVER! THE OTHERS HAVE EASIER ASSIGN-MENTS!
WHEEZE

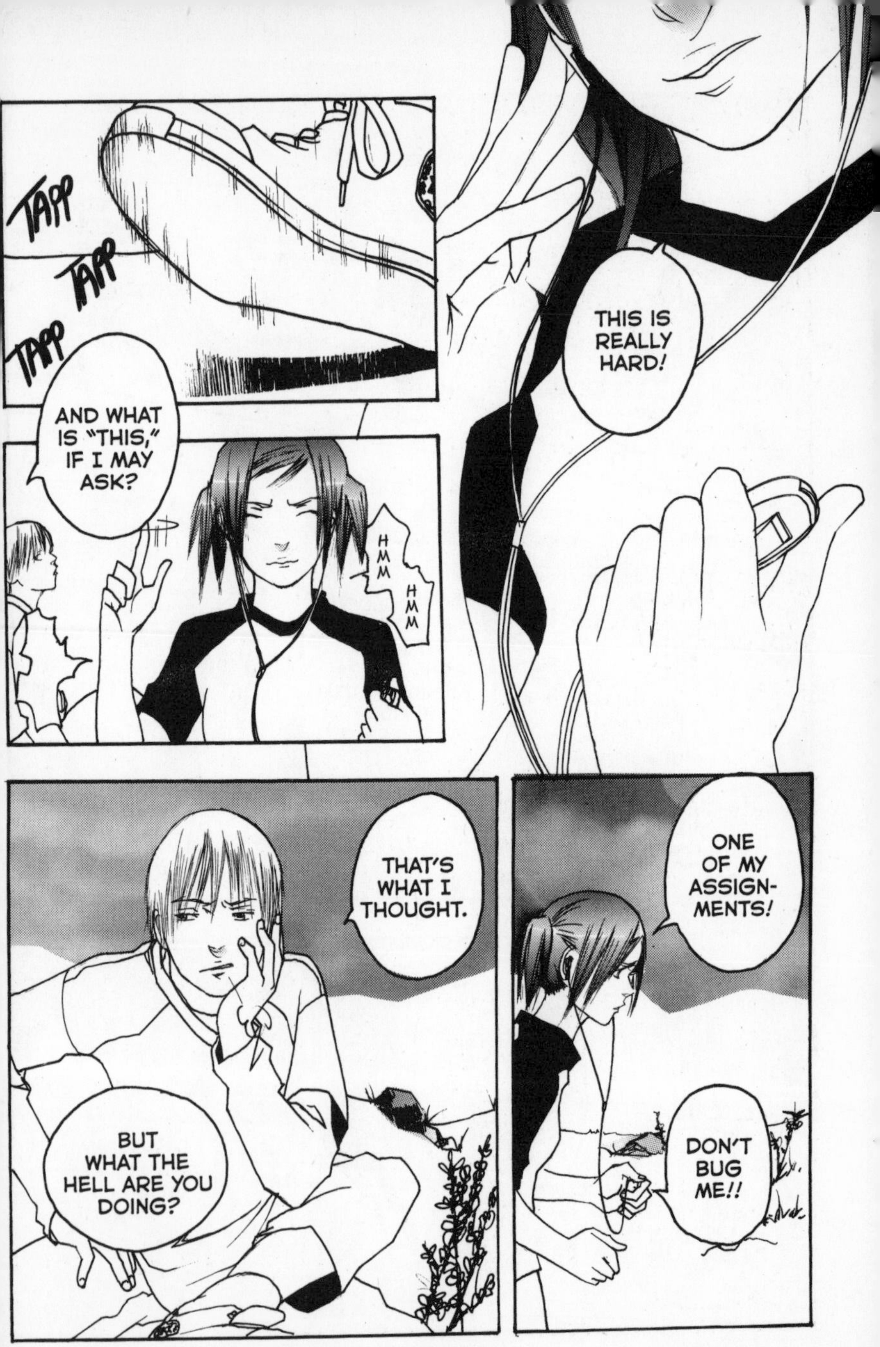
THIS IS REALLY HARD!
TAPP TAPP TAPP
AND WHAT IS "THIS," IF I MAY ASK?
HMM HMM
ONE OF MY ASSIGN-MENTS!
DON'T BUG ME!!
THAT'S WHAT I THOUGHT.
BUT WHAT THE HELL ARE YOU DOING?

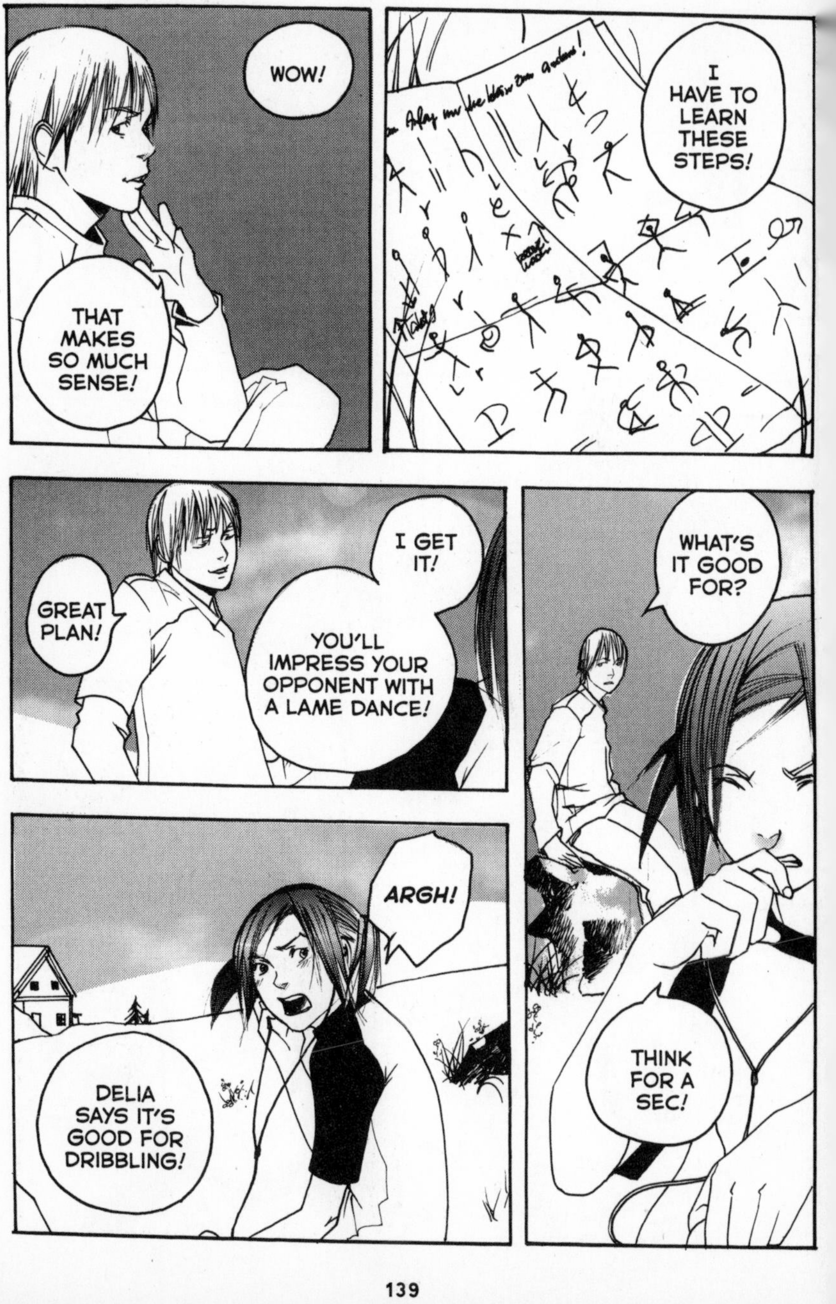
I HAVE TO LEARN THESE STEPS!
WOW!
THAT MAKES SO MUCH SENSE!
WHAT'S IT GOOD FOR?
THINK FOR A SEC!
I GET IT!
YOU'LL IMPRESS YOUR OPPONENT WITH A LAME DANCE!
GREAT PLAN!
ARGH!
DELIA SAYS IT'S GOOD FOR DRIBBLING!

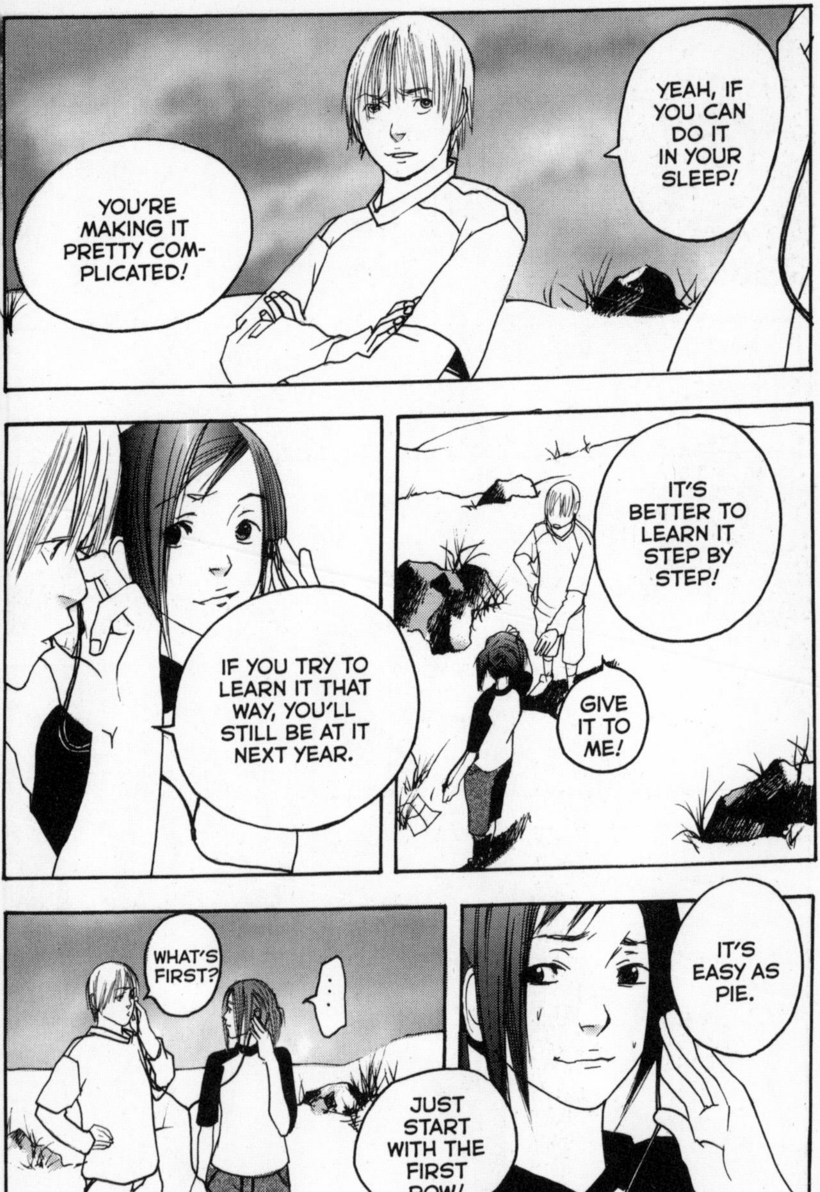
YOU'RE MAKING IT PRETTY COM-PLICATED!
YEAH, IF YOU CAN DO IT IN YOUR SLEEP!
IF YOU TRY TO LEARN IT THAT WAY, YOU'LL STILL BE AT IT NEXT YEAR.
IT'S BETTER TO LEARN IT STEP BY STEP!
GIVE IT TO ME!
WHAT'S FIRST?
...
IT'S EASY AS PIE.
JUST START WITH THE FIRST ROW!

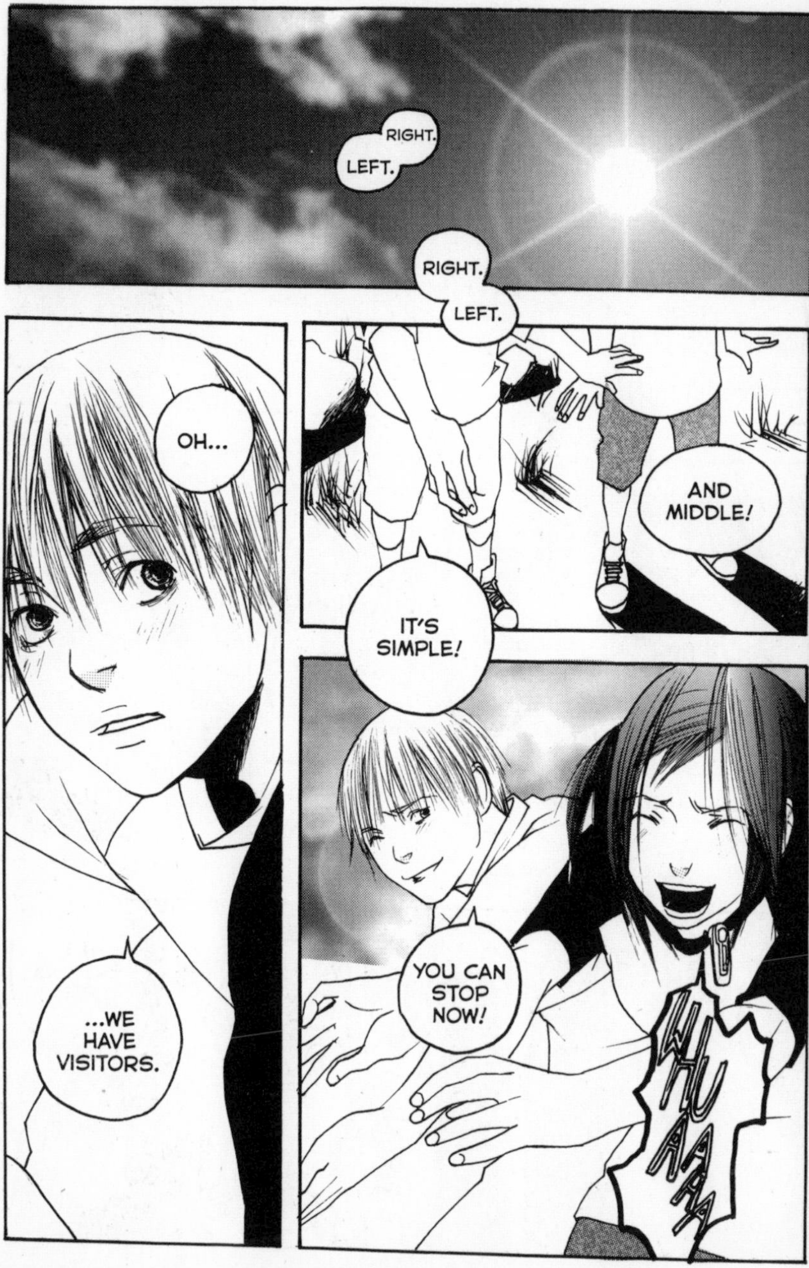
RIGHT.
LEFT.
RIGHT.
LEFT.
AND MIDDLE!
IT'S SIMPLE!
YOU CAN STOP NOW!
WHUAAAA
OH...
...WE HAVE VISITORS.

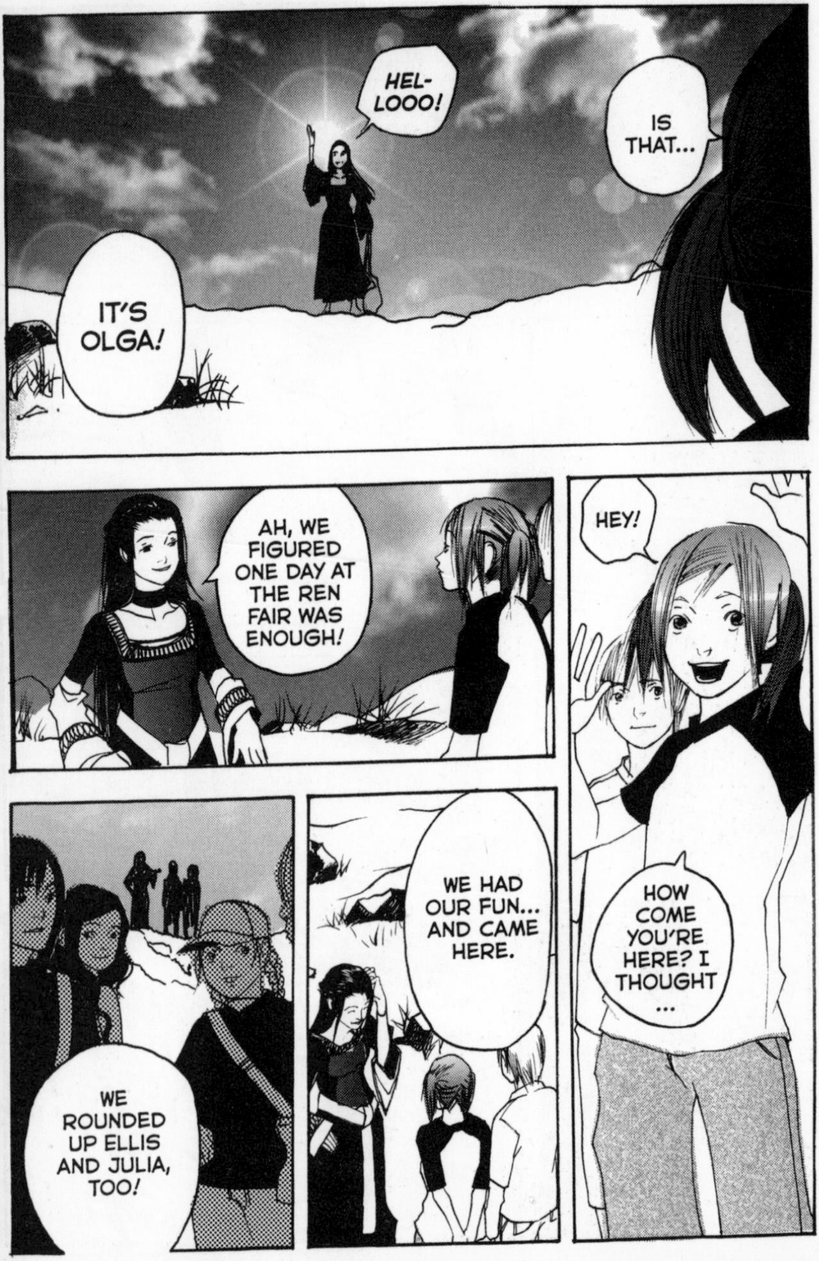
IS THAT...
HEL-LOOO!
IT'S OLGA!
HEY!
HOW COME YOU'RE HERE? I THOUGHT ...
AH, WE FIGURED ONE DAY AT THE REN FAIR WAS ENOUGH!
WE HAD OUR FUN... AND CAME HERE.
WE ROUNDED UP ELLIS AND JULIA, TOO!

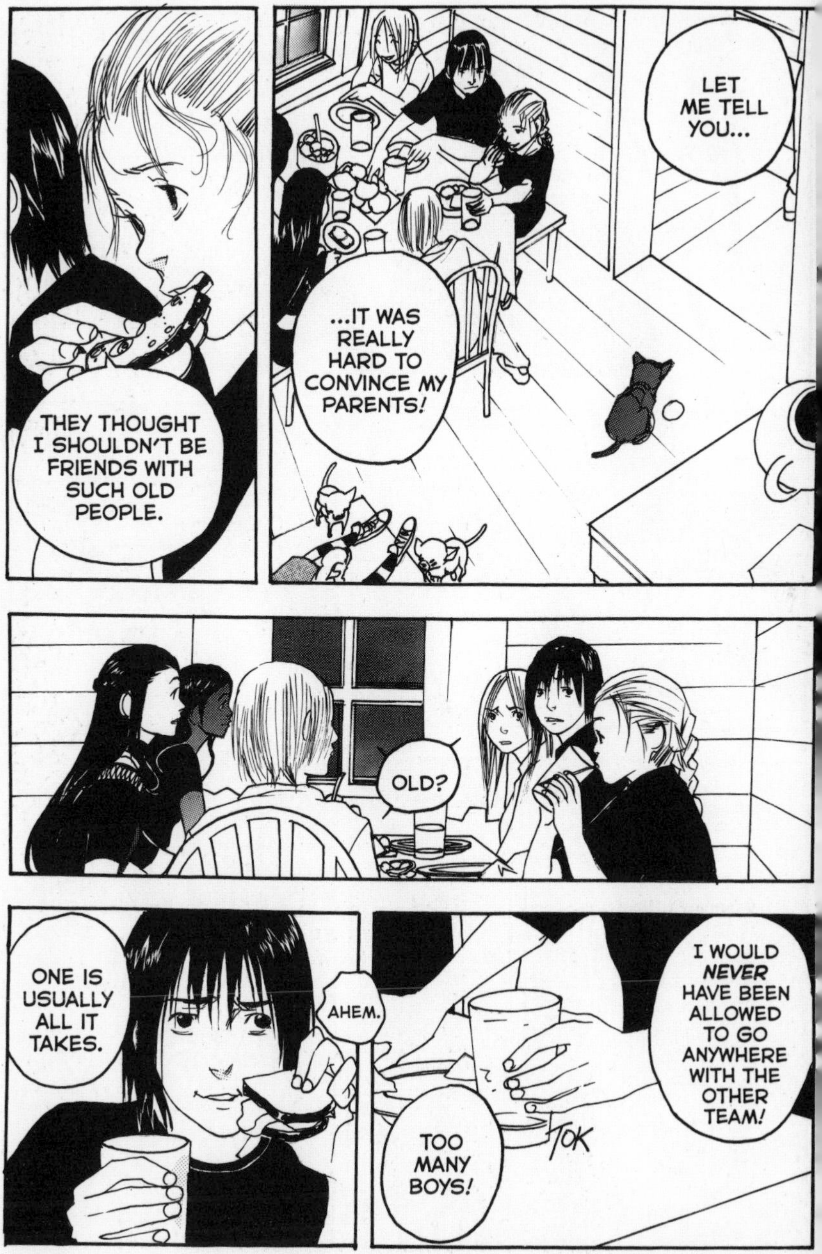
LET ME TELL YOU...
...IT WAS REALLY HARD TO CONVINCE MY PARENTS!
THEY THOUGHT I SHOULDN'T BE FRIENDS WITH SUCH OLD PEOPLE.
OLD?
I WOULD *NEVER* HAVE BEEN ALLOWED TO GO ANYWHERE WITH THE OTHER TEAM!
TOK
TOO MANY BOYS!
ONE IS USUALLY ALL IT TAKES.
AHEM.

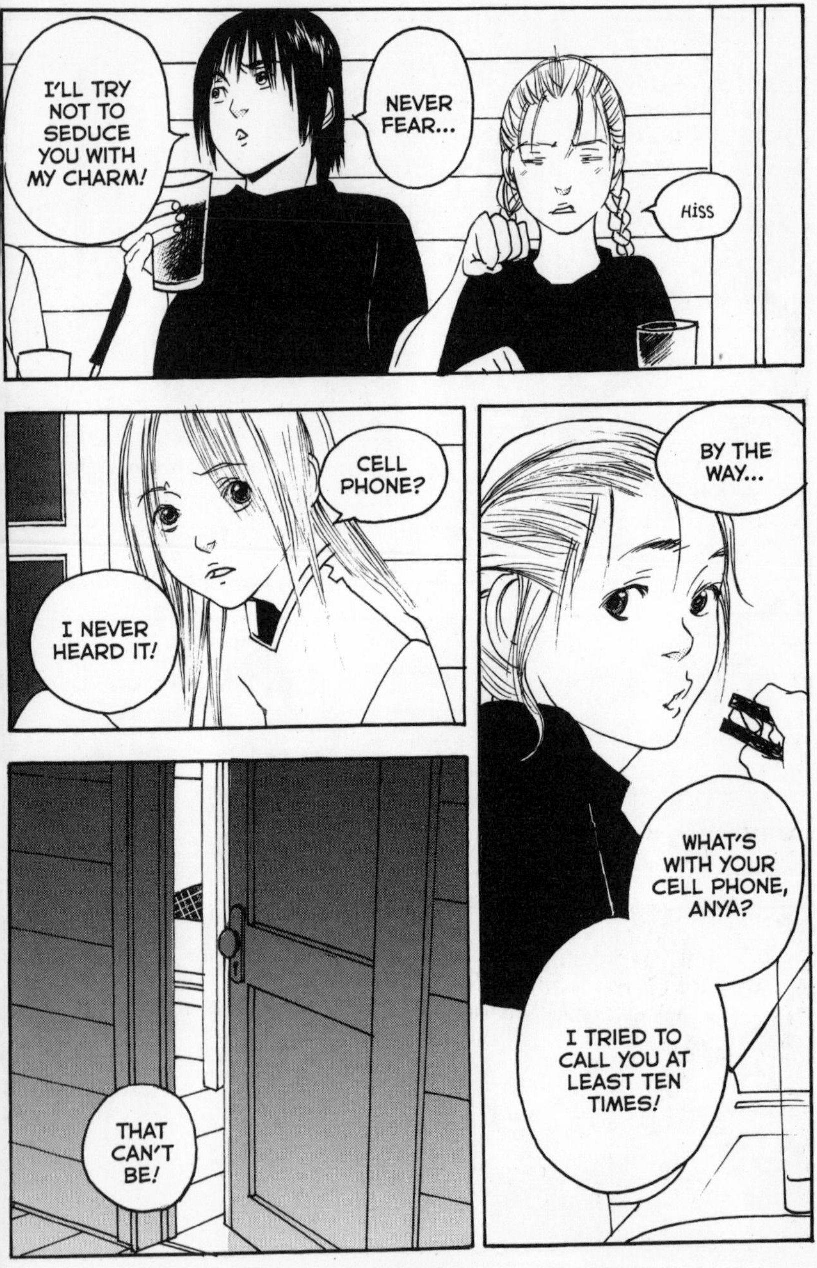
NEVER FEAR...
I'LL TRY NOT TO SEDUCE YOU WITH MY CHARM!
HISS
BY THE WAY...
WHAT'S WITH YOUR CELL PHONE, ANYA?
I TRIED TO CALL YOU AT LEAST TEN TIMES!
CELL PHONE?
I NEVER HEARD IT!
THAT CAN'T BE!

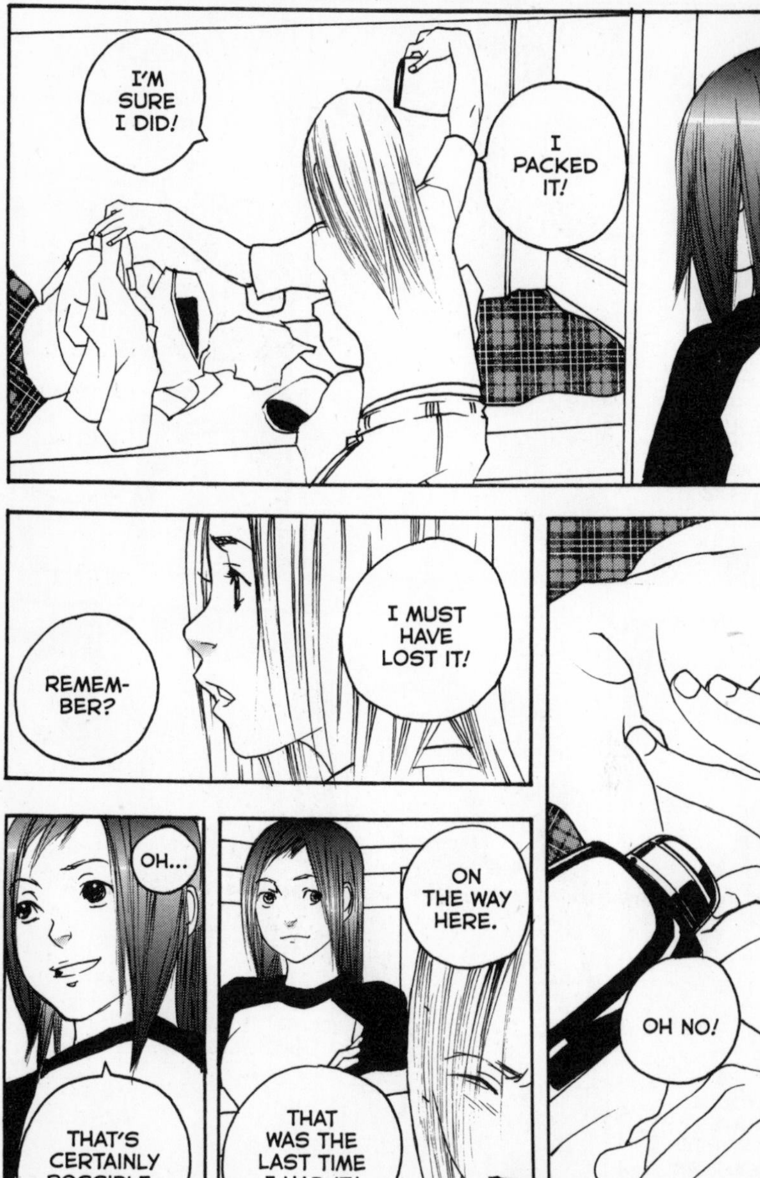

I PACKED IT!
I'M SURE I DID!
OH NO!
I MUST HAVE LOST IT!
REMEMBER?
ON THE WAY HERE.
THAT WAS THE LAST TIME I HAD IT!
OH...
THAT'S CERTAINLY POSSIBLE.

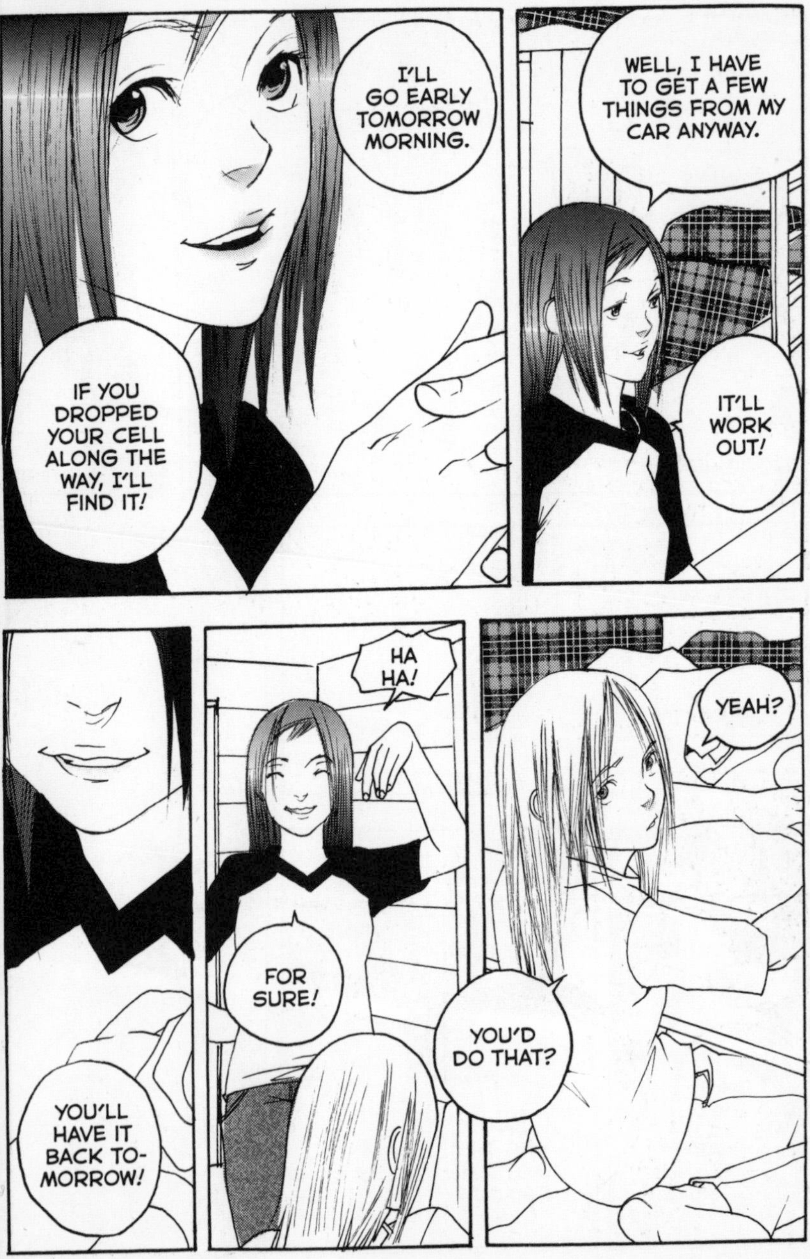
WELL, I HAVE TO GET A FEW THINGS FROM MY CAR ANYWAY.
IT'LL WORK OUT!
I'LL GO EARLY TOMORROW MORNING.
IF YOU DROPPED YOUR CELL ALONG THE WAY, I'LL FIND IT!
YEAH?
YOU'D DO THAT?
HA HA!
FOR SURE!
YOU'LL HAVE IT BACK TO-MORROW!

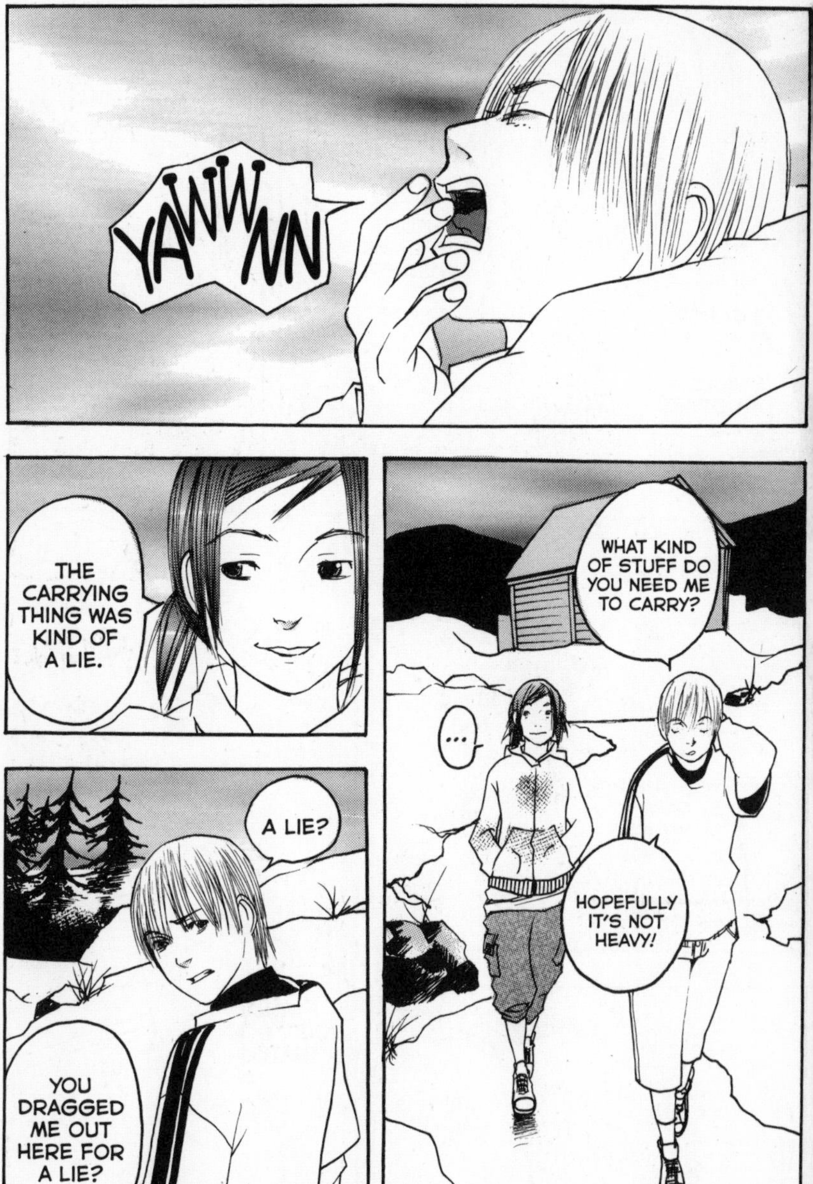
YAWWNN
WHAT KIND OF STUFF DO YOU NEED ME TO CARRY?
...
HOPEFULLY IT'S NOT HEAVY!
THE CARRYING THING WAS KIND OF A LIE.
A LIE?
YOU DRAGGED ME OUT HERE FOR A LIE?

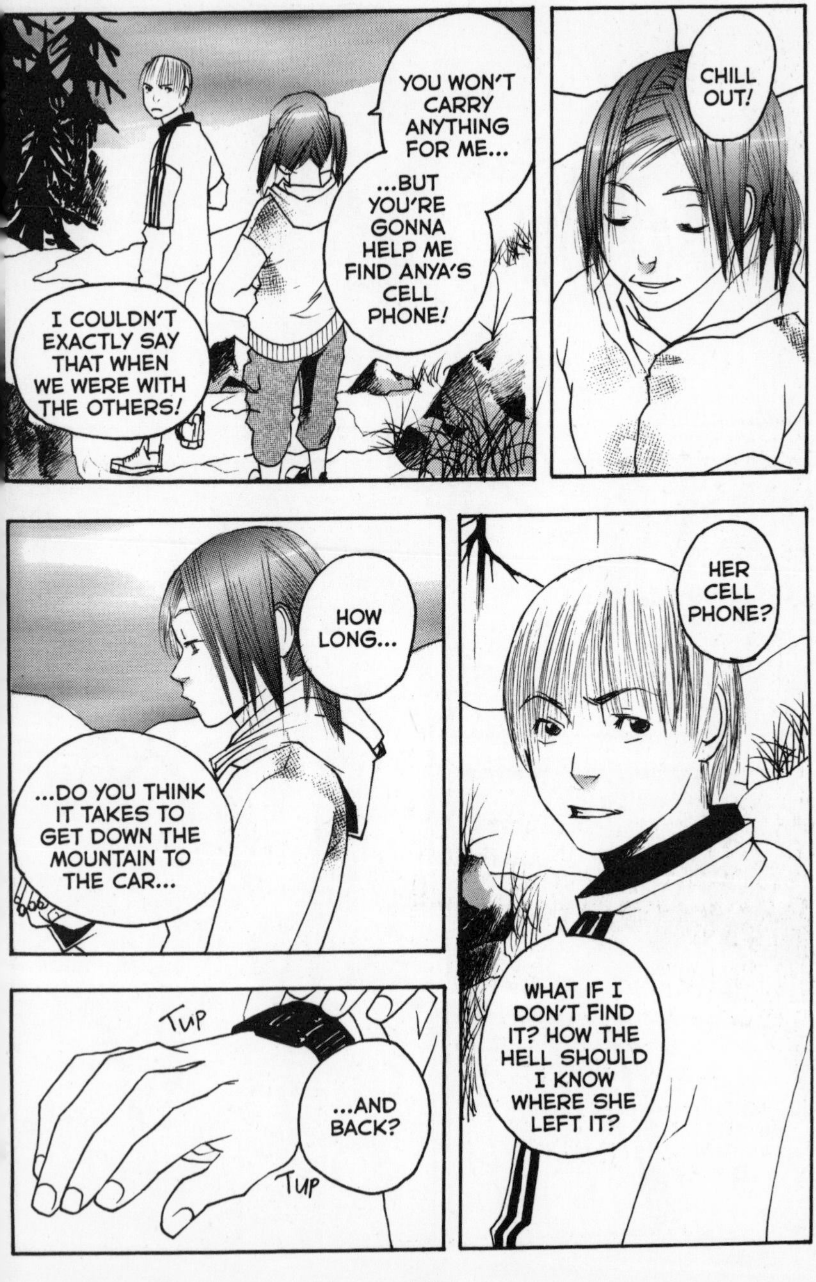
CHILL OUT!
YOU WON'T CARRY ANYTHING FOR ME...
...BUT YOU'RE GONNA HELP ME FIND ANYA'S CELL PHONE!
I COULDN'T EXACTLY SAY THAT WHEN WE WERE WITH THE OTHERS!
HER CELL PHONE?
WHAT IF I DON'T FIND IT? HOW THE HELL SHOULD I KNOW WHERE SHE LEFT IT?
HOW LONG...
...DO YOU THINK IT TAKES TO GET DOWN THE MOUNTAIN TO THE CAR...
TUP
...AND BACK?
TUP

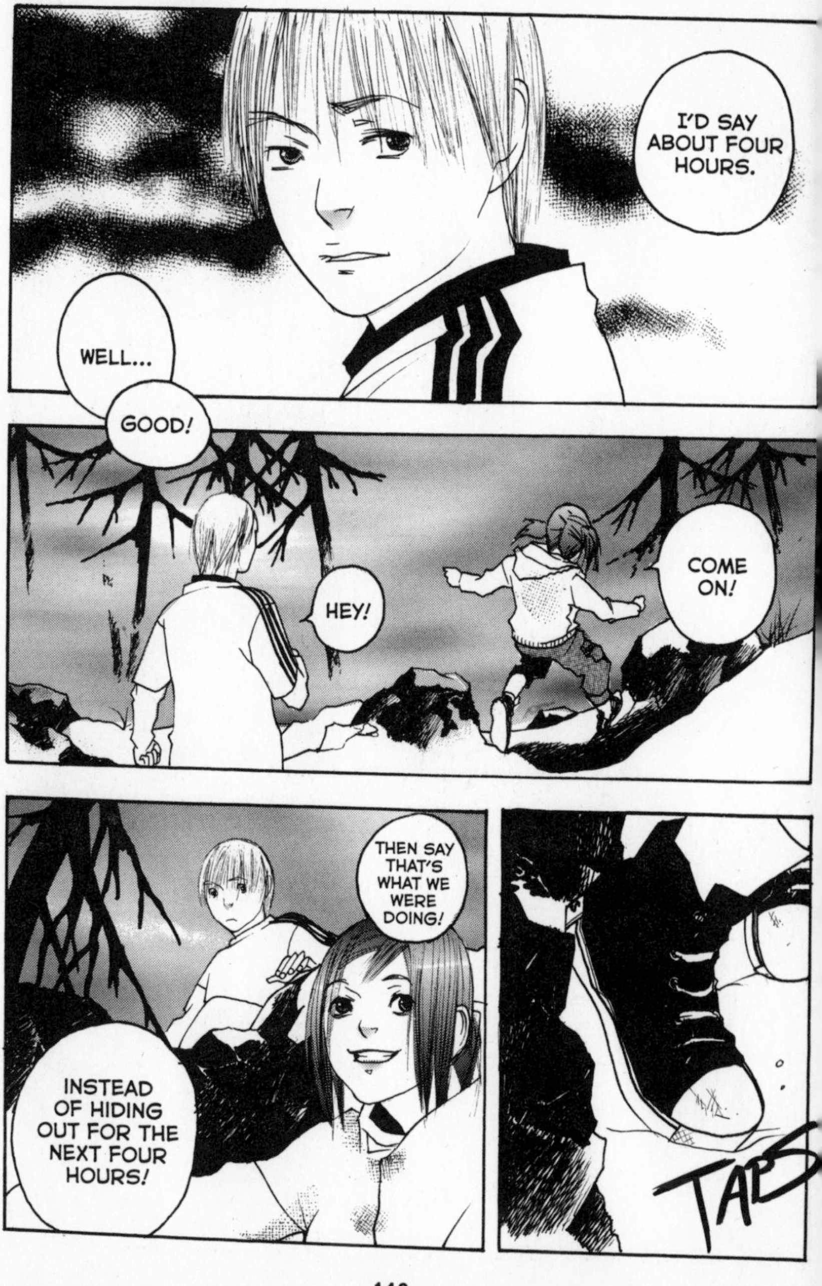
I'D SAY ABOUT FOUR HOURS.
WELL...
GOOD!
COME ON!
HEY!
TAPS
THEN SAY THAT'S WHAT WE WERE DOING!
INSTEAD OF HIDING OUT FOR THE NEXT FOUR HOURS!

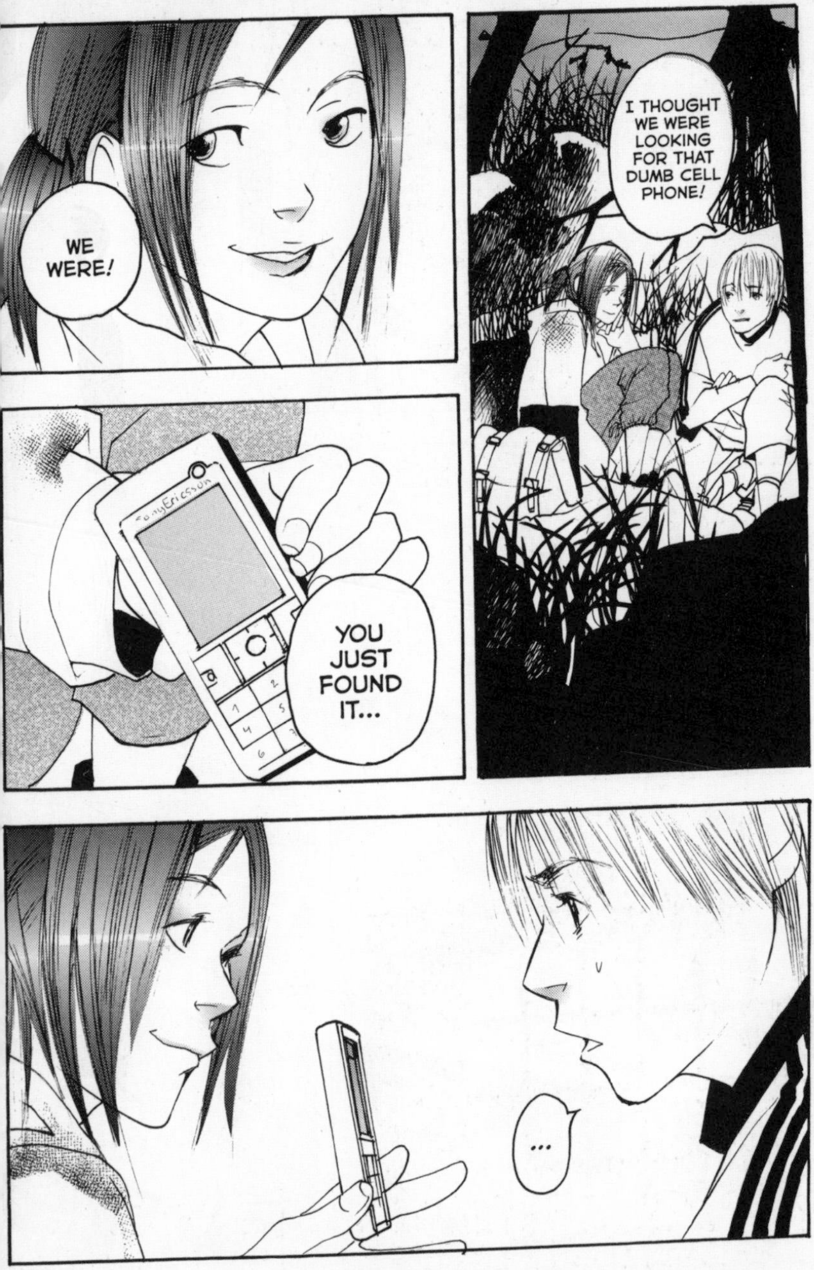
I THOUGHT WE WERE LOOKING FOR THAT DUMB CELL PHONE!
WE WERE!
YOU JUST FOUND IT...
...

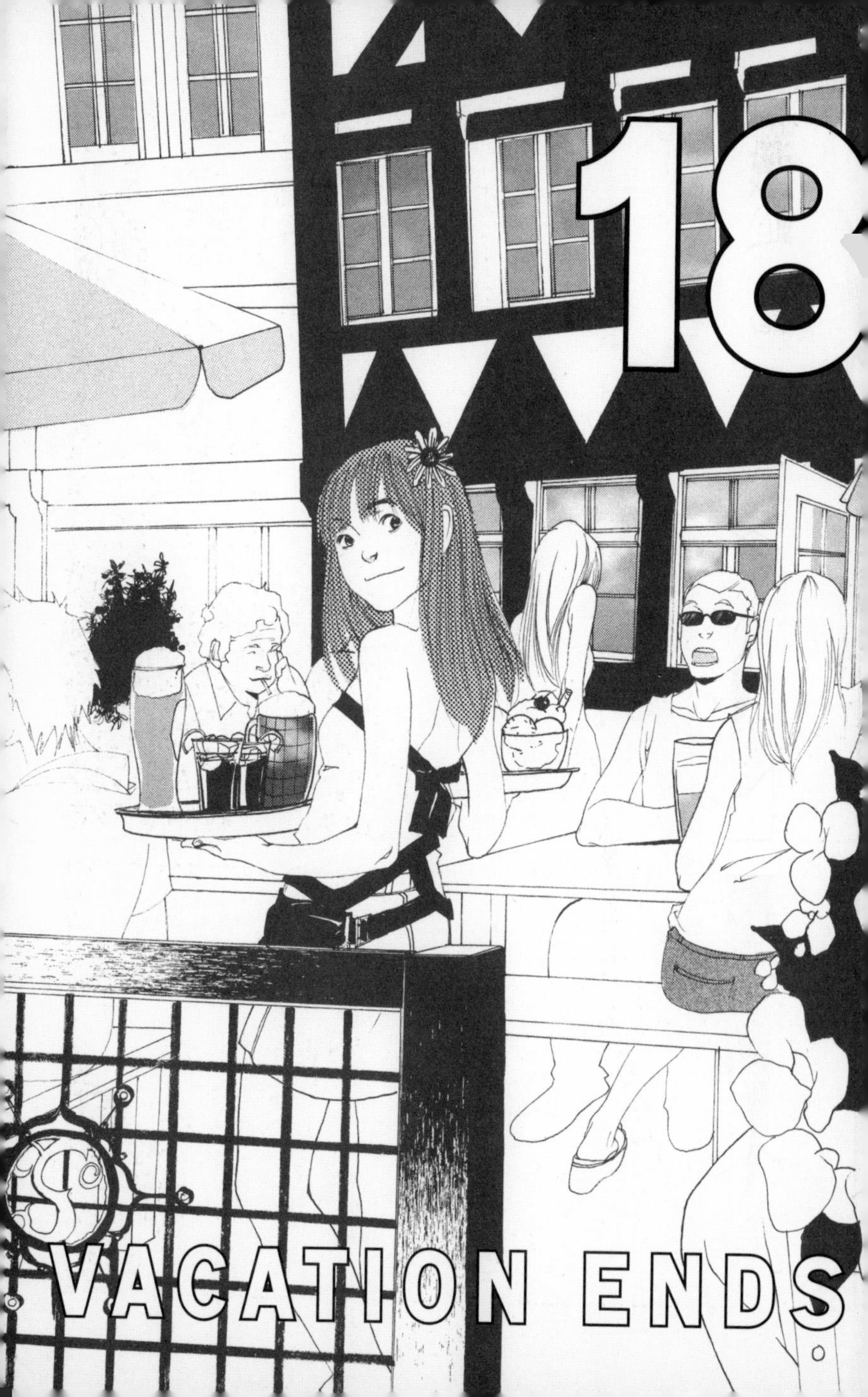
18
VACATION ENDS

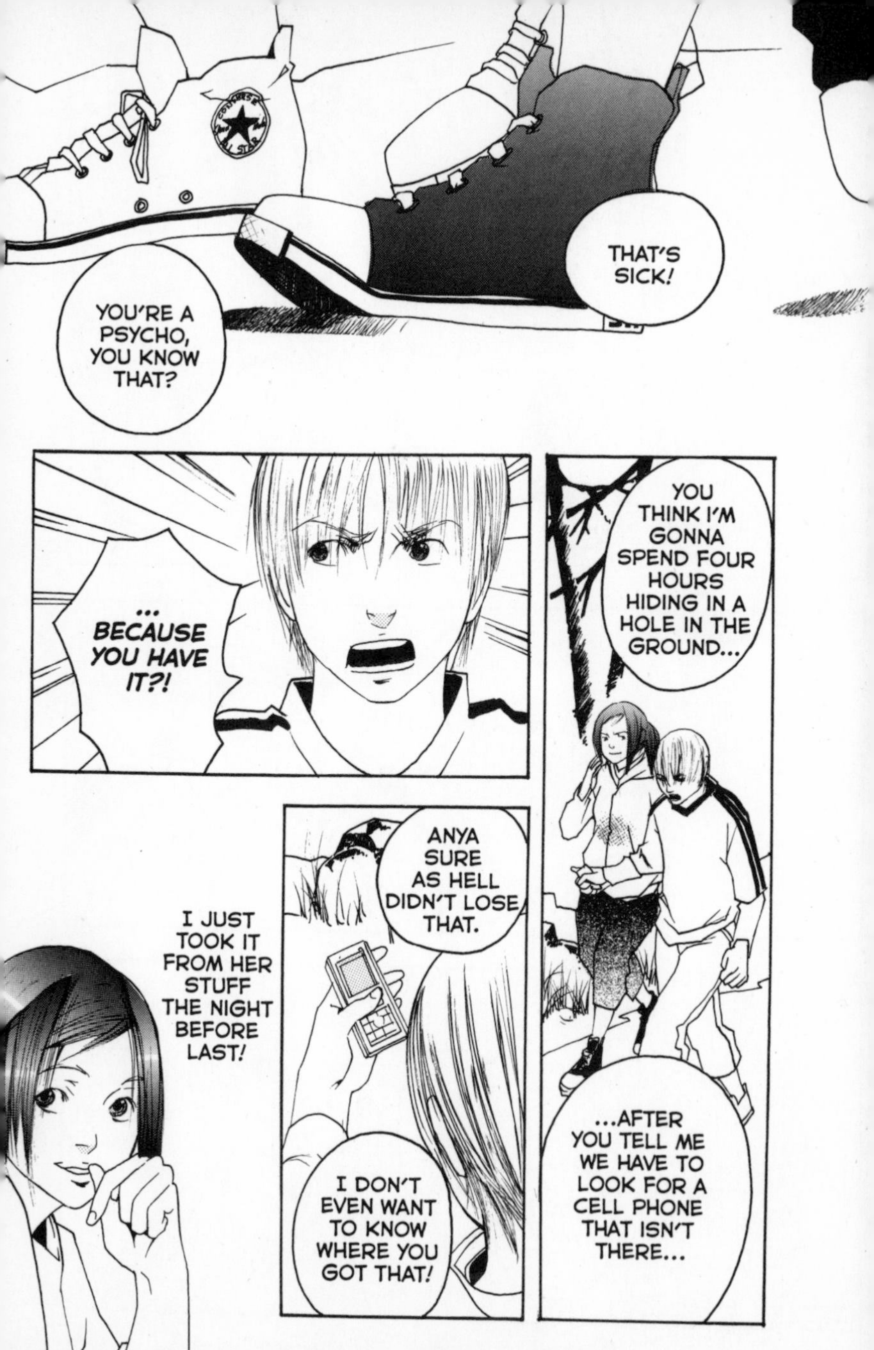
THAT'S SICK!
YOU'RE A PSYCHO, YOU KNOW THAT?
YOU THINK I'M GONNA SPEND FOUR HOURS HIDING IN A HOLE IN THE GROUND...
...AFTER YOU TELL ME WE HAVE TO LOOK FOR A CELL PHONE THAT ISN'T THERE...
...BECAUSE YOU HAVE IT?!
ANYA SURE AS HELL DIDN'T LOSE THAT.
I DON'T EVEN WANT TO KNOW WHERE YOU GOT THAT!
I JUST TOOK IT FROM HER STUFF THE NIGHT BEFORE LAST!

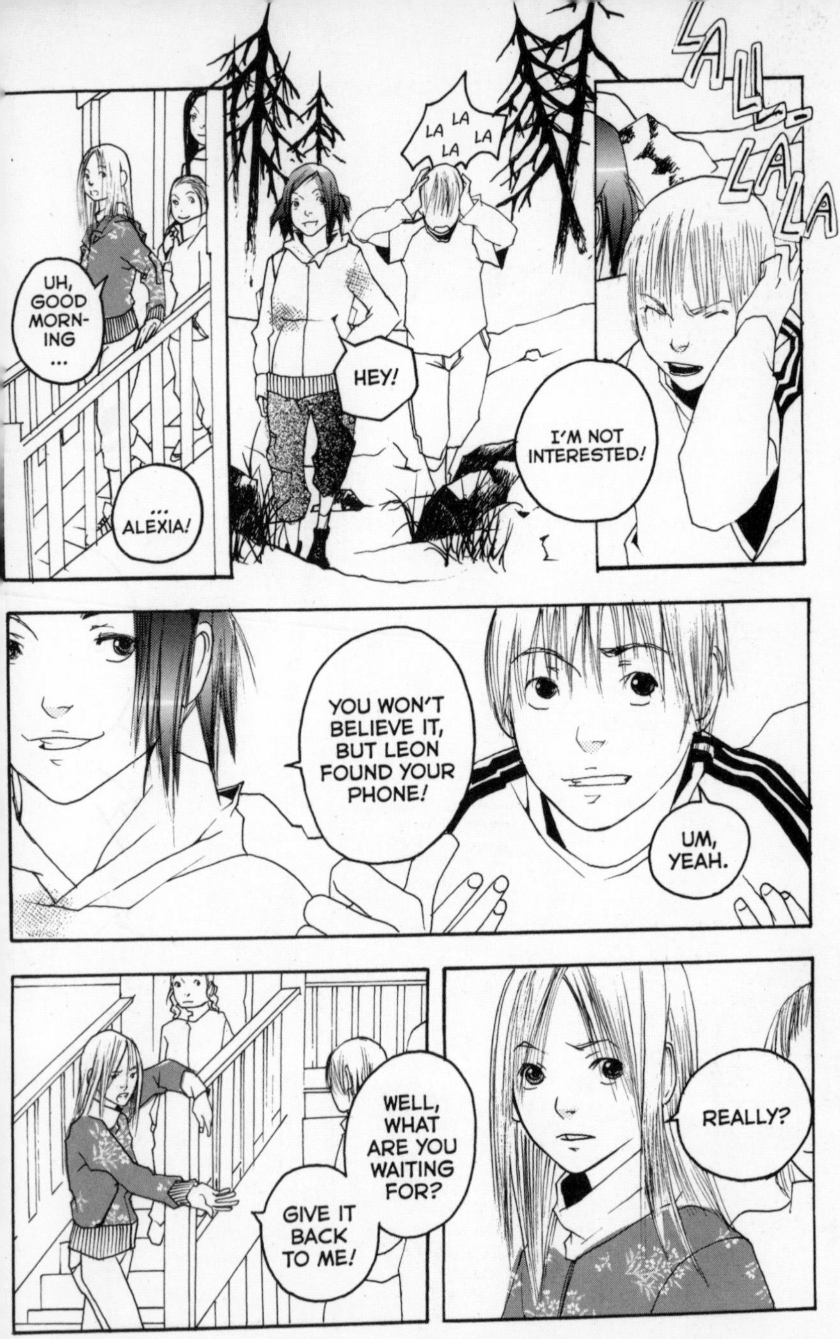
LALL-LALALA
I'M NOT INTERESTED!
LA LA LA LA LA
HEY!
UH, GOOD MORNING-ING ...
... ALEXIA!
YOU WON'T BELIEVE IT, BUT LEON FOUND YOUR PHONE!
UM, YEAH.
REALLY?
WELL, WHAT ARE YOU WAITING FOR?
GIVE IT BACK TO ME!

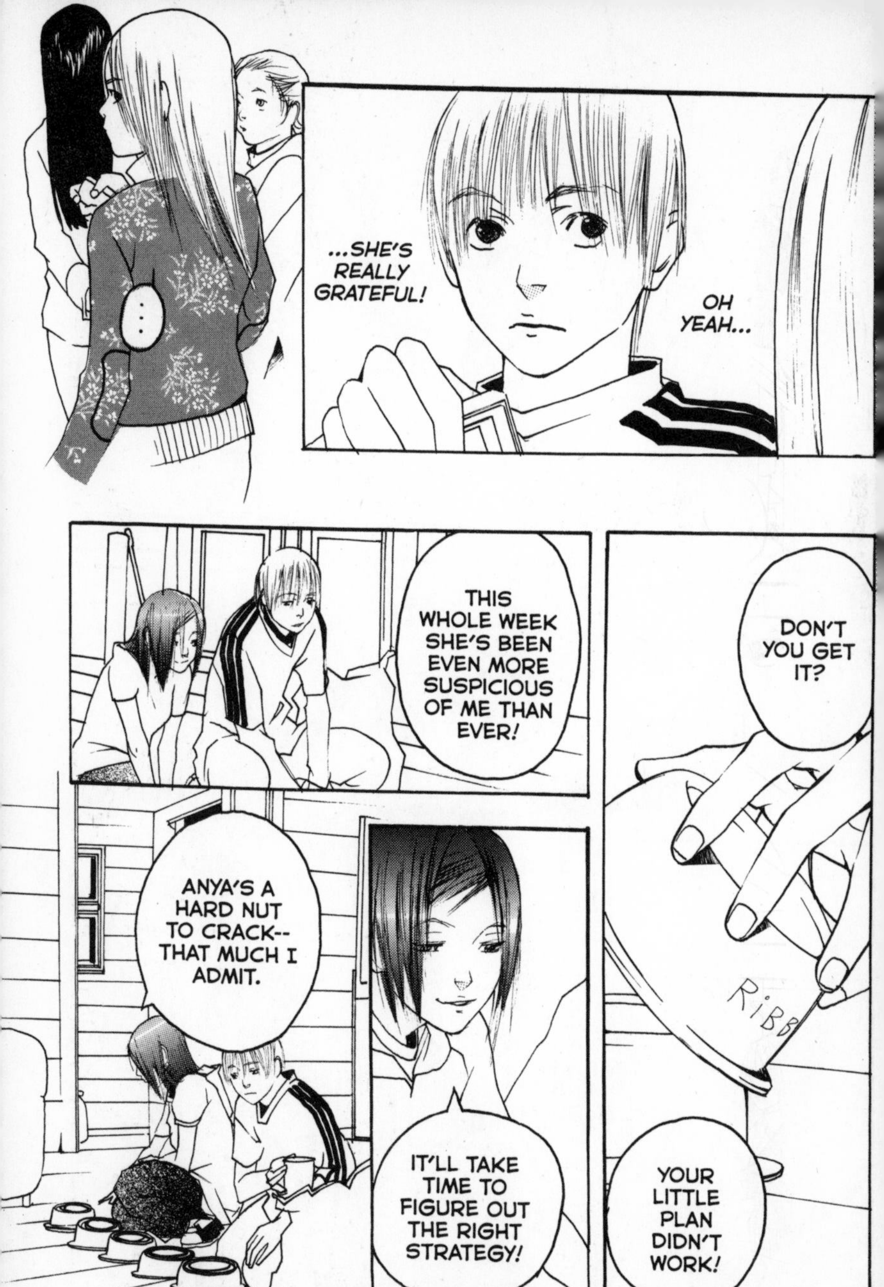
OH YEAH...
...SHE'S REALLY GRATEFUL!
DON'T YOU GET IT?
YOUR LITTLE PLAN DIDN'T WORK!
THIS WHOLE WEEK SHE'S BEEN EVEN MORE SUSPICIOUS OF ME THAN EVER!
IT'LL TAKE TIME TO FIGURE OUT THE RIGHT STRATEGY!
ANYA'S A HARD NUT TO CRACK-- THAT MUCH I ADMIT.
RiBB

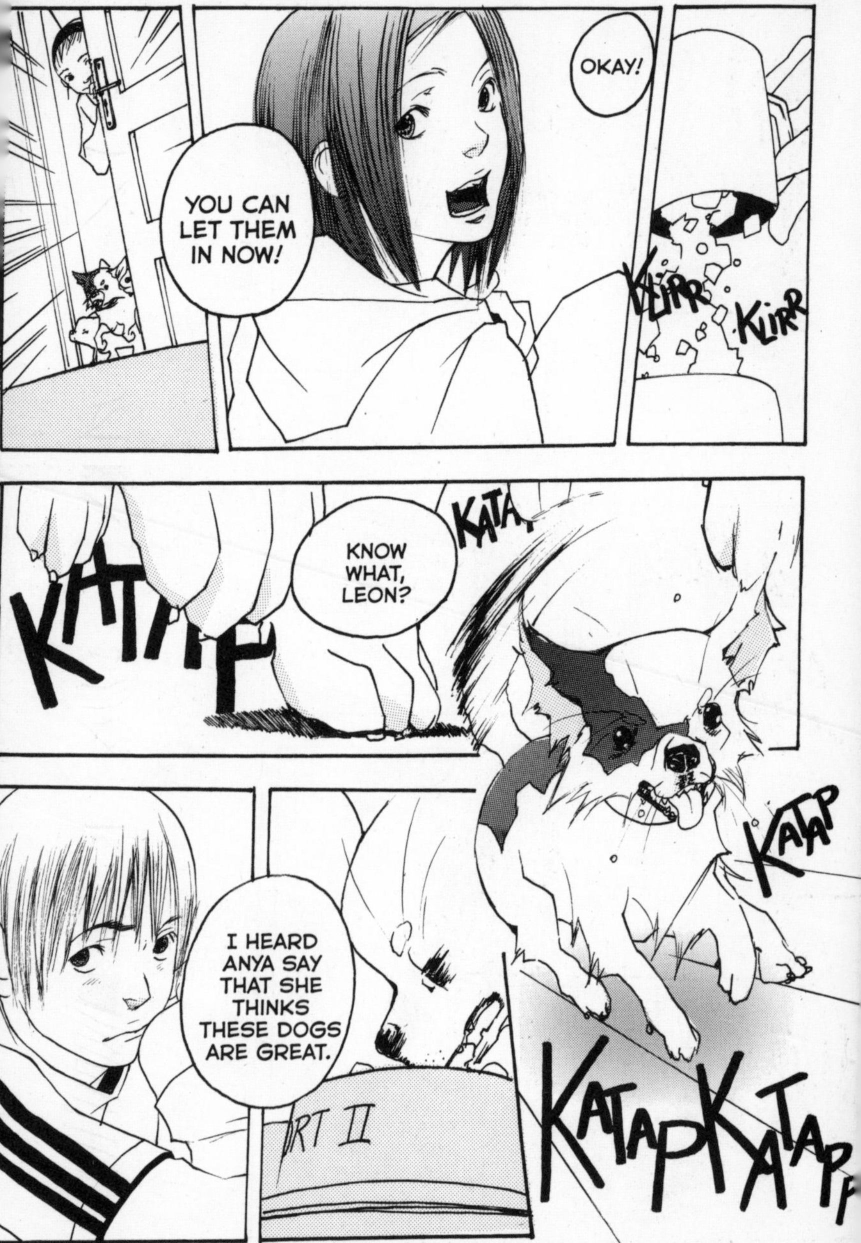
OKAY!
KLIRR
KLIRR
YOU CAN LET THEM IN NOW!
KATAP
KATAPKATAPP
KATA
KNOW WHAT, LEON?
KATAPP
I HEARD ANYA SAY THAT SHE THINKS THESE DOGS ARE GREAT.

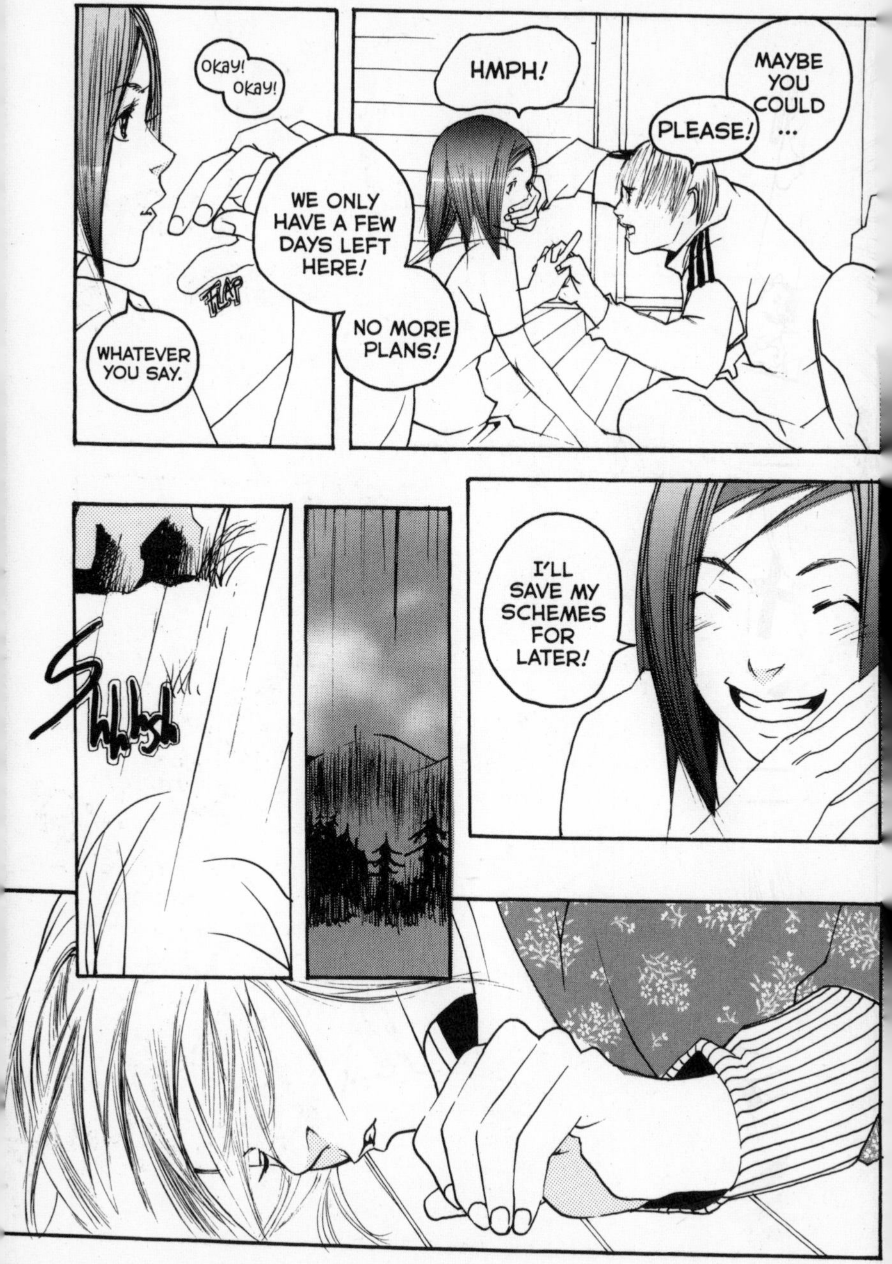
MAYBE YOU COULD ...
PLEASE!
HMPH!
WE ONLY HAVE A FEW DAYS LEFT HERE!
NO MORE PLANS!
Okay! Okay!
FLAP
WHATEVER YOU SAY.
I'LL SAVE MY SCHEMES FOR LATER!
Shhhsh

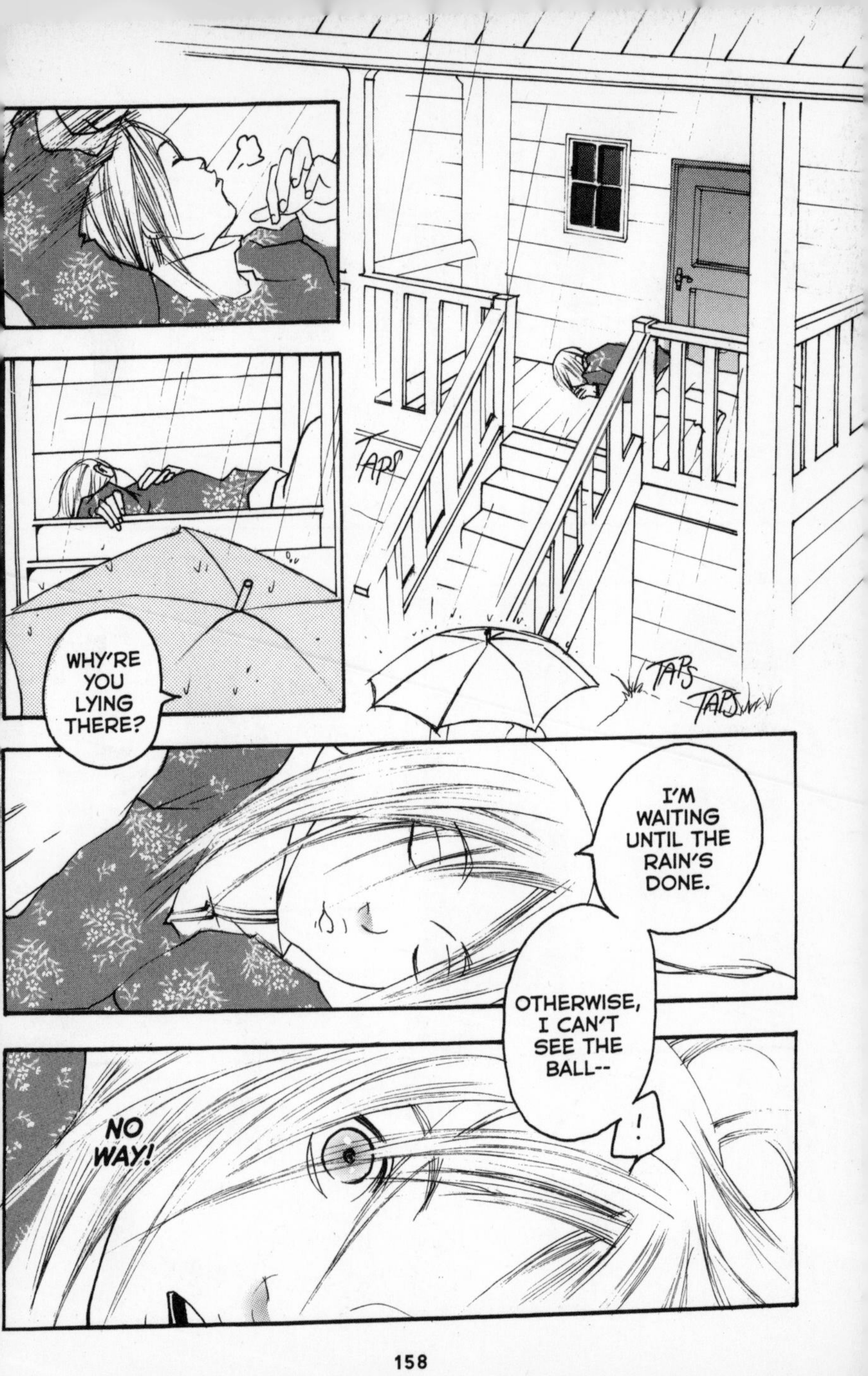
TAPS
TAPS
TAPS
WHY'RE YOU LYING THERE?
I'M WAITING UNTIL THE RAIN'S DONE.
OTHERWISE, I CAN'T SEE THE BALL--
!
NO WAY!

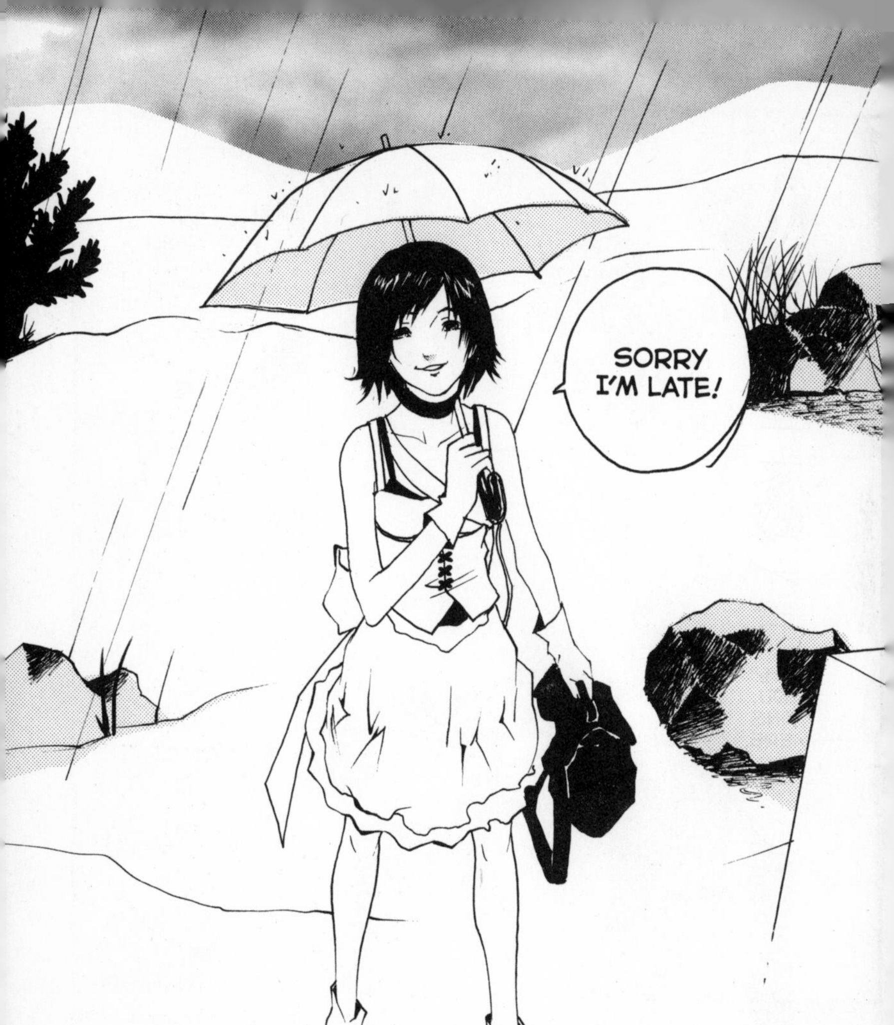
SORRY I'M LATE!
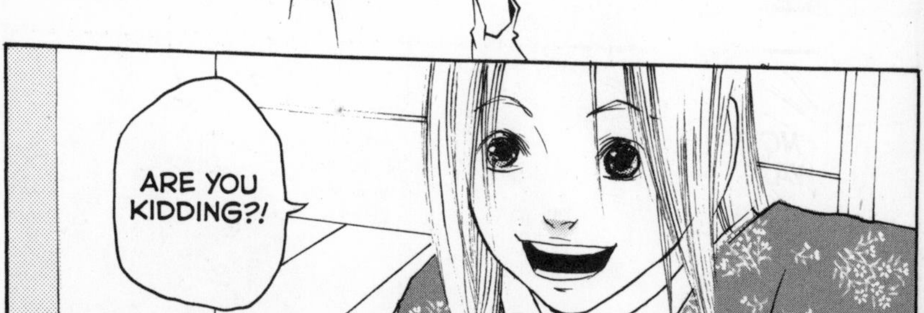
ARE YOU KIDDING?!

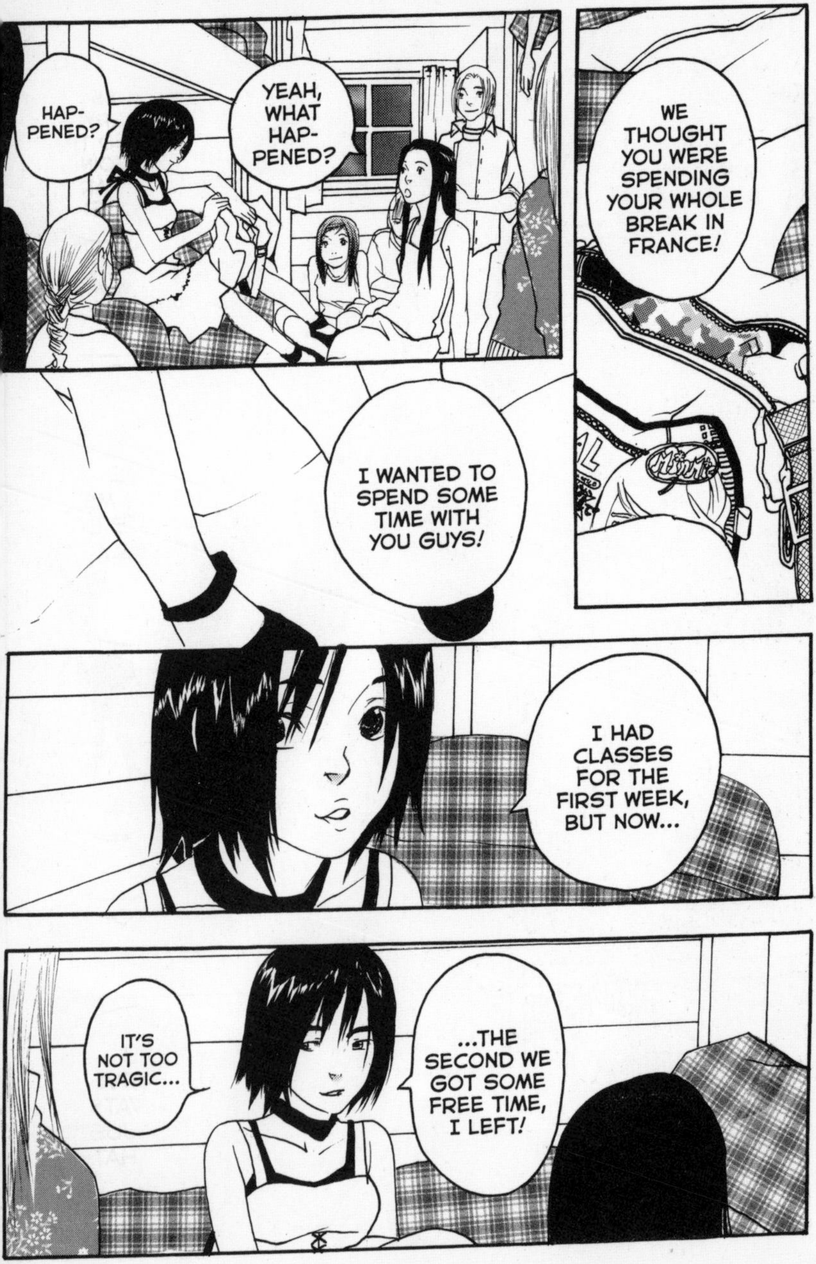

WE THOUGHT YOU WERE SPENDING YOUR WHOLE BREAK IN FRANCE!
YEAH, WHAT HAP-PENED?
HAP-PENED?
I WANTED TO SPEND SOME TIME WITH YOU GUYS!
I HAD CLASSES FOR THE FIRST WEEK, BUT NOW...
...THE SECOND WE GOT SOME FREE TIME, I LEFT!
IT'S NOT TOO TRAGIC...

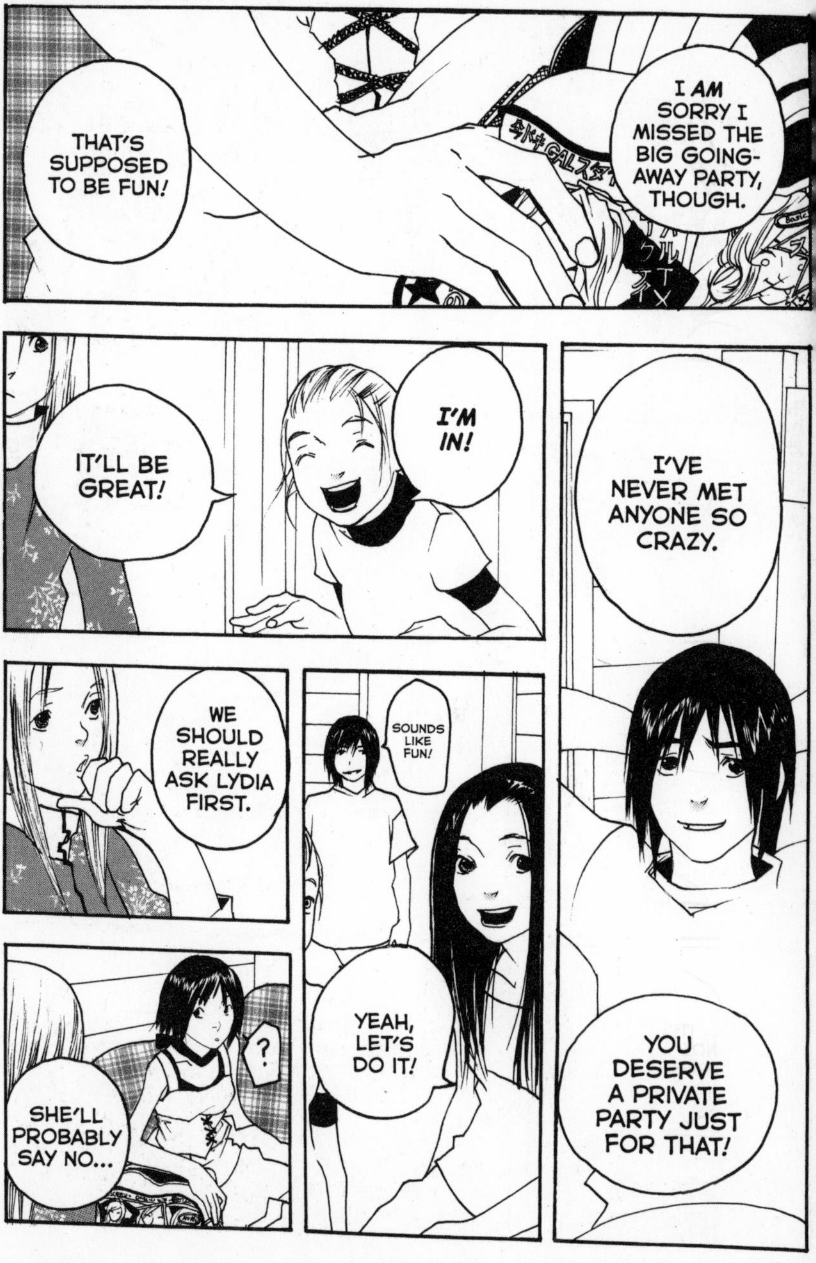
I AM SORRY I MISSED THE BIG GOING-AWAY PARTY, THOUGH.
THAT'S SUPPOSED TO BE FUN!
I'VE NEVER MET ANYONE SO CRAZY.
YOU DESERVE A PRIVATE PARTY JUST FOR THAT!
I'M IN!
IT'LL BE GREAT!
SOUNDS LIKE FUN!
YEAH, LET'S DO IT!
WE SHOULD REALLY ASK LYDIA FIRST.
?
SHE'LL PROBABLY SAY NO...

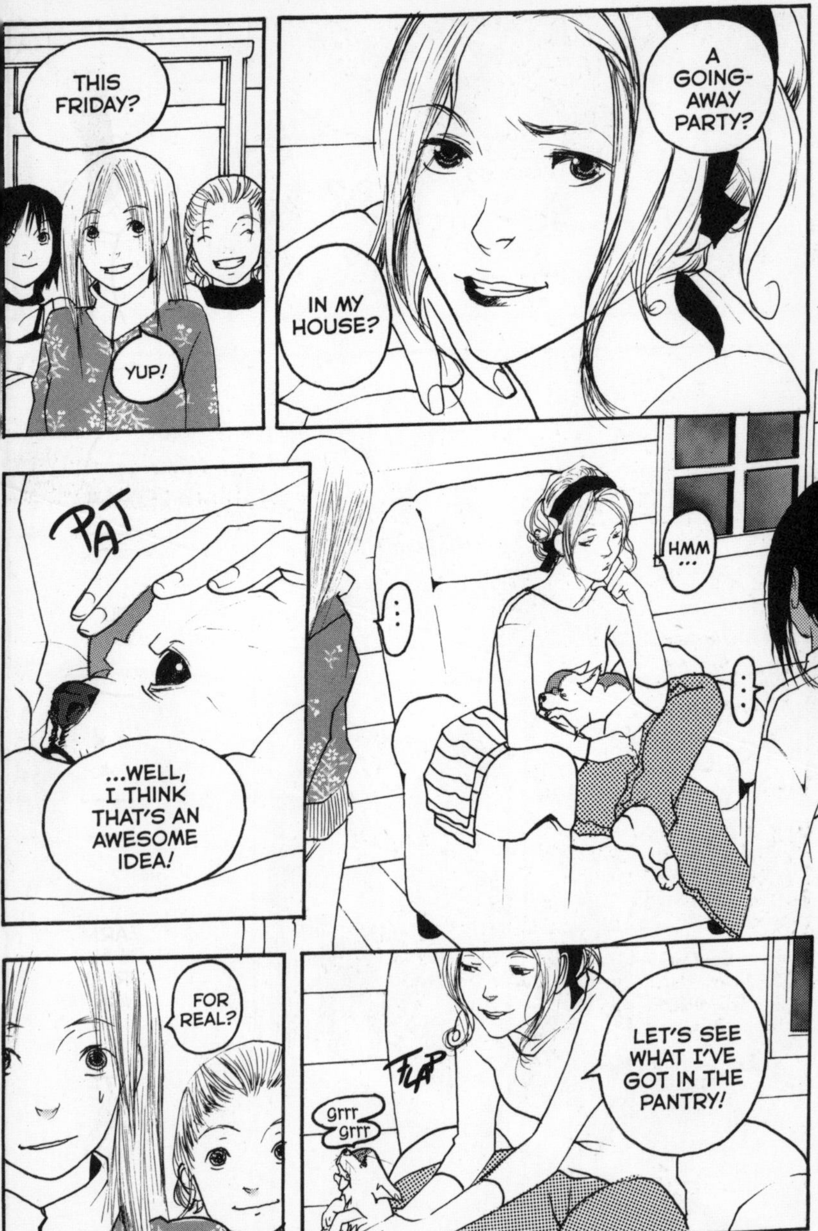
A GOING-AWAY PARTY?
IN MY HOUSE?
THIS FRIDAY?
YUP!
HMM...
...
...
PAT
...WELL, I THINK THAT'S AN AWESOME IDEA!
LET'S SEE WHAT I'VE GOT IN THE PANTRY!
FLAP
grrr grrr
FOR REAL?

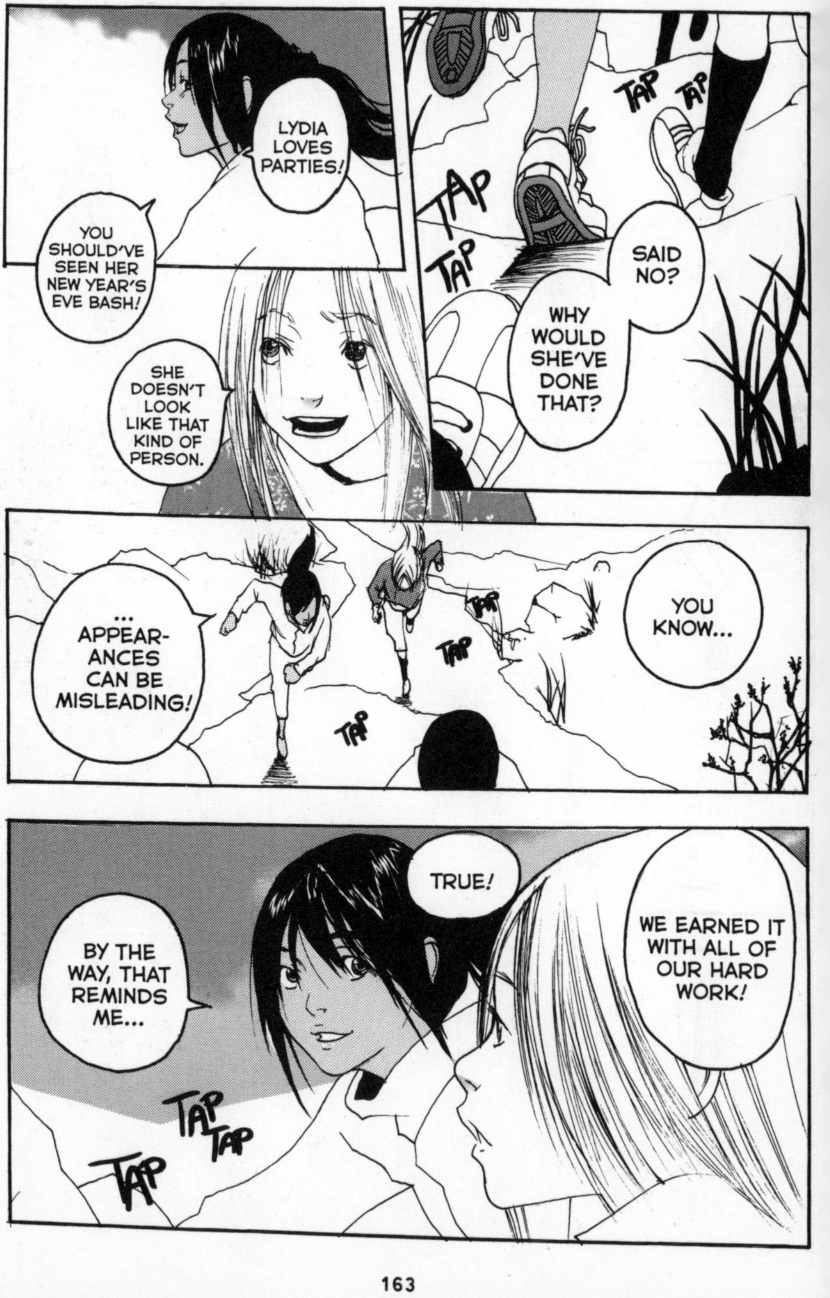
TAP TAP
TAP
TAP
SAID NO?
WHY WOULD SHE'VE DONE THAT?
LYDIA LOVES PARTIES!
YOU SHOULD'VE SEEN HER NEW YEAR'S EVE BASH!
SHE DOESN'T LOOK LIKE THAT KIND OF PERSON.
YOU KNOW...
TAP
TAP
TAP
... APPEARANCES CAN BE MISLEADING!
WE EARNED IT WITH ALL OF OUR HARD WORK!
TRUE!
BY THE WAY, THAT REMINDS ME...
TAP TAP
TAP

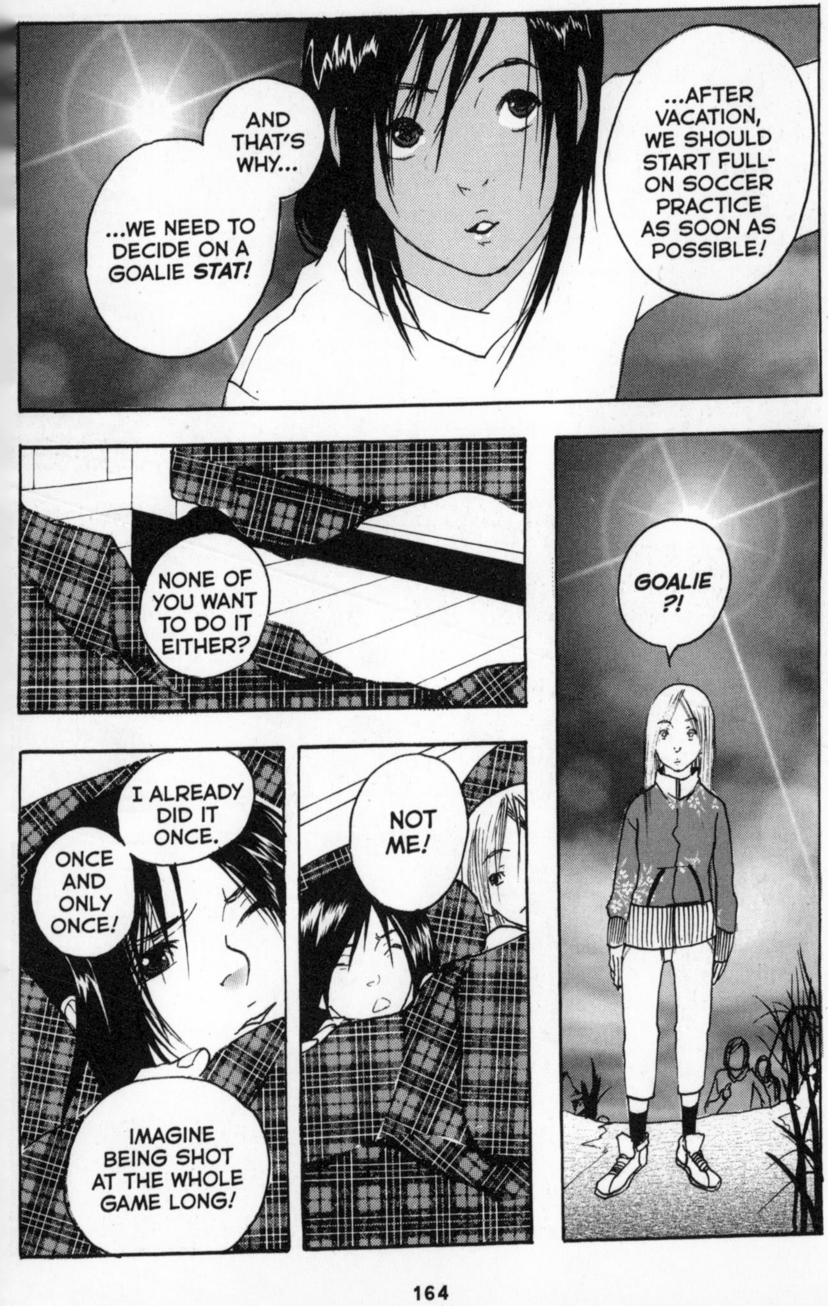
...AFTER VACATION, WE SHOULD START FULL-ON SOCCER PRACTICE AS SOON AS POSSIBLE!
AND THAT'S WHY...
...WE NEED TO DECIDE ON A GOALIE STAT!
GOALIE ?!
NONE OF YOU WANT TO DO IT EITHER?
NOT ME!
I ALREADY DID IT ONCE.
ONCE AND ONLY ONCE!
IMAGINE BEING SHOT AT THE WHOLE GAME LONG!

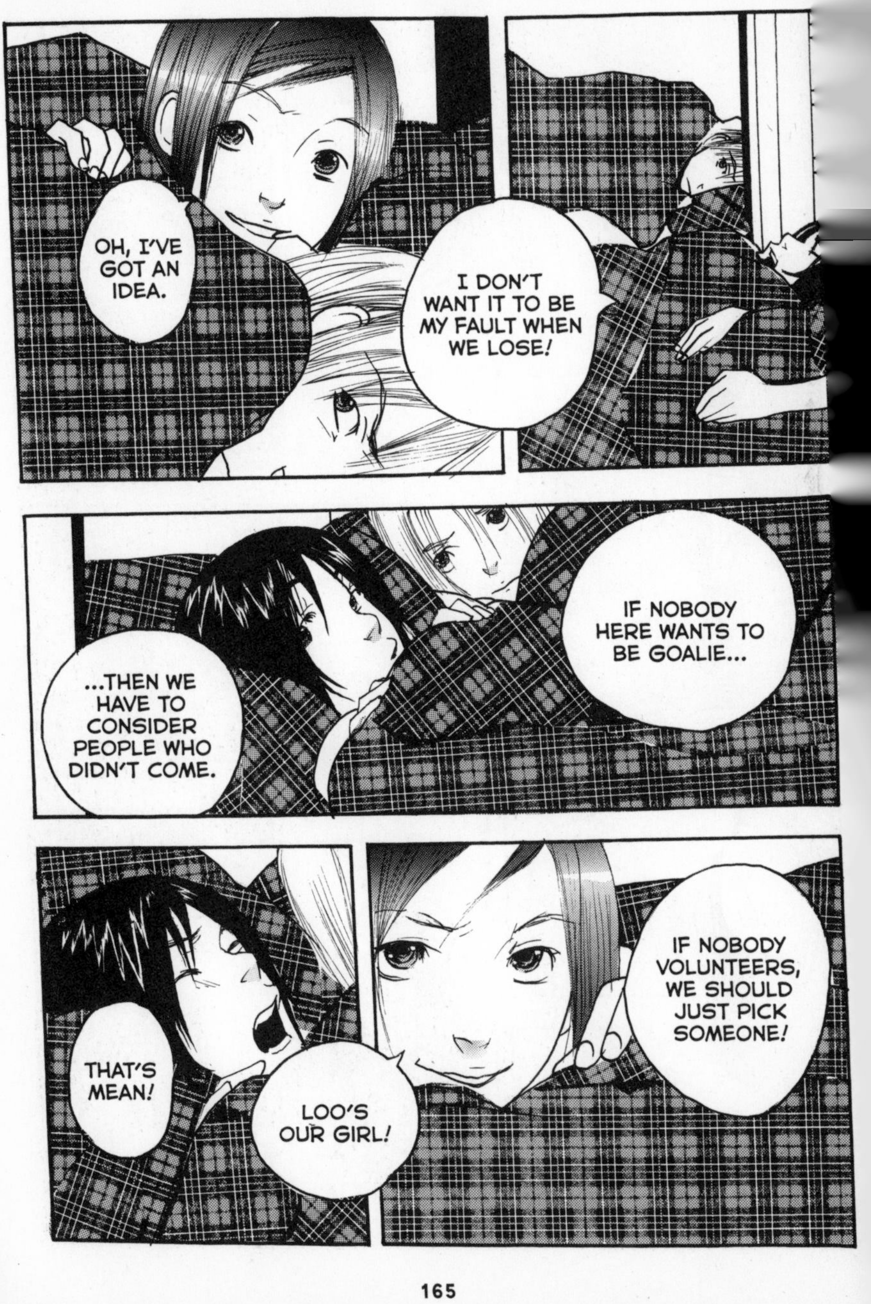
I DON'T WANT IT TO BE MY FAULT WHEN WE LOSE!
OH, I'VE GOT AN IDEA.
IF NOBODY HERE WANTS TO BE GOALIE...
...THEN WE HAVE TO CONSIDER PEOPLE WHO DIDN'T COME.
IF NOBODY VOLUNTEERS, WE SHOULD JUST PICK SOMEONE!
LOO'S OUR GIRL!
THAT'S MEAN!

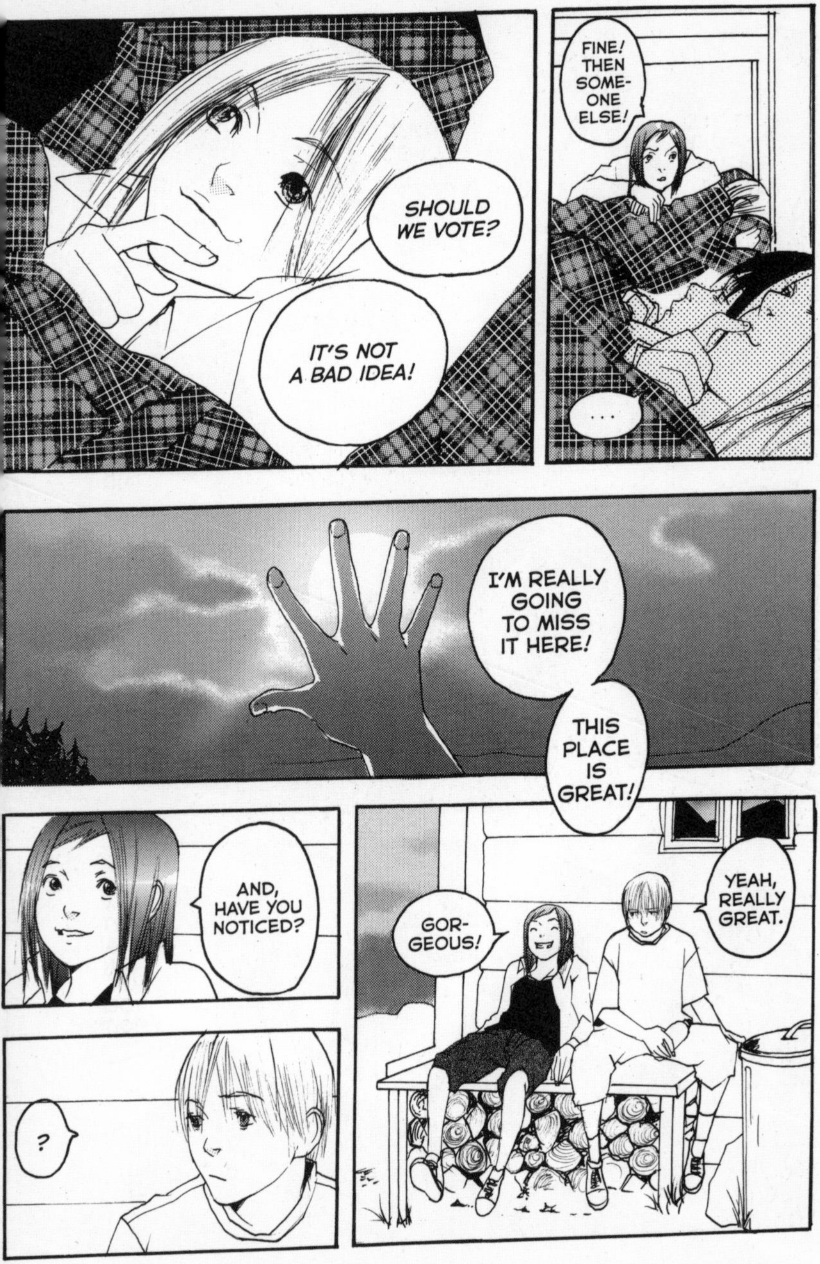
FINE! THEN SOME-ONE ELSE!
. . .
SHOULD WE VOTE?
IT'S NOT A BAD IDEA!
I'M REALLY GOING TO MISS IT HERE!
THIS PLACE IS GREAT!
YEAH, REALLY GREAT.
GOR-GEOUS!
AND, HAVE YOU NOTICED?
?

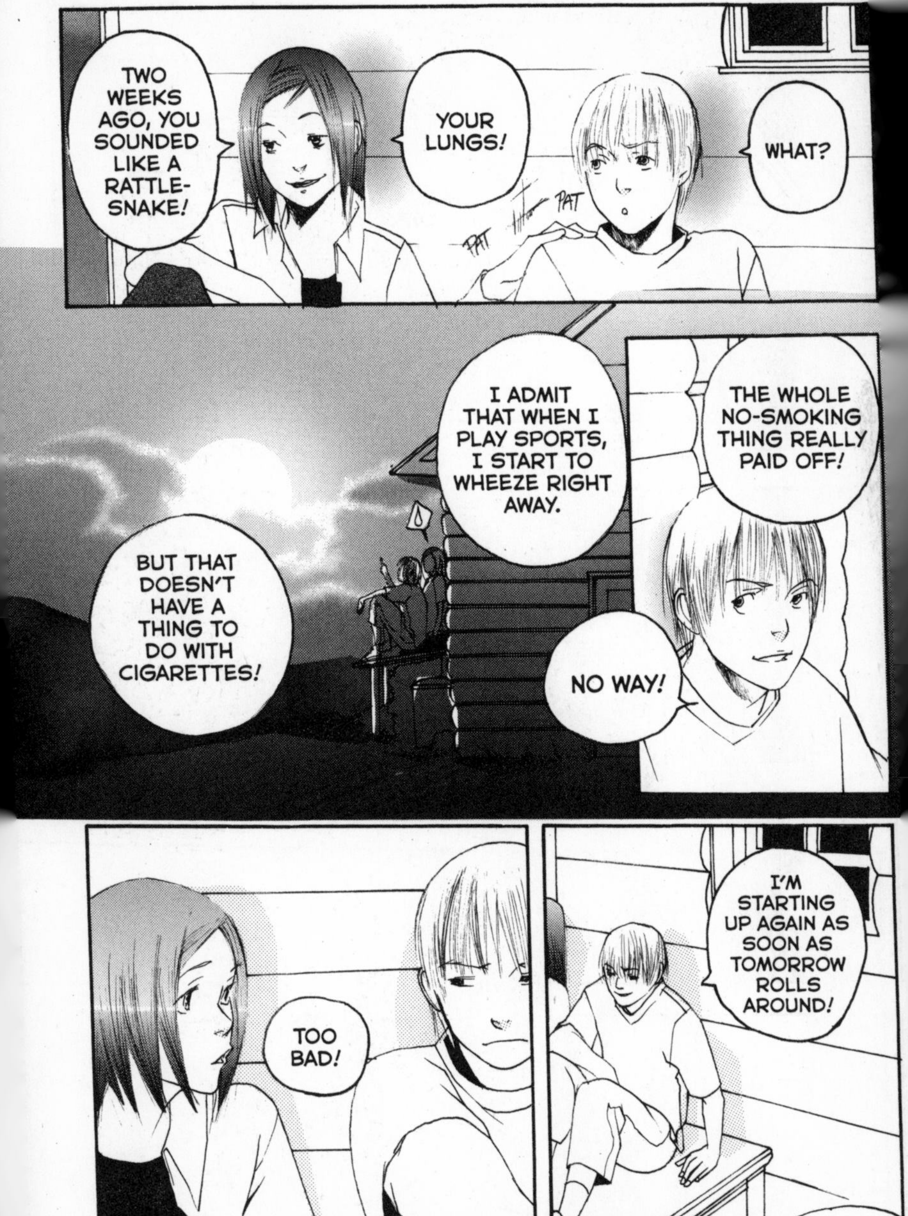
WHAT?
YOUR LUNGS!
PAT
PAT
TWO WEEKS AGO, YOU SOUNDED LIKE A RATTLE-SNAKE!
THE WHOLE NO-SMOKING THING REALLY PAID OFF!
NO WAY!
I ADMIT THAT WHEN I PLAY SPORTS, I START TO WHEEZE RIGHT AWAY.
BUT THAT DOESN'T HAVE A THING TO DO WITH CIGARETTES!
I'M STARTING UP AGAIN AS SOON AS TOMORROW ROLLS AROUND!
TOO BAD!

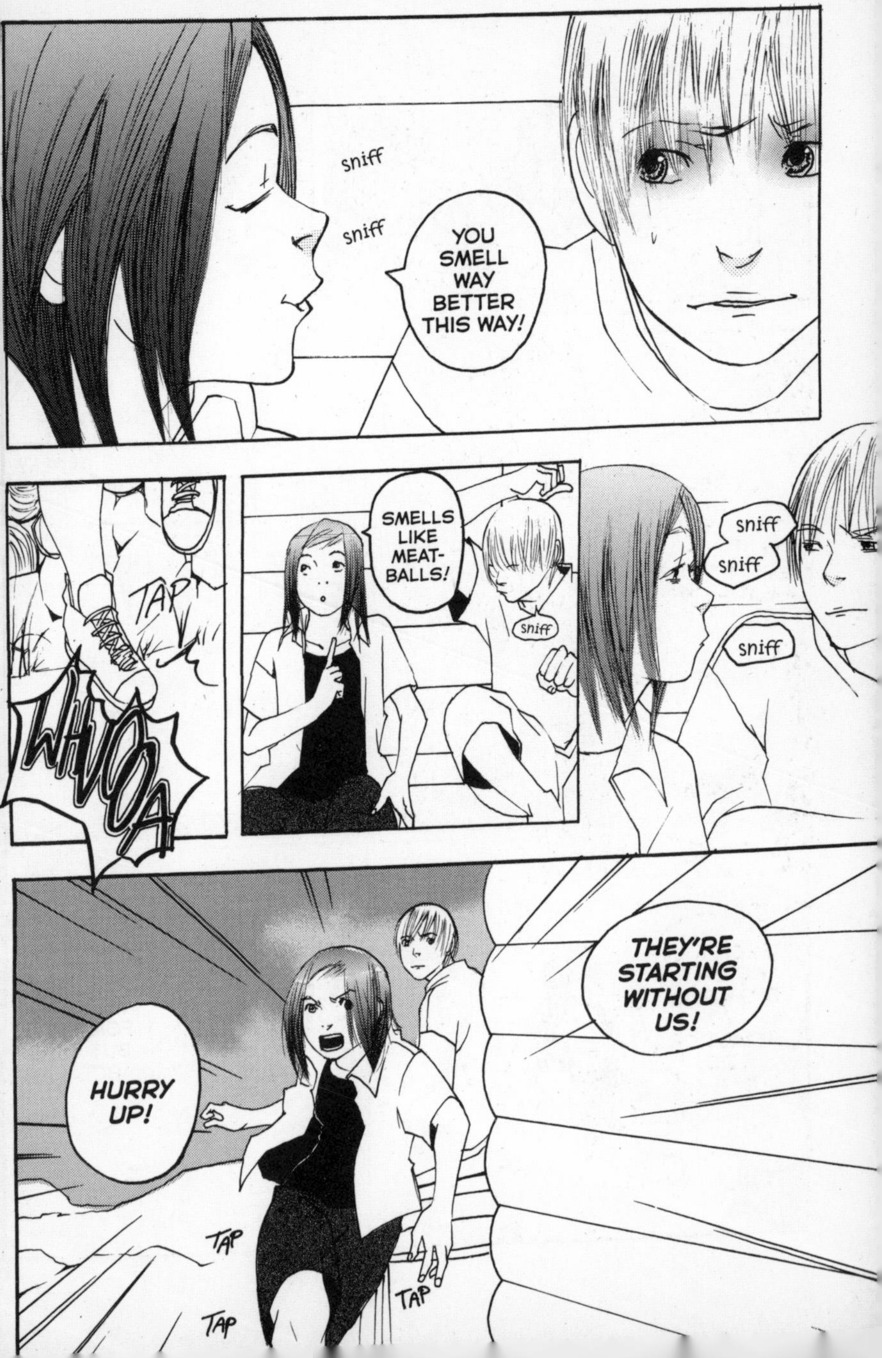
sniff
sniff
YOU SMELL WAY BETTER THIS WAY!
sniff
sniff
sniff
SMELLS LIKE MEAT-BALLS!
sniff
TAP
WHOOA!
THEY'RE STARTING WITHOUT US!
HURRY UP!
TAP
TAP
TAP

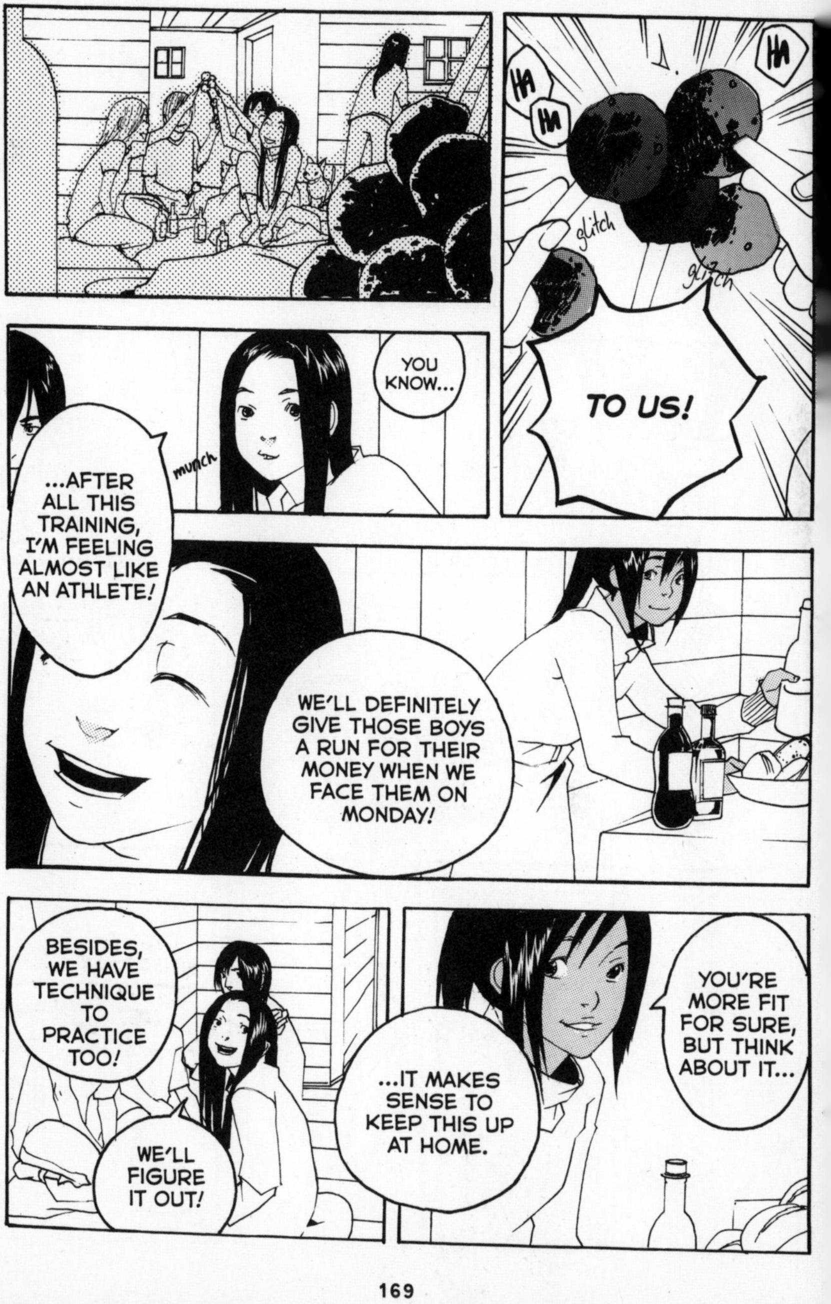
HA
HA
HA
glitch
glitch
TO US!
YOU KNOW...
munch
...AFTER ALL THIS TRAINING, I'M FEELING ALMOST LIKE AN ATHLETE!
WE'LL DEFINITELY GIVE THOSE BOYS A RUN FOR THEIR MONEY WHEN WE FACE THEM ON MONDAY!
YOU'RE MORE FIT FOR SURE, BUT THINK ABOUT IT...
...IT MAKES SENSE TO KEEP THIS UP AT HOME.
BESIDES, WE HAVE TECHNIQUE TO PRACTICE TOO!
WE'LL FIGURE IT OUT!

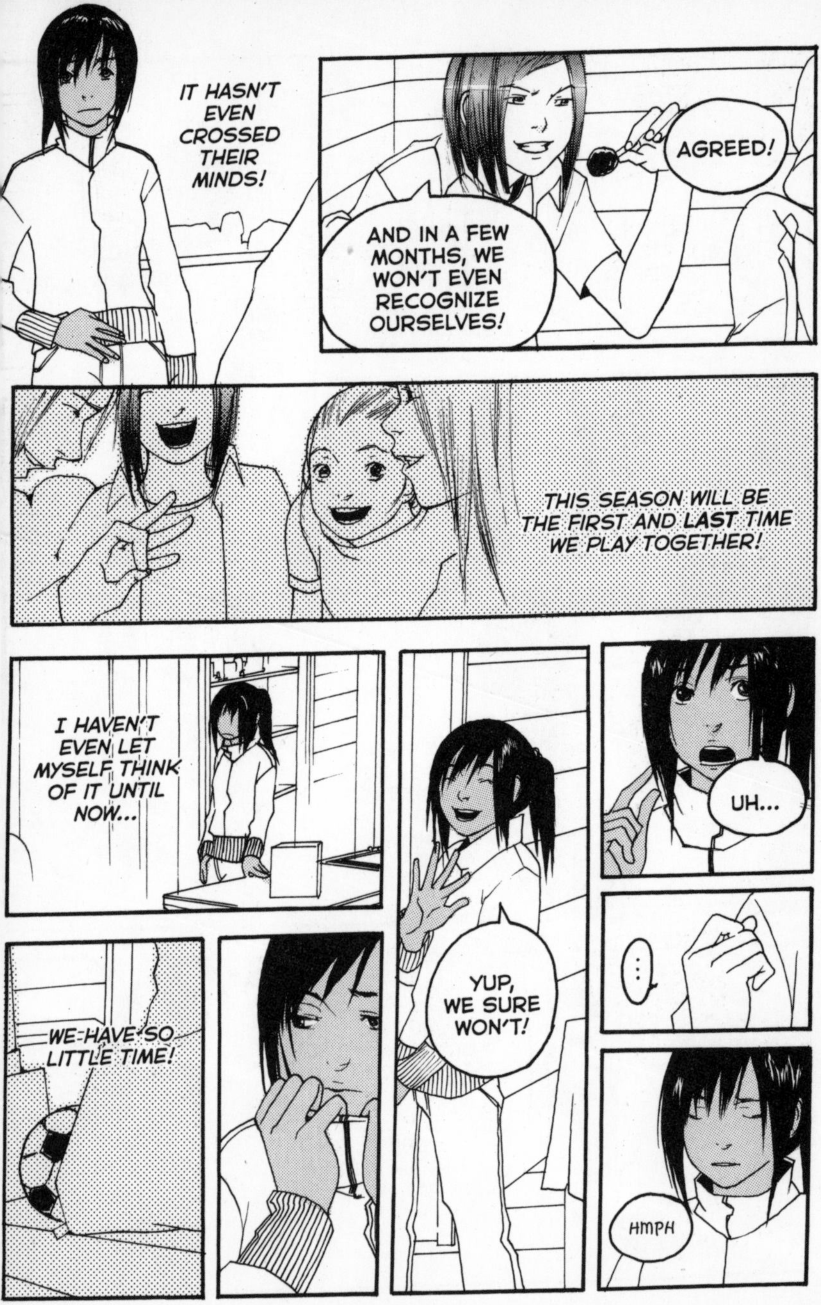
AGREED!
AND IN A FEW MONTHS, WE WON'T EVEN RECOGNIZE OURSELVES!
IT HASN'T EVEN CROSSED THEIR MINDS!
THIS SEASON WILL BE THE FIRST AND LAST TIME WE PLAY TOGETHER!
UH...
...
HMPH
YUP, WE SURE WON'T!
I HAVEN'T EVEN LET MYSELF THINK OF IT UNTIL NOW...
WE HAVE SO LITTLE TIME!

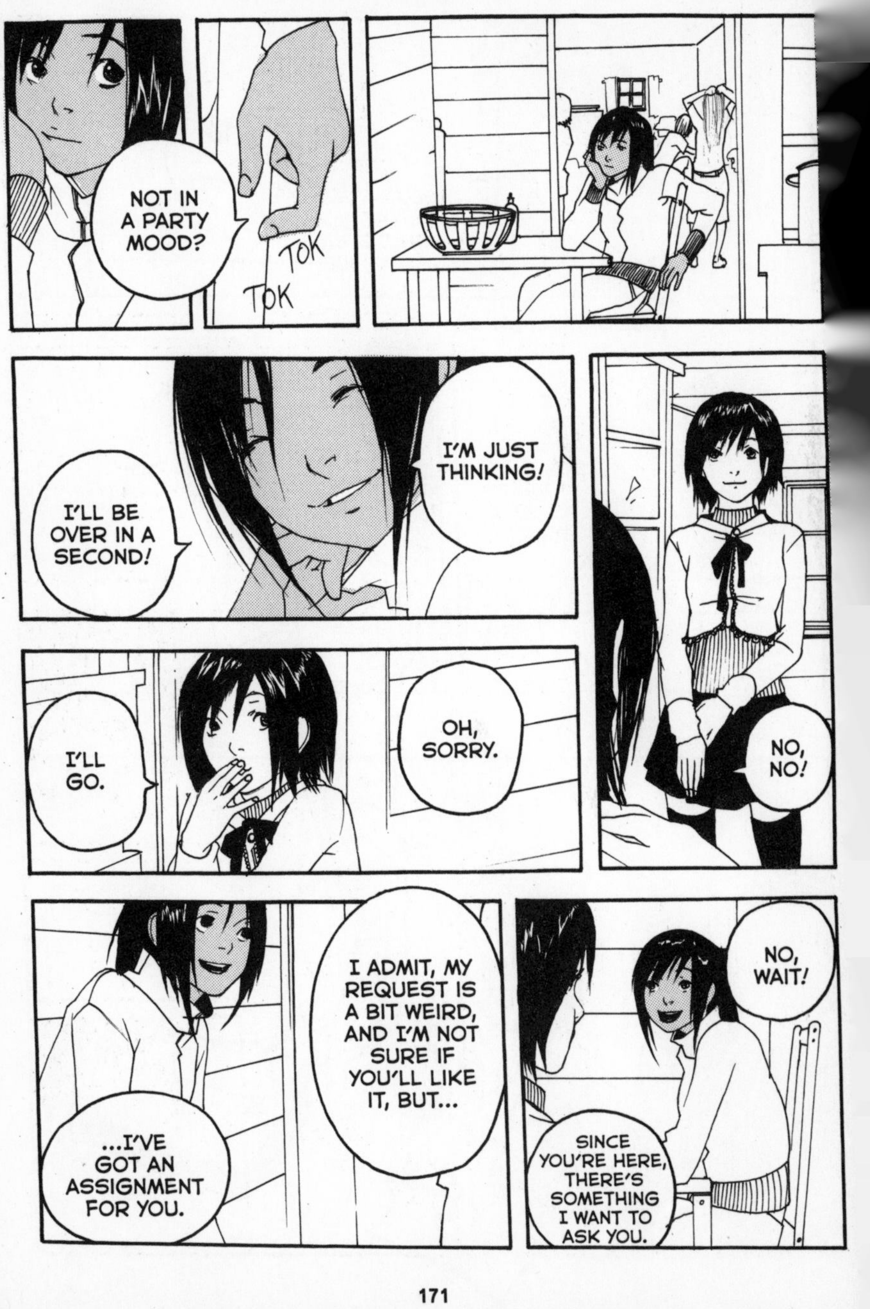
TOK
TOK
NOT IN A PARTY MOOD?
NO, NO!
I'M JUST THINKING!
I'LL BE OVER IN A SECOND!
OH, SORRY.
I'LL GO.
NO, WAIT!
SINCE YOU'RE HERE, THERE'S SOMETHING I WANT TO ASK YOU.
I ADMIT, MY REQUEST IS A BIT WEIRD, AND I'M NOT SURE IF YOU'LL LIKE IT, BUT...
...I'VE GOT AN ASSIGNMENT FOR YOU.

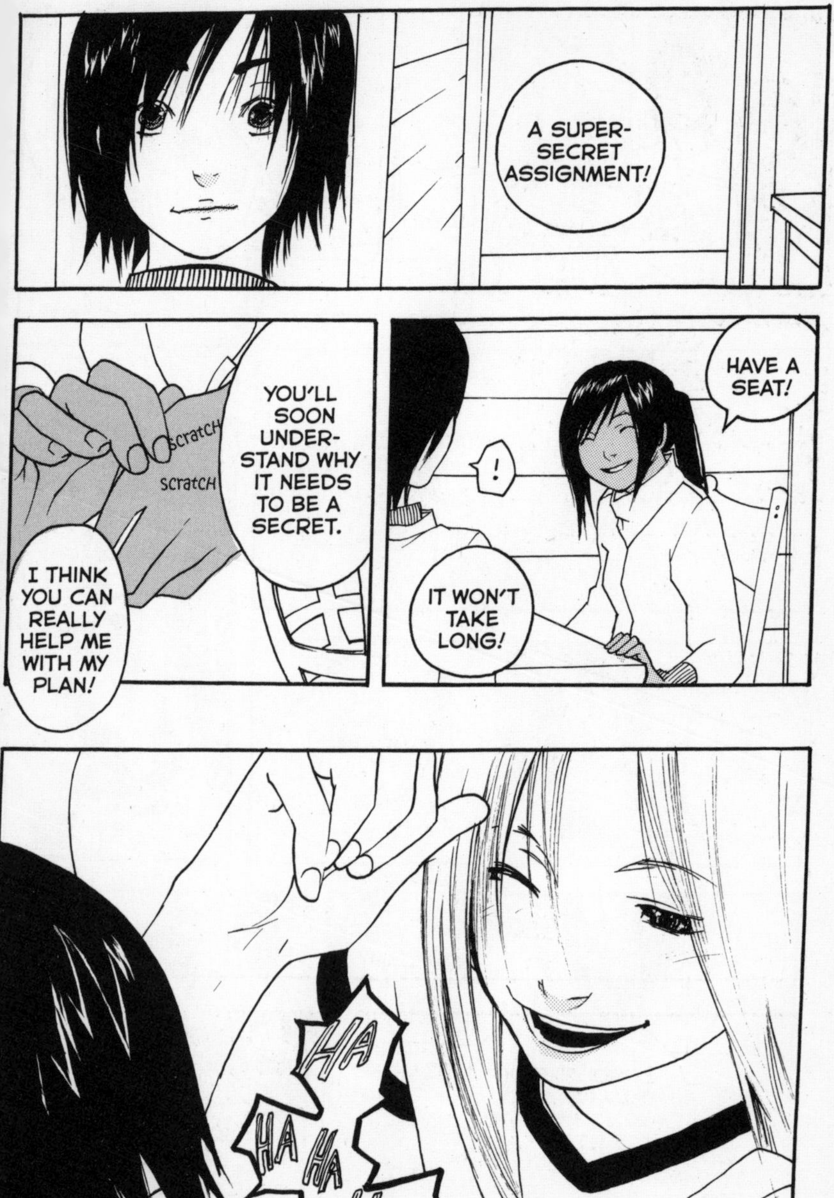
A SUPER-SECRET ASSIGNMENT!
HAVE A SEAT!
!
IT WON'T TAKE LONG!
YOU'LL SOON UNDERSTAND WHY IT NEEDS TO BE A SECRET.
SCRATCH
SCRATCH
I THINK YOU CAN REALLY HELP ME WITH MY PLAN!
HA HA HA HA HA

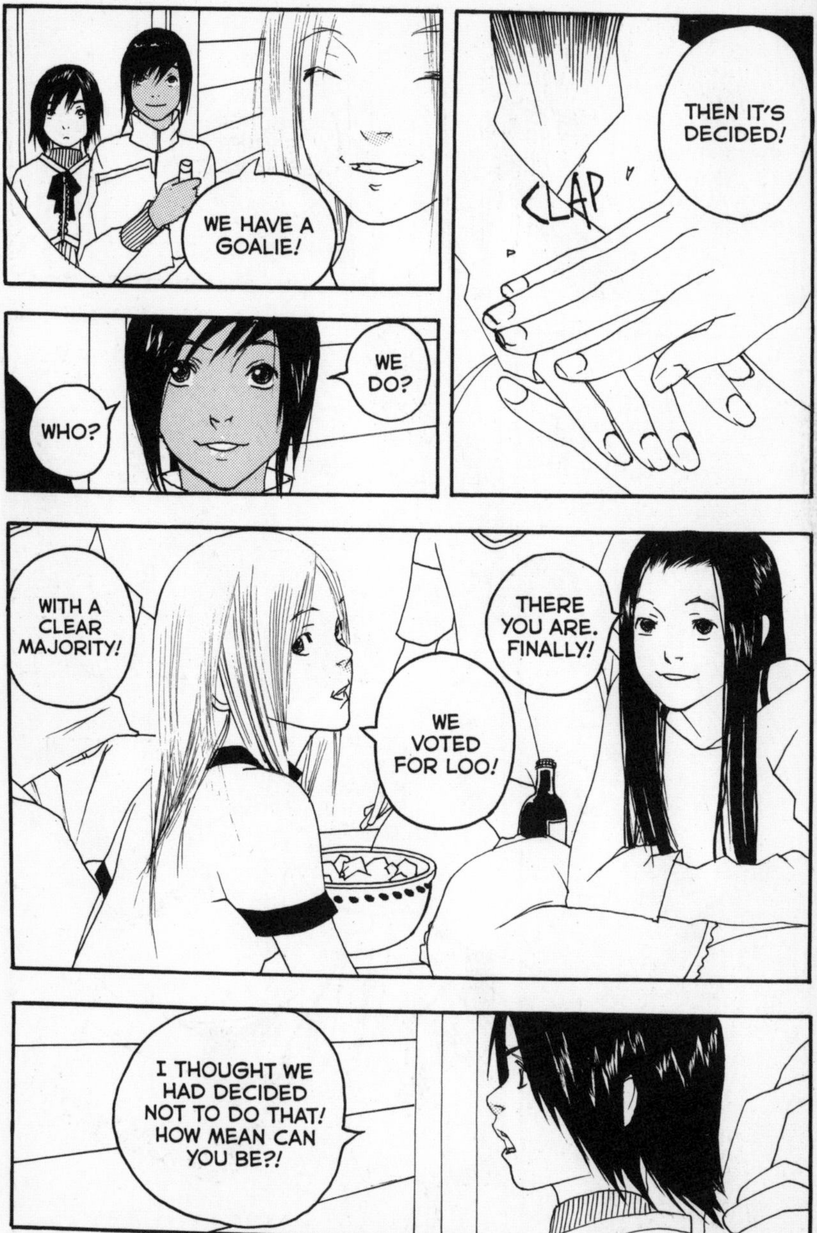
THEN IT'S DECIDED!
CLAP
WE HAVE A GOALIE!
WE DO?
WHO?
THERE YOU ARE. FINALLY!
WE VOTED FOR LOO!
WITH A CLEAR MAJORITY!
I THOUGHT WE HAD DECIDED NOT TO DO THAT! HOW MEAN CAN YOU BE?!

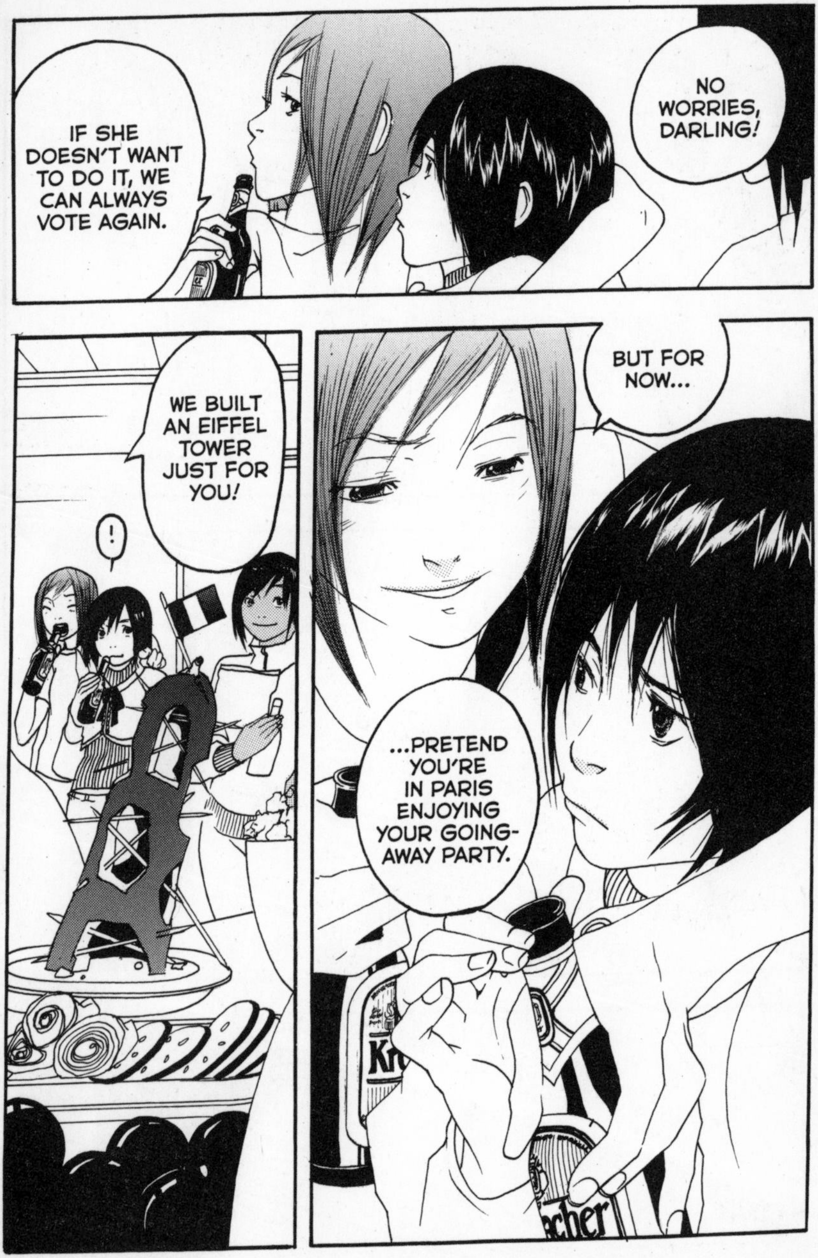
NO WORRIES, DARLING!
IF SHE DOESN'T WANT TO DO IT, WE CAN ALWAYS VOTE AGAIN.
BUT FOR NOW...
...PRETEND YOU'RE IN PARIS ENJOYING YOUR GOING-AWAY PARTY.
WE BUILT AN EIFFEL TOWER JUST FOR YOU!
!

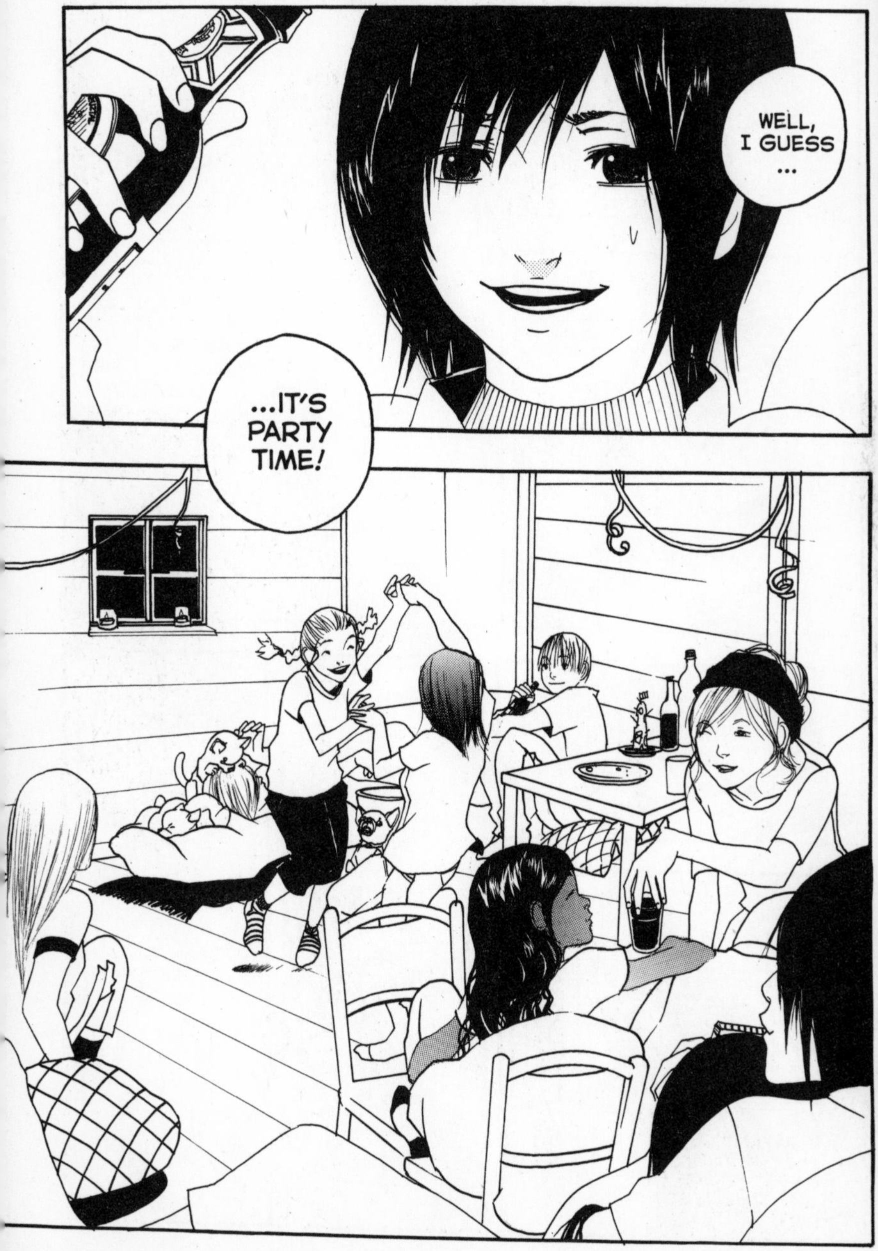
WELL, I GUESS ...
...IT'S PARTY TIME!

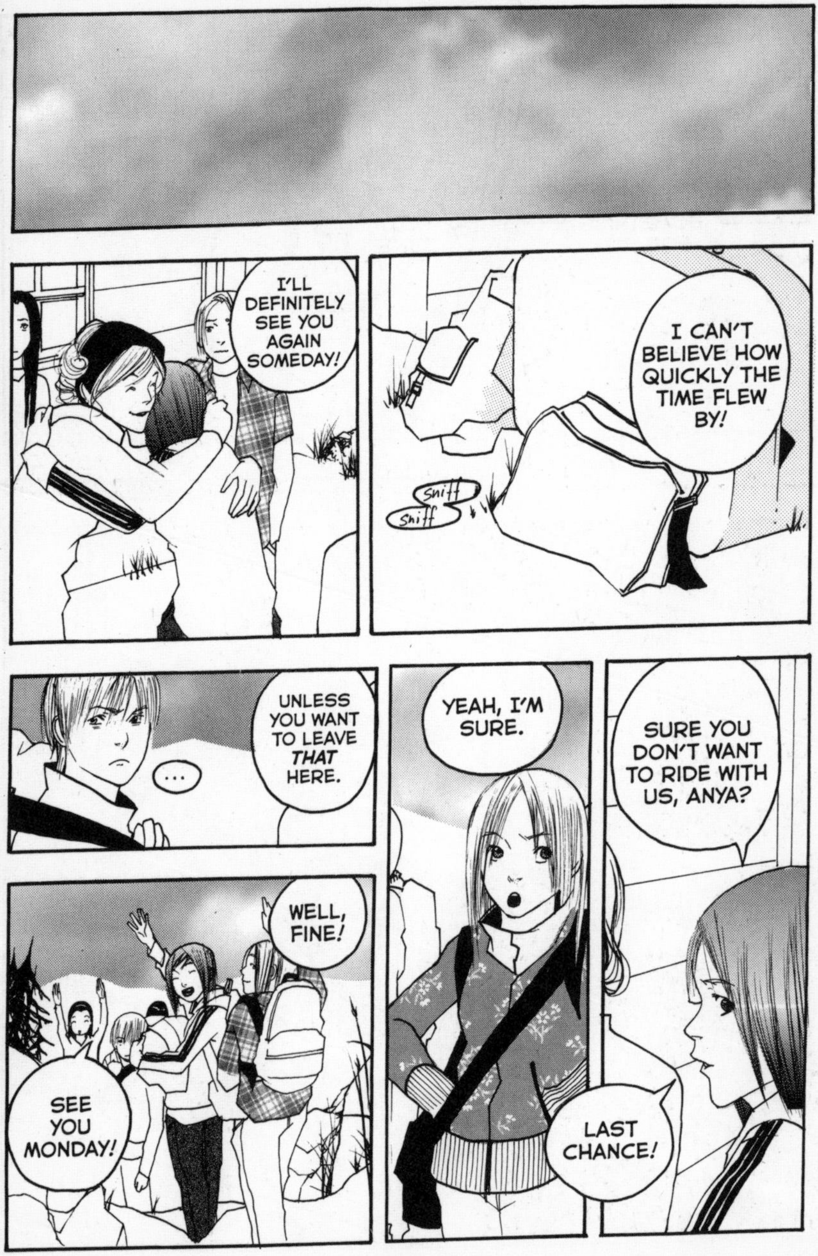
I CAN'T BELIEVE HOW QUICKLY THE TIME FLEW BY!
Sniff
Sniff
I'LL DEFINITELY SEE YOU AGAIN SOMEDAY!
SURE YOU DON'T WANT TO RIDE WITH US, ANYA?
LAST CHANCE!
YEAH, I'M SURE.
UNLESS YOU WANT TO LEAVE *THAT* HERE.
...
WELL, FINE!
SEE YOU MONDAY!

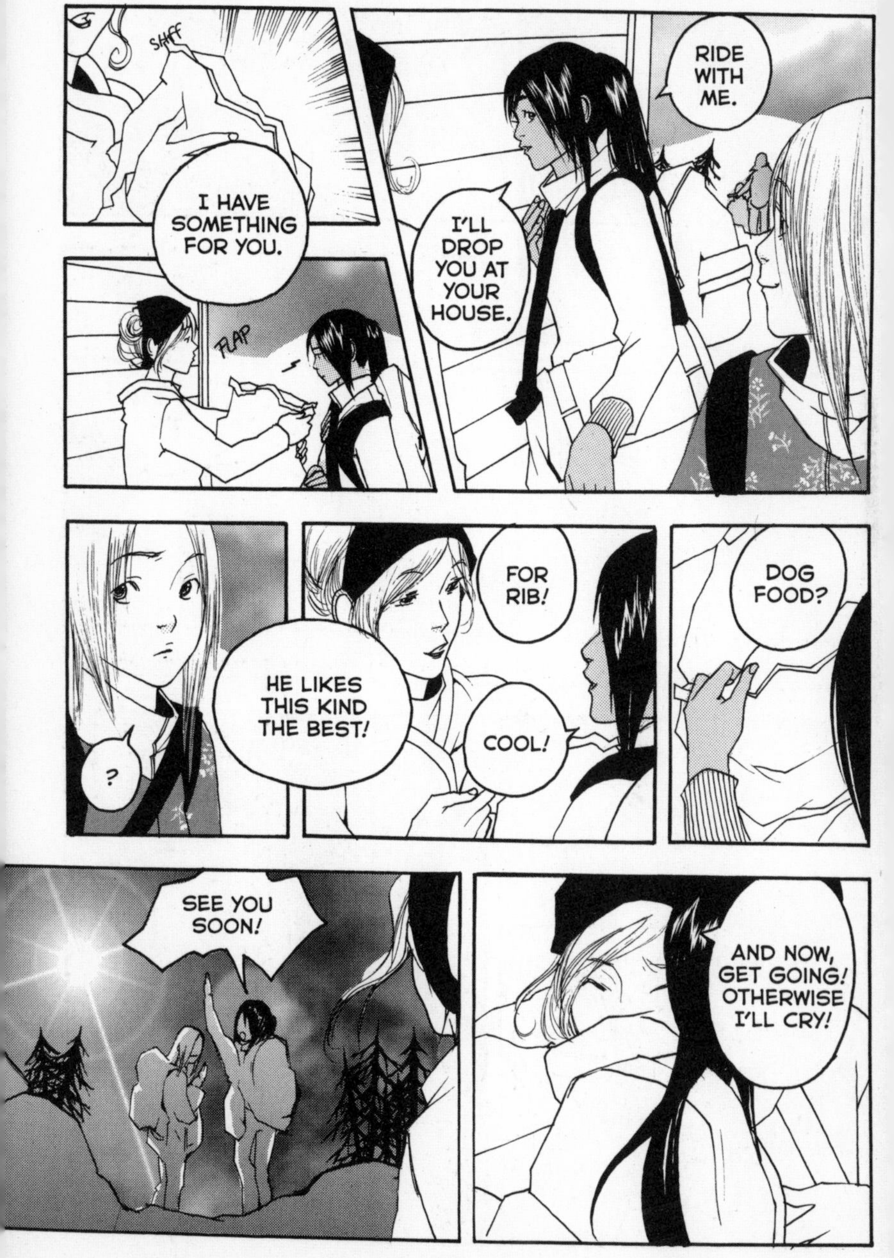
RIDE WITH ME.
I'LL DROP YOU AT YOUR HOUSE.
SHFF
I HAVE SOMETHING FOR YOU.
FLAP
DOG FOOD?
FOR RIB!
HE LIKES THIS KIND THE BEST!
COOL!
?
AND NOW, GET GOING! OTHERWISE I'LL CRY!
SEE YOU SOON!

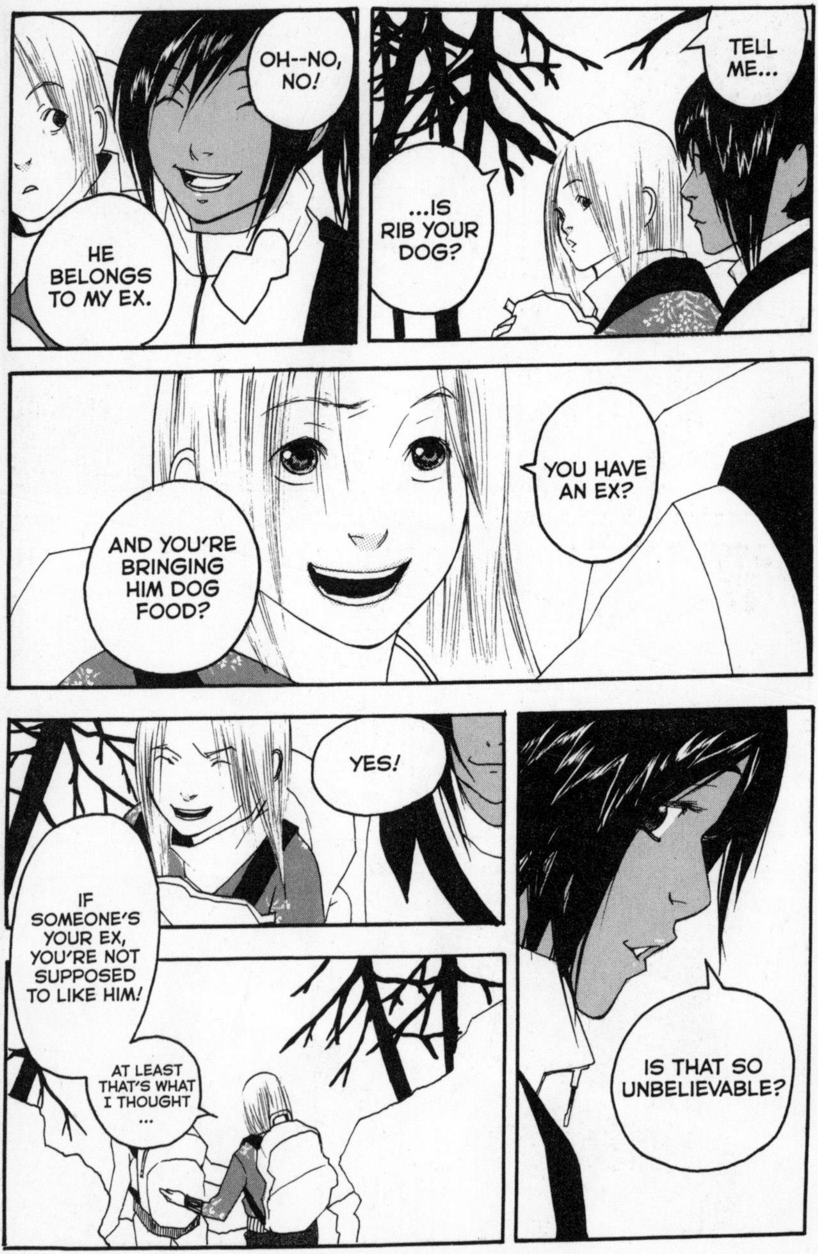
TELL ME...
...IS RIB YOUR DOG?
OH--NO, NO!
HE BELONGS TO MY EX.
YOU HAVE AN EX?
AND YOU'RE BRINGING HIM DOG FOOD?
IS THAT SO UNBELIEVABLE?
YES!
IF SOMEONE'S YOUR EX, YOU'RE NOT SUPPOSED TO LIKE HIM!
AT LEAST THAT'S WHAT I THOUGHT ...

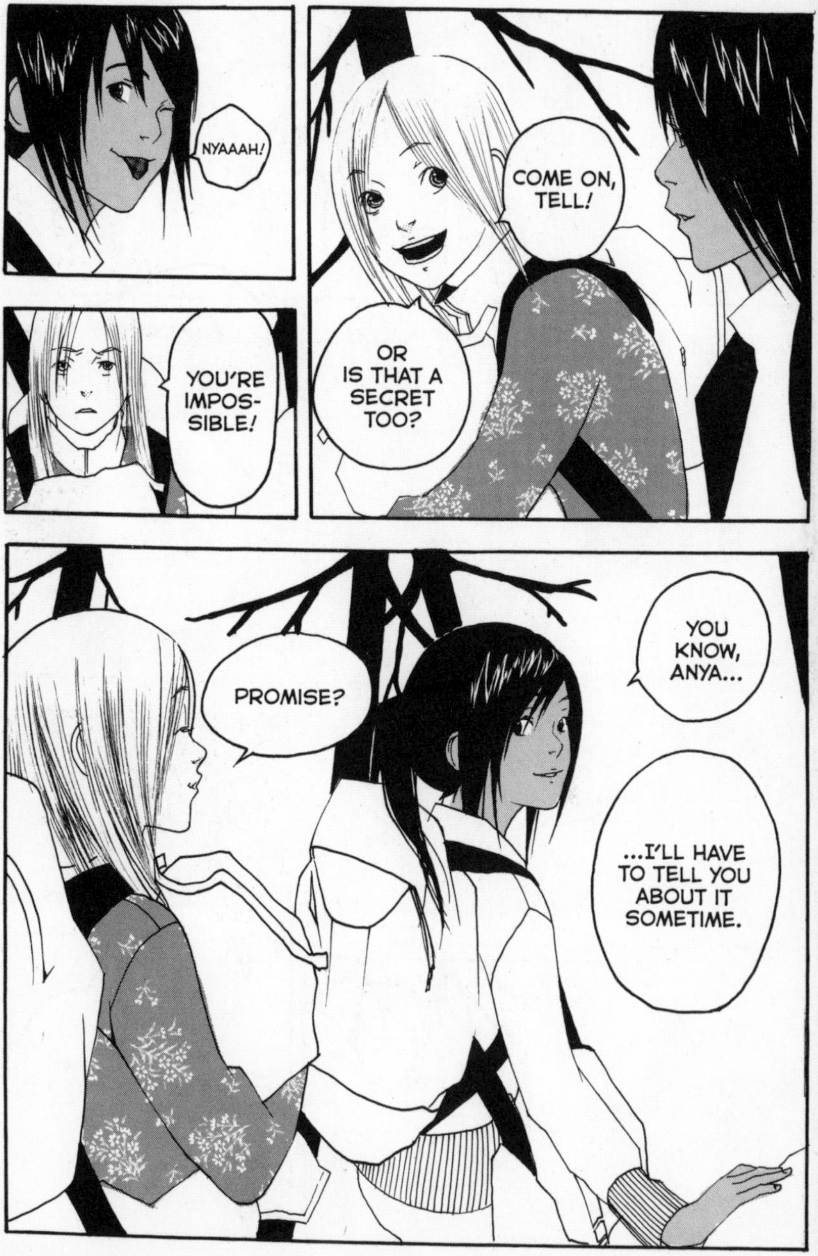
COME ON, TELL!
OR IS THAT A SECRET TOO?
NYAAAH!
YOU'RE IMPOS-SIBLE!
YOU KNOW, ANYA...
...I'LL HAVE TO TELL YOU ABOUT IT SOMETIME.
PROMISE?

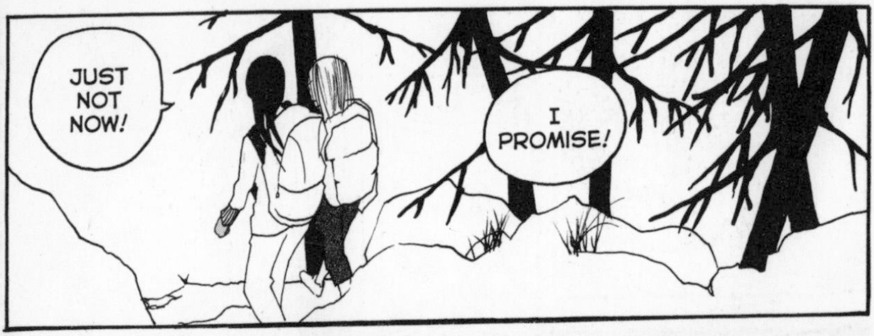
JUST NOT NOW!
I PROMISE!

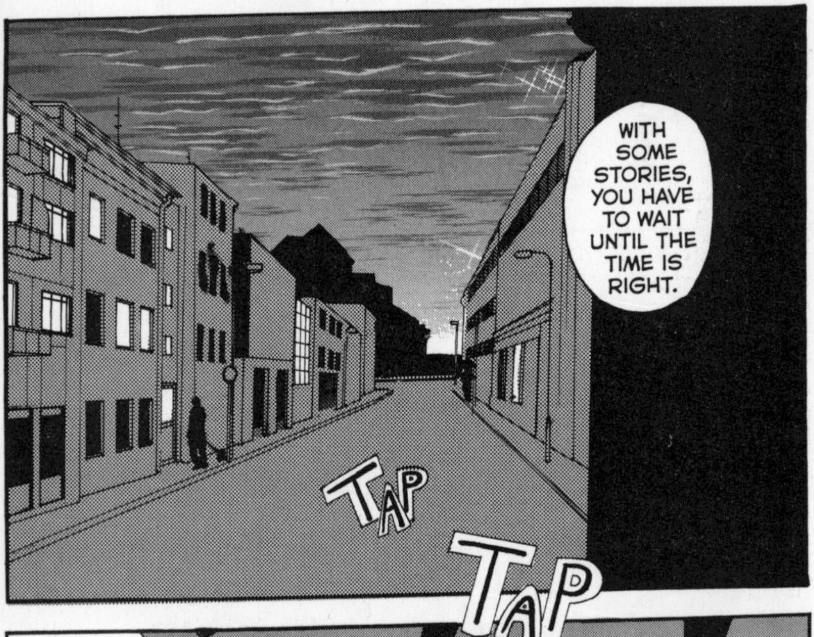
WITH SOME STORIES, YOU HAVE TO WAIT UNTIL THE TIME IS RIGHT.
TAP
TAP

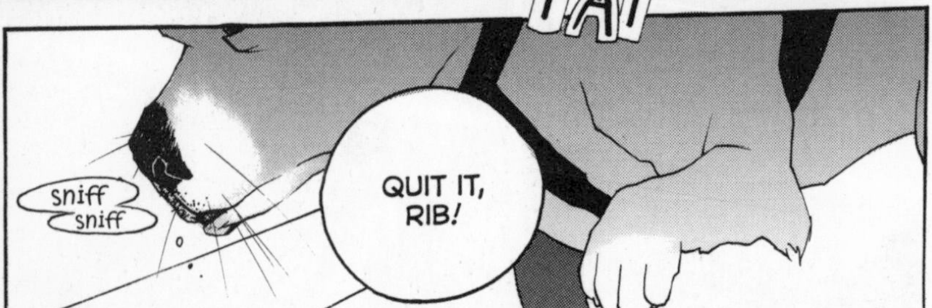
QUIT IT, RIB!
sniff sniff

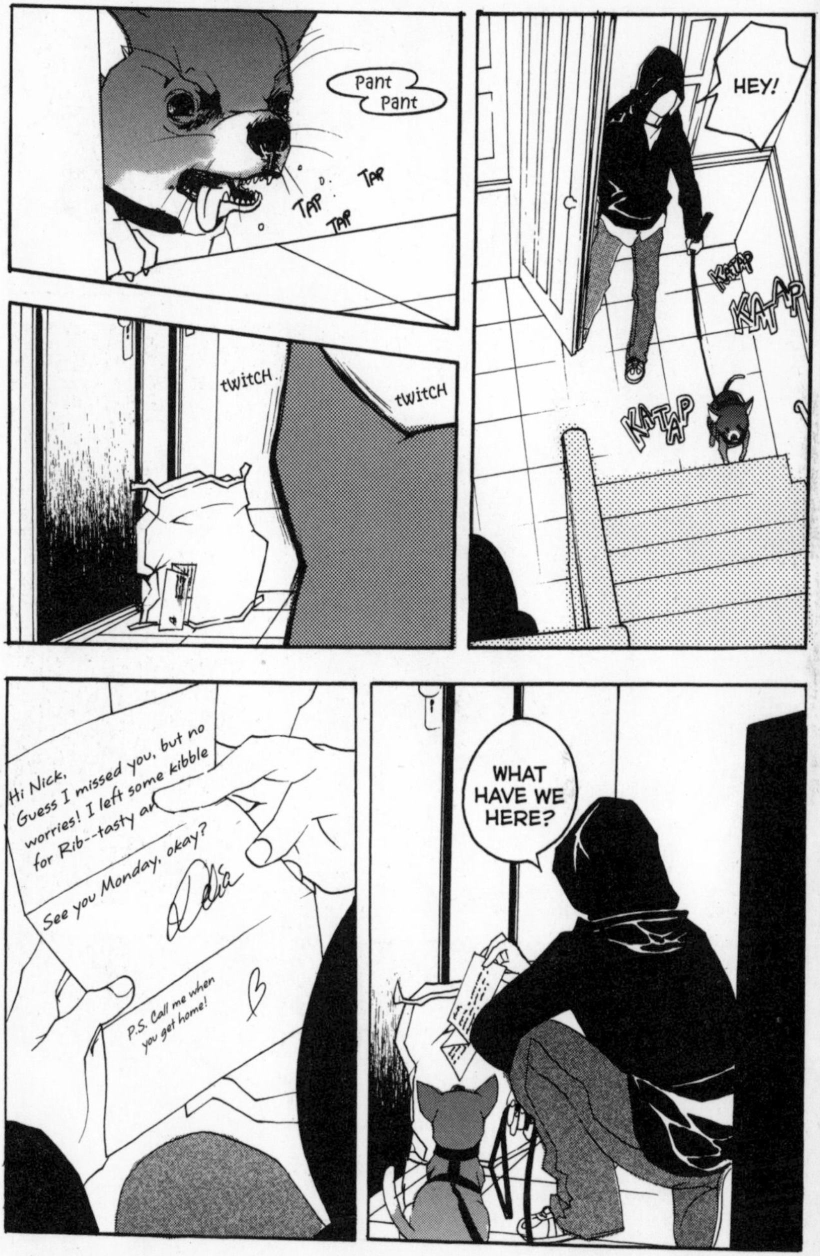
HEY!
KATAP
KATAP
KATAP
Pant
Pant
TAP
TAP
TAP
TWITCH
TWITCH
WHAT HAVE WE HERE?
Hi Nick,
Guess I missed you, but no
worries! I left some kibble
for Rib--tasty
See you Monday, okay?
P.S. Call me when
you get home!

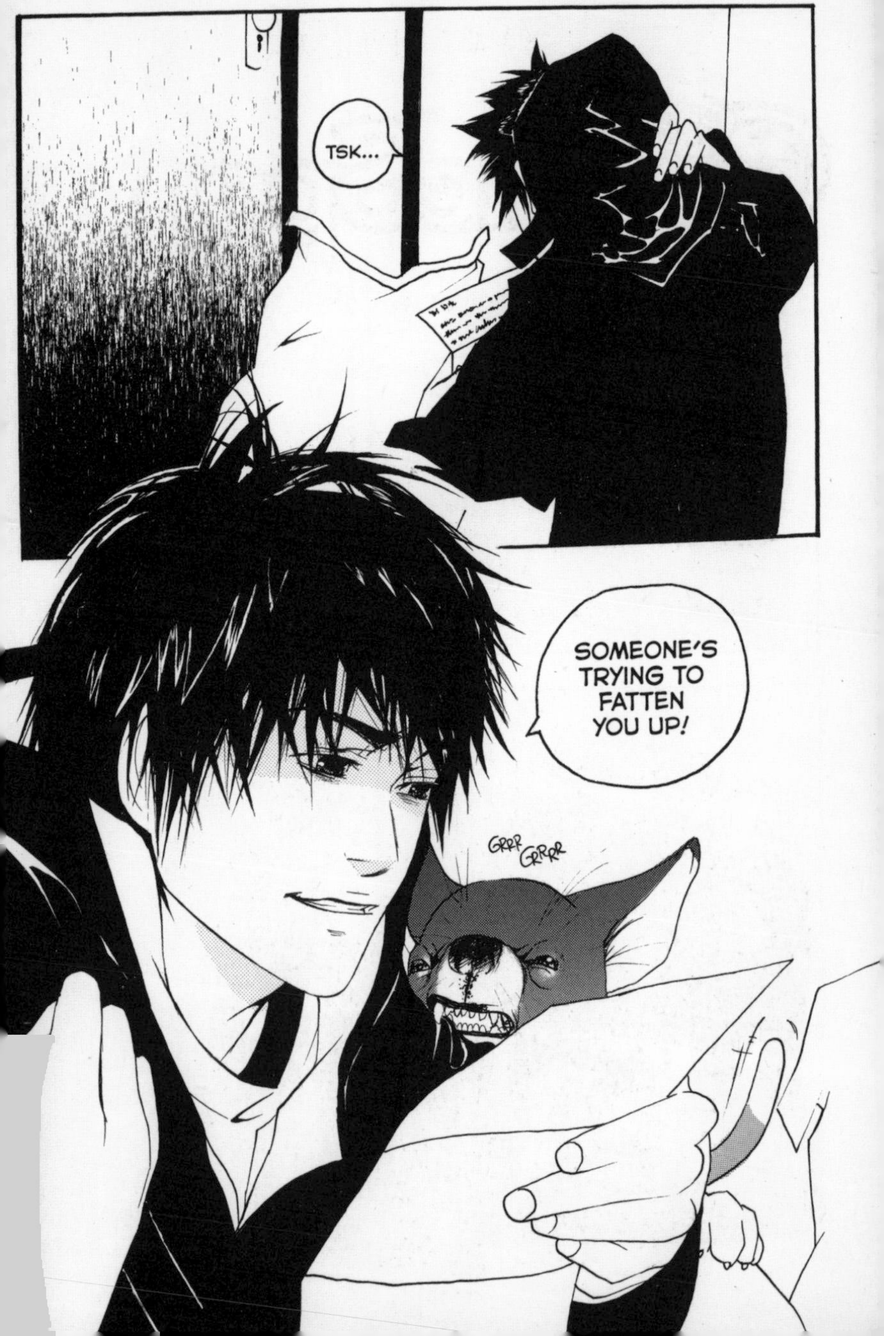
TSK...
SOMEONE'S TRYING TO FATTEN YOU UP!
GRRR GRRRR

NEXT TIME IN

GothicSports

The team's mountain retreat has shaped up more than their soccer skills—they've all gotten to know each other a little better. Now everyone is excited to bring their success to school for all to see.

But for some, soccer camp brought up more questions than it answered. Will Delia's past catch up with her? Will Anya ever come to terms with Leon? And what challenges await the team on and off the field now that vacation's over?

Find out this—and so much more—in Volume 4!

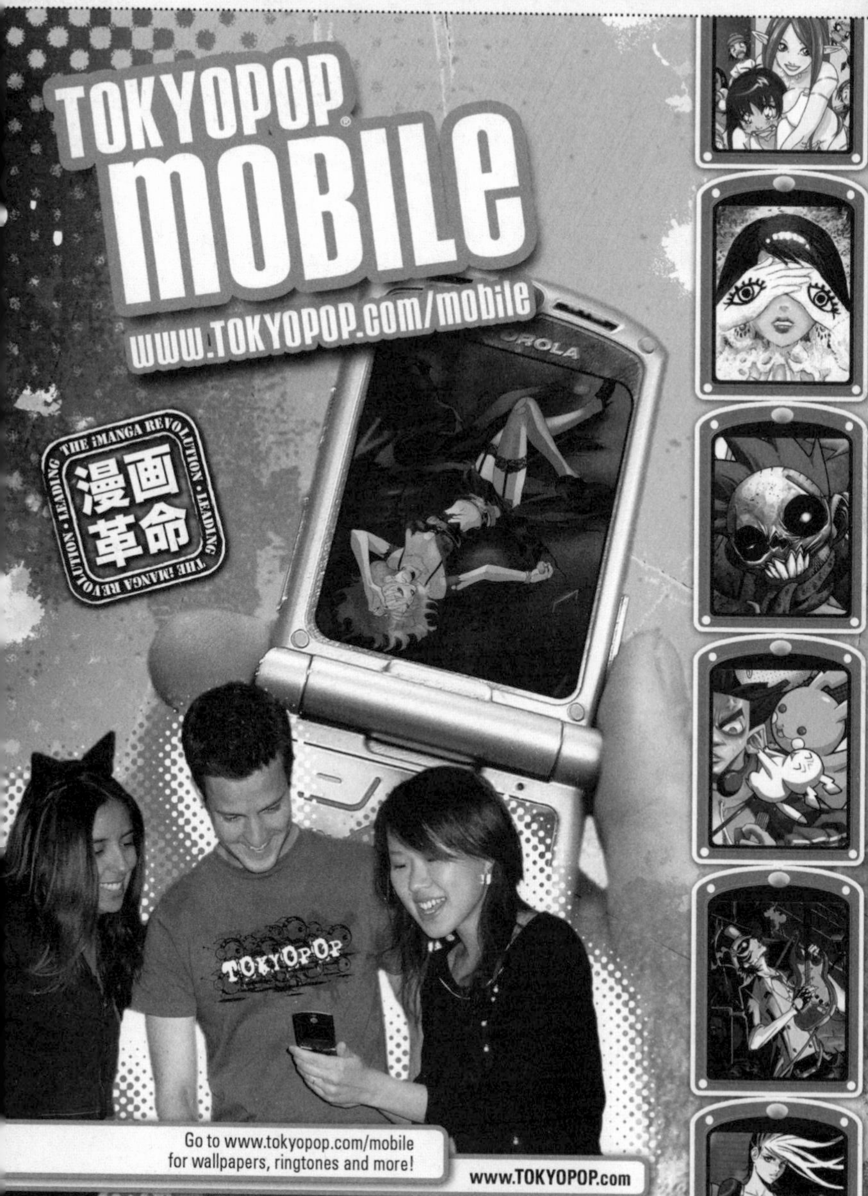
TOKYOPOP
MOBILE
www.TOKYOPOP.com/mobile
THE iMANGA REVOLUTION • LEADING
漫画革命
Go to www.tokyopop.com/mobile
for wallpapers, ringtones and more!
www.TOKYOPOP.com

April 18-20, 2008
at the Jacob Javits Center, New York City

New York Comic Con is Coming!

Find the best in **Anime, Manga, Graphic Novels, Video Games, Toys, and Movies!** NY Comic Con has hundreds of **Celebrity Appearances, Autographing Sessions, Screenings, Industry Panels, Gaming Tournaments, and Much More!**

Go to **www.nycomiccon.com** to get all the information and **<u>BUY TICKETS!</u>** Plus, sign up for special New York Comic Con updates to be the first to learn about Guests, Premieres, and Special Events!

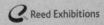 Reed Exhibitions

Follow the MAGICAL and MYSTERIOUS adventures of Mikan at the Alice Academy!

Young Mikan runs away to Tokyo after her best friend is transferred to an exclusive and secretive private school for geniuses. But there is more to Alice Academy than meets the eye—it is actually home to children with special powers. If Mikan wants to stay by her friend's side—and stay *alive*—she must discover the Alice that lives within her!

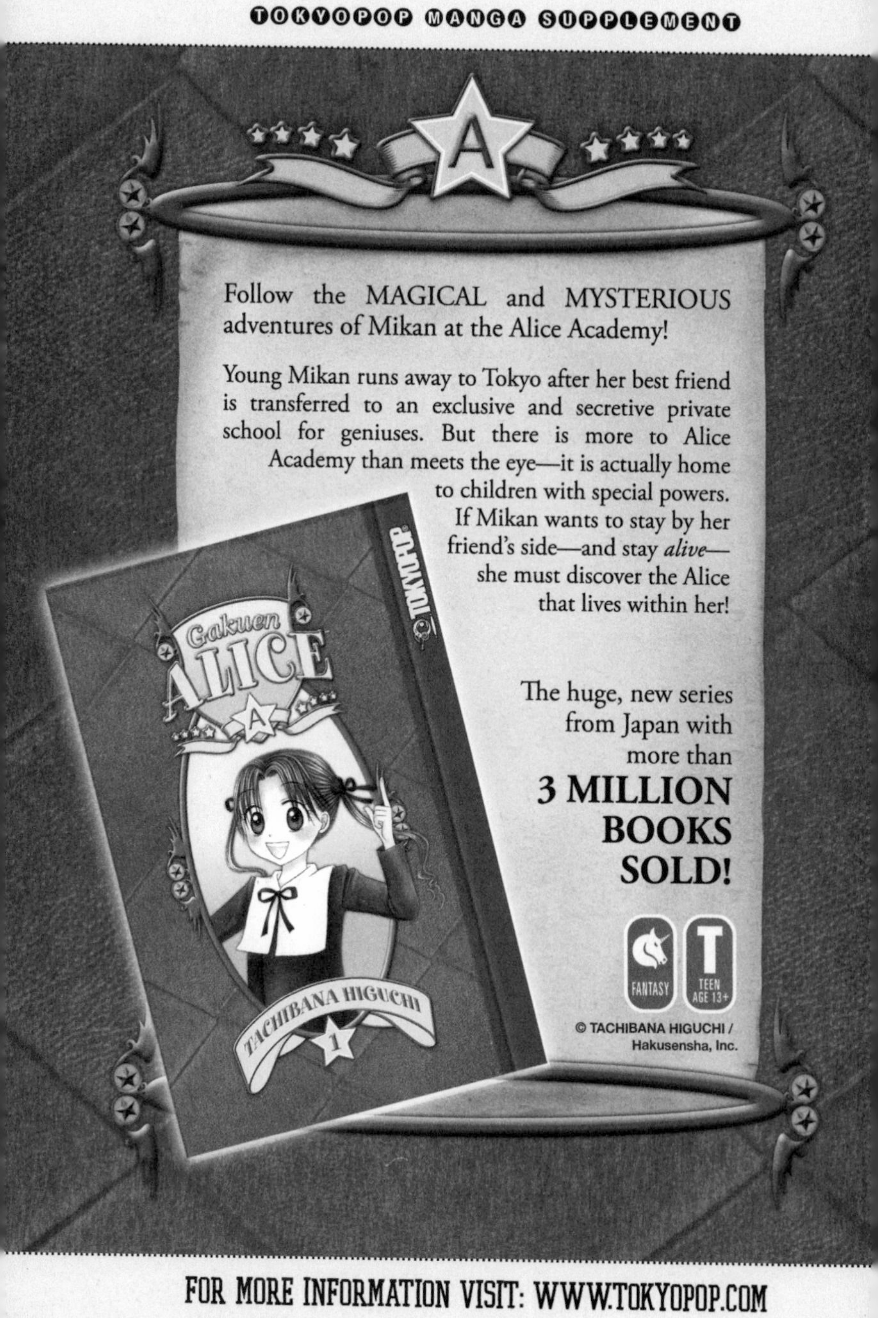
Gakuen
ALICE
A
TOKYOPOP
TACHIBANA HIGUCHI
1

The huge, new series from Japan with more than

3 MILLION BOOKS SOLD!

FANTASY

T
TEEN AGE 13+

FOR MORE INFORMATION VISIT: WWW.TOKYOPOP.COM

THE SPECTACULAR FANTASY EPIC NOW IN PAPERBACK!

THE TWELVE KINGDOMS™

THE TWELVE KINGDOMS
SEA OF SHADOW
FUYUMI ONO

For high-schooler Yoko Nakajima, life has been fairly ordinary—that is, until Keiki, a young man with golden hair, tells Yoko they must return to their kingdom. Whisked away to an unearthly realm, Yoko is left with only a magical sword, a gem—and a million questions about her destiny, the world she's trapped in, and the world she desperately wants to return to.

INSPIRED THE ANIME!

FANTASY

POP FICTION

FOR MORE INFORMATION VISIT: WWW.TOKYOPOP.COM

TOKYO
Pet Shop of Horrors™
TOKYOPOP
MATSURI AKINO
1

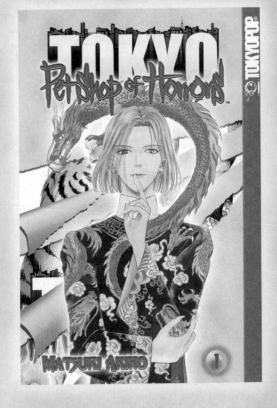

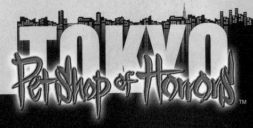

STOP!

This is the back of the book.
You wouldn't want to spoil a great ending!

This book is printed "manga-style," in the authentic Japanese right-to-left format. Since none of the artwork has been flipped or altered, readers get to experience the story just as the creator intended. You've been asking for it, so TOKYOPOP® delivered: authentic, hot-off-the-press, and far more fun!

DIRECTIONS

If this is your first time reading manga-style, here's a quick guide to help you understand how it works.

It's easy... just start in the top right panel and follow the numbers. Have fun, and look for more 100% authentic manga from TOKYOPOP®!